SHOCKING REVELATIONS FROM
THE #1 *NEW YORK TIMES* BESTSELLER

Obama's far-left domestic policy, his controversial votes on abortion, his history of opposition to the Second Amendment, his determination to raise capital-gains taxes, his impractical plan to achieve universal health care and his radical plan to tax Americans to fund a global-poverty-reduction program:

Obama's naïve, anti-war, anti-nuclear foreign policy, predicated on the reduction of the military, the eradication of nuclear weapons and an overconfidence in the power of his personality;

Barack and Michelle's twenty-year-long religious affiliation with the rage-steeped black-liberation theology of former Trinity United Church of Christ Reverend Jeremiah Wright;

Obama's connections with Kenya, the homeland of his father;

Obama's involvement in the slum-landlord empire of the Chicago political fixer Tony Rezko, who helped to bankroll Obama's initial campaigns and the purchase of Barack and Michelle's dream-home property;

The background and techniques of the Obama campaign's cult of personality, including the derivation of the words "hope" and "change."

The Obama Nation **is also available from**
Simon & Schuster Audio and as an eBook

— THE —
OBAMA NATION

Leftist Politics and the
Cult of Personality

JEROME R. CORSI, Ph.D.

POCKET STAR BOOKS
NEW YORK   LONDON   TORONTO   SYDNEY

Pocket Star Books
A Division of Simon & Schuster, Inc.
1230 Avenue of the Americas
New York, NY 10020

First Pocket Star paperback edition February 2010

POCKET STAR and colophon are trademarks of Simon & Schuster, Inc.

For information about special discounts for bulk purchases, please contact Simon & Schuster Special Sales at 1-866-506-1949 or business@simonandschuster.com.

The Simon & Schuster Speakers Bureau can bring authors to your live event. For more information or to book an event contact the Simon & Schuster Speakers Bureau at 1-866-248-3049 or visit our website at www.simonspeakers.com.

Designed by Joy O'Meara

Manufactured in the United States of America

10 9 8 7 6 5 4 3 2 1

ISBN: 978-1-4391-8969-6
ISBN: 978-1-4165-9810-7 (eBook)

In loving memory of my father, Louis E. Corsi,
and with deep appreciation
for the care with which he first introduced me to politics

~ CONTENTS ~

– PREFACE TO THE
PAPERBACK EDITION –

In titling this book "The Obama Nation," the play of word was fully intended.

The subtitle of the book, "Leftist Politics and the Cult of Personality," was meant to convey the argument that Obama's radical leftist politics, driven by the cult of personality he has intentionally manufactured, would be an *abomination,* in that the result of those policies would be to lead the United States in a costly and self-destructive direction both at home and abroad.

Now, with President Obama in the White House, the major thesis of *The Obama Nation* has been validated: Under an Obama presidency, the United States is becoming a militarily weakened and economically diminished nation. Instead of becoming more united, our internal conflicts are becoming more sharpened and more abrasive, even on the critically important issue of racial relations in America.

Barack Obama: A Radical Leftist Democratic Party Politician?

When *The Obama Nation* was published in August 2008, during the height of the presidential campaign, few Americans were prepared to accept that the Democratic Party would nominate a radical leftist, choosing instead to believe that a President Obama would gravitate to the political center and govern as a pragmatist, following the lead of the last Democratic Party president, Bill Clinton.

All too easily, Middle Americans were willing to give candidate Obama the benefit of the doubt that he was not an acolyte of Saul Alinsky or a follower of Saul Alinsky's famous handbook, *Rules for Radicals*. Equally incredible to independent voters was that Barack Obama might have followed Saul Alinsky's advice encouraging radical leftist political candidates to trim their long hair, buy business suits, and tell voters what the voters wanted to hear in order to win political office so as to enact their true goals, namely, to redistribute wealth according to a socialist agenda.

Instead, voters accepted Barack Obama's facile dismissal that he knew radical SDS bomb-throwing Weather Underground terrorist William Ayers only casually because they lived in the same neighborhood. Now, serious arguments are being made that Barak Obama not only began his political career with a fund-raiser held in Bill Ayers's living room, but that Bill Ayers may have played such a major role in Barack Obama's political career that Ayers assisted Obama as ghost writer in composing what ended up being Obama's campaign autobiography, *Dreams from My Father*,[1] although this idea has been both denied and ridiculed by Ayers.

Equally, voters gave Senator Obama a pass when he claimed he was not attending Trinity United Church of Christ in Chicago the day Reverend Wright gave his famous speech cursing the United States of America, even though Barack Obama had been a member of the church for some twenty years. Few took the time to examine the premises laid out in this book that charged the core of black-liberation theology blended a racially oriented view of Christianity with a radical leftist revolutionary political ideology. Rather than a one-time event, Reverend Wright's offending sermon derived from the fundamental tenets of black-liberation theology that all believers would be expected to understand and embrace.

In other words, few Americans voting in the 2008 presidential election were willing to entertain the idea seriously that the gifted orator promising "hope" and "change" could ever have had in mind Saul Alinsky's radical redistribution of wealth, or Reverend Wright's extremist analysis that American free-enterprise capitalism necessarily positioned the United States to be a racially exploitive imperialist nation that deserved to be opposed and defeated.

The experience of President Barack Obama in the White House has only validated the conclusion that this book, *The Obama Nation,* was an extremely accurate predictor of how President Obama would govern, explaining how Barack Obama's leftist education and radical political experience as a Saul Alinsky community organizer had shaped his political views and dictated the inevitable course of his political agenda in the White House.

Americans looking toward the 2010 mid-term elections will have the opportunity to reject the Democratic Party in Congress if the party continues to follow the leftist politics set by the Obama White House and implemented in Congress through Democratic majorities led by House Speaker Nancy Pelosi and Senate Majority Leader Harry Reid.

But what was almost inconceivable in Barack Obama's November 2008 presidential victory was that the Democratic majorities in Congress could be in jeopardy only two years later. This is due largely to the disillusion Middle American voters are experiencing, realizing that "hope" and "change" meant an expanded welfare-entitlement state, central government control of the private economy in domestic policy, and an apology for the historical record of the United States in foreign policy—all combined with a diminishment of U.S. power and influence around the world.

Obama's White House Czars

While other presidential administrations have appointed "czars" to manage policy areas outside the Cabinet members confirmed by the Senate, President Obama has appointed nearly thirty czars, according to Politico.com, with the vast majority being in positions outside those created by Congress or requiring Senate confirmation.[2] This extra-constitutional effort to concentrate administrative control in the White House outside the Cabinet is seen by many as mirroring the Obama-administration effort to impose government control on the private economy.

That many of the czars bear radical leftist political credentials has reinforced the impression that President Obama himself remains a radical leftist. Consider the following four czars:

- Green Jobs Czar Van Jones, who was forced to resign on Sept. 6, 2009, after a controversy arose over his involvement with Standing Together to Create a Revolutionary Movement, or STORM, a Bay Area radical group with Marxist roots, and his signing a petition in 2004 with 911Truth.org, a group that questions whether Bush administration officials "may indeed have deliberately allowed 9/11 to happen, perhaps as a pretext to war," as well as having called

Republicans a crude name in a video clip that was widely televised.[3]

- Regulatory Czar Cass Sunstein, who was confirmed by the Senate on Sept. 10, 2009, despite his views that the state should abolish marriage, authorizing only civil unions without issuing any marriage licenses whatsoever,[4] that the United States should be heavily taxed for carbon emissions in order to redistribute America's wealth to third-world nations,[5] and that organs can be removed from deceased individuals who did not explicitly consent to becoming organ donors.[6]

- Science Czar John Holdren, who wrote a series of books in the 1970s with Malthusian population alarmist Paul Ehrlich, in which he argued that to prevent ecological disasters, including either global warming or global cooling, government-imposed sterilizations, compulsory abortions, and laws limiting the number of children could be justified as steps needed to produce "sustainable well-being."[7]

- "Chief Diversity Officer" Mark Lloyd who authored for the progressive Center for American Progress a 2007 paper entitled "The Structural Imbalance of Political Talk Radio," which argued private broadcasters failing to provide "balance" should be heavily taxed, estimated at between $100 million to $250 million a year, as an alternative to reintroducing the Fairness Doctrine, in order to subsidize public broadcasting of diverse racial, cultural, and political views more attuned to the liberal political agenda.[8]

Those voters who believed a President Obama was a centrist politically were hard-pressed to explain why the

Obama White House included such radicals in positions of authority.

Trillion-Dollar Deficits and Continued High Unemployment

The U.S. Treasury has reported that the deficit for fiscal year 2009 was $1.4 trillion, or approximately 10 percent of the United States gross domestic product, far larger than the under $455 billion federal budget deficit run by President George W. Bush in fiscal year 2008.[9] Moreover, the Congressional Budget Office has announced that over the next ten years, from fiscal year 2010 through 2019, federal budget deficits could total $9.1 trillion, almost doubling the $11 trillion accumulated national debt since the establishment of the Republic that President Obama assumed when he took office.[10]

Through 2009, unemployment climbed to over 10 percent nationwide, despite President Obama's promise that unemployment would not exceed 8 percent if the $787 billion economic stimulus plan were passed by Congress and signed into law.[11] That government bailouts and trillion-dollar federal deficits did not reduce unemployment caused Middle Americans to question whether Obama administration policies were bringing an end to the recession.

Nor did Middle Americans take the rise of the stock market in 2009 as a sure sign the economy was emerging from the recession. That the stock market rallied to over 10,000 on the Dow Jones Industrial Average was arguably a result of yet another financial bubble caused by Federal Reserve Chairman Ben Bernanke's determination to hold federal funds rates at near zero. With financial institutions able to borrow at near-zero interest rates and invest those funds in the stock market, the dollar under the Obama administration was competing to replace the yen as the world's new "carry trade" currency of choice.

While the Obama administration argued that trillion-dollar deficits were needed to solve the economic problems inherited from the Bush administration, the size of the Obama deficits made "trillions" into the new standard for government deficits, replacing "billions." That a difference in size is a difference in magnitude was reflected in the vocal complaints of Chinese economic officials, who warned the Obama administration that printing money would inevitably cause the dollar to devalue, reducing the Chinese willingness to continue buying the U.S. Treasury debt needed to finance the deficit.

The Obama administration's refusal to consider reducing taxes to stimulate job creation in the private economy reinforced the impression of an ideologically driven White House that all too rapidly threatened to "tax the rich" in a manner that threatened to engage in class warfare to fund an Obama-administration expansion of entitlement programs into a European-style social welfare state.

This impression was underscored with the realization that 2009 was likely to be the first year in which nearly half of all Americans would not earn enough income to pay income tax, while fully 20 percent would pay no income tax and receive a federal check back in the form of an earned-income tax credit.[12] A nation in which half the population pays no income tax and half pays all the income tax is not a formula likely to produce social harmony, when those in the half not paying income tax have no negative incentive to vote themselves increased social-welfare benefits at the expense of the half paying income taxes.

What the American public witnessed in the first months of the Obama administration was a government takeover of a major segment of the automobile industry in the bankruptcy of GM and Chrysler, followed by a health-care-reform proposal in which the Obama administration appeared ready to impose government-funded health insurance on a segment of the economy with national health spending already estimated to account for approximately 17.6 percent of United States gross domestic product in 2009.

After a decree by White House pay czar Kenneth Feinberg that executive compensation would be limited to $500,000 at seven firms that had accepted federal bailout funds, many Americans began to perceive the Obama administration as ready and willing to affect a government takeover of major segments of the U.S. private economy.[13]

Meanwhile, the threat loomed that increasing interest rates may be needed to finance trillion-dollar Obama-administration federal-budget deficits projected into the foreseeable future, with the resultant risk that that increasing interest rates could trigger a double-dip recession in which even more jobs would be lost to unemployment and even more homes abandoned to foreclosure.

The Demise of the Dollar

As an indication of the extent to which the United States has become weakened under the Obama administration, the London G20 meeting in April 2009 formally decided, with the concurrence of President Obama, to fund an international plan to create a "one-world currency" alternative to the dollar for use in international trade, out of concern that the Obama White House had no plan to prevent the dollar from dropping dramatically in value.

In my 2009 book, *America for Sale: Fighting the New World Order, Surviving a Global Depression, and Preserving USA Sovereignty,* I argued that President Obama is working actively with the G20 to implement Columbia University economist Robert Mundell's proposal to fund International Monetary Fund Special Drawing Rights as an alternative to the dollar in international trade. Special Drawing Rights are international reserve assets that are calculated by the IMF in a basket of major currencies that are allocated to the IMF 185 member nation-states in relation to the capital, largely in gold or widely accepted foreign currencies that the IMF member nation-states have on deposit with the IMF.

Robert Mundell is considered the "Father of the Euro." In 1999, he won a Nobel Prize for his work on "optimum currency areas." The idea is that nation-state currencies, including the dollar, need to give way to a new official world currency. According to Mundell, international free-trade areas and regional markets best define an "optimal currency area." Mundell's argument is that nation-states such as the U.S.A. are not optimal currency areas because nation-state borders are artificial constraints that are imposed on the globe to create ethnic or historical divisions that do not necessarily represent how international markets operate. To make his concept clear, Mundell frequently cites former Federal Reserve chairman Paul Volker's frequently quoted dictum that, "A global economy needs a global currency."[14]

Mundell's goal was to first replace the U.S. dollar as the major currency held in foreign exchange reserves with a "one-world international currency" issued by the International Monetary Fund. Ultimately, Mundell argues all nation-state currencies, including the dollar, should be rolled into regional currencies, on the way to a "one-world currency" that would operate across the globe, both in nation-state domestic markets and global markets.

As a consultant to China, Mundell advised the Chinese to support his IMF proposal as a means of reducing their dollar exposure in international trade. The Chinese, with approximately $2 trillion in foreign exchange reserves, approximately 80 percent of which is held in dollar assets, want to reduce their exposure to the dollar out of concern that Obama administration trillion-dollar deficits will result in a dollar devaluation that could significantly reduce the value of their dollar holdings.

The G20 summit meeting in London in April, with the full concurrence of President Obama, took an important step to create a new one-world currency through the International Monetary Fund that is designed to replace the dollar as the world's foreign-exchange reserve currency of choice.

Point 5 of the final communiqué from the G20 summit in London on April 2, 2009 specified that, "We have agreed to support a general SDR which will inject $250 billion into the world economy and increase global liquidity," taking the first steps forward to implement Robert Mundell's proposal that Special Drawing Rights at the International Monetary Fund should be created as a foreign exchange currency to replace the dollar.[15]

Failure to Stop Iran from Enriching Uranium

On Thursday, June 4, 2009, President Obama fulfilled a campaign promise by giving a major policy address in a Muslim capital when he spoke at Cairo University in Cairo, Egypt.

Clearly, President Obama's intent was to establish a new reconciliation with the Muslim world by reaching out to Islamic moderates. Notably, the president referenced the "Holy Koran" five times and the "Holy Bible" only once. For the vast majority of those listening to the speech in Israel, including top government officials, President Obama's Cairo speech marked the beginning of a new relationship with the United States, in which U.S. support for Israel could no longer be assumed without qualifications. In the speech, President Obama commented that, "I have known Islam on three continents before coming to the region where it was first revealed."[16] This admission by President Obama that he had experienced Islam in presumably Kenya, Indonesia, and the United States was in sharp contrast to 2008 when the Obama campaign castigated any critic that dared to make reference to President Obama's past association with Islam.

Yet even the historic appeal President Obama issued to the Muslim world with his soaring rhetoric or the power of his charismatic personality as he stepped on the stage in Cairo were not sufficient to turn back the tide of the reality of centuries of conflict that have traditionally defined Middle Eastern politics.

In my 2009 book *Why Israel Can't Wait: The Coming War Between Israel and Iran,* I argued President Obama's Cairo speech capped an intensification of pressure on Israel that began almost immediately after the Obama administration took office. By insisting that Israel must stop immediately even all "natural growth" development in West Bank settlements, without requiring that Hamas or the Palestinian authority make any similar concessions, the Obama administration indicated to many experienced Middle East observers that President Obama considered Israel the main obstacle to establishing a two-state solution as a key objective on the path to achieving piece in the region.

Then, in the June 2009 post-election protests in Iran against perceived voter fraud in the re-election of President Ahmadinejad, President Obama chose to stay largely on the sidelines, missing an historic opportunity to intervene in support of the protestors in a move that might have led to peaceful regime change in Iran from within. Notably, President Obama refrained from calling for new presidential elections in Iran under international supervision. The Obama administration's apparent goal was to engage in direct negotiations with Iran, as candidate Obama had promised in the 2008 presidential campaign.

Then, in September 2009, the Obama administration unilaterally reversed Bush administration policy by withdrawing the missile shield from Eastern Europe, without getting any concession from Russia in return. The Bush administration had largely placed the missile shield over Poland and the Czech Republic out of concern that Iran's advances in medium-range missile technology represented a strategic military threat to the region.

The Geneva negotiations with Iran and the five permanent members of the UN Security Council—the United States, Britain, France, China, and Russia—plus Germany, which opened in October 2009, were marred by the UN International Atomic Energy Agency's disclosure confirming the existence of an up-to-then secret uranium-enrichment facility built underground by Iran close to Tehran. Despite enormous international pressure, Iran appears resistant to abandoning the enrichment of uranium in Iran, a condition Israel considers essential to preventing Iran from secretly developing a nuclear weapon that could be used against Israel.

Failure by the Obama administration to stop Iran from

enriching uranium increases the likelihood of a war between Israel and Iran. The major conclusion of *Why Israel Can't Wait,* based on interviews in Israel with top Israeli government officials, is that Israel will invoke its right of self-defense to launch a pre-emptive military strike on Iran, with or without the approval of the United States, when Israeli intelligence informs the government that Iran is capable of making an atomic weapon that could be delivered on Tel Aviv. With the Obama administration continuing to pressure Israel while making no progress on halting Iran's enrichment of uranium, President Obama has done nothing to slow the ticking of the clock toward an Israeli-Iranian military showdown.

The White House Strategy of Demonizing Critics

The demonization with which the Obama presidential campaign handled the publication of *The Obama Nation* was a clear indication of how the Obama administration would handle political critics of the Obama White House.

Following Saul Alinsky's advice in *Rules for Radicals* to ridicule your opponents, the Obama administration has characterized Tea Party protesters and the Middle Americans expressing at town hall meetings objections to Obama administration programs, including budget deficits, government bailouts, and proposed health-care reform as a form of professionally organized rabble-rousing promoted by Fox News.

The White House war of words with Fox News escalated when White House communications director Anita Dunn in October 2009 said on CNN that Fox News was "a wing of the Republican Party," in an attempt to discredit Fox News as a reputable news agency.[17] Then President Obama commented that Fox News was "operating basically as a talk radio format," supporting Anita Dunn's contention that Fox News was "either the research arm or the communications arm" of the Republican Party.[18]

Finally, the bureau chiefs of the five television networks decided that a White House attempt to exclude Fox News from an interview with White House pay czar Kenneth Feinberg was going too far. The pool informed the U.S. Treasury that Fox News was a member of the network pool and could not be excluded from the interview under the rules of pool coverage. The White House backed down after the bureau chiefs threatened not to cover the Feinberg interview if the White House shut out Fox News.[19]

Students of Saul Alinsky are aware that the radical political left is typically intolerant of political criticism, just as ideological true believers remain convinced only their political views deserve public expression. That President Obama demonizes and vilifies critics further reveals President Obama's leftist bias. How strong the First Amendment will remain under a full-term Obama presidency yet remains to be seen.

President Obama's Historic Drop in Approval Ratings

The White House war with critics has escalated as President Obama's popularity ratings have undergone a near-historic drop since Inauguration Day on January 20, 2009. Unfortunately for President Obama, while the frustration resulting from disappointing polls may intensify the temptation to lash out at critics, that tactic ironically is more likely to depress ratings even further. Even a quick study of President Nixon's presidency should make clear that attacking critics is almost always a losing strategy for a White House losing popular support.

As American voters are beginning to realize that President Obama is and always has been a radical leftist politician, the euphoria of "hope" and "change" campaign rhetoric has evaporated in the failure of the Obama administration to achieve tangible results. *The Obama Nation* predicted that an Obama presidency would be a repeat of the presidency of Democrat Jimmy Carter, not only in persistent economic woes and repeated foreign policy failures, but also in historically low popularity ratings. President Obama's ratings in office are making that prediction come true.

President Carter's average approval rating from January 1977 to January 1981 was 45.5 percent, the lowest for all modern presidents since the end of World War II. Carter's presidency was badly damaged by the OPEC oil embargo, double-digit interest rates, and the 444-day U.S. embassy hostage crisis in Iran. Carter was easily beaten by Republican challenger Ronald Reagan in the November 1980 presidential election, at the end of Carter's first term.

Moreover, comparisons with approval ratings for President George W. Bush indicate that Obama's strongly partisan approval ratings promise problems in the future, especially if the war in Afghanistan expands unfavorably and the economic downturn continues.

President Obama's 63 percent approval rating at the end of the administration's first one hundred days in office is identical to the 63 percent approval rating President Jimmy Carter received in 1977 at the same point in his administration, according to the Pew Research Center.[20]

Carter's presidency clearly shows that initially high approval ratings for Democratic presidents do not necessarily predict the success of the presidency.

While much is made of President Bush's low approval ratings of 23 percent, mainstream media commentators rarely note President Carter's ratings fell to a low of 28 percent in the period of June 29 to July 2, 1979.

LittleGreenFootballs.com has pointed out another comparison between Obama and Carter in that Georgia Governor Jimmy Carter also ran on a message of "change" in 1976, winning on a wave of emotion against the Republican Party following President Ford's decision to pardon President Nixon from any criminal offenses that may have been involved with the Watergate affair.[21]

Pew Research also reported President Obama has the most polarized early job approval ratings of any president in the past four decades, despite the administration's repeated assertions of bi-partisanship.[22] President Obama's 61-point partisan gap comes from relatively high support among Democrats (88 percent job approval rating) and exceptionally low job approval ratings from Republicans (27 percent). The next most partisan divide at the end of the first one hundred days in office was registered by President George W. Bush, with a fifty-one-point partisan divide caused by the sharp difference in strong approval expressed by Republicans (87 percent) and much lower approval ratings from Democrats (36 percent).

Interestingly, President Bush at the end of the first one hundred days in office had an 11 percent higher rating from voters of the competing party than President Obama enjoyed in 2009. President Bush's average approval ratings remained strong throughout his first term (62.2 percent), dropping only in his second term (36.5 percent).

A lesson from President Bush that President Obama should study is that sharp partisan differences can over time lead to decreasing overall approval rates.

Rasmussen's polling shows that President Obama has declined from a 62 percent approval index rating in January 2009 to under 50 percent, beginning only eight months later, in August 2009.[23]

Gallup further reported that President Obama's approval rating averaged only a 53 percent job approval rating in the third quarter of 2009, a nine-point drop from the second quarter that was the largest drop Gallup has ever measured for an elected president between the second and third quarters of his term, dating back to 1953.[24]

Perhaps most alarming of all for the Obama administration is that his popularity has declined dramatically among independent voters, the fastest-growing voter segment and the most determinative voting block in close elections nationwide.

CNN, typically a pro-Obama news source, reported in August 2009 that President Obama's job approval rating among independents had fallen from 66 percent in May to only 49 percent in August, a collapse in Gallup Poll data that CNN attributed to the rancor of the health-care debate and the dislike of independents for deficit spending, the growth of big government, and one-party control of Washington.[25]

The American public expects a president to produce concrete results creating jobs, defending the dollar, and protecting U.S. national security interests abroad. Concrete results, not campaign promises, are what generate presidential approval ratings.

If the Obama administration persists with a radical leftist agenda, not even his charismatic personality or his obvious gifts at speech making will be sufficient to earn President Obama a place in history as one of America's most popular presidents.

~ PREFACE ~

Who I Am and Why I Wrote This Book

In 2004, I coauthored *Unfit for Command: Swift Boat Veterans Speak Out Against John Kerry*,[1] with Swift Boat veteran John O'Neill, a highly successful attorney in Houston, Texas, and a longtime friend I first met more than forty years ago, in college. In the 1960s, John O'Neill attended the U.S. Naval Academy while I was attending Case Western Reserve University and we competed in intercollegiate debate.

Unfit for Command was a critical analysis of John Kerry's military service during the Vietnam War and his radical antiwar protest activities as a lead spokesperson for the Vietnam Veterans Against the War when he returned from Vietnam. Any implication that this book is a "Swift Boat" book is not accurate in that John O'Neill and the other members of the Swift Boat Veterans for Truth have had nothing to do with this book, its analysis and arguments, or my opposition to Barack Obama's 2008 presidential campaign.

My intent in writing this book, as was the case in coauthoring *Unfit for Command*, is to fully document all arguments and contentions I make, extensively footnoting all references, so readers can determine for themselves the truth and validity of the factual claims. My fundamental opposition to Obama's presidential candidacy involves public policy differences. While Obama's three complete years in the Senate have given him remarkably little time on the national political stage, we still have enough information from his slim Senate record, as well as his years in the Illinois state legislature, to see a pattern of voting on the far left on a wide range of policy issues, including abortion, taxes, illegal immigration, international trade, and national security.

In this book, I intend to argue that an Obama presidency would lead us into an "Obama Nation." The play on words is fully intended, because Obama's radical leftist politics, driven by the cult of personality he has intentionally manufactured, would be an *abomination* in that the result of those policies would be to lead the United States in a costly and self-destructive direction, both at home and abroad. After an Obama presidency, we would be a militarily weakened and economically diminished nation. Instead of being more united, our internal conflicts could well become more sharpened and more abrasive from four years of Obama leadership.

Obama has so doggedly positioned himself on the extreme left that it is doubtful he can credibly move to the political center without alienating his Democratic Party supporters on that extreme left as well as his youthful base. This, in many ways, was the liability Senator George McGovern faced in running against President Richard Nixon in 1972. After McGovern won the nomination on a radical antiwar platform, Nixon was able to show the vast majority of center-right voters that McGovern's policies spelled defeat in Vietnam, even though Nixon himself withdrew from the war less than two years later.

In the race against Barack Obama in the general election,

the Republican Party will have a decided advantage because of the prolonged, acrimonious primary campaign Obama and Hillary Clinton waged against each other in 2008. The Republican Party now has hours of video ready to be played back to American voters in campaign advertisements, repeating Clinton's and Obama's abrasive comments about the other.

Obama first drew my attention in 2004, when he stepped onto the national political stage by addressing the Democratic National Convention that nominated Kerry for the presidency. My preliminary decision to write this book was made in 2005, immediately after Obama was sworn in to the U.S. Senate. Since he was a child, Obama has been making statements that he intended to be president, and in 2005 I suspected he would attempt to use the U.S. Senate as a stepping-stone for the presidency.

So I began researching Obama and following him in the Senate; I'd frequently sit in the Senate gallery to observe him on the Senate floor, and watched him on C-SPAN as he debated and voted on legislation. I finalized the decision to write this book in March 2008, as Hillary Clinton continued her presidential campaign despite delegate numbers that made it likely Obama would win the 2008 presidential nomination in the Democratic Party. I calculated that publishing the book before the Democratic National Convention would likely have an impact, even if Hillary beat the odds and ultimately won the nomination. Yet, I did not write the book to promote Hillary Clinton's candidacy, nor did I publish it before the national nominating convention in the Democratic Party to assist her in getting the nomination on the convention floor. If Hillary Clinton were the nominee, I would oppose her too.

I have never been a registered member of the Republican or Democratic Party, unless voting in some particular state primary over the past forty years necessitated that result. The only political party I ever consciously joined is the Constitution Party, of which I am a registered member in the state of New Jersey, where I currently reside. Let me also clearly state that I am writing this book strictly to examine and oppose Barack Obama, not to support Senator John McCain or any other Republican Party or third-party candidate for the presidency.

While I intend to vote in 2008 for Chuck Baldwin, the presidential candidate of the Constitution Party, this book was begun before that party had chosen a 2008 presidential candidate and is not intended to be an argument for Chuck Baldwin. I also want to make clear the Constitution Party asked me to run as its presidential candidate in 2008, but I declined, preferring instead to remain with World Net Daily, where I am currently employed as a senior staff reporter.[2]

Obama is running to be the nation's first African-American president. Since the 1960s, I have been studying and writing about U.S. racial relations. In all my writings on that subject, I have been a strong opponent of any form of racial violence and a strong advocate for eliminating all forms of racial discrimination, inequality, and injustice.

In 2006, I supported Ken Blackwell in his campaign as the Republican candidate for governor of Ohio. Once again, my background studying racial relations was relevant, as Blackwell sought to be the first African-American governor of Ohio. Seeking to advance Blackwell's 2006 gubernatorial campaign, I coauthored with him a book titled *Rebuilding America: A Prescription for Creating Strong Families, Building the Wealth of Working People, and Ending Welfare.*[3] Many of my policy criticisms of Obama stem from arguments initially made with Ken Blackwell in writing *Rebuilding America*, especially the analysis of the importance of families in building middle-class wealth, reducing the incidence of teenage pregnancies, and alleviating poverty.

Blackwell, a conservative, had served in 2004 as Ohio's secretary of state, and so presided over his state's voting in the 2004 presidential election, which George W. Bush narrowly won over John Kerry. It was in Ohio that Bush secured the final electoral votes needed to be elected president in yet another historically close contest. I did not meet Blackwell or work with him in any capacity until 2005, months after the 2004 campaign was over.

My interest in U.S. racial politics dates back to my days as an undergraduate student in political science at Case Western Reserve University, in Cleveland. As a political science student, I wrote papers published in law journals on legal assistance for the poor and on the Detroit race riots of 1967.[4] The Hough Riots in Cleveland in 1966 led me to co-author, with two Case Western Reserve professors, a book titled *A Time To Burn?*[5] This was one of the first college textbooks on racial relations that used the race riots of the 1960s as a central focus of analysis. In 1966, I also studied Reverend Jesse Jackson's efforts to bring "Operation Breadbasket," begun by Reverend Martin Luther King's Southern Christian Leadership Council, to Chicago.

In 1967, while completing my senior year at Case Western Reserve, I worked full-time in downtown Cleveland with Edward Howard & Co., one of the nation's first public relations firms (it was established in 1925).[6] I was an assistant to William Silverman, Jr., the vice president, who served as public relations manager for Seth Taft, the Republican Party candidate opposing Democrat Carl B. Stokes to be mayor of Cleveland.

My duties at Edward Howard & Co. during the Stokes-Taft race included bird-dogging Carl Stokes in the field by following him on his public appearances and reporting back the contents of his speeches and any relevant information regarding attendees, crowd size, and audience reaction. My work was fully disclosed to the Stokes campaign and I was welcomed at virtually every Carl Stokes campaign event I chose to attend. I observed Reverend King in Cleveland as he visited the city to aid in a voter registration drive and campaign for Stokes in 1967. On November 7, 1967, Stokes was elected the first African-American mayor of a major U.S. city.

On July 23, 1968, in my last summer in Cleveland before moving to Cambridge, Massachusetts, there was a gun battle between Ahmed Evans, an African-American militant, along with his armed followers, and the Cleveland police in Glenville, an inner-city neighborhood. The shooting went on for an hour and a half, leaving seven people dead and fifteen wounded. Fifteen of the casualties were policemen. For the next five days, a riot flared in Glenville and the surrounding East Side communities; the burning and looting were typical of 1960s race riots.

In my first year at Harvard University, where I was pursuing a Ph.D. in political science, I coauthored with Louis H. Masotti, Ph.D., a report titled "Shoot-Out in Cleveland. Black Militants and the Police: July 23, 1968."[7] The report, then widely known as the "Masotti Report," was published as a staff report to the Eisenhower Commission, formally known as the National Commission on the Causes and Prevention of Violence, as well as in two commercially published editions.[8] I had studied under Masotti at Case Western Reserve both as a political science student and as a research associate at the Civil Violence Research Center, which Masotti headed.

As part of my studies at Harvard, I continued researching racial violence, student protests, and the antiwar movement as a research associate at the Lemberg Center for the Study of

Violence at Brandeis University. One of my projects involved studying the wide range of civil rights and protest literature of that time. For example, at Harvard Square in the late 1960s and the early 1970s, the Black Muslims frequently distributed such literature, including free copies of their newspaper. A subfocus of that study became the anti-Semitic diatribes the Black Muslim movement launched at Jews. I initially found the harsh feelings surprising; my assumption had been that oppressed African-Americans and Jews would be sympathetic to one another; the Jews have suffered centuries of their own oppression. While we found affinity between the intellectual views of Jews on the political left and the anger of African-American radicals, we also found antipathy in the black communities toward Jewish shop owners, who often became victims of burning and looting in urban race riots.

The Lemberg Center was where I conducted my first field studies of John Kerry and his participation with Vietnam Veterans Against the War. I personally observed various race riots, student demonstrations, and antiwar protests, and examined the literature that was distributed at these events as explanation and political justification.

In 1980 and 1981, after the takeover of the U.S. Embassy in Tehran, I was recruited as a political scientist by the U.S. Agency for International Development to assist the State Department on a psychiatrist-led team that had been organized to teach hostage survival skills to U.S. embassy employees and staff worldwide. For this work, I received a Top Secret security clearance. The project was led by psychiatrist David Hubbard, a noted expert on skyjacking.[9] My work included extensive psychological research and training, with instruction from Dr. Hubbard. I analyzed prison interview transcripts and films of a variety of convicted felons, including bank robbers, rapists, and terrorists.

By 1982, I had left academia to pursue a career in financial services that continues to this day. After coauthoring *Unfit for Command*, I decided to devote the majority of my time to writing about politics. As a Senior Staff Reporter for World Net Daily, I investigate and write about a wide range of issues, including the economy, oil policy, trade agreements, foreign affairs, and domestic politics. One or more of my articles are published nearly every day.

Islam is part of this book, both in examining Obama's background and in looking at policy areas including Islamic terrorism and our relations with Iran. I have been studying and writing about terrorism and Islamic extremism for over twenty-five years. This includes a game theoretic analysis of terrorism published by a noted journal at Yale University.[10]

I have written or co-written two books on Iran: *Atomic Iran* and *Showdown with Nuclear Iran*.[11] In the preface to *Atomic Iran*, I went on record supporting Islam as a genuine and important religion, with more than one billion believers throughout the world. I also acknowledged the proud three-thousand-year history of Iran, carefully distinguishing my opposition to the radical terrorists and clerics controlling the current Islamic Republic of Iran. I have opposed the United States' or Israel's going to war with Iran, arguing instead that we should support the millions of Iranian expatriates around the world and the thousands of brave freedom fighters within Iran who seek to bring true liberty to their country peacefully.

Finally, let me clearly state that this book has been written solely on my initiative. There has been no attempt made, nor will there be any attempt made, to communicate the shape or contents of this book with anyone in the Republican Party, the Democratic Party, the Constitution Party, or in any third party with a candidate running for the presidency.

In contrast to Hillary Clinton, Barack Obama has not been vetted, not even by Democrats. Even today he is largely an unknown to all but a small handful of dogged political professionals and a concentrated core of political junkies who inhabit Internet blogs. Thus, in this book I have pursued Obama's extensive connections with Islam and with radical racial politics, including those articulated by such extremists as Malcolm X and Louis Farrakhan, in order to bring these issues from the shadows where Obama has tried to keep them hidden. For this same reason, I have pursued Obama's extensive and continuing connections with Kenya, the homeland of his father, where Obama has continued to involve himself personally in advancing the goals of Raila Odinga, the radical socialist presidential contender who comes from Obama's home tribe. Even for Obama, his past is prelude, in a political world where voters legitimately see character as an important predictor of policy.

Hence, I also document Obama's emergence in Chicago politics through the Saul Alinsky school of radical community organizing. Alinsky used the battle cry of "Change" as a code word for a socialist redistribution of wealth. I have also examined Obama's involvement in the slum landlord empire of Chicago political fixer Tony Rezko.

The nation went into 2008 with a struggling economy and a continuing war in the Middle East. Radical Islamic terrorist enemies continue to plot our demise, while growing numbers of largely Hispanic illegal immigrants, many of them still citizens of their home countries, including Mexico, live in our midst with no firm purpose or requirement to become American citizens. Meanwhile, urban African-American poverty has become generational and persistent, hardened by the continuance of an alarming rate of teenage pregnancies and abortions. These problems of racial disadvantage have not been diminished by more than four decades of well-intentioned but ineffective welfare-state programs that many would argue have actually been counterproductive. I will argue that the policies reflected in Obama's legislative history or suggested in his presidential campaign are nothing more than a rerun of far-leftist solutions that have been tried many times but to no avail.

Obama's life story, a subject Obama himself put on the agenda by writing an autobiography, is relevant only to the extent it illuminates public policy goals and objectives Obama is likely to pursue. In the final analysis, what I seek to prevent by writing this book is an Obama presidency that would represent nothing more than a repeat of the failed extremist politics that have characterized and plagued Democratic Party presidential politics since the late 1960s. With Obama, the leftist political correctness enforced by his campaign has even intervened to prevent anyone from using his middle name, which happens to be Hussein.

Put simply, the argument here is that Barack Obama is more of a Michael Dukakis, a George McGovern, a Jimmy Carter, or a John Kerry than he is a Franklin Delano Roosevelt or even a John F. Kennedy.

——— THE ———

OBAMA
NATION

- INTRODUCTION -

Here are three short vignettes, or snapshots, that offer a first impression of Barack Obama's career and the 2008 presidential campaign. The first involves a short video clip in which Obama makes his opposition to the military abundantly clear.

1.

YouTube Video:

"In 52 Seconds, Why Barack Obama Cannot

Win a General Election"[1]

On the screen we see Barack Obama, wearing a business suit, white shirt, and dark tie. Behind him at right are the red and white stripes of an American flag. Obama is not wearing an American flag lapel pin.

In the head shot, Obama is looking directly into the camera, speaking deliberately, careful to articulate his words precisely. He has a positive but firm look to his face. The video clip looks as if it might have been prepared for a television ad.

Without any introduction, Obama begins, "I am the only major candidate to oppose this war from the beginning and, as president, I will end it.

"Second," he continues, "I will cut tens of billions of dollars in wasteful spending. I will cut investments in unproven missile defense systems. I will not weaponize space. I will slow our development of future combat systems and I will institute an independent defense priorities board to ensure that the quadrennial defense review is not used to justify unnecessary spending.

"Third," he says, without pausing, "I will set a goal of a world without nuclear weapons. To seek that goal, I will not develop new nuclear weapons. I will seek a global ban on the production of fissile materials. And I will negotiate with Russia to take our ICBMs off hair-trigger alert and to achieve deep cuts in our nuclear arsenals."

Given the title, "In 52 Seconds, Why Barack Obama Cannot Win a General Election," the poster appears to believe that this one short video would provide Obama's Republican rival in the 2008 presidential election with enough ammunition to defeat him.

Why? The video begins with Obama posturing himself as the most antiwar candidate on the left, opposing U.S. involvement in the Iraq War. Without mentioning her name, Obama reminds us in the first seconds of the video that Hillary voted for the war, no matter what she said later about her supposed opposition to it.

From there, Obama embraces a "no nukes," antiwar, *antimilitary* posture that places him even further left than Senator George McGovern, the last openly antiwar presidential candidate put forth by the Democratic Party.

In the 1972 presidential election, at the height of the Vietnam War's unpopularity, McGovern lost forty-nine states to President Richard M. Nixon. The only state McGovern carried was Massachusetts, which then, as now, was so "peacenik" that many Republican Party loyalists derisively referred to it as the "People's Republic of Massachusetts."

Obama made this video while trying to win enough primary contests to secure the Democratic Party presidential nomination in 2008. As the base of the Democratic Party has moved steadily to the far left of the political spectrum, Obama's antiwar rhetoric has served well in capturing that leftist base as well as youthful voters who want "change."

What the person posting this video knew is that a general election is a very different phenomenon from a primary. Being antiwar and so antimilitary that he was willing to embrace a "no nukes" policy, Obama was risking a strategy that would sell well in the primaries but cost him the general election. The video was obviously easily available for use by a Republican candidate for president or any group seeking to hamper Obama with television ads. Whether using the entire video or a few segments of it, a skillful opposition-oriented creator of TV spots could have a field day telling Republican and independent voters that a vote for Obama is a vote to leave the United States of America undefended in the nuclear age.

Yes, Obama was careful to qualify his comments by suggesting he would appoint a defense priorities board to verify military cuts independently. He also stated he would make no cuts in the U.S. nuclear arsenal without first negotiating those cuts with Russia. But if the television spot were produced, those parts of his statement would never get heard by the average viewer. What would be heard by most listeners is that Obama hates the military so much that he might leave the United States defenseless against our enemies, just to keep out of wars or to avoid having to use nuclear weapons.

So Obama is now boxed in. If he tries to move to the center in the general election or qualify his bold "no nukes" statement with a lot of conditions, he can easily be portrayed as a "flip-flopper"—all one has to do is play clips from this video as evidence against the more moderate positions he might articulate later.

Running on the political extreme may be a good primary strategy when a party's voters have moved to the political extreme, but since the 1950s, running on a political extreme has proven to be a very ineffective general election strategy.

"If the Democratic Party decides to run another antiwar candidate against the Republican nominee in 2008, Senator McGovern may be seen in retrospect to have done very well indeed." That is the basic message of "In 52 Seconds, Why Barack Obama Cannot Win a General Election." And unfortunately for Obama, the poster was probably right. The video received over two million views in less than three months on YouTube.

2.
John Fund
Reporter and Columnist, Wall Street Journal[2]

"While Republicans tend to nominate their best-known candidate from previous nomination battles [Richard Nixon, Ronald Reagan, George H. W. Bush, and now John McCain], Democrats often fall in love during a first date." This was among the perceptions of John Fund, a *Wall Street Journal* reporter and Fox News commentator, during the 2008 presidential primary campaign.

Still, Fund acknowledged that 2008 is the Democrats' presidential election to lose, for at least two reasons. First, it is extremely difficult for a party that has held the White House for two terms to extend into a third term. "People have Bush fatigue," Fund has said, "and they want to try something new. People loved Reagan and he got a third term, in effect, when his vice president, George H. W. Bush, was elected in 1988. Reagan could not run for a third term, but the voters liked Bush, so by electing Bush, the voters got what they wanted, a Reagan third term. It's very rare and hard to do."

Second, as the economy slowed down through the first quarter of 2008, the odds were increasing that it would be in a recession in November 2008. Recessions are never good for the party holding the White House. Evidence for that includes John F. Kennedy's defeat of Richard M. Nixon in 1960, on the heels of the "Eisenhower recession" of 1958.

Yet Fund has consistently argued that the Republican Party has an excellent chance to retain the White House in 2008. Why?

First off, Obama entered the primary season a virtually unvetted presidential candidate. Even among serious political professionals, few knew much about Obama's background, his political history, or his voting record. Obama appeared on the national scene when he gave the keynote address at the Democratic National Convention in Boston in 2004. When the presidential election is held in November 2008, Obama will have spent only three complete years in the U.S. Senate, having been sworn into the U.S. Senate on January 4, 2005.

"Mr. Obama is the closest thing to a rookie candidate on the national stage since Dwight Eisenhower, who was a beloved war leader," Fund wrote. "Candidates as green as Mr. Obama make first-timer mistakes under the searing scrutiny of a national campaign. Even seasoned pols don't understand how unforgiving that scrutiny can be. Ask John Kerry, who had won five statewide elections before running for president.

"In 2004, when Mr. Obama ran for the U.S. Senate, he had the good luck of watching both Blair Hull, the front-runner for the Democratic nomination, and Jack Ryan, the GOP nominee, self-destruct in sex scandals," Fund pointed out. "Mr. Obama's eventual Republican opponent, Alan Keyes, was an unserious candidate who won the votes of only 56 percent of Republican voters."

Fund's point is that Obama has not really been tested in a national campaign, yet the Democratic Party appears ready to nominate him as its presidential candidate for 2008.

"In 2000, then–state Sen. Obama challenged Congressman Bobby Rush, who was vulnerable after having been crushed in a bid to become mayor of Chicago," Fund argued. "Mr. Rush, a former Black Panther, painted Mr. Obama as 'inauthentic' and beat him 2–1."

Other unsuccessful Democratic presidential candidates considered "first dates" include Michael Dukakis, the former governor of Massachusetts, in 1988; Senator George McGovern in 1972; and Senator John Kerry in 2004.

Second, most people don't pay attention to elections until they have to. "Voters, unlike 'political junkies,' pay attention only in the fall, when the candidates are finally joined on issues of policy and ideology, not on issues of personality," Fund has insisted. "In the primary campaigns, the liberal mainstream media does not press Obama or Hillary on issues such as where they are going to find the funds to pay for all their spending programs. In the primaries, the media coverage is all about personality."

But, finally, in September and October, in the last stages of a general election, we get into a discussion about issues and ideology. When the campaign focuses on issues, conservatives benefit, Fund has maintained. "Republicans win when they decide to focus campaigns on issues.

"George W. Bush, despite all his faults, ran a campaign of contrasts and issues in 2000 and 2004, and won, even with a hostile audience in both cases," he has told audiences.

"Ronald Reagan was a master at that," Fund argues. "Reagan was all about compare and contrast. 'We are conservatives, they are liberals,' or 'their policies fail' and 'our policies work—choose.'" Reagan was behind Carter in the polls but the final debate turned the tide, when he framed the question clearly for voters. How did voters feel in 1980 they would be better off economically—with the failures of the Carter years or the promises of the Reagan years? Only then did Reagan win by a landslide.

"Michael Dukakis had a healthy lead in 1988 against the elder Bush at this time and right through the political conventions," Fund wrote. "Then came the GOP's dissection of his Massachusetts record and his tank ride.

"Bill Clinton was able to win with only 43 percent of the vote in 1992, thanks in part to Ross Perot's presence as a spoiler," he continued. "John Kerry had a six-point lead in the May 2004 Gallup poll over President Bush, then the wind-surfer crashed. All of those candidates had never run for national office before. Democrats paid a price for running a rookie."

Campaigns are important because campaigns have the potential to move voters and change votes. That's why we have them. If a presidential campaign becomes a campaign of "compare and contrast," Republicans tend to win. "We are still a center-right country," Fund has reminded audiences. "On any fundamental policy question—social, economic, or foreign policy—about 60 percent of the country will vote for the conservative side rather than the liberal side, provided the fall campaign turns to comparing and contrasting issues of policy and ideology, not personality."

Remarkably, in the sixty-four years since FDR won his fourth election only two Democrats have won a majority of the popular vote in a presidential election. Lyndon B. Johnson in 1964 won 61.05 percent of the popular vote, riding a wave of sympathy and emotion following the assassination of John F. Kennedy the year before. Then, in 1976, Jimmy Carter won a narrow majority of the popular vote, 50.08

percent, benefiting from the resentment President Gerald Ford's pardon of Richard Nixon generated after Watergate.

3.

Barack Obama

Recorded Comments at a Private Fund-Raiser,
San Francisco, April 6, 2008

On Sunday, April 6, 2008, at a private fund-raising event in San Francisco, Barack Obama was speaking to a small group of wealthy supporters. He was comfortable in the belief that his off-the-record comments were not being recorded, but unbeknownst to the senator, Mayhill Fowler, a member of the citizen journalism project of the Huffington Post, managed to gain entry to the event and recorded his remarks on a simple device with less than perfect sound quality.

On Friday, April 11, 2008, the leftist-oriented Huffington Post published an article by Fowler, including a link permitting readers to hear the recording of Obama's remarks for themselves.[3]

A firestorm of criticism immediately broke out, threatening to dislodge Obama from his then-presumptive nominee status and giving an advantage to Hillary Clinton. Behind in the delegate count as the April 22 Pennsylvania primary approached, Clinton was pressing hard to win, hopefully by a large double-digit margin. Hillary's strategy was to argue she had the superior chance to win the general election because she had the momentum, she could win the big states, and she might (possibly) end up with more of the popular vote.

The moment the secretly made Obama recording surfaced, Hillary had an unexpected weapon. She could argue Obama was an elitist, out of touch with middle-class American voters, an ironic argument for a former first lady whose recently disclosed income statements showed she and her husband, the former president, had made more than $100 million in income over the past seven years.

What Did Obama Say?

The offending sentence was uttered as Obama tried to explain to the prospective campaign donors why he was still behind in the Pennsylvania polls. Obama explained that in "some of these small towns in Pennsylvania, and like a lot of small towns in the Midwest, the jobs have been gone now for twenty-five years and nothing's replaced them." He went on to note, "And they fell through the Clinton administration, and each successive administration has said somehow these communities are gonna regenerate and they have not." Then came the offending sentence: "And it's not surprising then they get bitter, they cling to guns or religion or antipathy to people who aren't like them or anti-immigrant sentiment or anti-trade sentiment, as a way to explain their frustrations."

In only thirty-five words, which Obama had reason to expect would never be heard outside that room, he risked blowing a carefully crafted image designed to make him appear a unifier, a politician who had transcended politics, a large soul capable of embracing the poor and the lowly more effectively than had any person on the American political scene since at least Robert F. Kennedy.

Instead, Obama appeared elitist. Yes, he had been born of mixed blood and was raised by his grandparents. Nevertheless, he had attended elite schools—Punahou School in Hawaii, Occidental College and Columbia University, Harvard Law School, where he was elected the president of the law review.

Suddenly, we were reminded that Barack Obama was not an African-American descended from a slave and that he had never lived in an urban ghetto, except by choice, when working as a community organizer in Chicago.

Republican pundits had a field day. William Kristol, editor and publisher of the *Weekly Standard,* said Obama's comment made him think back to Karl Marx's statement that religion is the opiate of the people.[4] Conservative columnist George Will observed that Obama was implying that for working-class voters, "primitivism, superstition and bigotry are balm for resentments they feel because of American's grinding injustice."[5] On Fox News's *Hannity & Colmes* show, Karl Rove said Obama had hurt himself: "the more people hear about this and the more people listen to the entire speech, the more they're going to find this tone of arrogance and elitism coming through." Rove took the opportunity to reinforce red state sentiment for Republicans, arguing, "there is a sense in places like San Francisco that the United States consists of a narrow sliver on the East Coast and the narrow sliver on the West Coast and the rest of the country is uninteresting and unimportant, and that kind of attitude was evidenced in Senator Obama's comments."[6]

Who Is Mayhill Fowler?

Mayhill Fowler is an amateur who volunteers for blogs like the Huffington Post, working on her own time and money as "a citizen reporter" equipped with nothing more than a sound recorder and a digital camera. One blogger, resenting what Mayhill Fowler had wrought, retaliated by characterizing her as nothing more than "a 61 year old 'Wesley Girl' who landed in Oakland, California, and married well."

In "real life," Fowler is the wife of attorney James C. Fowler, a lifelong Democrat who is a partner in the prestigious law firm Bingham & McClutchen, one of whose clients is Alex Mehran, the wealthy San Francisco real estate developer who hosted the private fund-raising party where Obama spoke. Two San Francisco bloggers reported that Fowler had tried to get into one of two Obama fund-raiser events in the Bay Area a couple of months earlier, when former New Jersey senator Bill Bradley stood in as a proxy. They reported that both times Fowler was turned away, although evidently she had offered to pay to be allowed to attend, although she says she was invited and attended.[8]

Fowler's blog is a virtually unknown and unvisited site titled "Junehill, Owl and a Green Dog, Too."[9]

In the Internet age, however, no candidate should ever assume what is said or done will remain private or secret for long.

The Power of the Internet

Candidates are especially vulnerable in unguarded moments, which can be captured as audio and video and turned into personal vignettes, through which an Internet user can peer behind the candidate's carefully crafted public persona. The research for this book was greatly assisted by the hundreds of Internet reporters and bloggers who have recorded, documented, and analyzed virtually every word spoken by every candidate at every campaign appearance, going back virtually to Election Day 2004, the day the 2008 race for the presidency began.

Today, an average citizen at a remote campaign event can make world history armed only with a cell phone that can take electronic photographs or a pocket bar recorder that electronically picks up sound. Moreover, with the Internet's extensive ability to archive past records, researching even obscure points of interest becomes vastly more doable. The Internet today provides an information capacity many times greater than was available in the world's most extensive archives, including the Library of Congress and the National Archives, in the pre-Internet era. Presidential candidates today who presume some past incident will remain obscured from voters are merely fooling themselves.

Few people are prepared for the level of scrutiny they will undergo running for president. Even candidates in the presidential primary campaigns are unprepared for the scrutiny they receive when lucky enough to emerge as Democratic and Republican nominee for the general election. U.S. presidential election campaigns take all the oxygen out of the room, making it nearly impossible for any other news story to get the full attention the story may deserve. In the final days of a general election presidential campaign, news time gets compressed. The news cycle, in which an item may typically take a week to be introduced, debated, and finished, may in the final days of a general election presidential campaign get condensed into a few hours.

Yet with so much information coming at voters in a general election presidential campaign, how a candidate is framed becomes all-important. For example, a candidate successfully tagged as a "flip-flopper" may never overcome that disadvantage, as John Kerry painfully learned in 2004. Or, as Adlai Stevenson painfully learned twice, first in 1952 and again in 1956, a candidate pegged as an "egghead" may never shake that pejorative designation in the minds of general election voters. If a brief sound recording surreptitiously made in a closed-door fund-raiser in San Francisco successfully ends up tagging Barack Obama as an elitist, he may never escape that designation, no matter how much he protests that he came from a mixed-race family of modest means or that he was largely raised by his grandparents, who sacrificed for his education. He and other candidates have to contend not just with their direct political adversaries, but also with enthusiastic bloggers ready to pick up on every gaffe instantly and disseminate it worldwide like viral wildfire.

In the age of the Internet, how will Barack Obama transcend the issue of race when shared video clips abound showing his longtime pastor, Reverend Jeremiah Wright, wearing a dashiki and railing against the United States of America as a white establishment that inflicts the Middle East with unjust wars waged against Islam and keeps African-Americans economically oppressed at home in urban colonies of ghetto poverty?

PART ONE

ROOTS

Another special circumstance is history, where extraordinary beings, by their own self-centered maneuvers and through the prodding of the charismatic hunger of mankind, become (auto) biographies.

—ERIK ERIKSON, *Young Man Luther,* 1958[1]

Barack Obama, Jr., introduced himself to the American public with an autobiographical book, *Dreams from My Father: A Story of Race and Inheritance*. It was first published in 1995, when he was thirty-four years old, before he entered public life by running for the Illinois legislature.[2]

He tells us in the introduction he began the book in 1990, after being offered book contracts by several publishers who sought to capitalize on his election as the first black president of the *Harvard Law Review*, a position Obama held when completing the third and final year of law school at Harvard, in 1991.

In the introduction, Obama makes clear that he "resisted the idea of offering up my past in a book" because his past left him feeling exposed and "even slightly ashamed."[3] Obama openly admits he is offering us a psychological autobiography, not a chronological one. The dialogue is an "approximation of what was actually said or relayed to me" and the characters are "composites of people I've known, and some events appear out of precise chronology." Furthermore, while names of family and public figures in the autobiography are openly disclosed, Obama tells us "the names of most characters have been changed for the sake of privacy."

What we have then is a psychological autobiography, one that reflects Obama's inner perception of his personal past, not a chronological one. As psychiatrist Erik Erikson, famed for his psychohistorical analyses of Martin Luther and Mahatma Gandhi, has warned us, autobiographies written by political figures raise the questions of why the book was written, as well as what political message the author wanted to give his audience.[4] Erikson's suggestion is that a political autobiography is written by a politician who wants to deliver a carefully crafted political message that the author believes will advance his political career to a receptive and understanding audience.

In the first pages, Obama says people who see him as a "mulatto" resulting from the brief union of an African and an American do not know who he is and cannot "guess at my troubled heart," with the tragedy being "not mine, or at least not mine alone, it is yours, sons and daughters of Plymouth Rock and Ellis Island, it is yours, children of Africa."[5]

His project, Obama tells us, is to "search for my father" and through that search "find a workable meaning for my life as a black American."[6] For this reason, the book is subtitled "A Story of Race and Inheritance." As Obama further admits, only at his father's grave as an adult did he understand how much of his life he had spent trying to rewrite stories of his past, plug up holes in the narrative, and accommodate unwelcome details.[7]

In writing *Dreams from My Father*, Barack felt no need to be precise and accurate in the many stories related. In an autobiography where the chronology is admittedly hard to decipher, psychology is pushed to the forefront. What we are told by Obama outright is that much of the autobiography is not factually true, at least not as written. If Obama then is admittedly writing a psychological self-investigation, what are the political conclusions we are justified in drawing? If this is a story of race and inheritance, what is Obama telling us about race and what is the nature of the inheritance?

As Erikson found in his own analyses, to answer these questions we need to probe the text until we find the holes in the narrative and discover exactly what the unwelcome details are.

MYTHS FROM HIS FATHER

> Dreams from My Father *contains composite*
> *characters and other fictionalized elements—not*
> *exactly a portrait of sterling honesty or authenticity.*
>
> —SEAN WILENTZ, *The New Republic,*
> DECEMBER 19, 2007[1]

> *If Obama will lie about his parents, what won't*
> *he lie about?*
>
> —ANDY MARTIN, *ContrarianCommentary.com,*
> MARCH 2008[2]

In *Dreams from My Father,* Barack Obama paints a heroic picture of his father as a simple goatherd who emerged from a poor Kenyan village to become a Harvard-educated economist and then returned to Africa to fulfill his destiny. Unfortunately, the reality is much bleaker than the tall tale Obama spins in his book.

Since Barack Obama introduced himself to the American public with a book about his father, we will begin our inquiry there as well. Who was Obama's father and what was Obama's relationship with him? What life lessons did

Obama learn from his father and what impact did those lessons have on his public career in politics? We will also test Obama's story of his roots, not only to see how it informs us about who Obama is and what type of president he might be, but also to see exactly just how accurate the story he told us truly is.

Obama's Father, an Alcoholic Polygamist

Barack Obama Senior, Obama's father, was a polygamist who had already abandoned one wife and child in Africa when he met Obama's mother in Hawaii.

After being educated at Harvard, Obama Senior returned to Africa, abandoning Barack and his mother, to live the life of a chronic alcoholic. He ultimately killed himself in a drink-induced car accident, tragically driving drunk on the streets of Nairobi.

The truth was first disclosed by London's *Daily Mail* in a January 2007 exposé titled "A drunk and a bigot—what the U.S. Presidential hopeful HASN'T said about his father," the details of which remain unchallenged.[3] Sharon Churcher, the author of the piece, confirmed in a telephone interview from London that, as far as she knows, her original report remains accurate.[4] Rob Crilly, the freelance journalist in Africa who did much of the on-site, firsthand interviews with Obama Senior's family and acquaintances in Kenya, also said in a telephone interview from Nairobi that he has learned of nothing since 2007 that would contradict the *Daily Mail* story.[5]

Obama begins his *Dreams from My Father* with a scene from 1982, when Obama, having just turned twenty-one a few months earlier, is shaken, in his New York apartment, by a phone call from Africa telling him his father has been killed in a car accident.[6] The narrative omits that Obama Senior killed himself driving drunk.

A few pages later, Obama traces his father's history in Kenya back to the time his father herded goats while attending the local "British colonial school." Obama claims his father showed such "great promise" that he won a scholarship to study in Nairobi and then, "on the eve of Kenyan independence, he had been selected by Kenyan leaders and American sponsors to attend a university in the United States." Obama proudly tells the reader his father joined "the first large wave of Africans to be sent forth to master Western technology and bring it back to forge a new, modern Africa."[7]

Again, Obama carefully omits the underside of the story, that when his father headed off at age twenty-three to a university education in Hawaii, he was abandoning an African girl named Kezia, whom he had married at age eighteen. Nor does Obama mention that Kezia was then pregnant with his father's first child.

Obama magnifies his father's time in Hawaii, claiming he arrived at the University of Hawaii as the institution's first African student. Obama then boasts that his father "studied econometrics, worked with unsurpassed concentration, and graduated in three years at the top of his class." Obama further notes his father's friends "were legion, and he helped organize the International Students Association, of which he became the first president."[8]

He omits any mention of his father's continued success with women.

The *Daily Mail*, on the other hand, reports that Obama Senior was a "slick womanizer" who persuaded Obama's mother, Ann Dunham, a "naïve 18-year-old white girl, to marry him, without disclosing to her that he had left behind in Africa a wife he had not divorced." Obama presents a more dramatic version of his parents' romance, claiming his father met his mother in a Russian language course at the university, "an awkward, shy American girl, only eighteen, and they fell in love.[9]

"The girl's parents, wary at first, were won over by his [Obama Senior's] charm and intellect," Obama continues in his narrative; "the young couple married, and she bore them a son, to whom he bequeathed his name."[10]

Obama Junior was born on August 4, 1961.

In the next sentence, Obama intentionally skips over several more key details. After noting his father's decision to leave Hawaii for Cambridge, Massachusetts, Obama explains, "A separation occurred, and he returned to Africa to fulfill his promise to the continent. The mother and child stayed behind, but the bond of love survived the distances . . ."[11] The ellipsis that ends the sentence in the book omits the fact that Obama's mother divorced his father when she discovered "his bigamous double life," as the *Daily Mail* disclosed.

Two years later, Obama Senior won another scholarship, this time to pursue a Ph.D. at Harvard. Obama explains his father's decision to abandon his mother and him in Hawaii by saying that the scholarship from Harvard did not include "the money to take his new family with him."[12]

Yet even here we find Obama caught up in half-truths. Before Obama Senior accepted Harvard's limited scholarship, the New School for Social Research in New York City had offered him a generous scholarship that would have paid for his family to accompany him.[13]

In typical fashion, Obama does not make this important point chronologically, as he could have in the opening pages of the autobiography when he describes a central family drama that shaped his life. Exactly why did his father abandon the family to go to Harvard? At the beginning we are led to believe that Obama Senior had no choice—Harvard was his only option, or so we think, and the Harvard scholarship did not provide enough funds.

Instead Obama provides the true explanation some hundred pages later, and only in passing, as part of a conversation with his mother when she visits him at Columbia University in New York City: "The New School agreed to pay for everything—room and board, a job on campus, enough to pay for all three of us," she tells her son, after they go together to see the art film *Black Orpheus*. But in that conversation Obama focuses our attention on how going to the movie with his mother made him aware for the first time of the sexual excitement that she, "a white middle-class girl," felt for "the promise of another life: warm, sexual, exotic, different," one inhabited by vibrant black men.[14] Finally, Obama's mother explains why his father abandoned them to go to Harvard: "Harvard just agreed to pay tuition. But Barack [Senior] was such a stubborn bastard, he had to go to Harvard. How can I refuse the best education? He told me. That's all he could think about, proving that he was the best . . ."[15]

Again the narrative is scrambled. On a first reading, only the most aware readers—or those who already know the truth—will realize that the dialogue at Columbia refers back to the beginning of the book and explains how Ann Dunham Obama saw her husband's decision to go to Harvard, a key issue since the opening pages of the autobiography. Deciphering the truth takes much effort, almost requiring the reader to memorize the book as you go along, so you can unscramble where important discussions occur, put the parts together, and see some semblance of truth. The order of the book appears to be the chronology not of the events themselves, but the chronology of how Obama pieced together the truth about his father's failed life.

While at Harvard, Obama Senior had an affair with yet another woman, an American-born teacher named Ruth Nidesand; recall that he was still married to Obama's mother and to his abandoned wife in Africa. Then Obama Senior returned to Kenya and fathered two more children by Kezia. Somewhere during that period, he also married Ruth, after she followed him to Africa from Harvard.

The *Daily Mail* quoted a relative of Obama as saying, "We told him [Obama Junior] how his father would still go to Kezia and it was during these visits that she became pregnant with two more children. He also had two children with Ruth." The *Daily Mail* further reported that Ruth finally left Obama Senior "after he repeatedly flew into whiskey-fuelled rages, beating her brutally."

"Friends say drinking blighted his [Obama Senior's] life," the *Daily Mail* reported; "he lost both his legs while driving under the influence and also lost his job."

Drunken driving ended Obama Senior's "brilliant" civil service career as a top Harvard-trained econometrician in the newly independent government of Jomo Kenyatta, who was on a mission to bring his economically backward country into prosperity. According to the *Daily Mail,* even after losing both legs in the car accident, Obama Senior fathered yet another son, his eighth child, by yet another woman, and "continued to come home drunk." Then, shortly after Barack Obama Junior's twenty-first birthday, Obama Senior put an end to the sad drama by killing himself in yet another car crash, once again driving drunk.

The *Daily Mail* quoted Kenyan writer Philip Ochieng as

saying, "He [Obama Senior] was excessively fond of Scotch. He had fallen into the habit of going home drunk every night. His boasting proved his undoing and left him without a job, plunged him into prolonged poverty and dangerously wounded his ego.

"He was a menace to life," Ochieng said. "He had many extremely serious accidents. Both his legs had to be amputated. They were replaced with crude false limbs made from iron.

"He was just like Mr. Toad [from *The Wind in the Willows*], very arrogant on the road, especially when he had whiskey inside. I was not surprised when I learned how he died."

"Why didn't my father return?" is a question Obama admits in his autobiography has haunted him since the age of five or six.

In his autobiography, we learn that Obama's Kenyan father was Muslim, but only indirectly, when Obama explains to a girlfriend in Hawaii that his name is not "Barry," as he was then commonly called, but "Barack," a name Barack explains means "Blessed" in Arabic. He further explains that the name was his father's and says, "My grandfather was a Muslim." [16]

In 1986, four years after his father's death, Obama went to Africa for the first time, to be confronted with the truth of his father's life and to meet half-brothers and half-sisters he never knew he had. In Africa for the first time, Obama admits he was told the truth about his father, perhaps for the first time in his life.

Obama recounts an important conversation he had in Africa with his aunt Zeituni.

"Zeituni stopped walking and turned to me," Obama wrote in his autobiography. "'After your father went off to live with his American wife, Ruth . . . well, he would go to Kezia sometimes. You must understand that traditionally she was still his wife. It was during such a visit that Kezia became pregnant with Abo, the brother you haven't met. The thing was, Kezia also lived with another man briefly during this time. So when she became pregnant again, with Bernard, no one was sure who—' Zeituni stopped, letting the thought finish itself." [17]

Obama still wants to see his father as the victim. Zeituni, for instance, explains that "the problem [with Obama Senior] was that his heart was too big." [18] She also explains that Obama Senior was the first in the family to study abroad, the first in the family who had ever ridden in an airplane, and he had taken on too large a burden trying to help his family in Africa and lift Kenya into a modern economic age.

The *Daily Mail* concluded that "for all Mr. Obama's reputation for straight talking and the compelling narrative of his recollections, they are largely myth.

"We have discovered that his father was not just a flawed individual but an abusive bigamist and an egomaniac, whose life was ruined not by racism or corruption but by his own weakness," the *Daily Mail* wrote. "And, devastatingly, the testimony has come from Mr. Obama's own relatives and family friends."

The *Daily Mail* suggested that Obama chose to present his father in a favorable light as an electoral tactic. "Indeed, by offering up a conveniently plotted account of his personal history in this way," Churcher wrote, "he [Obama] might even have made a pre-emptive strike on those sure to pose the awkward questions that inevitably face a serious contender for the White House."

Regardless of the motives, in the autobiography Obama never states precisely how many wives his father had, or how many half-brothers and sisters he has from different mothers, whether the women were married to his father or not. Obama blames racism for breaking up his parents' marriage, not his father's polygamist ways, which began when he first left Africa, before he ever met Obama's mother in Hawaii.

Yet in the final analysis, Obama embraces the myth, accepting Zeituni's explanation that his father was a victim who suffered because his "heart was too big." In reality, Obama Senior was a bureaucrat of modest achievement who could not overcome a struggle with alcohol that ultimately caused his death.

Interview with an Uncle

A telephone interview with Sayid Obama, Barack Obama's uncle, from his home in Kisumu, Kenya, provides additional insight into the life of Barack's father. Barack Obama Senior was Sayid Obama's older brother.[19]

"My brother Barack was born in 1936," Sayid explained. "I was the much younger brother, the last born of the sons, born in the mid-1950s."

Sayid Obama said their father had livestock, including goats and cows, and that the sons in the family, including Obama Senior, worked to take care of the livestock, confirming a detail Obama related about his father. Working as a goatherd does not mean the family was poverty-stricken or otherwise disadvantaged in their tribal home, a misimpression that could easily be derived from reading Barack Junior's autobiography. Obama Senior's father was a tribal elder from a prominent and wealthy family in the village where they lived, Nyangoma-Kogelo, in the Siaya District in southwestern Kenya. Moreover, Obama Junior's tribal grandfather had considerable influence with the African leaders at the national level who were pushing for independence from British colonial rule.

"My brother was very bright, very intelligent and that is how he came to be identified to go and study in the United States," Sayid said. Clearly, Obama's father had to do something if he was going to escape Kenya, and an education in the United States must have seemed the chance of a lifetime. Sayid's account seems to agree with the story told by the *Daily Mail*, that Obama was seen as special, selected for U.S. study probably because of his family background and his demonstrated intelligence in local schools. So far the story holds that Obama Senior left Kenya for schooling in the United States, in the anticipation he would return to Kenya and assume an important position in the Kenyan government of Jomo Kenyatta after independence. Kenya achieved independence on December 12, 1963, when Jomo Kenyatta of the Kenya African National Union formed a government in which he served as both president and prime minister, ending a period of British colonialism that stretched back to the late nineteenth century. "It was on the eve of independence," Sayid continued, "and because the British occupied most of the senior posts in the government and Africans were taking over at independence, so some of the bright students were taken to the U.S. to go and study so they could take over the jobs that were previously being occupied by the British."

Sayid affirmed that he and his brother were both born into a religious Islamic family and were raised as Muslims. "I did not see my brother practice Islam," Sayid recalled, "especially after he came back from his studies in the United States; I did not consider him to be very religious." While Kenya is approximately 85 percent Christian, a Muslim minority dates back to 1730, when Arabs from Oman began occupying eastern Africa, dislodging the Portuguese colonists and taking over the slave trade in the eastern African coastal states, including both Kenya and Tanzania. Listening to Sayid, there is no doubt Obama Senior was a Muslim by birth and upbringing, even if his devotion as a Muslim remained in doubt. The facts are that the Obama family in Africa is a Muslim family of the predominantly Christian Luo tribe in the predominantly Christian country of Kenya.

"First my brother went to the University of Hawaii, where he met Obama's mother," Sayid confirmed, "then he got a scholarship to study at Harvard. Then after graduating, he came back to Kenya and occupied several posts in the government.

"First, I believe, he worked for Shell Oil," he continued. "Then, later, he went to work with the Ministry of Economic Planning and Development. He also worked with the Ministry of Tourism. I cannot say in which order, but I know he worked with those ministries."

Sayid also confirmed his brother had difficulties working with the government in Kenya after independence.

"Barack's main problem working with the government was tribalism," Sayid explained. "Tribalism in Kenya really is something you have to understand, if you want to understand Kenya's politics. During that time, because our family was close to Tom Mboya, who was a very corrupt but charismatic leader in Kenya, we suffered. The elite around President Kenyatta were from his tribe, the Kikuyu, Kenya's dominant tribe, and they were pledged to support the president, so all the people close to Mboya suffered, including my brother."

Mboya was from the Luo tribe, the same tribe of Obama's family. The Luo are Kenya's second-largest tribe, smaller in number than the Kikuyu.

In 1957, Mboya formed the People's Convention Party and was very close to Kwame Nkrumah of Ghana, who like Mboya and Kenyatta was a Pan-Africanist. Some ten years earlier, in 1946, Nkrumah and Kenyatta had formed the Pan-African Federation. In 1958, at an All-African Peoples' Conference in Ghana that was convened by Nkrumah, Mboya was elected conference chairman. (The Pan-African movement had roots in the United States. W. E. B. Du Bois is considered the father of Pan-Africanism. Du Bois's goal was to form a positive African identity to counter the crime of slavery.)

In 1960, Mboya joined his People's Convention Party with Kenyatta's Kenya African Union to form the Kenya African National Union, or KANU. Kenyatta had been imprisoned since 1952 for his role in the Mau Mau rebellion. Still imprisoned when the KANU was formed, Kenyatta was named KANU president in absentia.

On December 12, 1963, Kenyatta became prime minister of a finally independent Kenya. Mboya served under Kenyatta as minister of justice and constitutional affairs and later as minister of economic planning and development, until he was assassinated on July 5, 1969, by a Kikuyu tribesman. After Mboya's assassination, Kenyatta's political opponents charged that Kenyatta had been involved in the assassination to eliminate a political rival with a charismatic national following. Had Mboya succeeded Kenyatta as president and prime minister of the country, he most likely would have promoted the Luo tribe over the Kikuyu, who enjoyed power under Kenyatta.

When interviewing Rob Crilly, the freelance journalist in Africa who had contributed to the *Daily Mail*'s article on Barack Obama Senior, I asked why Obama failed to discuss his father's alcoholism and polygamy in his autobiography.

Crilly insisted Obama had discussed the truth, but he argued Obama made the truth difficult to discern in the book, especially since Obama first presents a highly sympathetic portrait of his father. When we first read the book, Crilly argued, Obama encourages us to see his father as a noble but poor African who emerges ultimately to get a degree at Harvard, one of the most prestigious universities in the world. Obama leads us to believe his father abandoned his mother and him only because economic restraints left his father no other choice. The problem, Crilly said, was that the truth, or what Obama chooses to reveal of the truth, comes only much later in the book, and then only in pieces.

Rejecting a simple conclusion, that the book is poorly written and confusing, we are left to ask once again: What is Obama trying to hide and why would he do so?

Obama Visits Africa

How many times did Obama visit Africa? Even on that question the autobiography is cloudy.

"Obama has been in Africa three times," Sayid insisted. "The first time was in 1986. Then he came again in 1992, when he was collecting material for his autobiography. Then the last time was 2006, when he visited Kenya as a U.S. senator."

In the third section of the autobiography, Obama Junior does not disclose clearly the date of the trip to Kenya he discusses, nor does he make clear that he took two separate trips before the autobiography was published. Rather, we are presented with what evidently is a composite of experiences from both trips, without any way of knowing which related experiences came when.

"The trip in 2006 was the second time Obama came with his wife," Sayid further specified. "He first came with her in 1992, when they were getting ready to get married. Then he visited with her as his wife, when he came back in 2006, as a U.S. senator."

Only in the epilogue to the autobiography does Obama disclose that his wife-to-be accompanied him to Africa on the 1992 trip.

Crilly recommended reading the last section of Obama's *Dreams from My Father* a second time, after we know more of the truth about his father. We would be surprised to discover that Obama allows elements of the truth to surface in the text, at the end of the book, in the third-section discussion of Obama's trip to Kenya. Even then, we get the truth obliquely, in a manner that still requires some considerable effort to decipher. We are forced to pit fragments of truth presented later in the book against the idealized version of his father's life presented initially in the book. Crilly said only then can one begin to see in the narrative the various holes and unwelcome details Obama was obviously still struggling to comprehend and accept.

In this section, Obama's aunt Zeituni confirms that his father's "luck changed" after he returned to Kenya and began working for the government.[20] Mark, Obama's half-brother from Ruth Nidesand, the American woman who followed Obama Senior back to Kenya from Harvard, tells Obama, "He [Barack Obama Senior, Mark's father as well as Obama Junior's father] was dead to me even when he was still alive. I knew that he was a drunk and showed no concern for his wife or children. That was enough."[21]

We learn that Obama's aunt Sarah, his father's sister, also ended up resenting Barack Obama Senior for dying without giving her any of the small inheritance Barack Obama

Senior may have had from the Kenyan government, possibly a small government pension or a small plot of land.[22] Sarah feared that any inheritance Barack Obama Senior may have had would go to Kezia, the first wife, whom Barack Obama Senior abandoned when he left Kenya to go to study in Hawaii, and to Kezia's many children, some of whom Barack Obama Senior fathered even after he returned from Harvard.

But these clues are scattered in the third part of the autobiography, not presented so clearly that a reader would get the full picture easily. Obama admits he had difficulty putting together the truth about his father and his family in Africa. When it comes to telling the story of his grandfather, Obama says: "If I could just piece together his story [that of his grandfather, Hussein Onyango Obama], I thought, then perhaps everything else might fall into place."

The problem is that the grandfather's tale turns out to be as complicated as the father's, filled with multiple wives and the resulting half-brothers and half-sisters, among them Barack Obama Senior. Nor was Kenya's history easy to understand, as Kenya struggled toward independence. Through it all, Obama Junior confesses he allowed himself fantasies "that I'd kept secret even from myself," the fantasy "of the Old Man's [Obama Senior, his father] having taken my mother and me back with him to Kenya."

Sayid Obama said his brother's drinking problem intensified after his troubles with the government began. But while Sayid Obama openly acknowledges Obama Senior's drinking problem, his explanation contradicts that offered by the *Daily Mail*. Perhaps Obama Senior's incompetence as a bureaucrat wasn't what caused his alcoholism; perhaps tribal jealousies blocked his advancement in the bureaucracy and so he took up drinking to relieve the frustration of a career stalled through no fault of his own.

The truth no one will ever know, not when more than two decades and family politics fueled by multiple wives and the claims of competing half-brothers and half-sisters stand between us and what really happened to Obama Senior before he died tragically, driving drunk in 1982.

Sayid Obama was not even sure how many wives his brother had: three or four, maybe more. There were at least three: the eighteen-year-old wife, Kezia, whom Obama Senior abandoned when he left Kenya to study in Hawaii; Ann Dunham, Obama Junior's mother, whom Obama Senior abandoned when he left Hawaii to study at Harvard; and Ruth Nidesand, the woman from Harvard who followed Obama Senior back to Kenya and married him there.

The number of children Obama Senior had is equally uncertain. Sayid Obama paused to think when asked how many. "About six," he concluded, although he could not say for sure.

A Family Looks Back

Sayid Obama is currently employed in Kisumu as a mechanical technician with a company that produces industrial alcohol used in pharmaceuticals and manure used in agriculture.

"I do practice Islam, but not that much," Sayid made clear. "I was born in a Muslim family in a predominantly Christian area. Whenever we were short of something, we were sent into our neighbors' homes to ask for it, and they did the same with us. I attended Christian schools and studied Christian religion. Still, I've lived my life studying the Koran.

"So, I have all these values," he continued, "but as much as I would want to identify with Christianity, I cannot belong there only. At the same time as I identify with Islam, I cannot belong there wholly. So, what I can say is that there are values in Christianity that are key to me and there are also values in Islam that are key to me.

"So, if somebody asked me what religion I belong to, sometimes I find that it is very difficult to answer.

"My brother was different," he distinguished. "I didn't see him actually practicing any religion, though he was raised into a Muslim family, as was I."

Was his father, Obama Junior's grandfather, wealthy?

"I would say he was better off than other people in the village," Sayid answered. "He traveled all over the world with the British for a long time. My father was older than Kenyatta and closer to the kings and all those people that we had before the British system of government ended."

Again, when one asks how Obama Senior got the chance to go to the United States for education, the family produces multiple versions.

"My brother [Barack Senior] got a better path in life because my father [Hussein Onyango Obama, Obama Junior's grandfather] worked with the British and knew the importance of going to school, so he made all his children go to school," Sayid elaborated, the second time the question was asked.

"Plus Barack Senior had something besides what his father imparted in him, which was that he was very intelligent, he was very good in school, and he didn't need anybody to push him to achieve whatever he wanted to achieve," he continued. "So, once he got the beginning from his father, the rest of it he managed to get by himself."

In the last part of *Dreams from My Father*, Obama Junior relates a story told by his stepgrandmother Sarah [the stepmother of his father and Sayid], not to be confused with

Obama's aunt Sarah, explaining how his father got accepted to go to the United States to study.[23]

According to Granny Sarah, as related in the closing pages of the autobiography, Obama Senior began working as an office boy, a clerk to an Arab named Suleiman, to support his wife Kezia and two children he and Kezia had at that time, Roy and Auma. Again, we find yet another conflict, this time with the *Daily Mail* story that Obama Senior abandoned Kezia to go to Hawaii when she was pregnant with their first child.

Then, according to the story told by Granny Sarah, two American women from a religious organization in Nairobi entered the picture and took an interest in Barack Senior, then working as a "clerk office boy" for the Arab businessman. These two women encouraged Barack Senior to take a correspondence course so he could get a secondary school certificate, a prerequisite to entering college.

According to Granny Sarah, Obama's father took the exam at the U.S. Embassy and, while waiting for the results, began using the office typewriter at night to write letters applying to study in American universities. Finally, the embassy sent a letter notifying Obama Senior that he had passed, and the university in Hawaii wrote back saying they would give him a scholarship.

So, according to the story told by Granny Sarah, Obama Senior's own determination and initiative got him the chance to study in the United States, a version different from the one in which Obama Senior was singled out as an exceptional student at his village school. Still, both versions have in common the fact that Obama Senior abandoned his wife to go to Hawaii, much as he abandoned Ann Dunham, his second wife, and his son Obama Junior, as he headed off to study at Harvard.

By the end of the book, Obama warms to Granny Sarah in the glow of her family saga, as she recalls for him the family history going back to the day she married his grandfather after he was abandoned by Akuma, his grandfather's first wife, the mother to Obama Senior. Still, if we read closely, we find in Granny's account evidence that she harbored resentments toward her stepson, Obama Senior, much as did Obama's aunt Sarah, although for different reasons.

Granny offers no altruistic or patriotic reason why her stepson Obama Senior left Kenya to study in the United States. Instead, what we get is Granny's resentment that Obama Senior, while in the United States, had married a white woman in Hawaii over the objections of the family in Africa. Moreover, Obama Senior abandoned Ann Dunham just as Hussein Onyango Obama, her husband and Obama Senior's father, had predicted he would do.

So too, if we read closely enough, we can detect Granny's umbrage when Obama Senior married yet a second white woman, Ruth Nidesand. Granny's unhappiness is unmistakable as she recounts how Ruth insisted Obama Senior bring into Nariobi the two children Kezia had with Obama Senior, a situation that predictably turned out to be a disaster for all involved. Even after he married Ruth, Obama Senior returned periodically to have yet more children by Kezia, children Ruth evidently no longer insisted move in with them as part of their family.

In the end, Granny Sarah offers no explanation why Obama Senior "fell from power," claiming only that she knew something had gone wrong when Obama Senior started arriving home to see them in a taxi instead of his usual Mercedes. She noted that Obama Senior ironically continued to arrive home bearing gifts, but now gifts "he could no longer afford." Nor could she resist adding that

Obama Senior, even after his fall, continued to "boast and laugh and drink with the men," as evidently "he still liked to do." [24]

Nevertheless, the Obama family in Africa is happy to accept Barack Obama Junior as one of them, especially now that he has achieved political success as a U.S. senator and is running for president.

"Barack Obama is a loving person who loves his family here in Africa," Sayid emphasized at the conclusion of the telephone interview. "There is no denying he has his roots and family here in Kenya. He is an American, but he also has a family he loves very much here in Africa.

"The American people should remember Barack Obama is a good person," Sayid summed up. "If only America would give him a chance to solve the problems, I believe Barack Obama has all it takes to be the U.S. president."

The Camelot Connection: An Obama Fiction

Michael Dobbs, writing in the *Washington Post,* probed yet another conflict with versions of the story Obama likes to tell about how his father got to the United States to study. [25]

The fascinating part of these stories is Obama's determination to connect himself and his African family with John F. Kennedy and the Camelot myth of the abbreviated presidency, as well as connecting to the Selma voting rights march in 1965 and the civil rights movement, identified with yet another martyr of the time, Reverend Martin Luther King, Jr.

Why Obama would want to connect himself with JFK is clear: JFK, along with FDR, occupies a central position in the pantheon of revered Democratic Party presidents.

All Democrat presidential contenders want themselves to be seen as the "next JFK." Why he would want to connect with King is equally clear: King, the only African-American for whom we celebrate a national holiday, became the embodiment of the civil rights movement the moment he pronounced at the Lincoln Memorial that he had a dream. Among Democratic Party politicians, Obama appears to be no exception in wanting to identify with both JFK and MLK. The problem is that the stories he told about JFK and about Selma to make the connections are fabrications: they are lies with no basis in fact or reality.

In a speech delivered from the pulpit of the historic Brown Chapel A.M.E. Church in Selma, Alabama, on March 4, 2007, Obama argued that he owed his very existence to Selma. A transcript of Obama's speech[26] and a video clip posted on YouTube.com[27] permit precise analysis of the exact words Obama spoke to the Selma congregation that day.

A few minutes into the speech, Obama began discussing the protests in Selma and Birmingham, Alabama, which were instrumental to the growth of the civil rights movement in the 1960s. He invented some dialogue in which he mused, "It worried the folks in the White House who said, 'You know, we're battling communism. How are we going to win hearts and minds all across the world if right here in our own country, John, we're not observing the ideals set forth in our Constitution? We might be accused of being hypocrites.'" So Obama went on rewriting history to invent the complete fabrication that Robert and Jack Kennedy were the ones who decided to do an airlift that brought Obama's father to America.

Unfortunately, JFK was not in the White House until January 20, 1961, and he did not participate in the decision that Tom Mboya made in Kenya to organize the 1959 airlift.·

Yet, in his mind Obama imagined differently, dramatizing his version of events by offering the Selma congregation yet more imagined White House dialogue, visualizing JFK making a decision he never made: "'We're going to go to Africa and start bringing young Africans over to this country and give them scholarships to study, so they can learn what a wonderful country America is.'"

Obama did not stop here.

"This young man named Barack Obama got one of those tickets and came over to this country," he continued from the pulpit in the historic Selma church. "He met this woman whose great-great-great-great-grandfather had owned slaves. But she had a good idea there was some craziness going on because they looked at each other and they decided that we know that in the world as it has been, it might not be possible for us to get together and have a child."

Obama's point in rewriting history was to argue that he owed his life to JFK.

Unfortunately for Obama, research by Michael Dobbs has set the historical record straight. Dobbs found conclusively that the 1959 airlift, which brought eighty-one Kenyan students to the United States, including Obama's father, happened before JFK was inaugurated president and did not benefit from any Kennedy family funding. The funding for the 1959 airlift came from a general appeal to the U.S. public that had been organized by the Kenyan political leader Tom Mboya.

The historical record is further established by a background memorandum prepared by Senator John Kennedy's office in August 1960, while he was running for president. The memo documents that JFK met with Tom Mboya—*but after the 1959 airlift had already occurred.* Mboya met with JFK in Hyannisport, Massachusetts, on July 26, 1960, while Kennedy was running for president.[28] Mboya's goal was to convince JFK to fund a second airlift of African students to the United States. The memo further documents that the State Department, despite intervention by Vice President Richard Nixon, had already turned down Mboya's request for a second airlift to bring to the United States two hundred African students who had received scholarships from U.S. schools.

The Kennedy family, utilizing the Joseph P. Kennedy, Jr. Foundation, decided to give Mboya a hundred-thousand-dollar donation to pay for the second airlift, in memory of JFK's brother who was killed in World War II. Knowing the Kennedy family was going to pay for the second airlift, Nixon prevailed on the State Department to reverse their earlier negative decision. The African-American Students Foundation, however, decided to accept the Kennedy Foundation's offer, preferring the willing generosity of the privately offered financing to the obvious hostility the State Department had initially expressed to the group's request. Mboya's decision was a rebuke to Nixon, who had failed to deliver the State Department until after the Kennedy family had stepped forward with funding.

At the time, the State Department was turning down Mboya's request in deference to the government of Jomo Kenyatta, who had argued against Mboya that young, talented Kenyans should stay home and attend Makerere College in neighboring Uganda, instead of traveling to the United States to be trained in American universities.

In 1959, some eight thousand individuals contributed money to the first airlift, including baseball star Jackie Robinson and actors Harry Belafonte and Sidney Poitier.

"There was enormous excitement when the Britannia aircraft took off for New York with the future Kenyan elite on board," Dobbs wrote. "After a few weeks of orientation, the students were dispatched to universities across the United States to study subjects that would help them govern Kenya after the departure of the British. Obama Sr. was interested in economics and was sent to Hawaii, where he met, and later married, a Kansas native named Ann Dunham. Barack Jr. was born in August 1961."

Dobbs corrected Obama, pointing out: "A more accurate version of the story would begin not with the Kennedys but with a Kenyan nationalist leader named Tom Mboya, who traveled to the United States in 1959 and 1960 to persuade thousands of Americans to support his efforts to educate newly emerging African elite. Mboya did not approach the Kennedys for financial support until Obama Sr. was already studying in Hawaii."

To recap: Obama Senior came to the United States to study in Hawaii on the first airlift, the one organized by Mboya and funded by some eight thousand individuals. JFK was involved in funding only the second airlift and played no part in the first airlift. So Obama is again lying about history to claim JFK had anything to do with bringing his father to the United States to study.

Obama's Selma speech was also inaccurate to claim that Selma and the civil rights movement were responsible for his birth.

Immediately following the part of the speech quoted above, Obama went on to say, "there was something stirring across the country because of what happened in Selma, Alabama, because some folks are willing to march across a bridge. So they got together and Barack Obama Jr. was born. So don't tell me I don't have a claim on Selma,

Alabama. Don't tell me I'm not coming home to Selma, Alabama. I'm here because somebody marched. I'm here because you all sacrificed for me. I stand on the shoulders of giants."

Almost as soon as the speech was given, bloggers across the Internet pointed out the fabrication. The Selma voting rights march Obama referenced in the speech happened in March 1965, but Obama Junior was born in August 1961. So there was no chronologically possible way Obama Senior and Ann Dunham decided to marry in the excitement of a Selma march that would not happen until more than three and a half years after they married and Obama Junior was born.

Obama's fabrications, both in his autobiography and in his Selma speech, hide what was most likely the reality, especially when we recall Sayid Obama's recollections that the Obama family in Kenya were supporters of Mboya, also a Luo tribe member. Barack Obama's African family most likely used Luo tribal influence to make sure their son was one of the privileged few who got on the 1959 airlift to the United States for schooling. Rather than being encouraged by two American religious workers and typing up applications at night in the office where he was working as a clerk, Obama Senior was most likely chosen by Mboya at the urging of Obama Senior's father, all done within the influence networks established by the Luo tribal hierarchy.

Either way, Barack Obama Junior's story that his birth was due to JFK or to the Selma voting rights march was made up completely out of thin air. Regardless of how Barack Obama Senior was selected to attend school in Hawaii, JFK had nothing to do with his getting here to study and Selma had nothing to do with Junior's being conceived.

Dobbs also reported that a letter among the Mboya

papers at Stanford University's Hoover Institution shows "most" of Obama Senior's early expenses in the United States were covered by Elizabeth Mooney Kirk, an international literacy expert who traveled widely in Kenya. Kirk wrote to Mboya in May 1962 to request funds "to sponsor Barack Obama for graduate study, preferably at Harvard." By then Obama had married Ann Dunham and Obama Junior had been born. Kirk's letter evidently makes no request by Obama Senior for sufficient funds to take his new American wife and child with him, as he departed Hawaii to pursue his studies in Cambridge, Massachusetts.

"It's a touching story—but the details are either untrue or grossly oversimplified," Dobbs generously wrote. "Obama's Selma speech offers a very confused chronology of both the Kenya student program and the civil rights movement."

In unraveling Obama's fabrications about who was responsible for his being born, Dobbs provides one other detail that proves useful. He notes that Philip Ochieng was another student on the first airlift with Obama Senior. Ochieng was on his way to study in Chicago, destined to return to Kenya, where he remains a prominent journalist. We encountered Ochieng earlier in this inquiry, recalling Obama Senior back in Kenya as a hopeless drunk whose love of Scotch and tendency to brag about his intellect caused him to lose his job as a failed bureaucrat in the Kenyan government.

Dobbs interviewed Ochieng and got the same story. Ochieng remembered Obama Senior as "charming, generous and extraordinarily clever," but also "imperious, cruel and given to boasting about his brain and his wealth."

Ochieng's account to Dobbs conforms with the story he told the *Daily Mail*, undermining the explanation Obama Junior offers in his autobiography for his father's failure, namely, Granny Sarah's story that Obama Senior was on the outs because he was from the wrong tribe. Obama Senior may have been of the wrong tribe to succeed in Kenyatta's government, but even Granny Sarah said enough to indicate that Obama Senior's fondness of drink was commonly known to his family in Africa.

Dobbs concludes his story by noting that Obama Senior returned to Kenya, where he became an aide to Mboya while Mboya headed the Ministry of Economic Planning and Development. "According to his old 'drinking buddy' Ochieng," Dobbs wrote, "he [Obama Senior] antagonized other officials with his 'boasting,' was 'excessively fond of Scotch' and ended up in poverty 'without a job.' He got into frequent car accidents, one of which led to the amputation of both legs. He was killed in another car accident, in 1982, at the age of 46."

If Obama owes his life to any politician, it is to Tom Mboya, not John Kennedy or Martin Luther King. Mboya was from the same tribe as Obama Senior, Mboya championed the Obama family, selected Obama Senior to study in the United States and arranged the financing to pay for the airlift. Had Tom Mboya not felt a tribal affinity for Obama's grandfather in Africa, Obama Senior may never have left Kenya.

Obama Senior "Lost" in Drinking Scotch

We learn more from Ochieng in an extraordinarily self-revealing essay he published in Africa in 2004, when Obama Junior was running for the U.S. Senate.[29] Ochieng confirms every important detail of what the *Daily Mail* and *Washington Post* reported him as saying. Ochieng knew Obama Senior well and his story in all three sources is consistent and easy to understand.

In his essay, Ochieng related that he first met Obama Senior in Tom Mboya's Nairobi office when Mboya was the secretary general of the Kenya Federation of Labor, prior to flying with him to the United States as part of the Tom Mboya airlift of 1959. Ochieng, like Obama Senior, was one of the hundreds of Kenyan students given scholarships to attend American universities.

This adds to the weight of the evidence that Obama Senior got this opportunity through political favor, based on his father's privileged position in the Luo tribe. Obama Senior had the high intellect and good grades that would certainly have been requirements, but it is doubtful he or any other Kenyan youth made their way to Hawaii simply by typing a university application at night with a borrowed typewriter.

Ochieng added, "Obama and I met up again on returning to Nairobi and remained drinking buddies for many years." In an acknowledgment to Hussein Onyango Obama, Ochieng wrote, "Like his father, although charming, generous and extraordinarily clever, Obama Senior was also imperious, cruel and given to boasting about his brain and wealth."

This boasting proved Obama Senior's undoing in the Kenyatta system, Ochieng judged, admitting there was also "tribalism in it." Left without a job, Obama Senior plunged into poverty with a dangerously wounded ego.

"Like me, he was excessively fond of Scotch," Ochieng admitted, repeating the story he told the newspaper. "In his later years, he had fallen into the habit of going home drunk every night."

Ochieng said Scotch "proved to be Obama Senior's final undoing," noting that driving a car "always excited him excessively.

"Obama Senior had many extremely serious accidents," Ochieng affirmed. "In time, both his legs had to be amputated and replaced with iron. But his pride was such that he could not tolerate 'crawling like an insect' on the road. I was not surprised when I learned how he had died."

By contrast, Obama's story of his father's life is dense, presented in anything but a straightforward manner, often glorified or embellished so as to mask much of the harsh and, for Obama, probably painful truth.

Obama Junior "Lost" from His African Roots

Ochieng's point in writing this insightful piece was not just to set the record straight on Obama Senior. More important, he sought to describe how Obama Junior, when first visiting the "Home Squared" of his father's native village during his 1992 trip to Africa, was confronted with the perplexing accusation, "You're lost!"

The expression comes from the Luo verb *lal,* which Ochieng explained means to disappear or be away for a long time without an explanation. "Simply by being born and growing up in America, Barack Junior had never been a Luo: He had *lal,*" Ochieng wrote.

From there, Ochieng argued Obama Senior "had lost his way by marrying a white woman—Barack Junior's mother." Ochieng confessed that he shared this plight. For decades he was estranged from his daughter, who was born of a white woman who left him while Ochieng was in the United States studying.

"Obama Senior left Ann—Junior's mother—almost as soon as Junior was born," he continued. "Junior met Senior only once. When he was 12. Senior visited him in Honolulu,

Hawaii, where Junior was growing up under the care of his white grandfather and grandmother. They never saw each other again." So too, the white mother of Ochieng's child left him when the child was born and the two had still not seen each other at the time he was writing the piece, even though the daughter was then in her early forties.

"Because I recognize myself in it," Ochieng admitted, "this is the most moving theme in Barack Obama's book—the scar that this fact left in Junior's mind, the enduring crisis of identity that will not go away."

Ochieng extended the analysis to a crisis he posited, "that all black people—no matter where they are—really live in two worlds and, therefore, have an identity crisis.

"One might even say that they live in no world," he continued. "Even in our native Africa, *walal* ('we are lost')." From here Ochieng reached back to "European imperialism" that "drove our forefathers' communal spirit away from the land," such that "we stopped being African.

"We started to think like Europeans," he went on. "But we never became Europeans either. We became ghosts flitting into and out of European imagination."

This brought Ochieng to the work of the Kenyan author Ngugi wa Thiong'o, whom Ochieng credits as "telling us for decades what we have refused to hear—that as long as we continue to worship European gods, European ideas on governance and European paradigms of development, all our endowments—labour, natural resources and markets—will continue to belong to Europe for the fleecing."

He goes so far as to charge that Obama Junior, by being elected a U.S. senator, "may himself be accused of surrender to a 'democracy' that is in essence an 'elective tyranny,' the white liberal's political prescription for perpetuating an economic-intellectual system that dehumanizes the black person."

Ochieng's argument proceeds not from responsibility, but from victimization. Most of us could claim to have ancestral roots in some sort of injustice or tyranny, somewhere during the nearly three thousand years of recorded or near-recorded history we have experienced together as human beings. Yet, not all of us feel as if we are victims to our ancestrial past.

Ochieng's self-examination, his contemplation of his common experience with the Obama family, gives us a glimpse into the "race and inheritance" Obama directed us to examine in the subtitle of his book. Is the lesson we are to learn one of resentment? Is the analysis one of "imperialism" and "exploitation"?

"I was more surprised when Obama Junior emerged, as if from the blue," Ochieng concluded. "I knew that Home Squared, Luoland, Kenya and Africa might soon be represented in the world's most powerful council."

As Obama Junior developed from Barry Obama to Barack Obama, his sense of *lal*, "being lost," never left him. Examining the truth about the Obama family becomes an important part of understanding Obama, at the very least because Barack Obama himself tells us that Kenya is an important part of who he is, even today. As Ochieng reminds us, where Barack Obama is, there also is Kenya. Where Obama is, there too is his search for his father.

— 2 —

STRANGERS IN
STRANGE LANDS

*I also think we were a little untethered, that our
lives involved a lot of sort of drifting in and out
of worlds, here and there.*

—Maya Soetoro-Ng, *Barack Obama's half-sister*[1]

While Obama Senior is at center stage in Obama Junior's autobiography, *Dreams from My Father*, his mother, Stanley Ann Dunham, is also onstage, but in a supporting role.

Obama spent the majority of his formative years in Hawaii, where he was raised by his grandparents: Stanley Armour Dunham, a World War II veteran from Kansas and struggling furniture salesman who ultimately tried selling life insurance, and Madelyn Lee Payne Dunham, also a Kansas native, who ended up with a management position in a prominent Hawaiian bank. Yet Obama spent three years growing up in Indonesia, after his mother moved them there so they could be with her second husband, an Indonesian-born Muslim whom she met studying at the University of Hawaii, just as she had met her first husband, Obama's father.

The Obama family story is far different from those of past presidential candidates. Even his mother's story is curious: What father would name his daughter "Stanley" after himself, just because he wanted a son? Being introduced her whole life as "Stanley Ann," the only child of the Dunham family, must have given her a lot to explain to her peers, from the first moment she set foot on the neighborhood playground or showed up for school.

Before we sort out the truth of Obama's childhood years in Hawaii, we have to sort out the truth of his brief sojourn in Indonesia. Once again, as we saw in the last chapter with Obama's stories about his father, we are more misled than assisted by Obama's autobiography, just as we will be again when we get to Hawaii. In 2007, the *Chicago Tribune* conducted more than forty interviews with former classmates, teachers, friends, and neighbors in Obama's childhood homes of Hawaii and Indonesia, as well as a review of public records, only to conclude that "several of his oft-recited stories may not have happened in the way he has recounted them." The *Tribune*'s explanation was that some of the stories "seem to make Obama look better in the retelling, others appear to exaggerate his outward struggles over issues of race, or simply skim over some of the most painful, private moments of his life." [2]

What does his childhood experience in Indonesia tell us about Obama the man, Obama the politician, and Obama the possible president of the United States of America?

High School on Mercer Island

Stanley Ann graduated in 1960 from Mercer Island High School, located on an island in the middle of Lake Washington in Seattle. The *Chicago Tribune* characterized Mercer

Island of the Eisenhower era as being "a rural, idyllic place," not the pricey community of corporate luminaries it later became (among those who live there today is Paul Allen of Microsoft fame).

Interviewed by the *Tribune*, many of her classmates at Mercer Island found Stanley Ann to be "strong willed and unconventional," a judgment undoubtedly influenced by hindsight, especially knowing she chose Obama Senior, followed by an Indonesian Muslim, Lolo Soetoro Mangunharjo, to be her husbands.[3] Raising the darker-skinned Obama Junior as her infant son also undoubtedly reinforced the judgment that Stanley Ann was "different," recollections that surfaced in the *Tribune* interviews in 2007, some forty-seven years after the Mercer Island High School class of 1960 had graduated.

"She touted herself as an atheist, and it was something she'd read about and could argue," the newspaper quoted Maxine Box, Stanley Ann's best friend in high school, as remembering. "She was always challenging and arguing and comparing. She was already thinking about things that the rest of us hadn't." Chip Wall, a retired philosophy teacher, said, "She was not a standard-issue girl of her times . . . She wasn't part of the matched-sweater-set crowd."

The *Tribune* noted that these classmate recollections belied Obama's campaign speech presentation of his mother, which the newspaper characterized as "If you have any lingering questions or doubts about the Hawaiian-born presidential candidate with a funny name, just remember that Mom hails from America's good earth." The paper noted this was Obama's "log cabin story," his version of Bill Clinton's "Man from Hope" tale.

Elaine Johnson, a classmate who used to wait for the school bus with Stanley Ann, confirmed to the newspaper that Stanley Ann did not like having a boy's name. Others said Stanley Ann felt no need to date and was not interested in having children. She was remembered as a girl whose mind was "in full tilt."

Stanley Ann's classmates remembered two teachers in particular, Val Foubert and Jim Wichterman, who "generated regular parental thunderstorms by teaching their students to challenge societal norms and question all manner of authority." Foubert taught English, but his texts were "cutting edge": *Atlas Shrugged*, *The Organization Man*, *The Hidden Persuaders*, *1984*, and the acerbic writings of H. L. Mencken. Wichterman's philosophy selections were not much better. "I had them read 'The Communist Manifesto,' and the parents went nuts," Wichterman told the newspaper, adding that parental protests, known then as "mother's marches," met any attempts to introduce discussions of sex or religion. Wichterman taught Sartre and Kierkegaard, as he encouraged his students to question the existence of God. Students called the hallway between Foubert's and Wichterman's offices "Anarchy Alley," apparently an apt description of the revolutionary ideas encouraged by the two teachers there.

The *Tribune* further reported that Stanley Ann did not want to leave Mercer Island and move to Hawaii. Her father felt business opportunities might be better in Hawaii. In the newly created state of Hawaii he hoped to revive his career as a furniture salesman, which had faltered in Seattle.

The *Tribune* quoted Neil Abercrombie, currently a Democratic congressman from the 1st District in Hawaii, as being part of the "long coffeehouse sessions" that Stanley Ann and Obama Senior enjoyed while courting at the University of Hawaii. "I think she was attracted to his powerful personality," Abercrombie told the *Tribune*, "and he was attracted to her beauty and calmness." Abercrombie noted Obama Senior's deep voice, which "made James Earl Jones seem like a tenor," and he described Stanley Ann as "the original feminist," quietly passionate in her arguments.

After Obama Senior was accepted at Harvard, Abercrombie told the *Tribune*, Stanley Ann disappeared from the University of Hawaii student gatherings. He excused Obama Senior's departure, saying, "I know he loved Ann, but I think he didn't want the impediment of being responsible for a family. He expected great things of himself and he was going off to achieve them."

Years later, Abercrombie caught up with Obama Senior during a trip to Africa. "He was drinking too much; his frustration was apparent," he recalled. To Abercrombie's surprise, the paper noted, Obama Senior never asked about his ex-wife or son. Abercrombie himself evidently found it so hard to explain this omission that he felt obliged to mention it to the interviewer.

A Muslim Stepfather from Indonesia

One fact that remains undisputed in the narrative is that Obama's mother chose another third world prospect for her second husband, deciding to follow Obama's Kenyan-born Muslim-raised father with an Indonesian-born Muslim, a second man of color to be her mate, this one destined to be Obama's stepfather.

The circumstances of exactly how or why Stanley Ann ended her marriage with Obama's father, like much else in the narrative, remain unclear. One version is that Stanley Ann divorced Obama Senior in 1964, when Obama Junior was three years old and Stanley Ann realized Obama Senior had returned to Africa to rejoin the previously undisclosed wife he had abandoned in Kenya. The other version is that Obama Senior, following the prescripts of Islamic sharia law, divorced Stanley Ann when he returned to Africa in 1963 to begin his work as a bureaucrat in the Kenyatta government.[4]

In his autobiography, Obama relates a conversation in New York, while Obama is in college at Columbia, in which his mother tells him his grandfather in Africa wrote a letter disapproving of her marriage with Obama Senior. "'He didn't want the Obama blood sullied by a white woman, he said,'" Stanley Ann tells Obama. "'And then there was a problem with your father's first wife . . . he had told me they were separated, but it was a village wedding, so there was no legal document that would show a divorce . . .'"[5]

Probing this issue, we find there is even uncertainty whether Stanley Ann and Obama Senior were ever married in a church. No marriage license for this first marriage surfaces in any of the now-growing volume of research being done, much of it for the first time, on Obama's life. In discussing Stanley Ann and Obama Senior's marriage, Obama comments, "In fact, how and when the marriage occurred remains a bit murky, a bill of particulars that I've never had the courage to explore. There's no record of a real wedding, a cake, a ring, a giving away of the bride."[6] Obama then suggests there was a small civil ceremony with a justice of the peace. Other sources say divorce papers confirm that a civil ceremony was held on Maui, on February 2, 1961, when Ann was three months pregnant with Obama.[7]

Yet even this remains murky. "No families were in attendance; it's not even clear that people back in Kansas were fully informed," Obama added. In retrospect, Obama finds everything about his parents' marriage a bit of a mystery. "The whole thing seems so fragile in retrospect, so haphazard," he wrote. "And perhaps that's how my grandparents intended it to be, a trial that would pass, just a matter of time, so long as they maintained a stiff upper lip and didn't do anything drastic."

Obama was skeptical his grandparents were beyond race when they first met their prospective son-in-law. "In 1960, the year that my parents were married, *miscegenation* still described a felony in over half the states in the Union," he wrote in the autobiography. He noted that in many parts of the South, "my father would have been strung up from a tree for merely looking at my mother the wrong way." Then he questioned about his grandparents, "Sure—but would you let your daughter marry one?"[8]

He notes in passing, without explaining fully, that his grandfather had experienced his own form of discrimination, which Obama suggests made his grandfather more sympathetic to Obama's father's courting his mother. "The condition of the black race, their pain, their wounds, would in his mind have become merged with his own," Obama wrote about Stanley Armour Dunham, "the absent father and hint of a scandal, a mother who had gone away, the cruelty of other children, the realization that he was no fair-haired boy—that he looked like a 'wop.'"[9] What Obama neglects to bring forward anywhere in the book is the real crux of his grandfather's tragedy, namely, that his grandfather's father had been a philanderer who abandoned his wife, and that in 1926, Stanley Dunham came home to discover his mother's dead body.[10] Obama's grandmother had ended her life by committing suicide, at least in part as a result of her abandonment by her husband.

At any rate, Stanley Ann married Lolo Soetoro in 1965, two years after her divorce from Obama Senior, before Obama Junior had turned four years old. Although Soetoro's age is also disputed, he appears to have been about thirty-five when he married the twenty-two-year-old Stanley Ann. Like Obama Senior, Lolo was a Muslim sent by his country to study in the United States. In Lolo's case, Indonesia's President Sukarno sought to develop an educated class of youth who could assist Indonesia to achieve economic success as the nation headed down the path of independence, much as Tom Mboya had sought to do in Kenya. Lolo and Stanley Ann met at the East-West Center on the University of Hawaii campus, the same campus where Stanley Ann met Obama Senior in a Russian class.

The parallels between how Stanley Ann met and fell in love with Obama Senior and Lolo Soetoro are too striking to ignore. Stanley Ann may have sought a relationship with a foreigner, or a Muslim, or a man of color. She may have wanted to protest the conventional ideas of her parents, or the comfortable conformity of the Eisenhower years. Clearly even after she and her small son had been abandoned by her first husband, Stanley Ann was willing to try virtually the same relationship all over again, only with a different man. Obama says his grandfather was amused to learn that *Lolo* means "crazy" in Hawaiian. Obama also described his future stepfather in racial terms, noting Lolo "was short and brown, handsome, with thick black hair and features that could easily have been Mexican or Samoan as Indonesian." [11]

Reporters and commentators trying to explain Stanley Ann's marriages often note she was an anthropologist, as if that professional designation settles everything. [12] We are expected to conjure up images of Stanley Ann as a Margaret Mead. Soon, Stanley Ann would be taking Obama with her on what would turn out to be her first field trip, to Indonesia to be with her new husband.

An enthusiastic belief in the 1950s and 1960s that the study of natives could help unlock questions of "natural right" probably explains why even Obama saw his mother in terms of "New Frontier" liberalism. Discussing his mother in Indonesia, Obama recalls "she was a lonely witness for secular humanism, a soldier for New Deal, Peace Corps, position-paper liberalism."[13] Stanley Ann passed away in 1995 from ovarian cancer at the age of fifty-two, the year Obama's autobiography was published. So we cannot ask her what her motivation was to marry Barack Senior and Lolo Soetoro. Did her motivation derive from some intellectual commitment to the third world, or an ideological commitment to ameliorate poverty in foreign countries less economically advanced? Was she rebelling against her parents, or the Christian religion, or the Kansas culture into which she was born? Perhaps her simple answer would have been that she loved both men.

In 1967, Stanley Ann moved to Jakarta, taking Obama Junior with her. They were joining Lolo, who had been suddenly called back to Indonesia when a military coup overthrew Sukarno and brought Suharto to power. Once in Indonesia, Obama realized how different his stepfather had become. In Hawaii, Lolo had been engaging, even fun. But in Indonesia, gone was the stepfather that Obama remembered playing chess with his grandfather for hours. What happened? Finally, one of Lolo's cousins in Indonesia explained to Obama's mother that when the military purged Sukarno, all the students studying abroad were summoned home without explanation, their passports purged. When Lolo got off the airplane in Indonesia, the army whisked him away. He was conscripted to the jungles of New Guinea for a year. "And he was one of the lucky ones," the cousin explained. "Students studying in Eastern Bloc countries did much worse. Many of them are still in jail. Or vanished."[14]

Amazingly, the pattern of failure we saw with Obama

Senior was being repeated. Lolo was being disappointed by internal politics in Indonesia, much as Obama Senior found government service in Kenya disappointing. In Indonesia, the army and the government were fighting; the communists and Muslims were vying for power, all against the background of U.S. meddling in Southeast Asia, in a period that turned out to be the prelude to the Vietnam War. In Kenya, Obama Senior returned home to Africa, only to find a political environment where tribal rivalries competed for power against a background in which the national hero Jomo Kenyatta was rejecting Tom Mboya, Obama Senior's family supporter. Obama Senior, Tom Mboya, and Jomo Kenyatta were all Luo, but Kenyatta, a member of the majority Kikuyu tribe, had begun to turn against Mboya, believing that Mboya wanted his job.

In Indonesia, Lolo Soetoro found himself on the outside as a result of the political conflicts within Indonesia, just as Barack Obama Senior found himself on the outside as a result of the political and tribal conflicts within Kenya. Lolo, like Obama Senior, turned to the bottle, easing his disappointment in an angry alcoholic daze.

Obama observed that in Indonesia, Lolo and his mother no longer talked with enthusiasm about their future. "That was what had drawn her [Stanley Ann] to Lolo after Barack had left," Obama Junior wrote of his stepfather and father, "that promise of something new and important, helping her husband rebuild a country in a charged and challenging place beyond her parents' reach." [15]

We can almost feel Obama's intense hurt: "On some nights, she [Stanley Ann] would hear him [Lolo] up after everyone else had gone to bed, wandering through the house with a bottle of imported whiskey, nursing his secrets." [16] Obama also tells us that the last time he saw his stepfather was some ten years after he left Indonesia, "when my mother helped him travel to Los Angeles to treat a liver ailment that would kill him at the age of fifty-one." [17] What Obama omits is that the liver disease that killed his stepfather was brought on by acute alcoholism, much as his father had committed what some would see as a car-assisted suicide.

In the midst of the personal drama being played against the background of this Indonesian turmoil, on August 15, 1970, Obama's half-sister, Maya Soetoro-Ng, was born to his mother and his stepfather. Obama devotes the entire second chapter of his autobiography to his time in Indonesia, but remarkably, he makes only one reference in passing to Maya's birth.

By 1971, Stanley Ann's marriage with Lolo began falling apart and Obama Junior was sent back to Hawaii, ultimately to be raised by his grandparents. Yet there is a discrepancy: Maya Soetoro has consistently said Obama lived in Indonesia for five years, putting the dates of Obama's stay from 1968 to 1973, not for three or four years, as Obama has maintained, from 1968 to 1971. [18] The autobiography, as we have repeatedly noted, is not written in strict chronological order and cannot be relied upon to provide precise dates and documentation.

Regardless of the year, the truth is that Obama wanted to leave Indonesia. The "new arrangement" did not sound bad to Obama when his mother explained it. "It was time for me to attend an American school," he wrote in the autobiography. "I'd run through all the lessons of my correspondence course. She said that she and Maya would be joining me in Hawaii very soon—a year, tops—and that she'd try to make it there for Christmas." Obama was sent home to Hawaii by himself, alone on an airplane. When he saw his grandparents waiting for him at the airport he realized "I was to live with strangers." [19]

Stanley Ann did return to Hawaii after that, but primarily to take steps with the University of Hawaii to pursue a postgraduate degree in anthropology. For three years, Obama lived with his mother and his sister in a small apartment a block away from Punahou School, the private school Obama attended on his return to Hawaii. When his mother was ready to return to Indonesia to get on with the field work that her master's degree in anthropology would require, Obama did not want to go. When Stanley Ann told Obama she wanted him to return to Indonesia with her and his half-sister, he "immediately said no."[20] Rebelling, Obama decided to stay in Hawaii, confident he had "arrived at an unspoken pact with my grandparents: I could live with them and they'd leave me alone so long as I kept trouble out of sight." Subtly, Obama is saying not that he would stay out of trouble, but only that he would keep hidden the trouble he seemed to be planning to find.

By returning to Indonesia alone and abandoning a son who refused to go back to Indonesia, Stanley Ann went "native," as many commentators have harshly suggested. To explain to himself why now his mother and sister were abandoning him, Obama rationalized, deciding it was best for him to be alone, so he could finally sort out his search for identity as an African-American. "Away from my mother, away from my grandparents, I was engaged in a fitful interior struggle," he explained in the autobiography. "I was trying to raise myself to be a black man in America, and beyond the given of my appearance, no one around me seemed to know exactly what that meant."[21]

Throughout the autobiography, Obama's African father is never far away. Even as Obama discusses his stepfather and Indonesia, he seems drawn to comment over and over again that the move to this strange and distant land made him realize he was not where he belonged. We are again reminded of Obama's concern he is "lal," or lost in Indonesia, and his feeling that his African father is missing. "He had left paradise," Obama wrote about his Kenyan father's abandoning them in Hawaii to go to Harvard, "and nothing my mother or grandparents told me could obviate that single, unassailable fact." [22] In Indonesia with his stepfather, Obama misses his father, who is then in Kenya. Obama's distress over being abandoned by his father is a concern Obama repeats throughout the autobiography, without ever finding anyone who can give him an explanation that eases his pain. Anticipating the move to Indonesia, Obama commented, "I was too young to realize that I was supposed to have a live-in father, just as I was too young to know I needed a race." [23] Abandonment and the search for identity are central themes of Obama's autobiography, as they must also be central themes of his life.

Interestingly, Obama did not include a separate dedication page in *Dreams from My Father*. Instead, he included the dedication in the introduction, mentioning his mother, his grandparents, and his siblings "stretched across the oceans and continents." Missing are mentions of his father and stepfather.

Revealingly, the autobiography opens with an epigraph from the Bible, 1 Chronicles 29:15. The words seem to capsulize Obama's experience of life as expressed in the book. "For we are strangers before them, and sojourners, as were all our fathers." Strangers in strange lands, if we adapt the title from Robert Heinlein's novel, is a phrase that somehow seems to sum up what Obama Junior is telling us about his life experience through his thirty-fourth year, when the autobiography first was published.

In other words, it would appear the life-lesson Obama

draws in the autobiography, a lesson Obama means to teach us about life, is that we are all necessarily strangers here on earth, merely sojourners, as were our fathers before us. The Christian Bible, even in the chapter of Chronicles that Obama quotes, urges us to resolve this feeling of alienation with the realization that we are all children of God. With the New Testament, we are further advised that only in Christ and through Christ can we find our true identity. If Obama is on a search for identity, then our question must be this: How does Obama resolve the crisis of abandonment and identity that his life experience so poignantly causes him to feel? Is it in Christianity, as Obama solidly proclaims?

Before we get there, however, we must address another question, regardless of whether it is politically correct: Was Obama ever trained in Islam? Obama and his presidential campaign vehemently deny he ever had anything to do with Islam. But is that the truth?

Barry Soetoro, Muslim

As well as we can determine, Obama Junior lived in Jakarta for four years, from 1968 to 1971, from the time he was six years old until he was ten. During that time, the evidence will show, he received Islamic instruction and attended mosque worship with his father.

Obama's 2008 presidential campaign website has a page devoted to proving "Obama Has Never Been a Muslim, and Is a Committed Christian." [24] The website includes an excerpt from a letter the Indonesian Embassy wrote to Obama stating, "Sekolah Dasar Negeri Besuki in Menteng, Jakarta, Indonesia has always been a public school. It has never been an Islamic Madrassa type of school."[25] In another section, Obama's campaign website is unequivocal in its firmness and clarity. "Barack Obama is Not and Never Has Been a Muslim," it proclaims in bold type. "Obama never prayed in a mosque. He has never been a Muslim, was not raised a Muslim, and is a committed Christian who attends the United Church of Christ."[26]

Clearly, the Obama 2008 campaign views the issue of Obama's association with Islam as radioactive. The message comes through loud and clear—if one could prove Obama is, was, or ever has been a Muslim, his chances of ever being president of the United States would be diminished.

The controversy began when *Insight* magazine asserted that Obama had attended a radical madrassa school in Indonesia, where jihad, or holy war, was taught. "Although Indonesia is regarded as a moderate Muslim state," *Insight* wrote, "the U.S. intelligence community has determined that today most of these schools are financed by the Saudi Arabian government and they teach a Wahhabi doctrine that denies the rights of non-Muslims."[27] CNN expended resources and attracted substantial media attention by refuting *Insight*'s contention that Obama attended a madrassa in his years in Indonesia.[28]

Unfortunately, both *Insight* and CNN missed the point. We too find no evidence Obama ever attended a madrassa. A madrassa is an Islamic religious school where instruction is given from the Koran. When we think of a madrassa, many recall news reports showing religious schools in Saudi Arabia where boys recite the Koran under the supervision of a senior Islamic teacher. Yet the conclusion that Obama did not attend a madrassa in Indonesia does not mean he received no Islamic education in Indonesia. Obama *did* attend a government-run public school in Indonesia and he *did* receive Islamic instruction, including study of the Koran. Here the Obama campaign makes a mistake. I accept Obama's statement that he is a Christian, but take exception to the claim that Obama was not introduced to Islam as a child.

The best authority for the argument that Obama received Islamic education in Indonesia is Obama himself. In his autobiography, some hundred pages after he discusses chronologically his time in Indonesia, Obama relates an otherwise unconnected discussion he had with the activist community organizer who brought him to Chicago years later. Out of the blue, Obama clearly states, "In Indonesia, I had spent two years at a Muslim school, two years at a Catholic School." Then he admits, "In the Muslim school, the teacher wrote to tell my mother that I made faces during Koranic studies."

To further dismiss any significance we might have attributed to his childhood religious education, both in Islam and in Christianity, Obama quickly added, "My mother wasn't overly concerned. 'Be respectful,' she said." Then Obama made sure we understood he was disrespectful not only in his Koran studies, but also in the Christian education he received in Indonesia. "In the Catholic school, when it came time to pray, I would pretend to close my eyes, then peek around the room," he wrote. "Nothing happened. No angels descended. Just a parched old nun and thirty brown children, muttering words."[29]

Understandably, these quotations, especially as they relate to Islam, are nowhere to be found on Obama's 2008 presidential campaign website.

When the issue of Obama's receiving Islamic instruction in Indonesia first surfaced, Obama's campaign communications director, Robert Gibbs, said firmly, "We will not be swift-boated and we won't take allegations that are patently untrue lying down."[30]

Perhaps, Gibbs should have read Obama's autobiography more carefully.

Tracking Down Barry Soetoro in Jakarta

Given this admission to anchor the inquiry, researchers have uncovered quite a few supporting details.

The Laotze blog, run by an American expatriate in Southeast Asia, documents that Obama, registered under the name "Barry Soetoro," with serial number 203, entered the Catholic Franciscan Assisi Primary School on January 1, 1968, and was enrolled in Class 1B.[31] School documents listed Barry Soetoro as an Indonesian citizen born in Honolulu, Hawaii, on August 4, 1961.

According to the blog, his religion was listed as Islam.

School documents recorded Barry's father as "L. Soetoro Ma," a worker in the director general's office in the TNI Topography division of the Indonesian army. School records indicate Barry attended the Franciscan Assisi Primary School for three years, until Class 3. (The school is named "Asisi," which is an apparent misspelling of "Assisi," since it is run by Franciscan nuns of the Catholic religious order established by Saint Francis of Assisi, Italy. A sign posted on the outside of the building spells the school name as "Asisi," according to many photos posted on the Internet and widely shown on Jakarta television. Given the language difficulties, we assume here the school is properly spelled "Assisi," after the religious order.)

Obama made clear in his autobiography, "It had taken me less than six months to learn Indonesia's language, its customs, and its legends."[32] Obama wrote that family fortunes improved in Indonesia as his father's wealthy brother-in-law, who had "made millions as a high official in the national oil company,"[33] intervened to help Lolo get a job in the American oil company. "We moved to a new house in a better neighborhood; a car replaced the motorcycle; a television and hi-fi replaced the crocodiles and Tata, the ape. Lolo could sign for our dinners at a company club," Obama wrote.[34]

Israella Darmawan, Obama's first-grade teacher at the Catholic school he first attended in Indonesia, cast doubt on Obama's claim he learned to speak Indonesian. Darmawan told the *Chicago Tribune* that she attempted to teach him Indonesian by going over pronunciation and vowels. Obama struggled greatly with the Indonesian language, Darmawan reported, and as a result his studies suffered.[35]

Where exactly Obama lived during the four years he was in Indonesia is strangely hard to determine. The 1971 move that occasioned Obama's leaving the Catholic school is widely assumed to have been from 16 Haji Ramli Street to an undetermined address on Dempo Street, although there are some conflicts in the available record. An Indonesian newspaper reported that a student who attended the public school with Barry Soetoro said the Soetoro family lived in Dempo Street at that time. This is where the problem begins. When the newspaper sent reporters out to ask Dempo Street neighbors about the Soetoro family, they surprisingly could not remember the Soetoro family ever living there.[36]

Obama describes his first home as being "in a still developing area on the outskirts of the town." The house was "modest stucco and red tile, but it was open and airy, with a big mango tree in the small courtyard in front."[37] That physical description does not match the Indonesia television news videos showing the house on 16 Haji Ramli Street. Nor does it describe the Dempo Street address. The Indonesian newspaper that investigated the Obama "lost house" on Dempo Street did not describe the location as being a rural address on the outskirts of the city, but as an attractive neighborhood in the center of Jakarta, near Amir Hamzah Park. The account is further confusing because Obama in his autobiography does not give any addresses for the two residences he discusses having in Jakarta. The house on H. Ramli Street is located close to the Assisi school.

Also, the sequence of schools Obama attended does not make sense, not in relation to Obama living in the Dempo Street home last.

Obama went to a Catholic school first, when the family had little money and was struggling because Lolo was out of political favor. Then, in 1971, he ended up at the second school, the government-run public school. That's how the official records at the schools list Obama's school attendance and that's how Obama describes going to school in Indonesia in his autobiography.

Yet the way Obama tells the story in the second chapter of the autobiography, his mother and he were in Indonesia for a while, living in a poor rural home on the outskirts of Jakarta when the family's fortunes changed because Lolo's wealthy brother-in-law got him a job with an American oil company, allowing them to move to a better house.

Assuming Catholic private education would involve some tuition and that public education would be tax-supported, the logical conclusion would have been for Obama to go to the International School once their finances improved. Obama himself notes this in his autobiography when he comments that most of his mother's efforts when they first arrived in Indonesia centered on his education. "Without the money to send me to the International School, where most of Djakarta's foreign children went," he wrote, "she had arranged from the moment of our arrival to supplement my Indonesian schooling with lessons from a U.S. correspondence course." Obama describes at length how hard the correspondence course was for him, especially having to wake up at four in the morning so he could be force-fed breakfast and forced to study English lessons by his mother for three hours before he left for school and went to work. Yet he neglects to specify which school he was attending at this time. We assume this was when he was attending the Catholic school, since that was the one he attended first in Indonesia, but it may also have been when Obama first arrived and the family was living in the countryside.

We have already established that Obama wrote the autobiography to hide key points, but it is hard to decipher what Obama might be trying to hide by not being clear about the specific location of the houses where he lived in Jakarta and the dates he attended the two schools. One possibility is that Obama still was not ready to discuss openly how far his stepfather had fallen economically just before sending him back to Hawaii. Perhaps he did not attend school when he first arrived in Indonesia, not until the family's economic fortunes changed, permitting them to move to 16 Haji Ramli Street.

Still, Obama spells out none of this in the autobiography so it can be easily understood or followed. Looking closely at Obama's narrative, what dominates the story are the holes. This appears to be the case even for the Indonesian media trying to track down the truth today, especially about the "lost house" on Dempo Street.

It's very likely that Obama's stay in Indonesia involved three houses and three moves. The move to H. Ramli Street from the rural residence outside the city, after Lolo's finances improved and he had some money to afford the move, was probably the first. The people currently living on Dempo Street may not remember Obama simply because he did not live there long before he returned to Hawaii.

It's also possible there were only two moves and the house that was invented was the first house. Jakarta was a big city even in the late 1960s, but Obama's autobiography makes his first home in Indonesia sound as if he moved into the middle of a wild jungle, complete with exotic birds, baby crocodiles, reptiles, and an ape. Was this residence just his imagination? The truth is that we do not know for sure how many moves there were or where Obama was living when he attended the government-run public school. Unfortunately, what Obama writes about his time in Indonesia is not precise enough, with regard to locations or dates, to help us to sort it out. Obama was young when he was in Indonesia and maybe some of the details of the experience are obscure, even to him. Or, maybe he is trying to minimize intentionally the extent to which the experience placed him in an Islamic setting where he received public school education in Islam. Again, we simply don't know.

A *Los Angeles Times* report seems to establish conclusively that Obama was living on H. Ramli Street when he attended the Catholic Franciscan Assisi Primary School, which was located just around the corner, within walking distance.[38] The newspaper quoted Zulfan Adi, who described himself as one of Obama's closest childhood friends. Adi told the newspaper he often visited the Soetoro home, "a small flat-roofed bungalow at 16 Haji Ramli Street." Adi further told the newspaper, "This was a middle-class neighborhood but Haji Ramli Street was a dirt lane where Obama used to while away the hours kicking a soccer ball."

He remembered that in the rainy season the street turned to "thick, mucky soup," and Obama and his friends wore plastic bags over their shoes to walk through it.

Adi said neighborhood Muslims worshipped in a nearby house. When the muezzin sounded the call to prayer, Adi remembered seeing Lolo and Barry walk together to the make-shift mosque. "His mother often went to the church," Adi told the *Times,* "but Barry was a Muslim. I remember him wearing a sarong."

The *Times* also interviewed Israella Darmawan, Obama's first-grade teacher at the Catholic school. "At that time, Barry was also praying in a Catholic way, but Barry was a Muslim," she told the newspaper. "He was registered as a Muslim because his father, Lolo Soetoro, was a Muslim."

The paper noted that Darmawan, sixty-three years old at the time of the interview, still teaches in Obama's old classroom, as she has done for thirty-nine years.

Indonesian TV Seeks Out Barry Soetoro

In February 2008, Detik TV in Jakarta, Indonesia, ran a helpful multipart series of news reports that showed the locations associated with Barack Obama's time in Indonesia and featured interviews with people who were Obama's friends at the time.

Detik TV reporter Nadhifa Putri and cameraman Ari Saputra produced the reports. The reports all began with a video clip from an Obama campaign speech given in the United States, where the audience is chanting in rhythm, "O-ba-ma, O-ba-ma," clearly showing to the Indonesian television audience the great emotional appeal Obama is able to evoke in his U.S. campaign appearances. Almost every one of the Indonesian television news reports included up front a visual sequence that dissolved to show a widely reproduced file photo of Barry with his father and mother in Indonesia. The visual image of the Indonesian Lolo Soetoro, together with his white wife and two children, strongly identified the family as Indonesian.

To American researchers looking into Obama's background, the Indonesian TV news reports are helpful both because the Indonesian TV channel went out on location, bringing a cameraman to record the local scenes where Obama had been in Indonesia and to interview on camera those who knew him then. The Indonesian inquiry is convincing precisely because it is conducted by local news operations that can be expected to know what they are reporting.

One of the first TV news reports showed video clips of the Catholic Franciscan Assisi Primary School and fully documented Obama's attendance there.[39] In a group picture of the schoolchildren, Barry Soetoro can be seen clearly in the back row. The video also identified the Assisi school as being in the Menteng District of Jakarta, the same location as H. Ramli Street.

Another report actually showed a video of the Soetoro family residence on Jl. K. H. Ramli Tengah, as it is today.[40] A separate report even interviewed the current residents, Zulfian Mirzan and his wife, who bought Obama's childhood home from his half-sister Maya in 2005. These new buyers paid about 500 million rupiah, the equivalent then of about $54,500, again providing a strong indication the residence was a desirable home in an attractive neighborhood.[41]

This second report showed the interior of the home, including the room with the single bed across the hall from the master bedroom, which supposedly was Barry Soetoro's room. The house, modest by U.S. standards, appeared recently remodeled, clean, and comfortable. Again, the impression was in accordance with the reputation of the Menteng District, which travel guides frequently bill as one of Jakarta's more affluent residential areas, one where bureaucrats and diplomats frequently choose to reside.

Sometime in 1971, Obama was enrolled in Sekolah Dasar Negeri Besuki, a public school in the Menteng District. Here the evidence is that Obama did receive the Islamic instruction in the Koran that he refers to in his autobiography.

Obama always acknowledged his stepfather was Muslim, though he did his best to downplay Islam as an important force in his stepfather's life. "Lolo followed a brand of Islam that could make room for the remnants of more animist and Hindu faiths," he wrote in the autobiography. "He explained that a man took on the powers of whatever he ate: One day soon, he promised, he would bring home a piece of tiger meat for us to share."[42]

On July 9, 2006, the Jakarta daily *Banjarmasin Post* published an interview with Rony Amir, a classmate of Barry Soetoro's at the Franciscan Assisi Primary School.[43] Translated from Indonesian to English, what the Indonesian paper says is politically incorrect to the extreme, judged by current U.S. standards. Just for starters, the article's title translates roughly as "The Negroid Fat Child Who Worked Hard in the Prayer Room."

Amir recalled Obama's enjoying football and marbles, as well as being a Muslim. "We often asked Barry to the prayer room close to the house, when he lived in Street H Ramli, in the Menteng Dalam area of Jakarta," Amir said. "He looked funny wearing a sarong because his body was fat, he was black, and he had curly hair." Amir remembered that

Barry was always laughing, and liked to socialize. "Barry did not differ from the other children in Menteng Dalam who liked to play marbles and football," he told the newspaper. "The only thing that distinguished him was that his body was big and fat, and he was black." Amir speculated that Obama had to change his religion if he planned to run for the president of the United States, because America would never elect a Muslim president. According to the Indonesian press, Amir currently works in Bank Mandiri in Jakarta.[44]

Another report in the Detik TV series documented that Obama lived "in the middle of Muslims" in Jakarta.[45] The highlight of this video is an interview with Zulfan Adi, who, as we have seen, attended the Assisi Primary School with Obama. Adi shows viewers the Muslim prayer room where he and Barry Soetoro played as children of nine or ten years old.

A translation for much of the second Detik TV video is provided by the "Expat in Southeast Asia" Laotze blog. Referring to Barry Soetoro, reporter Nadhifa Putri states in Indonesian "juga hidup tengah-tengah orang muslim," which translates "he lived his life in the middle of Muslims." The reporter then states, "Barry yang punya wajah lucu sering dimainkan teman-teman pernah dipakaika sarong meski tak pernah ikut solat," which translates "Barry had a funny face and his friends made fun of him by putting a sarong on him even though he didn't pray." The blog comments, "The emphasis here is that even though Barry was a Muslim and was in the mosque and was wearing Islamic clothes, that he was only 'playing' and not really 'praying.' I suppose you can interpret that any way you wish."[46]

In the second part of the video, Zulfan Adi points out on camera the now famous prayer room, the "Musholla Al-Rahman," or Al-Rahman Prayer Room, where he and Barry Soetoro were together as children praying, or playing, if we acknowledge the current political spin coming out of Indonesia. Either way we look at it, praying or playing, the video changed the terms of the debate. Now all that is in dispute is whether any Obama praying ever occurred in the Muslim prayer room in Indonesia, not whether Barry Soetoro had ever been in one.

Kaltim Post Cyber News in Indonesia interviewed teachers and students at the government-run public school at SDN 1 Menteng, Jakarta.[47] The newsmen showed up on a Friday to find all the children from age six years old dressed in Muslim clothes, a requirement in all Indonesian public schools since 1970. In 1971, Barry was registered in Class 4 at the school. *Kaltim Post* interviewed Tine Hahiyary, the teacher who had been principal of the school from 1971 to 1989. Tine Hahiyary affirmed that Barry Soetoro had been registered as a Muslim and actively took part in the Islamic religious lessons. "I remembered that Barry studied 'mengaji,'" she told the reporters. *Mengaji* involves recitation of the Koran, a clear indication Barry did more than just "play" at being Muslim while he attended the public school.

Poskota, another Jakarta newspaper, interviewed Emirsyah Satar, currently the CEO of the national airline, Garuda Indonesia Airline. Satar remembered young Barry both as playing football and as being Muslim. He too recalled Barry coming to the prayer room wearing a sarong. He told *Poskota* that Obama was "quite religious in Islam, but after marrying Michelle, he changed his religion."[48] The newspaper also reported that Barack Obama was recorded officially at the school as an Indonesian citizen born in Honolulu, Hawaii, on August 4, 1961.

Researching thoroughly the many news investigative reports done on Obama's Muslim background by the mainstream media in 2007, we even find confirmation there from

Obama's sister that he was Muslim in Indonesia. "My whole family was Muslim," Maya Soetoro-Ng told the *New York Times* when interviewed about her early days in Indonesia. "Most of the people I knew were Muslim." [49]

Interestingly, in the first quarter of 2007, when most of the investigative reports were being written in the mainstream media linking Obama to Islam, Hillary Clinton was still the presumptive Democratic Party presidential nominee. A year later, when Clinton's presidential candidacy was in doubt, these kinds of investigative reports disappeared from mainstream media coverage, leaving in place only the Obama campaign's denial that Obama ever had anything to do with Islam.

Islam Instruction Required

Further confirmation that Indonesian secular public schools in 1971 required instruction in Islam comes from two academic studies done by Lambert Kelabora, then a lecturer in Indonesian education at La Trobe University in Melbourne, Australia. Writing in *Asian Survey* in 1976, Kelabora wrote that Sukarno's defeat of the Partai Komunis Indonesia, or PKI, the Communist Party of Indonesia, in an unsuccessful coup led to changes in the status of religious instruction in the Indonesian public school curriculum. "With the victory over the PKI in their hands," Kelabora wrote, "Moslem groups had no difficulty in arguing that it was religion that had saved the country from Communism, and that it was time to make religion compulsory for everyone in order to strengthen the moral fibre of the nation." [50] The result led to the intensification of Islamic studies throughout Indonesian institutions, "in the communist prison camps, in factories, in offices, and in all educational institutions."[51] The study of Islam was made mandatory in all Indonesian educational institutions in the country, including pre-primary schools. All students were required to increase their study of Islam to four lessons a week, some 10 percent of the curriculum, elevating the study of Islam "to *the most important subject* in the school curriculum."[52]

In a 1979 paper in *Comparative Education,* titled "Assumptions Underlying Religious Instruction in Indonesia," Kelabora stressed "the changing political and security situation in the country since 1949 has made religion a compulsory subject for all, from pre-primary to tertiary level, from the communist prison camps to factories and government establishments."[53]

Even Kim Barker, a *Chicago Tribune* foreign correspondent, in an article focused on "debunking the myth Obama had attended a Madrassa," admitted that Barry Soetoro attended the mosque with his father to pray. Barker interviewed Israella Darmawan, Barry's first-grade teacher at the Assisi Primary School. Barker reported her as saying, "Sometimes Lolo went to the mosque to pray, but he rarely socialized with people. Rarely, Barry went to the mosque with Lolo."[54] As much as Barker tried to diminish the fact, the evidence here and in Darmawan's earlier interview with the *Los Angeles Times* is that Barry Soetoro not only received religious instruction in Islam at the secular public school in Indonesia, but also went to the mosque to pray with his father even when he was in Catholic school.

Columnist Nicholas Kristof of the *New York Times* asked Obama about his Islamic education.[55] After acknowledging that he once got in trouble for making faces during Koran study classes in his elementary school in Indonesia, Obama recited for Kristof the opening lines of the Arabic call to prayer. The opening lines of the Adhan, the Muslim call to prayer, translated, read as follows, with each line repeated twice:

> *Allah is supreme! Allah is supreme!*
> *Allah is supreme! Allah is supreme!*
> *I witness that there is no God but Allah.*
> *I witness that there is no God but Allah.*
> *I witness that Muhammad is his prophet . . .*

Kristof said Obama recited the prayer "with a first-rate accent," and that, "In a remark that seemed delightfully uncalculated (it'll give Alabama voters heart attacks), Mr. Obama described the call to prayer as 'one of the prettiest sounds on Earth at sunset.'"[56]

The lines of the Adhan are very similar to the Shahada, the Muslim declaration of faith, which articulates the oneness of God and the acceptance of Muhammad as his final prophet. Recitation of the Shahada is one of the Five Pillars of Islam and is performed daily by Muslim faithful worldwide.

A Window to His Mother's Heart

As the second chapter of his autobiography moves toward conclusion, Obama's mother tells him yet another glorified version of his father's saga, how Obama Senior "had grown up poor, in a poor country, in a poor continent; how his life had been hard, as hard as anything that Lolo might have known." Stanley Ann stresses that Obama Senior "hadn't cut corners" or "played all the angles." Instead, she instructs her son, Obama Senior was "diligent and honest, no matter what it cost him." She tells Obama that his dad "had led his life according to principles that demanded a different kind of toughness, principles that promised a higher form of power."[57] She encourages Obama to follow his father's examples, because it "was in the genes."

Obama takes this as a message "to embrace black people generally." He says Stanley Ann would bring home books on the civil rights movement, the recordings of Mahalia Jackson, the speeches of Martin Luther King. "Every black man was Thurgood Marshall or Sidney Poitier; every black woman [civil rights pioneer] Fannie Lou Hammer or Lena Horne," she told Obama, making sure he got the message that to be black "was to be the beneficiary of a great inheritance, a special destiny, glorious burdens that only we were strong enough to bear."[58]

For Obama, the search for identity is resolved in the inheritance of race. That is the key we have been looking for, to explain why a book that explains Obama's "dreams from my father" is subtitled "race and inheritance." So, if we reread the dedication from 1 Chronicles, only verse 29:15 needs to be read, "For we are strangers before them, and sojourners, as were all our fathers." The message appears to be: *Obama does not need to be a stranger or a sojourner anymore, so long as he resolves the journey for identity by embracing his inheritance from his race.*

Gone, evidently, for Obama is the need to read the earlier verse, 1 Chronicles 29:11, in which we are admonished that the identity and inheritance for all is in God: "Thine, O Lord, is the greatness and the power, and the glory, and the victory, and the majesty: for all that is in the heaven and in the earth is thine; thine is the kingdom, O Lord, and thou are exalted as head above all."

Moreover, the race Obama embraces is not that of his mother, although he does have that choice. Nor is the race he embraces even precisely that of his Kenyan father. The race Obama embraces is his African race. Even though

Obama is not descended from a slave, the identity he seeks is African-American. Obama embraces an African-Americanism that is born out of slavery, and he embraces it as the son of a free Kenyan educated at Harvard.

In the very next paragraph, his mother instructs Obama he must carry his burdens "with style," adding what Obama suggests was one of her common refrains, "Harry Belafonte is the best-looking man on the planet." [59]

The sexual attraction of his mother to her African husband jumps out from the page, as it does once again, later in the book, when Stanley Ann visits Obama while he is in college at Columbia and insists they go together to view a film she says is one of her favorites, *Black Orpheus*. We discussed this incident before, pointing out that the day they went to see this film was the day Obama learned his father had been offered a scholarship from the New School in New York City that would have permitted him to bring his wife Ann and him along. Instead, as we saw then, Obama Senior took the less generous scholarship and went to Harvard, abandoning his wife and son in Hawaii.

The incident with *Black Orpheus* has even more significance in the context of the discussion here. Obama recalled in his autobiography that he was reluctant to see the film; it was an old art film with a Brazilian cast, made in the 1950s. But his mother was insistent, telling Obama it was the first foreign film she ever saw. Then, Stanley Ann told Obama, probably for the first time ever, of her disappointment when she was sixteen years old and graduating from Mercer Island High School. She had been accepted into the University of Chicago, but "Gramps wouldn't let me go." [60] That's when her father moved the family to Hawaii, setting his daughter on the path to meet Obama Senior and then later Lolo. How different her life might have been had she gone to Chicago, the city where Obama ended up. The resentment in her comment is hard to miss, as is the excitement she feels at going to see this particular film.

About halfway through the film, Obama tells us, he had seen enough and looked to his mother, to see if she was also ready to go. But her face, Obama tells us, was "lit by the blue glow of the screen" and "set in a wistful gaze." Obama gets an insight. "At that moment," he wrote in the autobiography, "I felt as if I were being given a window into her heart, the unreflective heart of her youth." What Obama writes next appears to be the psychological understanding of his mother he had struggled to obtain since he could first remember. "I suddenly realized that the depiction of childhood blacks I was now seeing on the screen, the reverse image of Conrad's dark savages, was what my mother had carried with her to Hawaii all those years before, a reflection of the simple fantasies that had been forbidden to a white middle-class girl from Kansas, the promise of another life: warm, sensual, exotic, different." [61]

Instead of embracing his mother at this moment, Obama tells us he turned away, "embarrassed for her." [62]

"The emotions between the races could never be pure, even love was tarnished by the desire to find in the other some element that was missing in ourselves," Obama ended the section by observing. "Whether we sought our demons or salvation, the other race would always remain that: menacing, alien, and apart."

The *Life* Magazine Story That Doesn't Exist

Obama's second chapter about his experience in Indonesia ends with a bizarre but important story. He tells us that in the embassy library he came across a picture in *Life* magazine of "the black man who tried to peel off his skin." Evidently the man had tried to lighten his skin with a chemical process and the result was a disaster. The experience caused Obama to feel the moment of self-doubt he suggests comes to every black child in America "undergoing similar moments of revelation." [63]

Obama tells us "that seeing that article was violent for me, an ambush attack." The photograph told him "there was a hidden enemy out there, one that could reach me without anyone's knowledge, not even my own." He began noticing things on the imported shows playing on Indonesian television: "Cosby never got the girl on *I Spy*, that the black man on *Mission: Impossible* spent all his time underground." [64] He noticed there was nobody like him, meaning no one black, in the Sears, Roebuck Christmas catalog and that Santa Claus was a white man.

What was Obama's moment of self-doubt? "I still trusted my mother's love—but I now faced the prospect that her account of the world, and my father's place in it, was somehow incomplete." [65]

The only problem with the story is that it is all made-up.

As columnist Richard Cohen wrote in the *Washington Post*, this violent awakening incident that permanently altered Obama's vision was at best a fantasy. *Life* reported no such issue ever existed. "When the *Tribune* told Obama that *Life* magazine historians could find no such story, Obama suggested it might have been *Ebony*—'or it might have been . . . who knows what it was?'" [66] Cohen wrote. Yet the *Chicago Tribune* contacted the magazine, and *Ebony*'s archivists could find no such article, either. [67]

In an A&E television biography, Obama provides yet a third explanation of where he saw this story: "I remember seeing this magazine that talked about blacks who had used skin bleaching agents to make themselves lighter. That's when I first realized I was African-American and also that there were all sorts of implications to race, and there were power relationships in race. I couldn't articulate all that at the time, but I remember feeling shocked by that."

As Obama spoke, the screen showed a variety of skin lightener print advertisements, including one for Black and White, a cream that was made by Plough Chemicals, and another advertisement for Mercolized Wax Cream, but the print advertisements shown on the screen were from the 1950s, not the period 1968 through 1971, when Obama was in Indonesia. With this explanation the story became even fuzzier, less defined. "Barack didn't show the article to his parents," the narrator continued, "but he couldn't forget the memory about the man who wanted to change the color of his skin." What exactly did Barack see? An article or advertisements, or does it make a difference?

The entire episode suggests what psychologists call "hypothetical lying," in other words, imagining something that has not happened, but imagining it with so much precise detail that the made-up memory functions for the person as if it were real. Skin-lightening chemicals had been marketed to African-Americans in the press for decades. Academic researchers have documented that powders and skin bleaches were being offered in the African-American press as far back as the 1850s.[68] Obama didn't have to get the idea from an article he saw in *Life*. The story of *Life* magazine is apocryphal at best. At any rate, the memory of the event/nonevent is so firmly planted in Obama's mind that it seems to have become an emotional truth for him, as equally powerful psychologically as a real experience.

Has Obama lost the ability to tell the difference between

something that actually happened and something he invented? As we have seen, Obama also had the ability to project John Kennedy and the civil rights movement into situations that never happened, just so he could claim his birth had something to do with Camelot and Martin Luther King. How much more imagining, hypothetical lying, or just plain lying is Obama capable of doing?

For those making a decision to vote or not vote for Obama to be president of the United States of America, the most powerful office in the world, these are questions that one cannot avoid asking. Hopefully they can be answered as well.

Earlier in the second chapter, Obama recalls going to the library in Indonesia and seeing a photo of a "Japanese woman cradling a young, naked girl in a shallow tub: that was sad; the girl was sick, her legs twisted, her head fallen back against the mother's breast, the mother's face tight with grief, perhaps she blamed herself . . ."[69]

That description matches W. Eugene Smith's possibly most famous photograph, "Tomoko Uemura in Her Bath," taken in 1971. The photo was first published in a Smith photo essay in *Life* on June 2, 1972. Obama does not mention *Life* magazine, but he adds the psychological detail that perhaps the girl's mother blamed herself. The girl suffered from Minamata disease, a type of mercury poisoning resulting typically from industrial waste absorbed by fish, and it is doubtful the mother was at fault. Still, we cannot help wondering if Obama was blaming his mother for his plight, possibly for bringing him to Indonesia, possibly for marrying his father in the first place.

The problem for Obama is that June 2, 1972, is after the date Obama wants us to think he left Indonesia.

If Obama did see the Tomoko Uemura photo in Indonesia, as he said he did, then maybe his sister, Maya Soetoro-Ng, is right and Obama did not leave Indonesia until 1972, or possibly even 1973.

What difference does this make?

To begin with, the puzzle just adds to the growing list of factual discrepancies or outright fabrications that Obama manufactures, very likely on an ongoing basis. Even Indonesian television reporters can't identify with certainty the addresses where Obama lived with his family. If Obama stayed longer than he says, he may have attended the Catholic school for two years and the government-run public school for two years, as he also says on page 154 of the autobiography that he did.

Two years' attendance at the government-run public school would add an additional year of Islamic studies to Obama's time in Indonesia, including *mengaji,* reciting Koranic verses, a study usually reserved for true believers in Islam.

The question comes down to where Obama was registered for fourth grade.

Hillary Clinton was widely criticized for issuing a press release[70] attacking Obama for being overly ambitious, citing Obama's third-grade class in Indonesia, in which his teacher, Fermina Katarina Sinaga, asked the class to write an essay titled "My dream: What I want to be in the future." Obama wrote, "I want to be president."

As we saw earlier in this chapter, the *Kaltim Post* Cyber News reported Obama was enrolled for fourth grade in the government-run public school at SDN 1 Menteng, Jakarta. The *New York Times* has published a 1972 yearbook photo showing Obama with his fifth-grade class at Punahou School in Hawaii.[71] Records at the Catholic Franciscan Assisi Primary School indicate Barry attended there for three years, from Class 1 until Class 3. Yet Obama told us in his autobiography he was at the Catholic school in Indonesia for only two years. The discrepancy would be resolved, however, if Obama's family's economic fortunes changed midyear, requiring Obama to register in public school before the school year was completed. Yet if Obama left Indonesia in 1971, in time to register to be with the fifth-grade class at Punahou, it is doubtful he was still in Indonesia when Smith's famous photograph of Tomoko Uemura was first published. One could then conclude that while *Life* magazine made a great impression on Obama, his memory of the particulars of the magazine and what he saw in it were fuzzy at best, some twenty-three or twenty-four years later, when he wrote his autobiography.

This, in turn, reinforces another major conclusion we can draw about *Dreams from My Father*. We are left wanting if we thought we would get a precise chronological account of Obama's life and experience. The book is instead more of a psychological autobiography, in which the main driving force behind the book's organization and execution is Obama's attempt to explain to the reader how his identity formed, evidently in relation to "race and inheritance," as Obama directs our attention in his subtitle. Factual accuracy, then, is not the book's primary concern, as should be obvious from Obama's admission he has changed names and invented scenes. As much as we have tried, ferreting out the factual record remains a problematic investigative exercise, which evidently is what Obama intended. This psychological autobiography, as written, leaves Obama much room in which to hide.

So, being left with the mission of determining just what the book tells us about Obama's psychological development, we are resolved to explore in the next chapter just how

Obama's identity search progressed. The reality Obama was facing was abandonment by his father, followed by his mother's leaving him. His race was conflicted, being half African from his father and half Caucasian from his mother. We will see in the next chapter that Obama comes out embracing his African side as he develops his particular African-American identity.

On this journey to self-discovery, Obama also gives us sufficient evidence to conclude he turns out radical, internalizing a black rage that can be explained only from the ideological Far Left that Obama tells us he embraced intellectually in his formative years.

BLACK RAGE, DRUGS, AND A COMMUNIST MENTOR

My blackness was there, dark and unarguable. And it tormented me, pursued me, disturbed me, angered me.

—FRANTZ FANON, *Black Skin, White Masks,* 1967[1]

Did Barack Obama's search for his real father simply fold into his search for a secure black identity?

—SHELBY STEELE, *A Bound Man: Why We Are Excited About Obama and Why He Can't Win,* 2008[2]

Obama describes himself in *Dreams from My Father* as a "misfit"[3] as he enters Punahou School back in Hawaii. The expensive, "prestigious prep school," located on carefully manicured, gate-enclosed grounds, is "an incubator for island elites."[4]

The story Obama tells of his years at Punahou is one of a building rage focused on his race. In paragraph after paragraph of the autobiography, Obama offers stories of suffering what he saw as racial scorn, from which he internalized a growing racial alienation. Obama perceived himself a victim who sought refuge in drugs and the writings of black authors, including some of the most politically extreme.

Unfortunately, and as with so much of Obama's self-told life story, what we are given to believe does not jibe with facts and reality, especially not after the hard light of the truth that many expert researchers have uncovered. Yet the psychological reality Obama conveys in the autobiography when discussing his formative years in Hawaii tells us a lot about how Obama saw himself when he wrote the book and very likely how he sees himself today.

Now we find Obama, back in Hawaii for high school, struggling with his identity as an African-American, finding within himself a depth of racial rage that may still inform his life decisions and his politics today.

Obama's mentor in these years? It turns out to be a well-known communist journalist and poet, Frank Marshall Davis, who ended his writing career and spent his final years in Honolulu.

Obama: Angry in Hawaii

Hawaii in 1971 was in many ways the most racially diverse state in the union. Obama had just been accepted to a school that the island's upper class fought to get their children admitted to. Obama had been on a waiting list and his grandfather had to use influence from his boss, a Punahou graduate, to get Obama in.

The only serious wage earner in the extended Obama family at this time was Obama's grandmother, Madelyn

Dunham, who by December 1970 had worked her way up to be the Bank of Hawaii's first female vice president.[5] In those days, female vice presidents of banks were rare not only in Hawaii, but anywhere in the world. As a vice president, Madelyn Dunham would have earned enough to be well off, even if not rich. Dedicating themselves to the future of their grandson, the Dunhams missed an opportunity in the mid-1970s to use Madelyn's bank salary to buy a single-family home in the hills overlooking Diamond Head at a then relatively affordable price. Had they done so, the Dunhams might well have been positioned to benefit from the windfall profits realized by many islanders when the Japanese swooped into Hawaii in the 1980s with abundant cash available to buy prize residential properties.

Madelyn's husband, Stanley Dunham, according to the account Obama gives in his autobiography, continued struggling in furniture sales as he experimented with selling insurance to supplement their income, two activities Obama describes in the autobiography as being less than lucrative. Obama's mother separated from her husband and came back from Indonesia shortly after she sent Obama home to Hawaii by himself. She was determined to stay in Hawaii probably long enough to get her course work completed at the University of Hawaii, so she could then complete the field work needed to write a thesis and get a master's degree in anthropology. Working as a graduate student, Stanley Ann was unlikely to have been an income producer for the family. While Obama's classmates at Punahou lived in "split-level homes with swimming pools,"[6] he worked at a burger chain and Baskin-Robbins before graduating.[7]

Obama and his sister Maya lived with their mother for most of the three years she was back in Hawaii, in an apartment separate from the grandparents. Then Stanley Ann left her son once again, this time taking her daughter back with her to Indonesia, where she planned to write her master's thesis on Indonesian blacksmithing. Through these years, Stanley Ann's marriage with her second Muslim husband had completely deteriorated and they were headed toward the divorce they would finalize in 1980. When his mother and sister went back to Indonesia, Obama moved back into his grandparents' modest apartment. Through all this time, Madelyn saved what she could from her bank salary, the family's only substantial source of income, to pay Obama's tuition at this privileged private college-preparatory school. If Obama had a scholarship to pay some or all of his tuition at Punahou, he makes no mention of it in the autobiography.

"A young black man struggles for acceptance at an institution of privilege, where he finds himself growing so angry and disillusioned at the world around him that he turns to alcohol and drugs."[8] That is how *Chicago Tribune* correspondents Kirsten Scharnberg and Kim Barker sum up the version of his life Obama likes to present today to the voting public. Unfortunately, the reporters note, the reality of Obama's narrative "is not that simple."[9]

The truth would have to be phrased much more harshly. A young man of mixed race identifies more with his African blood, rejecting his white mother and his African father, both of whom have abandoned him, as well as rejecting the white grandparents who have sacrificed economically to raise him, as he struggles to fit into an elite prep school, where radical anticolonial political philosophy, drugs, and an older socialist mentor help him find his identity as an African-American, in the heritage of his Muslim father. Once again, we remember that the subtitle of the autobiography, "A Story of Race and Inheritance," is what *Dreams from My Father* is really all about.

Much of this drama went on in Obama's head as he sought refuge in his bedroom, reading angry African-American authors expressing their black rage in print. As he withdrew inward, he began experimenting with drugs and drinking alcohol, using marijuana and cocaine, but stopping at heroin, as he describes the experience to us in the autobiography.

On the outside, teenage Barry Obama, as he was known at Punahou, went out for the school basketball team and did his best to fit in socially, while struggling to make modest grades. Obama's friends at the time do not remember Obama as an angry black kid. Instead they remember him as fairly normal, just one of them.

A member of the varsity squad, though not a starter, Obama was called "Barry the O'bomber" by teammates because of his long shots. The *Chicago Tribune* interviewed Alan Lum, the Punahou basketball coach, who remembered Obama as not shy about confronting coaches when he felt he was not getting enough playing time. "'Coach, we're killing this team,'" Lum recalled Obama as saying. "'Our second string should be playing more.'" Obama and his teammates won the Hawaii state high school basketball championship in 1979. A photo of Barry Obama taking a jump shot in his Punahou basketball uniform has been widely seen.

How were his grades at Punahou? The one time Obama Senior visited him in Hawaii, the only memory Obama Junior had of his father in person, the two of them fought over Barry's laziness about homework. Obama Senior decided to be the Grinch that stole Christmas, demanding his son turn off the television and quit watching that animated movie so he could turn his attention to his next day's assignments. "Barry, you do not work as hard as you should," his father reprimands him. "Go now, before I get angry at you." Obama writes that he dutifully but resentfully obeyed, going to his room and slamming the door, only to be saved by his grandfather, who, after Obama's father had left their apartment, came into Barry's room to tell him his father "had no right to come in and bully everybody, including me, after being gone all this time." [10]

Barry's report on his father's visit was less than enthusiastic. "After a week of my father in the flesh," he wrote, "I had decided that I preferred his more distant image, an image I could alter on a whim—or ignore when convenient." As for the real-life father, Barry further comments, "If my father hadn't exactly disappointed me, he remained something unknown, something volatile and vaguely threatening." [11] In writing that, Obama is also letting us know he had grown accustomed to his grandparents, and their inability or unwillingness to discipline him.

Ray: A Real Hard-Luck "Black Friend" in Hawaii?

Obama's autobiographical account of Punahou glosses over his first years after returning from Indonesia, almost immediately jumping forward to focus on Obama's teenage years. He invents a character he names only as "Ray," evidently to protect his privacy. Obama says he and Ray became easy friends, "due in no small part to the fact that together we made up almost half of Punahou's black high school population." [12] Of the school's 1,700 students, most were white.

Reading carefully, we notice Obama describes himself as a "black student," not a mixed-race student, or half African-American and half white. Although Ray was a senior in high school when Obama was a sophomore, the "big brother" age difference probably enhanced their friendship. As Obama tells the story, what held him and Ray together was race. Almost all of their conversations and exploits together ended up being one sort or other of a lesson about race, as Obama tells the story in the autobiography.

The *Chicago Tribune* tracked down the real "Ray" and found him to be Keith Kakugawa. Like Obama, Kakugawa is mixed-race, in his case half African-American and half Japanese, a native Hawaiian, something Obama never discloses when discussing Ray in the autobiography. In his interview with the newspaper, Kakugawa, now a convicted drug felon, said he always considered himself mixed-race, but he said he had never been the "prototypical black guy" Obama portrayed him being.

The *Tribune* further reported that Kakugawa remembered "long, soulful talks" with the young Obama and that his friend confided his longing and loneliness. But Kakugawa told the *Tribune* those talks were not about race. "Not even close," he said, though he added Obama was dealing "with some inner turmoil" in those days. "But it wasn't a race thing," Kakugawa went on. "Barry's biggest struggles were his feelings of abandonment. The idea that his biggest struggle was race is [bull]." [13]

Keith Kakugawa's story after Punahou, as reported by several media sources, was a hard-luck one, filled with failure, drug offenses, and a series of prison stays that stretched over decades.

The *Wall Street Journal* found Kakugawa, homeless in Los Angeles, just as he was released from a California state prison in March 2007 after a third drug conviction. [14] The *Journal* reported that Obama received a phone call from his long-lost friend just after coming off the Senate floor to prepare for a primary campaign trip to New Hampshire.

Without advance warning, his office patched through to his cell phone a call from Kakugawa. The two had not spoken with each other for some thirty years, not since Kakugawa left Hawaii in 1977. Then Kakugawa was full of promise, emerging from Punahou with college scholarships that reflected his outstanding performances in track and football. Kakugawa was calling from a pay phone in a run-down section of Los Angeles, looking for some help from his now-famous friend who was running for president from the U.S. Senate.

According to the *Journal* report, Kakugawa said his phone discussion with Obama was "short, sweet and to the point. He really acted like he didn't have a lot of time to spend with me." From there, the *Journal* further reported that aides in Obama's office took all subsequent calls from Kakugawa, not referring them to Obama. The aides advised Kakugawa to get help from social services agencies and said that Obama would help by working with the agencies. That exchange, the *Journal* reported, left Kakugawa upset. "Everybody's just abandoned me," the *Journal* reported Kakugawa as saying.

ABC News caught up with Kakugawa and he told the same story about Obama's alienation at Punahou.[15] "Everybody said they always saw him [Obama] smiling and happy. I didn't," Kakugawa told ABC. "I got to see the turmoil, I got to see how he really felt. Here's a kid who was growing up as an adolescent in a tough situation. He felt abandoned, he felt that his father abandoned him and his mother was always pursuing her career."

Obama confirmed Kakugawa's identity to the *Chicago Tribune* two days before Kakugawa contacted the campaign. Obama told the newspaper Kakugawa's incarceration was "a shame," before he complained, "Suddenly everybody who's ever touched my life is subject to a colonoscopy on the front page of the newspaper."

By then, Obama had realized that this level of intense scrutiny is a price paid by those running for president. What he may still not realize is the extent to which autobiographies that invent names and hide identities of key characters in the story invite scrutiny.

Despite Kakugawa's problems with drugs, his recent interviews suggest that the alienation Obama felt at Punahou was about his being abandoned by his parents, not from being a black kid in an elite white school. If Obama did not voice as much racial alienation with Kakugawa as he claims in the autobiography, perhaps their relationship was focused on drugs, a problem Kakugawa seems unable to shake, even today.

"I blew a few smoke rings, remembering those years," Obama wrote in a now-famous sentence reflecting on his college days at Occidental. "Pot had helped, and booze; maybe a little blow when you could afford it." [16]

Why Obama chose to disclose he smoked marijuana and used cocaine at all remains a mystery. Perhaps Obama felt the information would eventually come forward from his school buddies. So, to minimize the damage from this concealed fact, Obama possibly judged self-disclosure was the best route. In the paragraph where Obama makes this disclosure, he is quick to note he stopped short of using "smack," heroin. Obama says he backed off from heroin when "Micky," probably another invented name, "pulled out the needle and the tubing." Obama explains his revulsion, by claiming, "I'd looked at him standing there, surrounded by big slabs of salami and roast beef; and right then an image popped into my head of an air bubble, shiny and round like a pearl, rolling quietly through a vein and stopping my heart . . ." [17]

Obama told several reporters that he stopped taking drugs sometime during his college years. Did Obama ever use drugs in his days as a community organizer in Chicago, or when he was a state senator from Illinois? How about in the U.S. Senate?

In the autobiography, however, Obama links drug use with his blackness. He writes, "Junkie. Pothead. That's where I'd been headed: the final fatal role of the young would-be black man." [18] Had any white author written these words, they would have been hounded as a "racist." But Obama doesn't stop here. In the next few sentences, he links his drug use to his search for identity. He denies the "highs" had been about "me trying to prove what a down brother I was," arguing instead, "I got high for just the opposite effect, something that could push questions of who I was out of my mind, something that could flatten out the landscape of my heart, blur the edges of my memory." [19]

Blackness, identity crisis, and drugs: the three went together for Obama, at least according to his autobiography.

Black Rage

As we have just seen, Kakugawa says the source of Obama's discontent at Punahou was being abandoned by his parents, not race rage. Yet in passage after passage, Barry Obama uses the invented character of Ray to experience repeated acts of racial insult and engage in countless talks where they share black anger at the perceived insults and other affronts Obama feels they have suffered.

Conservative columnist Ann Coulter has characterized Obama's *Dreams from My Father* as a "dimestore *Mein Kampf*," in that "nearly every page—save the ones dedicated to cataloguing the mundane details of his life—is bristling with anger at some imputed racist incident." [20]

Coulter analyzes a passage in which Obama describes a "black party" that Ray threw at Schofield Barracks, about thirty miles out of town, on a Saturday night after a basketball game. Obama used his grandfather's Ford Granada to drive two white friends to the party, "Jeff" and "Scott," obviously more pseudonyms, especially since Obama introduces them into the story without mentioning last names. Everything was fine until Obama noticed Jeff and Scott were "smiling a lot," isolated by themselves, "huddled in a corner." [21] Obama concluded Jeff and Scott were uncomfortable being the only whites, so he excused himself to Ray and headed out, his two white friends with him.

Once back in the car, Jeff put an arm on Obama's shoulder and said what Obama took as a racial insult. "'You know, man,'" Obama quotes Jeff as saying, "'that really taught me something. I mean, I can see how it must be tough for you and Ray sometimes, at school parties . . . being the only black guys and all.'"

Those words spark one of the longest paragraphs in the autobiography, or what Coulter describes as "a full-page psychotic rant about living by 'the white man's rules.'" [22] Obama loses his composure, beginning the tirade by admitting "a part of me wanted to punch him right there. [23]

"We were always playing on the white man's court, Ray had told me, by the white man's rules," Obama goes on, launching into a very intellectual explanation of what he felt. The essence of the rant is that the white man had all the power, such that if a coach or teacher came to Obama's defense, Obama felt "it was his decision to make, not yours, and because of that fundamental power he held over you, because it preceded and would outlast his individual motives and inclinations, any distinction between good and bad whites had negligible meaning." The only option was to withdraw "into a smaller and smaller coil of rage, until being black meant only the knowledge of your own powerlessness, of your own defeat." Obama concluded by charging that this logic had a final irony: "Should you refuse this defeat and lash out at your captors, they would have a name for that, too, a name that could cage you just as good. Paranoid. Militant. Violent. Nigger."[24]

How severe was the racial injustice Obama truly suffered in this incident? Remember, he was attending one of the most elite educational institutions in Hawaii. Punahou was founded in 1841 to provide education for the children of Congregational missionaries. Its alumni include AOL founder Steve Case and eBay founder Pierre Omidyar, as well as luminaries from the Dole family (the pineapple powerhouse that has dominated the Hawaiian islands for generations), prominent government officials, military leaders, actors and actresses, literary figures. The current tuition for the 3,700 students lucky enough to be admitted is nearly seventeen thousand dollars. According to the school website, the campus "covers seventy-six acres at the edge of lush Manoa Valley and students occupy 44 school buildings, including three libraries and learning centers; computer areas and language labs; an impressive physical education facility (that includes a gymnasium, 50-meter pool, Mondo track, playing fields, racquetball and tennis courts, and weight and training facilities); and art facilities that include jewelry, ceramics and glassblowing."[25]

Where does Obama's racial angst come from? Obama is not a descendant of a slave, he did not grow up in an urban ghetto in an impoverished family, he was not unjustly prosecuted for some crime he did not commit. Where is the social injustice he has suffered? Perhaps Kakugawa is right.

What Obama had experienced to this point in his life was not intense racial injustice, but the abandonment of his father, followed by the abandonment of his mother. His white Midwestern grandparents loved him enough to provide him room and board in their home, modest as it may have been, and to pay a tuition his mother most likely could not afford, and which his father showed no interest in paying, even if he had the means. Yes, Obama was mixed-race, but what had he suffered from being born to an African father and a white mother? Beyond a confused identity, Obama never suffered poverty and he ended up the Harvard-educated son of a Harvard-educated father.

Borrowed Ideas from Frantz Fanon?

Is it possible that Obama invents "Ray" in his autobiography just to tell stories of black rage, especially when friends at Punahou, including his basketball buddies and even Keith Kakugawa himself, do not remember "black rage" associated with Barry Obama at the time? In 1995, Obama did not seek to find his high school friend to find out how he was doing and to ask permission to tell his story. From all accounts, Obama was taken aback when he received Kakugawa's phone call in 2007. Instead of reaching out to offer his friend personal assistance, Obama referred him to his staff and instructed them to tell Kakugawa to find help at a social services agency. Obama offered to help, but only at a distance. Where is the empathy for the past friendship of a classmate whose story Obama wove into his legacy?

Could the stories we find in *Dreams from My Father* have been borrowed, if not directly, then indirectly? In inventing "Ray," could Obama be merely dramatizing stories he had imagined from books as if they had happened in his own life? The borrowing is not a plagiarizing of words, but a borrowing of ideas, which Obama then overlays on circumstances in his life, either partially real or totally imagined, in order to express a black rage he wants to own. When he writes about his time in high school in Hawaii, Obama makes sure we understand that this black rage was the nexus of his own life at that time.

In *Dreams from My Father*, Obama himself provides us abundant evidence to conclude that his ideas of racial rage came from reading. Obama tells us that at Punahou, he "gathered up books from the library—Baldwin, Ellison, Hughes, Wright, DuBois." At night he would "close the door to my room, telling my grandparents I had homework to do, and there I would sit and wrestle with words, locked in suddenly desperate argument, trying to reconcile the world as I'd found it with the terms of my birth." [26] But there was no escape to be found, Obama confessed. "In every page of every book, in Bigger Thomas and invisible men, I kept finding the same doubt; a self-contempt that neither irony nor intellect seemed to deflect." [27]

Obama's search for identity had become a search for the racial overtones of the parental abandonment from which he suffered. Obama's black rage came from the books he read, a borrowed intellectual pattern he could place on his life.

Kakugawa has told reporters he has not read Obama's autobiography, so he has neither affirmed nor denied the truthfulness of the stories Obama tells. But we have our first hint that the important reality for Obama in high school involved not the mean streets of a racially oppressed city, but his bedroom, where, unknown to his grandparents, he searched for personal answers in the writings of black authors who had famously struggled with their own dreams and demons.

Many of the black-rage paragraphs Obama wrote in *Dreams from My Father* bear a striking resemblance to passages Frantz Fanon wrote in his first book, *Black Skin, White Masks*, first published in 1952. For instance, Obama has a whole section parsing out the meaning of the phrase "white folks." He ends up noting, "Ray assured me that we would never talk about whites without knowing exactly what we were doing. Without knowing that there might be a price to pay." [28]

On reading this one senses a similarity to Frantz Fanon, the African psychiatrist whose revolutionary writings were so influential in shaping the revolutionary political left of the 1950s and 1960s. In the first chapter of *Black Skin, White Masks*, titled "The Negro and Language," Fanon wrote, "The black man has two dimensions. One with his fellows, the other with the white man. A Negro behaves differently with a white man and with another Negro." [29] So too, Obama advises Ray to talk one way with him and another way when whites are present.

Let's take another passage. The dialogue introducing Ray begins, "Man, I'm not going to any more of these bullshit Punahou parties." [30] From there, Ray and Barry complain that the girls avoid them because they are black. "I'm saying, yeah, it's harder to get dates because there aren't any black girls around here," Ray says. "But that don't make the girls that are here all racist. Maybe they just want somebody that looks like their daddy, or their brother, or whatever, and we ain't it." [31]

Again we find a similar passage in *Black Skin, White Masks*, in chapter 3, "The Man of Color and the White Woman," where Fanon writes, "When the question is put directly, then, the white man agrees to give his sister to the black—but on one condition: you have nothing in common with real Negroes. You are not black, you are 'extremely brown.'"[32] Obama, like Fanon, assumes sexual attraction involves same-race consciousness.

The connection with Fanon may still seem slim, until we get to chapter 5, "The Fact of Blackness," in *Black Skin, White Masks*, where Fanon claims, "For several years certain laboratories have been trying to produce a serum for 'denegrification'; with all the earnestness in the world, laboratories have sterilized their test tubes, checked their scales, and embarked on researches that might make it possible for the miserable Negro to whiten himself and thus to throw off the burden of that corporeal malediction."[33]

Recall the story Obama told about an African-American tragically harming himself by using chemicals to alter his skin. As we saw in the previous chapter, *Life* researched the archives and reported that the article never existed. The same was true of *Ebony*. So if the source was not *Life* or *Ebony*, perhaps Obama got the idea from Fanon's speculation here that a serum was being produced for "denegrification."

In his autobiography, Obama tells us he read Fanon at Occidental College.[34] Fanon's political philosophy should have resonated with Obama, especially since Fanon's writings defined much of the anticolonial movement that swept across Europe and Africa in the 1950s and 1960s. During the Algerian revolution in 1954, Fanon went to Algeria and joined the Front de Libération Nationale, the radical socialist party then fighting for independence from France. In his classic study of the Algerian revolution, *A Savage War of Peace*, historian Alistair Horne wrote that Fanon "became one of the revolution's most articulate and extreme ideologues, and a violent exponent of anti-colonialism in any shape." Horne notes that Fanon died of leukemia in 1961, at only thirty-six years old, so respected that Independent Algeria "honored his name with a university and a boulevard."[35]

Fanon achieved world fame with *Black Skin, White Masks* in 1952 and the book was almost certainly known to Obama Senior, especially given the role Obama Senior planned to play in the Kenyatta government following independence. The revolution in Algeria against the French set the stage for Jomo Kenyatta and Tom Mboya's anticolonial revolution against the British in Kenya. We do not know if Obama Senior ever shared Fanon's writings with his son, but much of the expression of black resentment Obama offers in *Dreams from My Father* appears strongly influenced by Fanon's pages. Many ideas appear similar enough that Obama could easily have internalized Fanon's arguments into his own thought.

What Obama expresses in *Dreams from My Father* is not the inner-city black rage of decades of racial discrimination since slavery, as expressed by Stokely Carmichael or Eldridge Cleaver. Nowhere in the book does Obama write anything that would be included in classic critiques of American racial relations such as were penned by Gunnar Myrdal in *An American Dilemma*[36] or Harvard-trained psychologist Kenneth Clark in his 1964 book *Dark Ghetto*.[37] The racial crisis Myrdal and Clark trace back to slavery involves a twentieth-century reality of urban African-American poverty, racial segregation in housing and schools, and income inequality among the races caused by employment discrimination.

Obama's black rage, by sharp contrast, is anticolonial in nature. As we saw above, Obama objected that the "white folks" wrote the rules and the "black folks" seeking to adapt had no choice but to put the white mask over their black faces, even if doing so violated their feelings of authenticity to self-determine the rules for themselves. Obama railed against the same form of racial oppression his father must have felt under British colonialism. In his autobiography we learn Obama's racial rage developed as a teenager, after he returned from Indonesia. But while attending the elite Punahou School in the multicultural society of Hawaii, Obama never experienced educational inequality nor seems to have encountered any of the racial discrimination that inner-city African-Americans experience. Obama lived in an apartment with his grandparents, but he did not live in an impoverished inner-city ghetto. Obama's crisis is a crisis of racial identity. Even though colonized blacks in Africa suffered racial injustice and economic discrimination, what Fanon struggles to recover is a racial identity identified by his race and by Africa, free from the colonial racial identity imposed on African blacks by their elite European oppressors.

Obama too writes of his struggles to find his own racial identity: "In fact, you couldn't even be sure that everything you had assumed to be an expression of your black, unfettered self—the humor, the song, the behind-the-back pass—had been freely chosen by you. At best, these things were a refuge; at worst, a trap."[38] Or, as Fanon wrote, "Every colonized people—in other words, every people in whose soul an inferiority complex has been created by the death and burial of its local cultural originality—finds itself face to face with the language of the civilizing nation; that is, with the culture of the mother country's cultural standards."[39] We are reminded of Ochieng's comment that we quoted in the first chapter, that Kenyans have become ghosts "flitting into and out of European imagination."

This is the crux of the problem, both for Obama and for Fanon: "The colonized is elevated above his jungle status in proportion to his adoption of the mother country's cultural standards."[40] Obama introduces his invented Ray into the autobiography to object to going to white parties. What Obama cannot cope with is the real-life Ray who telephones him homeless, a drug addict suffering the street abuse of real-life poverty in today's urban America. Ray, much like Obama's mother watching *Black Orpheus*, appears to embarrass Obama.

We can see Fanon reflected in Obama when Obama tells us he felt "a warning whenever a white girl mentioned in the middle of a conversation how much she liked Stevie Wonder; or when the school principal told me I was cool. I did like Stevie Wonder, I did love basketball, and I tried my best to be cool at all times. So, why did such comments set me on edge?"

These comments set Obama on edge for the same reason colonialism set Fanon on edge: Fanon did not want to put the white colonial mask in front of his black face any more than Obama wanted to internalize white stereotypical ideas of who blacks were in the 1970s. In the final analysis, both Obama and Fanon share the same worst fear, namely, losing their self-determined identities in the definitions and language that a dominant white culture sought to impose on them in order to hold them in subjugation.

Obama's Communist Mentor

In writing about his time at Punahou, Obama singled out a friendship with a poet he only identifies as "Frank." In introducing Frank, Obama says he "lived in a dilapidated house in a run-down section of Waikiki."[41] Obama then provides enough background information about Frank to make identifying him easy for experts. "He had enjoyed some modest notoriety once, was a contemporary of Richard Wright and Langston Hughes during his years in Chicago—Gramps once showed me some of his work anthologized in a book of black poetry," Obama wrote. He adds Frank was "pushing eighty" when he met him. The only poet who fits that description completely is Frank Marshall Davis, a newspaper journalist and poet who was widely known in the 1950s to be a communist.

The first identification of "Frank" with Frank Marshall Davis was made by Gerald Horne, a contributing editor to *Political Affairs*, an openly Marxist political review.[42] In March 2007, Horne gave a speech at New York University on the occasion of the Communist Party USA archives being placed at an NYU library. In that speech, he discussed Frank Marshall Davis, noting that Davis, who was born in Kansas and lived much of his adult life in Chicago, had moved to Honolulu in 1948 at the suggestion of his good friend, actor Paul Robeson. In the 1940s, Robeson was an outspoken critic of segregation and racial discrimination in the United States. At the time, Robeson was a strong advocate of the Soviet Union and a member of the Communist Party USA.

Horne also documented Davis's friendship with the Dunham family in Hawaii. "Eventually, he [Frank Marshall Davis] befriended another family—a Euro-American family—that had migrated to Honolulu from Kansas and a young woman from this family eventually had a child with a young student from Kenya East Africa who goes by the name of Barack Obama, who retracing the steps of Davis eventually decamped to Chicago."[43] Horne further documented that Frank Marshall Davis was "a decisive influence in helping him [Barack Obama] to find his present identity as an African-American, a people who have been the least anti-communist and the most left-leaning of any constituency in this nation."[44] After Horne's speech, the identity of "Frank" was never in doubt, nor was his importance in the development of the young Barack Obama.

On December 5, 1956, Frank Marshall Davis appeared in executive session before the U.S. Senate subcommittee investigating "the scope of Soviet activity in the United States." It was one of the McCarthy-era committees seeking to expose communists considered to be a security threat.[45] Invoking his Fifth Amendment rights against self-incrimination, Davis refused to answer a direct question if he was then a communist. A year earlier, in 1955, the Commission on Subversive Activities organized by the government of the territory of Hawaii identified Davis as a member of the Communist Party USA. The committee singled out for criticism several articles Davis had published in the *Honolulu Record* that were critical of the commission.[46] The commission also found objectionable a 1951 story Davis published, titled "Hawaii's Plain People Fight White Supremacy," in the November 1951 issue of a New York City communist tabloid.

The two African-American writers Obama mentions to give "Frank" some context both had communist connections as well. Langston Hughes and Richard Wright were the two African-American writers most identified with the Communist Party USA in the 1930s. Hughes, a prolific writer best known for his 1921 poem "The Negro Speaks of Rivers," told the Senate Permanent Subcommittee on Investigations in 1953 that he had been a communist sympathizer.[47] Hughes further testified there was a period of his life when he believed in the Soviet Union's form of government and that books he authored were written to follow the communist line. Richard Wright, best known for his 1940 novel *Native Son*,[48] was the Harlem editor of the communist newspaper *Daily Worker* in 1937.

John Edgar Tidwell, a professor of English at the University of Kansas, who produced an anthology of Davis's poems, also confirms Davis joined the Communist Party.

Tidwell argues that Davis's radical poetry and newspaper articles "put him on a collision course" with the House Un-American Activities Committee and the FBI.[49] In his autobiography, *Livin' the Blues*, Davis himself tells us that being pursued by the U.S. government didn't bother him: "I knew I would be described as a Communist, but frankly I had reached the stage where I didn't give a damn. Too many people I respected as Freedom Fighters were listed as Red for me to fear name calling."[50] And again, "The genuine Communists I knew as well as others so labeled had one principle in common: to use any and every means to abolish racism."[51] Davis wrote to give "the widest possible publicity to the many instances of racism and the dissatisfaction of Afro-Americans with the status quo."[52]

In truth, many prominent African-American intellectuals and writers of the 1930s gravitated toward communism in their frustration at what they perceived as little or no progress fighting racial discrimination and inequality in the United States. Davis admitted to being "brainwashed for years after the Bolshevik revolution."[53] He believed that Russia had no colonies and "was strongly opposed to the imperialism under which my black kinsmen lived in Africa, and that those American forces which most staunchly resisted our own demands for equality were the most rabid foes of Russia."[54] So Davis saw Russia as an ally as determined as was he "to stamp out discrimination." Like so many other communists in the United States, white and black alike, Davis felt betrayed when Stalin signed the nonaggression pact with Hitler in 1939. For many in the Communist Party USA, that was the last straw of betrayal. After that, Davis worked with any group determined "to wipe out white supremacy."[55] He admitted, "I made no distinction between those labeled Communist, Socialist, or merely liberal."[56]

As noble as Davis's fight against racism was, investigative reporter Cliff Kincaid reminds us that the Obama/Communist Party connection through Davis had an "ominous" side as well. "Decades ago, the CPUSA had tens of thousands of members, some of them covert agents who had penetrated the U.S. Government," Kincaid wrote in *Accuracy in Media*. "It received secret subsidies from the old Soviet Union."[57]

The Black Poet and the Grandmother Crisis

Obama says he and his grandfather, Stanley Dunham, would stop by Davis's home. As Davis shared his whiskey "with Gramps out of an emptied jelly jar,"[58] Davis would entertain them by reading his poetry.

But the key role Frank Marshall Davis plays in the autobiography is not to provide Obama with words from his poems as a voice for Obama's black rage. Instead Davis is the mentor Obama seeks for wisdom and advice, for instance when he has a crisis with his grandmother that was so traumatic Obama still mentions it today.

Obama begins the story by recalling a day when he heard his grandparents arguing. Evidently, his grandmother had been harassed by a panhandler when she was waiting for the bus one morning to go to work at the bank. The incident so upset her that she asked Stanley to drive her to work, so she could avoid taking the bus. Obama did not understand why she was so upset until his grandfather explained, "It *is* a big deal. It's a big deal to me. She's been bothered by men before. You know why she is so scared this time? I will tell you why. Before you came in, she told me the fella was *black*."[59] Stanley whispered the word "black" and Obama said, "The words were like a fist in my stomach, and I wobbled to regain my composure."[60]

So upset by the incident that he could not stay home, Obama sought out the advice of his friend Frank. Later that evening, drinking with Frank Marshall Davis at the poet's Waikiki home, Obama told him the story of his grandmother and the black panhandler. As Barry most likely expected he would be, Frank was sympathetic. Listening closely to Barry, Frank explained to Obama that his grandmother was right to be scared. "She understands that black people have a reason to hate," Davis told him. "That's just how it is. For your sake, I wish it were otherwise. But it's not. So you might as well get used to it."

Those words sealed the deal for Barry Obama. Frank had just told him he was right to reject his grandparents. Despite all they had done for him, his grandparents were still "white folks" and "white folks" are racists. What else could Barry expect?

Obama said Davis's words made the earth shake under his feet. When he steadied himself, he knew "for the first time that I was totally alone." Gone were both his father and mother. Now Obama could feel justified concluding he had been abandoned by his grandparents as well. Looked at objectively, how could it have been otherwise? Obama's grandparents were white and Obama was in the process of forming his identity as an African-American. Clearly, in this story, the person Obama identified himself as being was not his grandmother, it was the black panhandler.

The story was obviously seminal in forming the adult Obama. Some thirty years later, Obama was still telling the story, this time to a national audience as he was running for president.

On March 18, 2008, Obama gave a speech in Philadelphia to answer a wave of criticism over the black liberation theology sermons given by Reverend Jeremiah Wright of Trinity Church in Chicago, which Obama attended. The speech was one of the most important Obama had to give during the Democratic primary campaign, as the Wright controversy threatened to sink his poll numbers as he and Hillary Clinton headed toward the Pennsylvania primary a month later. In the speech, Obama made reference to the incident with his grandmother and the panhandler. He explained he could no more disown Reverend Wright than he could disown his own grandmother, "a woman who loves me as much as she loves anything in this world, but a woman who once confessed her fear of black men who passed by her on the street, and who on more than one occasion has uttered racial or ethnic stereotypes that made me cringe."[61]

The comment in Obama's Philadelphia speech caused conservative columnist and blogger Steve Sailer to quip that Obama had thrown his eighty-five-year-old grandmother "under the wheels of the bus."[62] Remember, this grandmother was the same Madelyn Dunham who had used her bank vice president's salary to provide room and board for Obama, plus the tuition and other expenses he needed to attend high school at an institution as refined as Punahou. Never, in telling the bus stop story in the autobiography or decades later in his campaign apology in Philadelphia, does Obama take the time to acknowledge that Madelyn was at that bus stop to go to work and earn a living from which he would benefit.

Obama may have titled the speech "A More Perfect Union," but the invitation he issued that day to bring the question of race up to a new national dialogue involved not lofty questions of first principles but a descent into his private, personal psychology. Obama's Philadelphia speech demanded we go back to his childhood and judge his grandmother. The choice there was his, not ours. "Why is he talking about his grandmother?" an observer listening to Obama for the first time could ask, when the reason for the speech was criticism Obama was receiving over the extreme black rage expressed against the United States by his preacher's liberation theology sermons. What Reverend Wright had to do with this grandmother was that evidently both played an important role in shaping Obama's racial identity.

Malcolm X and "White Blood"

In relating his development at Punahou, Obama singles out the impact Malcolm X's autobiography had on him. "His repeated acts of self-creation spoke to me," Obama writes, "the blunt poetry of his words, his unadorned insistence on respect, promised a new and uncompromising order, martial in its discipline, forged through sheer force of will." Obama is quick to add that he rejected Malcolm's "talk of blue-eyed devils and apocalypse" as baggage that Obama believes Malcolm X himself abandoned at the end of his life, when Malcolm X was seeking some distance from Elijah Muhammad and the Black Muslim movement.

But a key point in Malcolm X's autobiography had a major impact on Obama: "And yet, even as I imagined myself following Malcolm's call, one line in the book stayed me. He spoke of a wish he'd once had, the wish that the white blood that ran through him, there by an act of violence, might somehow be expunged." [63]

The allusion is to chapter 12, "Savior," in Malcolm X's autobiography. Malcolm was relating one of the earliest speeches he gave in 1953 in Detroit, when he first became a minister in the Nation of Islam. [64] In the speech, Malcolm railed at the white man who had raped his grandmother on the Caribbean island of Antigua, fathering his mother, Louise.

"Turn around, *look* at each other!" Malcolm told the congregation. "What shade of black African polluted by devil white man are you? You see me—well, in the streets they used to call me Detroit Red. Yes! Yes, that raping, redheaded devil was my *grandfather*! That close, yes! My *mother's* father!" Malcolm X was clearly preaching in a frenzy, angry that blacks had been polluted by white blood at one time or another in ancestral time. Malcolm X detested miscegenation, consistent with his ideas that black Muslim women would and should be faithful and pure to their black Muslim husbands. Then, Malcolm said, "If I could drain away his blood that pollutes *my* body, and pollutes *my* complexion, I'd do it! Because I hate every drop of the rapist's blood that's in me!"

The passage takes up one paragraph in Malcolm X's autobiography, a book of 455 pages. Yet it is the one that stuck in Obama's mind. We are drawn back to the imagined *Life* magazine with the story Obama remembered of a black man who tried to rip off his black skin, or of Frantz Fanon's imagination that a serum had been invented that would turn black skin white. These are the images that have stuck in Obama's mind. Yet it turns out not that Obama wants to become white, a classic African-American psychological issue, but rather the haunting image here is the reverse. Obama wants to will all the white blood out of himself so he can become pure black.

Reflecting on the Malcolm X passage cited above, Obama wrote, "I knew as well that traveling down the road to my self-respect my own white blood would never recede into mere abstraction. I was left to wonder what else I would be severing if and when I left my mother and my grandparents at some uncharted border."[65]

At this point, Obama's story of race and inheritance

appears complete. His race, he self-determines, is African-American. In making that determination, he rejects everyone white, including his mother and his grandparents.

We do not have to speculate about this. Obama tells this to us outright; his words are direct, defying us to miss his meaning.

KENYA, ODINGA,
COMMUNISM, AND ISLAM

*You do not work hard enough, Barry. You must
help in your people's struggle. Wake up, black
man!*

—Barack Obama Senior[1]

*If Obama's not a closeted Marxist then why
should I vote for him?*

—Comment posted by "fwslusser" on the
NewRepublic.com, April 16, 2008[2]

On February 25, 2008, during the Democratic primary campaign, the Drudge Report published a photo, which the Hillary Clinton campaign later denied distributing in Texas and Ohio, showing Senator Barack Obama in Africa dressed in a headscarf and robe, with a walking stick in his right hand.[3]

According to Matt Drudge, Obama campaign manager David Plouffe accused the Clinton campaign of "shameful offensive fear-mongering" for circulating the photograph. The photo turns out to be authentic, taken in Kenya during Barack's five-nation taxpayer-funded trip to Africa in August 2006. The Obama campaign denied the photo proves any connection between Obama and Islam.

The controversy over the photo published by Drudge spurred greater examination of Obama's current ties to the politics in Kenya, the home of Obama's father. While the photograph was hardly convincing evidence that Obama is secretly Islamic, Obama's 2006 trip to Kenya evidenced his continued ties to a Raila Odinga, a fellow Luo tribesman, who was running for president of Kenya as a Muslim sympathizer with well-known communist political roots.

Obama's support for Raila Odinga is understandable, not just because his grandfather and father, like Odinga, were from the Luo tribe, but also because Obama's roots include an intellectual connection to decades of anticolonial political philosophy and U.S. African-American radical political writings that he had studied since his teenage years at the elite preparatory Punahou School in Hawaii.

Obama's trip back to Kenya occupies the concluding chapters of his autobiography. The "roots" trip described in the book appears to condense the first two of three excursions Obama made to his father's homeland, in 1986 and then again in 1992. Obama's third trip to Kenya, in 2006, his first as a U.S. senator, was much more than a personal trip. By supporting his fellow Luo tribesman, Raila Odinga, in his battle to share the presidency of Kenya, Obama not only plunged back into the Kenyan battles of domestic politics that destroyed his father, he also set a course to become an influence in Kenyan politics of today.

Thus, we have to examine Obama's support of Odinga,

a radical leftist politician educated in communist East Germany who has emerged from the tribal battles that have dominated Kenya's politics for centuries. Odinga, now sharing a co-presidency after being appointed prime minister under President Mwai Kibaki, appears to have allied with radical Muslims in Kenya whose main agenda is to advance aggressively the cause of Islam in Africa. We have to ask whether Obama, by supporting Odinga openly in Kenya, lent his name also to endorse Odinga's leftist politics and Odinga's alliance with radical Muslims pushing Islam in Kenya.

Senator Barack Obama, a Kenyan Tribal Elder

The photograph of Obama in African garb was originally published by Han-Geeska Afrika Online on September 1, 2006.[4]

The photo shows Sheikh Mahmed Hassan dressing Obama as a Somali elder. The photo is authentic; it was taken during Obama's visit to Wajir, a rural area in northeastern Kenya, near the borders with Somalia and Ethiopia. The BBC photographed Obama wearing the same red shirt, khaki pants, and wristwatch on Sunday, August 27, 2006, when Obama toured the slum area of Kibera.[5] There is little doubt Obama wore the Somali elder garb, but we can easily find dozens of photos of U.S. politicians wearing local costume during overseas travel.

On February 4, 2008, the tabloid *National Examiner* published the photo in an article that asserted Obama was wearing "Muslim attire" on a trip to the Kenyan homeland of his natural father. The Obama campaign decried the *National Examiner*'s sensationalism, arguing that Obama was dressed in traditional tribal garb, not "Muslim attire," much as, again, President Bush or other U.S. leaders take on local clothing or traditional native costumes when meeting in foreign countries. The Obama campaign was right: Somalia is almost entirely Sunni Muslim, so in that sense the Somali elder garb would of course be Islamic. Regardless, the photo does show Obama's acceptance as an African, a fellow Kenyan in the homeland of his father.

A DVD documentary titled *Senator Obama Goes to Africa* shows the enthusiastic reception Obama got on his 2006 tour of Africa, including his third visit to Kenya.[6] The documentary was produced by Bob Hercules, a Chicago-based independent filmmaker, and cameraman Keith Walker, who have previously collaborated to produce a documentary on the Chicago-based radical organizer Saul Alinsky. Accompanied by his wife, Michelle, Obama visited the South African jail where Nelson Mandela was held for twenty-one years and visited a Darfur refugee camp in Chad. The emotional highlight of the trip was Obama's visit to his father's home in Kisumu, Kenya. Obama got a celebrity's welcome at the small airport in his father's hometown. Supplied with a key to the village on a red ribbon that Obama placed around his neck, Obama led the camera crew on a "roots" trip back home in Kenya for the first time since becoming a U.S. senator.

In a staged public event at the Kenya Medical Research Institute in Kisian, Obama and his wife took an AIDS test, to demonstrate to the local people in a public forum that the test was safe. At the door of a mobile AIDS testing facility provided by the U.S. Centers for Disease Control, Obama was photographed with a microphone, speaking to the assembled crowd. Standing prominently in front of Obama, facing the crowd as Obama spoke, was Raila

Odinga. Positioned there, almost as a bodyguard, Odinga was clearly visible to the crowd as a principal in the scene, closely associated with his Luo tribesman, the U.S. senator from Illinois. The documentary film does not identify Odinga by name in this scene.

At the time, Odinga and his Orange Democratic Movement were contesting President Mwai Kibaki for the leadership of the country. Kibaki is a member of Kenya's largest tribe, the Kikuyu. The Luo tribe, of which Obama and Odinga are members, is Kenya's second-largest tribe. The Orange Democratic Movement, or ODM, was named after Viktor Yushchenko's "Orange Revolution" in the Ukraine, with the same intent to take control of the government by winning the presidency.

The primary message of the AIDS event in Kisian was a universal message, namely, that AIDS testing is safe. The documentary notes that in Kenya 1.3 million people, or 6.7 percent of the population, are living with HIV/AIDS. Another 1 million children are orphaned due to AIDS.

"One of the reasons we are here today is because HIV/AIDS has ravaged the community," Obama told the assembled crowd. "Too many people, too many children have gotten sick. So one of the things we're going to do here in front of this van today is that my wife and I are going to get tested for HIV/AIDS, because if you know your status, you can prevent illness." The Centers for Disease Control suggested to Obama that as many as a half-million Kenyans would take the HIV/AIDS test after they saw him and his wife safely do it themselves.

Still, what was understood by Kenyans who were at the event or saw videos of it later was that Obama, by being seen this prominently with Odinga in public, had injected himself into the presidential contest on the side of his tribesman.

Obama and Odinga had skillfully transformed a health message delivered by a foreign dignitary into a low-key stump speech for Odinga, with Obama effectively endorsing Odinga's candidacy to be president of Kenya simply because of how Odinga was positioned and filmed at the event.

Obama's tour of a slum in Kibera led to an appearance by Charity Ngilu, the Kenyan minister of health. "By Barack going to Kibera, we also saw the minister of health came," Michelle Obama says in the documentary. "I'd be very interested in knowing how many times she has been to Kibera. But, again, by him coming it kind of forces her to come as well and to be a part of that community. So, it's a good way to leverage your visibility on behalf of average Kenyans and not just the dignitaries."

After the visit to Kibera, Obama told the press, "I think people feel neglected, like nobody is listening to them. And people feel those in power don't care. I don't think that's just here in Kenya, it's also in the States."

Obama visited Kenya while President Kibaki was locked in a presidential election contest against Raila Odinga. During his visit, the Kibaki administration objected that Odinga was using Obama's visit to win votes. Obama's repeated public appearances with Odinga and his almost daily criticism of the Kibaki government added to the Kibaki administration's dismay at how the U.S. senator conducted himself in their country.

A report by Chicago's Channel 2 CBS news team, which covered Obama in Kenya, gives a completely different impression of the trip than the Hercules-Walker produced documentary does. The Channel 2 television news segment broadcast in Chicago shows Obama in Kenya making public comments critical of the Kibaki government.[7] Two separate video segments in the news broadcast documented that Obama spoke at the offices of Kenya's oldest newspaper, the *Standard*, where he accused the Kibaki government of suppressing freedom of speech, and at the University of Nairobi, where he accused the Kibaki administration of corruption. The Channel 2 broadcast noted that criticizing the Kenyan government was "something he [Obama] has done almost every day since he arrived in Kenya last week." The news report also showed repeated clips of Odinga accompanying Obama at various speaking appearances in Kenya, so much so that the news broadcaster commented in the background that Odinga "has been at Obama's elbow here fairly often."

The Channel 2 news team also interviewed on camera Kenyan government spokesman Alfred Mutua, who accused Obama of meddling inappropriately in Kenyan presidential politics. Mutua said politely but pointedly that "I think Obama has to look at critically where he is receiving his advice from. Just because somebody somewhere wants to run for president, and he is using Senator Obama as his stooge, as his puppet, to be able to get where he wants to get."

When President Mwai Kibaki finally agreed to meet Senator Barack Obama at the end of his trip to Kenya, Obama used the opportunity to claim the Channel 2 news team had been forced to pay a bribe in a "shake-down" corruption scheme. Obama charged "expeditors" demanded from Channel 2 exorbitant fees, just to walk the news cameramen through customs without being harassed with allegations that their cameras were stolen equipment.[8] On camera in the Channel 2 interview, government spokesman Mutua showed the notices the government had placed in several Nairobi newspapers to refute Obama's accusations, which Mutua claimed were unfounded. Matua said Channel 2 had been charged only legitimate customs duties. At the end of the report, Channel 2 acknowledged that all disputed fees had been repaid by the government.

The Legacy of Jomo Kenyatta, Tom Mboya, and Odinga Odinga

By supporting Odinga, Obama entered the four-decades-old political conflict between Jomo Kenyatta and Tom Mboya that had destroyed his father's career.

Kenyatta, a member of the Kikuyu tribe, had been working on Kenyan independence since 1929, when he traveled to England to argue the case in front of the Colonial Office and the British Parliament. After World War II the independence movement swept Africa. Kenyatta was arrested by the British on October 22, 1952, and imprisoned, much as the Dutch white settler apartheid government in South Africa imprisoned Nelson Mandela on August 5, 1962.

Kenyatta had played a role organizing the Mau Mau rebellion, a key force in convincing the British that unlike South Africa, the white settlers in Kenya would never be able to sustain a minority-white-dominated government. Although the etymology of the term *Mau Mau* remains debated today, there never was a Mau Mau tribe in Kenya, or anywhere else. The Mau Mau was a movement that the colonial Kenyan government banned in 1950. The majority of the Mau Mau were members of the Kikuyu tribe. Kenyatta was not released from prison until August 1961.

In May 1963, Kenyatta's political party, the Kenya African National Union, or KANU, won the country's first free presidential elections. On June 1, 1963, Kenyatta successfully organized a government, positioning himself to become the first prime minister of an independent Kenya. Kenyan independence was declared on December 12, 1963, with Kenyatta as prime minister. The next year, the country's minority party, the Kenya African Democratic Union, or KADU, dissolved itself and merged into the KANU. Kenya became a republic, and Jomo Kenyatta was declared the first president.

As we learned earlier, Tom Mboya was a member of the Luo tribe, the same as Obama's family. Mboya came to national prominence in Kenya in 1953, when he became treasurer of Kenyatta's first political party, then called the Kenyan African Union, or KAU. In 1955 and 1956, the British Labour Party paid for Mboya to study industrial management at Ruskin College in Oxford University. While Mboya was in England, the British effectively ended the Mau Mau rebellion. In 1957, back in Kenya, Mboya formed the People's Convention Party and began a campaign for representation in Kenya's legislature.

In 1960, Mboya and Odinga Odinga, the father of Raila Odinga, formed the KANU, by merging the People's Convention Party into the KANU, and Kenyatta, still imprisoned for his role in the Mau Mau rebellion, was named KANU president in absentia. Mboya made a move for national unity by campaigning for Kenyatta's release from prison. This decision effectively united the Luo behind the Kikuyu, with Kenyatta fingered as the likely national leader when Kenya achieved independence. In Kenyatta's government, Mboya was initially given the position of minister for justice and constitutional affairs. Then, in 1964, he moved to minister for economic planning and development.

Mboya liked to characterize himself as an African socialist, though according to U.S. standards, Mboya would have been seen as a supporter of capitalism and private enterprise.

Throughout his career, Mboya was a strong supporter of the United States.[9] We saw earlier that Mboya met with John F. Kennedy, before JFK won the 1960 presidential election, to secure Kennedy family financial support for the second air-lift of young Kenyan students to study in U.S. universities.

Odinga Odinga, then commonly known as "Double-O," always displayed a willingness to be more and more openly communist, even if the move to the far left of the political spectrum meant he would inevitably distance himself from the more moderately socialist Mboya. Babafemi Badejo, the biographer of Raila Odinga, commented that Mboya was "more socialized in the individualistic and materialistic approach to politics of the Kikuyu, who were strong on accumulation," while Odinga Odinga favored "the communal basis for politics in Kenya" that was "generally considered as communism."[10] Badejo also noted that, in the complicated tribal politics of Kenya, Mboya was "born a Luo, as a result of parentage," but "his birthplace was in the heart of Kamba land," the territory of yet another tribe. So, in Badejo's words, Mboya "grew up amongst Kamba children and spoke their languages, and had several experiences that made him first a Kenyan."[11]

The result was that Mboya could support Kenyatta even though Mboya was Luo and Kenyatta was Kikuyu. Mboya could cross tribal lines because he was considered a "Kenyan first." Mboya was willing to support Kenyatta primarily because he shared Kenyatta's enthusiasm that the future of Kenya rested with the United States. Still, Kenyatta never stopped worrying that the Luo tribe was secretly planning a coup to place Mboya and the Luo in power, after ousting Kenyatta and his Kikuyu tribesmen, who enjoyed positions of power throughout the Kenyan government.

Even though both Mboya and Odinga Odinga were

Luo, they were often at odds politically. As Badjeo wrote, "The legacy of the cold war led to a perception that Odinga Odinga was a Communist with allegiance to the Soviet Union and Communist China, while Mboya was seen as epitomizing the virtues of capitalist free enterprise, and allied to the United States of America."[12] Odinga Odinga and Mboya became Luo rivals, each striving to be president.

Another dimension entered into the conflict between Mboya and Odinga. There was a generational difference between the two, with Odinga Odinga estimating that he had been born in 1911, while Mboya was twenty years younger, born in 1930. Odinga Odinga frequently charged that the younger Mboya was arrogant toward him, treating him not as a colleague, but more as a tribal chief from a bygone era.

In 1964, when Kenya became a republic and Kenyatta became the country's first president, Odinga Odinga became the first vice president. The move was an attempt to unite the Kikuyu tribe, with their member Kenyatta at the head of the government, and the Luo tribe, with their member Odinga Odinga as number two. The arrangement reflected the dominant position of the Kikuyu tribe as Kenya's largest tribe, followed by the Luo. Over time, the arrangement proved unstable. Kenyatta was pro-West and he looked to the United States to help build Kenya. Odinga Odinga, as vice president, was now widely thought to be a communist who looked to the Soviet Union for Kenya's future.

In 1966, when Kenyatta ousted Odinga Odinga from the vice presidency, Mboya did nothing to assist his fellow tribesman. Odinga Odinga resigned from the KANU and formed the Kenya People's Union, or KPU, a truly communist African political party.

As the 1960s drew to a close, Mboya became increasingly agitated that Luo tribesmen he supported were being pushed out of government to make way for the Kikuyu tribesmen whom Kenyatta was promoting. On July 5, 1969, Mboya was assassinated in Nairobi by a Kikuyu tribesman, a fateful move that sent Obama Senior's career into a tailspin. Later that year, Odinga Odinga was placed under house arrest after he verbally accosted Kenyatta at a public function in Kisumu and a riot broke out that killed some eleven people and injured dozens more. Kenyatta did everything possible to make sure Odinga Odinga remained in political obscurity, a situation that lasted until Kenyatta died in 1978.

Raila Odinga's politics, like the politics of his father, Odinga Odinga, are on the far left. Raila Odinga was educated at the Technical University in Magdeburg in East Germany, where he graduated in 1970 with a degree in mechanical engineering. There he heard Fidel Castro lecture and he named his first-born son Fidel. On July 31, 1982, junior military men of the Luo tribe in the Kenyan Air Force led a coup against President Daniel arap Moi, but it failed. For his suspected involvement in the coup, Raila Odinga was arrested, charged with treason, and incarcerated without trial for nine years. He was released in February 1988 and then rearrested in September 1988, this time for his involvement with the clandestine Kenya Revolutionary Movement and for facilitating travel to Libya for Kenyans seeking to get military training under Colonel Muammar Qaddafi.

It should be noted that Odinga Odinga was a Christian who saw that his son, Raila Odinga, was also baptized a Christian. Odinga Odinga went by the double name to emphasize how completely he rejected his Christian name. Odinga Odinga also refused to allow his children to be baptized with European Christian names.[13] Raila Odinga today professes to be an Anglican.

In a country of 30 million people, some 85 percent of

Kenyans are Christians, with a minority Islamic population of about 10 million. The majority of both the Luo and Kikuyu tribes are Christian, and President Mwai Kibaki is also Christian. These distinctions will become important later, when we sort out why Raila Odinga decided to side with radical Islamic forces in Kenya in order to improve his chances of winning an electoral victory against President Kibaki in the election scheduled for December 2007.

Tribesmen Unite

This Kenyan history helps us understand Senator Obama's current position in a Kenyan political drama that has been unfolding since the 1950s. As we also saw earlier, Barack Obama Senior had been sponsored by Mboya to go on the first airlift in 1959 to go to the United States to study. When Obama Senior returned to Kenya in 1965, he worked for a short while for an American oil company and then within a few months became a senior economist in the Ministry for Economic Planning and Development, while Mboya was heading that ministry.

This context also helps us understand what Auma Obama told her younger half-brother, Obama Junior, when she visited him in New York while he was attending Columbia University. Auma is the daughter of Obama Senior and Kezia, Obama Senior's first wife, whom he abandoned in Africa in 1959 when he came to study in the United States. In New York, Auma told Obama the truth about his father, perhaps for the first time. In Africa, Auma had witnessed the downfall of Obama Senior firsthand, not only from within the country, but also from within the family.

In his autobiography Obama presents his talk with Auma

as an extended heart-to-heart talk. Auma explained to Obama Junior that their father, or the "Old Man," as Auma called him, got into trouble when he began to speak up after the death of Mboya and the arrest of Odinga Odinga. Auma explained their father "would tell people tribalism was going to ruin the country and that unqualified men were taking the best jobs. His friends tried to warn him about saying things in public, but he didn't care." This, in Auma's explanation, was the reason their father suffered his downfall. "Word got back to Kenyatta that the Old Man was a troublemaker, and he was called in to see the president," she continued. "According to the stories, Kenyatta said to the Old Man that, because he could not keep his mouth shut, he would not work again until he had no shoes on his feet."[14]

If we fast-forward to 2006, Obama Junior, by endorsing Raila Odinga during his visit to Kenya, positioned himself to be seen by Kenyans as an important U.S. senator who was joining forces with his Luo tribal kinsman. This positioning further sided Obama with Raila Odinga as he ran against President Mwai Kibaki in the December 2007 presidential election in Kenya. Remember: Obama and Odinga are Luo, while Kibaki is Kikuyu.

As understood in Kenya, Barack Obama Junior essentially picked up an old tribal fight, with both men fighting old battles to vindicate their fathers. Raila Odinga wanted to redress the perceived wrongs done to his father by Kenyatta and the Kikuyu tribe. Obama wanted to redress the same perceived wrongs done to his father. Both arguably could feel the injustices to their fathers had been righted if together they could establish a new government in Kenya in which the Luo tribe would gain power for the first time with Raila Odinga beating Mwai Kibaki in the December 2007 elections.

Senator Barack Obama came full circle with his father's

past by openly supporting Raila Odinga during his visit to Africa in 2006. He took up his father's battle with Kenyatta and joined forces with the most extreme Luo in Kenyan politics, Raila Odinga, the son of the communist Odinga Odinga, who was ousted by Kenyatta.

By supporting Odinga, Senator Obama is also seen in Kenya as siding with the extreme left wing of Kenyan politics, going back to the overt communism of Odinga Odinga. Odinga's current party, the Orange Democratic Movement, or ODM, is a leftist-socialist political party that stops short of being openly communist.

In January 2008, Odinga told the BBC that Obama's father was his maternal uncle, thus claiming Obama is his cousin.[15] A Reuters report published the same day contradicted Odinga, quoting Obama's uncle as saying Obama's mother came from the same area as Odinga, but is not a blood relative.[16] In the sense that both Senator Obama and Raila Odinga are Luo tribesmen by blood, they are both "cousins" within Kenya's African tribal understanding. Yet Senator Obama and Raila Odinga are not cousins, as Americans more narrowly define family relations. Still, Senator Barack Obama could claim to be a citizen of Kenya, as well as of the United States. Obama can trace his heritage back to his mother, who was born in the United States and was an American citizen when he was born, and to his father, who was born in Kenya and was a Kenyan citizen when Obama was born.

More than a Thousand People Killed

After the December 27, 2007, presidential vote, Raila Odinga charged he had been denied the presidency by voter fraud. After the election, Odinga pressed for a power-sharing arrangement in which he would be the prime minister in a government where Kibaki was president, with the two factions sharing power evenly in the cabinet. Odinga's claim led to widespread fighting that killed more than a thousand people in the weeks after the election and left more than 350,000 Kenyans displaced. While proving involvement is difficult, many in Kenya assumed the postelection violence was supported, if not organized, behind the scenes by Odinga and his Orange Democratic Movement.

In a horrifying incident following the election, at least fifty people, including women and children, were killed when an angry mob forced Kikuyu Christians into an Assemblies of God Pentecostal church and set fire to it, hacking with machetes any of the Christians who tried to escape the flames. The violence occurred in the village of Eldoret, about 185 miles northwest of Nairobi. The massacre in the church was part of youth gangs' violence aimed at harassing the Kikuyu Christian minority, which before the election numbered around 20 percent of Eldoret's five hundred thousand people. After the church burning, the vast majority of Eldoret's Kikuyu Christian minority fled the city, in fear for their lives.[17]

Christian missionaries reported that more than three hundred Christian churches were severely damaged or destroyed in the wave of violence that swept the country, but mosques were left undisturbed. The violence was not only Luo against Kikuyu, it was also Muslims against Christians, reflecting the divisions that opposed Kibaki and supported Odinga.

Another horrific report came from the *Telegraph* in London. Members of President Kibaki's Kikuyu tribe were attacked in Nairobi slums by ethnic groups, including Luo youth and men who engaged in gang rapes of women and gang sodomy of boys as young as five years old.[18] The *Telegraph* reported the vast majority of the victims were assaulted in their homes and all had been targeted because of their Kikuyu tribal membership. Mobs slashed their way into homes, attacking everyone they found with machetes and clubs. Youths raped women in front of their husbands and many wives were then dragged from their homes and killed.

Even as Kenya entered this postelection violence, Senator Obama has continued to insert himself into Kenyan politics. On January 1, 2008, two days before the Iowa caucuses, Obama called Secretary of State Condoleezza Rice to discuss Kenya. According to Robert Gibbs, communication director for Obama's presidential campaign, Rice called back as Obama was driving from Sioux City to Council Bluffs, Iowa. At Rice's request, Obama taped a message for Kenya after he completed a campaign rally in Davenport, Iowa, the next day. In the message, broadcast by the Voice of America into Kenya, Obama called for calm. "Despite the irregularities in the vote tabulations, now is not the time to throw that strong democracy away," Obama said. "Now is a time for President Kibaki, opposition leader Odinga, and all of Kenya's leaders to call for calm, to come together, and to start a political process to address peacefully the controversies that divide them." He also stressed, "Now is the time for this terrible violence to end."[19]

On January 8, 2008, in the final hours of the New Hampshire Democratic primary, Obama told reporters he had telephoned Raila Odinga in Kenya. After the call, Obama indicated Odinga was willing to meet with Kibaki. "Obviously he [Odinga] believes that the votes were not tallied properly," Obama told reporters, almost as if he were running for election in Kenya. "But what I urged was that all the leaders there, regardless of their position on the election, tell their supporters to stand down, to desist with the violence and resolve it in a peaceful way with Kenyan laws." Reporters asked if Obama had telephoned Kenyan President Kibaki. "I have not spoken to President Kibaki as yet," the senator answered, "but I hope to get in touch with him some time soon. I want to see if I can be helpful." [20] It is unclear whether Senator Obama ever spoke with Kibaki after their rough meeting in 2006.

The postelection violence in Kenya reached such a disturbing level that former UN secretary-general Kofi Annan traveled there to begin mediating talks between Odinga and Kibaki.

Supporters praised Obama's intervention in Kenya, arguing his personal involvement prefigured a personal style of diplomacy that would serve the candidate and the nation well should he win the Democratic nomination and be elected president. Moreover, Odinga's charge against Kibaki, namely, that there had been irregularities in the vote tabulation, was certain to play well with liberal Democrats who still believe George W. Bush stole the 2000 presidential election from Al Gore.

Obama critics counter that the voter irregularity argument was a complete smoke screen. If Odinga had won the election in December, the postelection violence perpetrated by Odinga supporters and Luo gangs against Kibaki supporters and Kikuyu tribesmen would not have been necessary. If Odinga lost, regardless of whether the vote count was close or not, the wave of violence created a crisis such that Odinga's idea of power-sharing, something never contemplated before the vote was taken, could be presented as a suddenly reasonable and suspiciously convenient solution. Even in Kenya, many Odinga opponents were less than enthusiastic about Senator Barack Obama's decision to interject himself into Kenyan presidential election politics. Respected international correspondent Maina Waruru wrote in *Africa News*, "In ethnically charged and divided Kenya, some people are praying that his [Barack Obama's] recent victories in the primaries does not translate into a win of his party's ticket and eventually his rise into the presidency."[21] In other words, having a Luo in the White House might catapult the Luo tribe into becoming the most powerful tribe in Kenya.

Waruru further added that the Kikuyu "fear Barack would ride roughshod on Kenya and perhaps remove Mwai Kibaki, a Kikuyu, in favor of Raila Odinga, a Luo like Obama, by means either military or political." These fears were intensified by a perception in Kenya that Obama, Secretary of State Rice, and Undersecretary of State for African Affairs Jedayi Frazer were all "pushing Kibaki into agreeing to a power-sharing deal with Odinga, something many of Kibaki's tribesmen did not like." He concluded by observing, "These events have thrust far off U.S. politics into Kenyan villages and intertwined U.S. and Kenyan politics together, never mind they are as different as night is from day."[22]

Obama's involvement in Kenyan presidential politics has raised additional questions in the United States:

- Would an Obama presidency mean the United States would seek a much more activist role in African domestic politics, simply because of Obama's family roots, which run back to Kenya through his father?
- If Obama were to be involved in Kenyan politics as U.S. president, would his political goal simply be to stop violence, such as that which erupted after the recent election? Or would Obama seek to advance the

same policy goals that his tribesman Odinga has in his Kenyan co-presidency with Kibaki?

- If so, what would an Odinga presidency or co-presidency mean to Kenya?

Odinga's Agenda to Advance Islam in Kenya

Although Odinga professes to be an Anglican Christian, concerns even today continue to circulate, especially among Kenya's Christian leaders, that Odinga intends to pursue an undeclared radical Islamic political agenda. Prior to the December 2007 presidential election, there were rumors that Odinga had signed a secret agreement with radical Muslim leaders. A memorandum of understanding, or MOU, which Odinga had signed with radical Muslims, was posted on the website of the Evangelical Alliance of Kenya, a national Christian religious organization established in 1975.[23] Once the document was public, Odinga had to admit that he had entered into an agreement with Muslim leaders in Kenya.[24] Still, there is concern in Kenya that the document posted on the Internet by the Evangelical Alliance might not be the authentic MOU. As we will see, a Kenya television news report showed a second version of the document, which may have superior claims to be the authentic document.

What appears documented by Kenyan newspaper and television news reports is that Raila Odinga, representing the Orange Democratic Movement, or ODM, and Sheikh Abdullah Abdi, the chairman of the National Muslim Leaders Forum, or NAMLEF, signed an agreement on August 29, 2007.

First, let's analyze the document posted by the Evangelical Alliance, realizing that the document might not be the actual one signed. Just posting the document created a controversy in Kenya. Among the more disturbing declarations in the MOU is the first "whereas clause," in which Odinga appears to profess to recognize "Islam as the only true religion."

In this version of the agreement, NAMLEF agreed to support Raila Odinga's candidacy for the presidency of Kenya in 2007 as "the only presidential candidate who has the interests of the Muslim community at heart," and the candidate who "has pledged to fully reinstate and protect the rights of the Kenyan Muslims, when he becomes the fourth President of the Republic of Kenya."

In return, Odinga promised that within six months of becoming president of Kenya he would "re-write the Constitution of Kenya to recognize Shari'a as the only true law sanctioned by the Holy Quran for Muslim declared regions."

Odinga also promised "to disband the imperialist Anti-Terror Police Unit (ATPU) that was set up for the sole purpose of terrorizing, harassing, intimidating and deporting innocent Kenyan Muslims to Guantanamo Bay." Odinga also agreed "to popularize Islam, the only true religion, in Coast and North Eastern Regions by ordering every primary school in Kenya in the regions to conduct daily Madrassa classes."

The *Nation*, a Nairobi newspaper, confirmed that Odinga and Sheikh Abdullah Abdi had signed a memorandum of agreement. On November 28, 2007, a group of Muslims made the MOU public, explaining they chose to support Raila Odinga and oppose President Kibaki out of "the need to protect the interests of members of the religious community who have suffered oppression under successive governments since independence in 1963." [25]

The newspaper quoted Odinga as saying the agreement signed was "very innocent," despite allegations to the contrary by his political rivals. Odinga also told the *Nation* that this was not the first time such an agreement had been signed with members of the Muslim community.

Establishing sharia Islamic law in the coastal and northeastern regions of Kenya would give Islam an even stronger hold on the Horn of Africa. Islam is already the dominant religion in nearby Somalia and Sudan.

Further confirmation of the authenticity of the MOU came from a press conference held during the election campaign and broadcast in Kenya by Nairobi-based NTV. The NTV report showed Sheikh Abdullah Abdi, the chairman of NAMLEF, discussing the MOU point-by-point.[26] NTV ended the news report by showing the three-page MOU clearly enough for the document to be recognized. This document appeared different in format and content from the document posted by the Evangelical Alliance. The camera ended by zooming in on the document so the signatures of Sheikh Abdullah Abdi and Raila Odinga could clearly be recognized by the viewer.

The agreement shown in the NTV news report appears to have been transcribed on Kenyan websites.[27]

This second version appears less inflammatory, without specific language that would require Raila Odinga to establish sharia in certain sections of Kenya. NAMLEF agreed to support Odinga's candidacy for president, to the exclusion of all other presidential candidates. NAMLEF also agreed to "mobilize the Muslim constituency countrywide" to support Odinga for president. NAMLEF pledged to provide counsel to Odinga's presidency and to maintain "open links of communication" during the presidency. Odinga agreed "to embrace NAMLEF totally as his partner of choice in seeking the backing of the Muslim community." He agreed that as president he would initiate "deliberate policies and programs to redress historical, current and structural marginalization and injustices on Muslims in Kenya." He further agreed to outlaw the targeting and profiling of any Kenyan community, including the Muslim community, and to set up a commission "to inquire on deliberate schemes and actions of government, its agencies or officers, to target or interfere with the welfare and social well being of Muslims in Kenya." Finally, Odinga agreed that as president he would equally represent Muslims in all public appointments.[28]

Christian missionaries in Kenya strongly objected to Odinga and NAMLEF signing what had been a secret agreement. They feared Odinga's alliance with Islamic elements in Kenya posed a grave threat to the Christian church in Kenya, as strongly suggested by the postelection violence. Even though Odinga professes to be a Christian, the missionaries in Kenya have argued that ODM and NAMLEF have come together on the theory that "the enemy of my enemy is my friend." Raila Odinga opposes the Kibaki government, despite the backing Kibaki enjoys from the United States. Kibaki, a Christian, has resisted the spread of Islam in Kenya. For their own separate reasons, Odinga and Sheikh Abdullah Abdi have joined forces. Sheikh Abdullah Abdi has agreed in writing to swing Islamic voters to Odinga in Kenya and Odinga has agreed to support Islam should he become president.

Obama Senior, the Socialist Economist

Further insight into Obama Senior's leftist ideology and his alliances within the Kenyan politics of the 1960s can be gained from a paper he published in the *East Africa Journal* in July 1965. The paper, "Problems Facing Our Socialism," was among several critiques submitted to analyze the "African Socialism" then being promoted by many African nations after achieving independence.[29] The journal described Obama as "currently in Nairobi working for his doctorate." Obama Senior "read his economics at Harvard University" and his dissertation was on "an economic model of the stable theory of development." However, Obama Senior left Harvard to return to Kenya before he finished his thesis. He never finished his dissertation and so never received his Ph.D. from Harvard.

Professors David William Cohen and E. S. Atieno Odhiambo, in their 2004 book *The Risks of Knowledge*,[30] explain that Obama Senior wrote the paper in response to a blueprint for what was then called a "mixed economy," one combining a version of liberal capitalism, seen as necessary to attract foreign capital, with a version of domestic socialism, seen as the most equitable way of distributing to the masses Kenya's anticipated economic gains under independence. Specifically, Obama Senior was commenting on what was circulating then in Kenya as the write-up of this blueprint known as the "Sessional Paper Number 10 of 1965," entitled "African Socialism and Its Application to Planning in Kenya."

In this debate within Kenya, Obama Senior lined up behind communist Odinga Odinga, opposing the liberal socialism of Tom Mboya. As Cohen and Odhiambo explained, "The debates pitted the liberal internationalist Mboya against endogenous communitarian Odinga Odinga and radical economists Dharam Ghai and Barack Obama, who critiqued the document for being neither African nor socialist enough."[31] This reference establishes that Obama Senior was considered at the time to be "a radical economist" and leaves no doubt that Obama Senior had gravitated from his longtime family supporter Tom Mboya to the more extreme communist position openly advocated by and identified with Odinga Odinga. It provides further confirmation that Senator Obama in embracing Raila Odinga truly follows in his father's footsteps.

What, then, was Obama Senior's critique of Mboya's version of "African Socialism"? A key argument of the paper is that communal ownership of land, not private property, will encourage economic growth without developing "have" and "have-not" economic classes. For this reason he recommends "clan co-cooperatives" as the best way for Kenya to introduce land reform, with individual land ownership restricted to very small farms, regardless whether the owner was the president of the country or the common man.

Expressing an ideal like this, Obama sides himself with socialists on the extreme left, if not Marxian communists outright. He objected that at that time, "many qualified Africans are employed by commercial firms and are given very pompous titles," but only for the purpose of publicity. In contrast, he advocated a government-enforced policy of "Africanizing" key positions, with Africans truly put in charge of foreign companies operating in Kenya as well as in charge of Kenyan companies financed by foreigners.

To avoid the concentration of economic power in the hands of the wealthy, Obama Senior saw no limit to the amount of taxes that could be charged, provided "the benefits derived from public services by society measure up to the cost in taxation which they have to pay." To make his point clear, Obama Senior added, "Theoretically, there is nothing that can stop the government from taxing 100 percent of income so long as the people get benefits from the government commensurate with their income which is taxed." He favored taxing the rich, arguing, "I do not see why the government cannot tax those who have more and siphon some of these revenues into savings which can be utilized in investment for future development, thereby reducing our reliance on foreign aid."

Obama also expressed concern that corporations in Africa would become, as they had in Europe and the United States, a vehicle for concentrating wealth. "Yet one who has read Marx cannot fail to see that corporations are not only what Marx referred to as the advanced stage of capitalism," he wrote, "but Marx even called it finance capitalism by which a few would control the finances of so many and through this have not only economic power but political power as well."

He further suggested the Kenyan government consider nationalizing various Asian and European enterprises then operating in the country. "One need not be a Kenyan to note that when one goes to a good restaurant he mostly finds Asians and Europeans, nor has he to be a Kenyan to see that the majority of cars running in Kenya are run by Asians and Europeans," he wrote. "We have to give the African his place in his country and we have to give him this economic power if he is going to develop." Obama Senior asked, "Is it the African who owns this country? If he does, then why should he not control the economic means of growth in this country?"

Odinga Wins

On April 13, 2008, the Associated Press reported President Mwai Kibaki had named rival Raila Odinga as prime minister, effectively entering into a power-sharing agreement that established Odinga as a coequal head of state.[32] As part of the agreement negotiated by the two, cabinet posts were to be divided equally between Kibaki's Party of National Unity and Odinga's Orange Democratic Movement. Reuters reported a few days later that Kenyans were beginning to express disgust at the inflated cabinet, which by some estimates would require up to $1 billion, about 5 percent of Kenya's Gross Domestic Product, "in salaries, limousines, bodyguards, support staff and sitting allowances."[33]

Commenting on the postelection violence in Kenya, *New York Sun* columnist and international businessman David Jonsson wrote, "Although the propaganda being put out by the press considers the events the result of vote counting, tribal conflicts and ethnic cleansing, deeper issues exist concerning the clash of ideologies between Muslims and Christians."[34] Jonsson sees the recent events in Kenya as signaling the resurgence of Islam in Kenya, a process likely to speed up now that Odinga has forced himself into a power-sharing arrangement with Kibaki. He argues we are witnessing the growth of a leftist/Marxist alliance with Islam that is striving, under the banner of "Change," to spread the growth of Islamic states worldwide. Jonsson also sees a direct tie between the "Change" themes of the Obama presidential campaign in the United States and the senator's support of Odinga's Islamic goals in East Africa. "Real Change for Africa" was perhaps not coincidentally the theme of Raila Odinga's 2007 presidential campaign.[35]

Kenyan Justice Minister Martha Karua, in an interview with the BBC shortly after the postelection violence broke out in Kenya, charged that Odinga and his Orange Democratic Movement were "planning mayhem if they lost." Karua further charged the Kibaki government had not expected "the magnitude of the violence and for it to be ethnic cleansing." Asked directly if she was charging the ODM leadership with "calculatedly planned ethnic cleansing," she responded, "Absolutely yes, that's what I'm saying categorically." The BBC reported Odinga's response that the allegations were "outrageous." In turn, Odinga charged Karua "knows where the truth lies—that all that we are having is a result of the order that the government has given to the police: to shoot particularly members of certain ethnic communities."[36]

A Father's Legacy

Obama Junior wrote in his autobiography, "All my life, I had carried a single image of my father, one that I had sometimes rebelled against but had never questioned, one that I had later tried to take as my own."[37]

If Obama does win the presidency in 2008, he will be the first president in our history to have an extended family in another country. Granted, Obama's brothers and sisters in Africa are half-brothers and half-sisters. Even his "Granny" is not a paternal grandmother, but the second wife of a grandfather who was equally as polygamist as was Obama's father.

What personal ties to the White House will come from Kenya?

Are all members of the family equally satisfied and finally resolved that they have inherited what they deserve from Obama Senior?

If Obama wins the presidency in 2008, Kenyan prime minister Raila Odinga will correctly perceive that for the first time ever a fellow Luo tribesman is running the United States of America.

Now, with President Kibaki agreeing to share power with Odinga, Obama can claim at least one electoral victory, in that the proclaimed results of Kenya's December 27, 2007, election have been effectively canceled.

Will Obama fulfill his father's legacy in Kenya by continuing to support Odinga as prime minister? Only time will tell.

Dick Morris Arrives in Kenya to Help Odinga

In November 2007, during the election campaign between Raila Odinga and Mwai Kibaki, well-known American political consultant and analyst Dick Morris showed up in Kenya, announcing he was going to work pro bono as an Odinga presidential campaign strategist. NTV broadcast a press conference in Kenya where Raila Odinga and Dick Morris appeared together to make the announcement.[38] "I met with Dick in New York during a recent visit and I was absolutely thrilled when he said he would be willing to come and help us here," Odinga said at the press conference. "I told him I would work in his campaign pro bono, for free, and I'm going to do that," Morris affirmed. "I think we are going to win this election."

The NTV television news report introduced Morris to Kenya as the "principal architect" of Bill Clinton's reelection in 1996. NTV also noted that Morris worked with the little-known United Kingdom Independence Party in the 2004 elections, helping them win twelve of England's seventy-eight seats in the European Parliament, and was a consultant to Viktor Yushchenko's presidential campaign in the Ukraine during the so-called Orange Revolution of 2004. Kenyans listening to the report easily drew the connection between Odinga's Orange Democratic Movement and Yushchenko's revolution of the same name.

Elsewhere Morris expressed support for Odinga with language that echoed Obama's criticism of the Kibaki government in Kenya in 2006. Morris even incorporated into his press statement Obama's 2008 catchword, "change." Morris told the press he was confident Odinga would win because "he has a clear reputation for courage and for integrity and for change. I am delighted to be here in Kenya and to help you get rid of the corrupt government."[39]

Obviously displeased to have such a high-profile consultant enter the picture on the side of the opposition, the Kibaki government notified Morris within a few hours of arriving that he had entered Kenya on a tourist visa and was not permitted to work on Odinga's presidential campaign, even if he was donating his services for free. Morris entered Kenya on a Tuesday, held the press conference with Odinga on Wednesday, and was whisked out of the country by the Kibaki government on Thursday. Kenyan government spokesman Alfred Mutua told ABC News, "If he [Morris] comes back and breaks our laws with impunity, we are going to treat him like we do all illegal immigrants. We will lock him up, take him to court and deport him in handcuffs."[40]

Morris's showing up in Kenya makes no sense outside the Obama-Odinga connection. Odinga critics speculated that Morris had been recommended by former Clinton associates working for Obama. The argument was that Obama decided to help Odinga when polls showed Odinga likely to lose the vote count against Kibaki in the December 2007 election. In the United States, Morris had been openly critical of Hillary Clinton's campaign against

Obama. Maybe Morris could help Odinga win, just as he had helped Yushchenko win. Regardless of how Morris was recruited to Kenya, the Kibaki government was not amused by the November surprise.

"Friends of Senator Obama" and Odinga's Campaign

In the days immediately after the Kenya December 2007 presidential election, a new set of documents began circulating on Internet websites in Kenya. One was allegedly an internal memo smuggled out of the Odinga campaign's accounting section.[41] An eight-page document accompanying the internal memo appeared to be an executive strategy summary, "Positioning and Marketing of the Orange Democratic Movement and the People's President—Hon. Raila A. Odinga," allegedly prepared by the party's core strategy team.[42]

The funding memo listed seventy-two top individuals and organizations allegedly contributing to Odinga's presidential campaign, including over $1 million from "Friends of Senator BO," widely interpreted as friends of Senator Barack Obama, and a second contribution of approximately $1 million from Seif-Al-Islam Qaddafi, the son of Muammar Qaddafi, the leader of Libya. Dick Morris was also allegedly listed as having made a "pro bono" contribution to Odinga's campaign of about a half million dollars, perhaps representing the value of his contributed services as a consultant.

These documents have caused a controversy in Kenya, especially worrying several prominent Christian missionaries who were already concerned that Odinga had linked his

2007 presidential campaign to radical Muslims seeking to expand Islam in Kenya. "Friends of Senator Barack Obama" is insufficient proof to link any campaign contribution from the U.S. senator or his donors to Odinga in Kenya. No Kenyan news agency as yet has validated these documents as authentic. However, the mention of Senator Barack Obama on the list has ignited fears in the same Christian missionaries working in Kenya that have expressed concern over the now-authenticated memorandum of understanding Odinga signed with Sheikh Abdullah Abdi. Credible sources in Kenya believe the documents should not be dismissed without further investigation, especially given that both documents first emerged in a similar manner. We can draw no conclusion from the ODM funding and strategy documents, except to list them in the category of "loose ends" from Kenya that remain to be resolved.

PART TWO

THE MAKING
OF A RADICAL
POLITICIAN

Everything was absolutely ideal on the day I bombed the Pentagon. The sky was blue. The birds were singing. And the bastards were finally going to get what was coming to them.

—BILL AYERS, *Fugitive Days*, 2001[1]

Bill Ayers lives in his neighborhood. Their kids attend the same school. They're certainly friendly, they know each other, as anyone whose kids go to schools together.

—DAVID AXELROD, *Obama campaign manager*[2]

When Ben Smith of RedState.com questioned Obama's campaign manager, David Axelrod, about Obama's relation to the radical 1960s SDS Weatherman bomber Bill Ayers, Axelrod tried to dodge the question. Axelrod claimed, as we see in the quotation above, that yes, Obama was acquainted with Ayers, but he was not such a "friend" that Obama endorsed Ayers's violent terrorist behavior or embraced his anti-American revolutionary ideas.

That Axelrod is "spinning" should be apparent just from the facts: Obama's children are grade-school age, while the Ayers children are already adults.[3] There is no way Obama's children ever went to school with Ayers's children, even if Ayers and Obama have lived in the same neighborhood much of their adult lives.

Criminal charges against Ayers were dismissed because of prosecutorial misconduct during the years Ayers was a fugitive in the Weather Underground. Today, Ayers lives in Hyde Park, Chicago, and likes to present himself as the "Distinguished Professor of Education" at the University of Illinois at Chicago.

Still, in his 2001 book *Fugitive Days*, Ayers openly admits his involvement in the 1970s bombings and the role he played as a radical revolutionary leader at the head of the SDS Weather Underground. Ayers bombed the U.S. Capitol in 1971 and the Pentagon in 1972 as part of his revolutionary antiwar activities. He was a leader in the extreme leftist Students for a Democratic Society, better known simply as SDS, during the Vietnam War.

Axelrod has no choice but to deny Obama was a friend of Ayers because, as we are arguing here, Obama and Ayers share more anti-American sentiments than Axelrod can afford the voting public to realize.

Ayers's violent revolutionary activity during the Vietnam War is potentially so radioactive that a close association of Obama with Ayers, revealing a shared far-left political ideology, could easily block Obama from the White House, and not just in 2008 but forever. Axelrod tried to explain away Obama's association with Ayers as incidental, in the attempt to reframe the relationship as trivial. Axelrod is betting that American voters will forgive Obama for knowing Ayers if Obama's only guilt is "guilt by association." That is why Axelrod argues Obama knew Ayers only because they lived in the same neighborhood and their kids went to the same school.

Axelrod is an accomplished political operative and he knew exactly what he was doing in responding to the question about Ayers. Axelrod's problem is Obama maintained the relationship with Ayers over many years because it was politically useful to Obama, especially as he first ran for political office from the impoverished, largely African-American South Side of Chicago. Now that Ayers is no longer useful to Obama, Axelrod wants to drop him.

As we have seen, Obama emerged from his teenage years in Hawaii as an angry youth, bitter at the abandonment he suffered from both his African father and his unconventional white mother. He searched to find his identity as an African-American by reading black radical political writers including Malcolm X and seeking out communist Frank Marshall Davis to be his mentor. All these years, Obama retreated into himself, using drugs, relying on marijuana and cocaine to express his inner rebellion. Obama tells us all this himself in his autobiography, *Dreams from My Father*, as we have seen.

In Chicago after his college years, Obama developed an extensive collection of radical leftist friends, mentors, and political associates. Obama used many of these political friends to advance his career in Illinois politics, in which leftism is a virtue. Today, however, on the national front, in his run for president, these same friends have become politically inconvenient and potentially destructive. The way Obama distanced himself from Ayers is typical of how he has distanced himself from others in his Chicago past. Obama begins by denying that the association was meaningful, then argues that the views of the other person were never his own, and ends up with a denunciation of the other person that somehow still does not completely cut the tie.

That presidential candidate Obama has to sever ties with so many key people in his past should alone raise questions about his character for the serious voter.

Axelrod wants to position Obama as a New Age politician who transcends wedge political issues, including race, so Obama can be seen as a unifier, above the fray that usually divides liberals and conservatives. This positioning will not be easy, once we examine his Chicago mentors: Obama's tutelage in Saul Alinsky's community organization methodology; the network of 1960s radicals Obama befriended in Chicago, including Bill Ayers; the "Chicago Way" patronage package offered to Obama by Chicago's corrupt political fixer Tony Rezko; his relationship with the black-liberation theology of Reverend Jeremiah Wright and Trinity United Church of Christ; and his history with Louis Farrakhan and the Black Muslims.

One by one, Obama has systematically dropped nearly all these Chicago political friends and associations, in what has become a pattern of lying about or otherwise intentionally misrepresenting these Chicago relationships. One by one, Obama has claimed he is now disappointed by what he has learned about these former associates, and has asserted that what they represent about the past is not who he is today. One by one, Obama reveals himself to be just another politician calculating from expediency.

The problem is that Obama *sought out* his relationships with the Alinsky organization, the Ayers-Dohrn radicals, the scandal-ridden Rezko, Reverend Wright and black-liberation theology, and Farrakhan and the Black Muslims. At the time he *wanted* these ties.

As much as Obama might like to define these relationships as irrelevant to his platform as a presidential candidate, the issue of character remains important to the vast majority of voters. Every president faces unanticipated problems and crises. The only way to predict what a candidate will do once elected is to look at the past, including examining the people the candidate invited into his or her immediate orbit of personal friends, professional associates, and mentors, including their pastors and religious advisors.

Also, our focus on Chicago is justifiable. Obama has spent most of his adult life in Chicago politics. He came to Washington for the first time in 2004, when he was elected U.S. senator from Illinois. By contrast, Obama has spent nearly a quarter century of his life in Chicago.

Obama, we argue here, is and always has been a radical on the far left. He is at heart a coldly calculating politician, driven more by winning at all costs than by the lofty principles he espouses.

For proof of this last point, study carefully what we present in the next chapter concerning how Obama undercut state senator Alice Palmer after she named him as her successor and introduced him to her key supporters and fund-raisers.

Obama, we argue here, learned well from Machiavelli, the political inspiration of his community organizer mentor, Saul Alinsky.

THE IDEOLOGY OF
"CHANGE"

The Prince was written by Machiavelli for the Haves on how to hold power. Rules for Radicals is written for the Have-Nots on how to take it away.

—SAUL D. ALINSKY, *Rules for Radicals*, 1971[1]

Obama was raised largely in Hawaii and he attended college in California and New York City. Yet he ended up working in the poverty-ridden housing projects on the mean streets of Chicago's South Side.

No one in Obama's paternal or maternal family, except for a great-uncle, had ever resided in Chicago. In *Dreams from My Father*, Obama tells us he had been to Chicago only once, just before his eleventh birthday, when Obama took a monthlong trip to see the mainland with his grandparents and his sister Maya.[2] However, from studying the life of Martin Luther King, Jr., Obama knew Chicago well, long before he ever lived there. Chicago was "ground zero" of the northern civil rights protest movement Martin Luther King led in the 1960s. The South Side, as Obama himself said, is "the capital of the African

American community in the country."[3] Obama has also called Chicago "the birthplace of community organizing."[4] In Chicago, Obama matured, beginning as a community organizer and ending up as a politician.

"His work as a community organizer was really a defining moment in his life, not just his career," Obama's wife, Michelle, told *U.S. News & World Report* in 2007.[5] As Obama prepared to run for his first elective office, the Illinois state senate in 1995, he defined his approach as a political "third way," in that he wanted to define an alternative to the civil rights movement that would advance the cause beyond where King's nonviolent civil disobedience had left the movement. Obama's "third way" involved an attempt to produce a new form of politics by combining community organizing with traditional politics.[6] As Saul Alinsky framed the debate, Obama's "third way" necessarily involved an excursion into the "ideology of change."[7]

So, how did Obama decide to live in Chicago? Why did Obama go to Chicago? How does Chicago fit into Obama's persona as a politician?

To answer these questions, we will also have to delve beyond his autobiography, *Dreams from My Father*, into Obama's second book, *The Audacity of Hope*,[8] a title Obama borrowed from his radical pastor, Reverend Jeremiah Wright.

The story of how Obama got to Chicago begins with the story of how Obama ended his college years. What drew Obama to Chicago's South Side was the prospect of pursuing revolutionary change from within the system, succeeding where his Kenyan father had failed.

College Years, Drugs, and Radical Politics

In *The Audacity of Hope*, Obama tells us he was a "pure product" of the 1960s. As the child of a mixed marriage, he explains his "life would have been impossible, my opportunities entirely foreclosed, without the social upheavals that were then taking place."[9] Born in 1961, Obama explains he absorbed much of the 1960s through his mother, whom he describes as "an unreconstructed liberal" who was inspired by the civil rights movement and believed in "tolerance, equality, standing up for the disadvantaged." But rather than admiring those values, Obama puts his mother down, saying her "understanding of the sixties was limited," both because of the distance of leaving the mainland and living in Hawaii or Indonesia since 1960, and by "her incorrigible, sweet-natured romanticism."[10]

Obama distinguishes himself from his mother's "pre-1967 liberalism," implying his leftist views came from the years during which the Far Left hardened. What made 1968 a dividing line? In 1968, the civil rights and antiwar movements were both radicalized. For those of us who lived through those years as politically conscious adults, even the mention of 1968 immediately triggers the memory of Reverend Martin Luther King, Jr., being assassinated on April 4 and Robert F. Kennedy being shot on June 5 and dying the next day. Then there are the images of Jerry Rubin, Abbie Hoffman, and their street protests, and the resulting police riots during the Democratic National Convention that nominated Hubert Humphrey for president on August 29, 1968, in Chicago. Obama tells us directly that his understanding of the 1960s came from his "adolescent rebellion," and that he had become "fascinated with the Dionysian, up-for-grabs quality of that era."

Obama also wrote that he found his vision of the 1960s through books, film, and music, being soaked in "images of Huey Newton, the '68 Democratic National Convention, the Saigon airlift, and the Stones at Altamont."[11] Huey Newton was the co-founder of the Black Panther Party, the Saigon airlift (which didn't occur until 1975) represented the final defeat of the United States in the Vietnam War, and the 1969 Altamont Speedway Free Festival was known as "Woodstock West," an ill-conceived drugfest and rock concert marred by at least one homicide and multiple accidental deaths. "If I had no immediate reason to pursue revolution," Obama wrote, "I decided nevertheless that in style and attitude I, too, could be a rebel, unconstrained by the received wisdom of the over-thirty crowd."[12]

Still involved with drugs at the time, Obama admitted, his "rejection of authority spilled into self-indulgence and self-destructiveness."[13] In 1979, he entered the largely white, prestigious, private, liberal arts Occidental College in Los Angeles. There Obama began to realize that his form of rebellion contained within itself "its own excesses and its own orthodoxy," which is a candid admission that even rebellion reinforced by marijuana and cocaine was no longer enough for Obama. Evidently, Obama's drug use had become habitual. At Occidental, Obama describes himself as being "as indifferent toward college as most everything else."[14] In the autobiography, Obama describes a college party at Occidental, complete with drugs and alcohol, blended with Billie Holiday music. "I fell back on the couch and lit a cigarette, watching the match burn down until it tickled my fingertips, then feeling the prick on the skin as I pinched the flame dead," he wrote. "*What's the trick? The man asks. The trick is not caring that it hurts.*"[15] Put simply, Obama told us, "I had learned not to care."[16]

Obama wrote that his friends at Occidental were chosen carefully: "The more politically active black students. The foreign students. The Chicanos. The Marxist professors and the structural feminists and punk-rock performers." Obama said they smoked cigarettes and wore leather jackets, and at night they discussed "neocolonialism, Frantz Fanon, Eurocentrism and patriarchy."[17] As we saw earlier, in chapter 3, Frantz Fanon's revolutionary writings were instrumental in shaping Obama's own political analysis of race, which we described as an anticolonial socialism Obama's father would have understood and believed. In the autobiography, Obama tells of how he explained to a girlfriend, Regina, that reading Joseph Conrad's *Heart of Darkness* was important, not because the book was about Africa or the black people in Africa, but because it taught him about the white European who wrote it. "So I read the book to help me understand just what it is that makes white people so afraid," he told her. "Their demons. The way ideas get twisted around. It helps me understand how people learn to hate."[18]

When Obama discovered Occidental had a transfer program with Columbia University, he applied. "I figured that if there weren't any more black students at Columbia than there were at Oxy, I'd at least be in the heart of a true city, with black neighborhoods in close proximity."[19] At Columbia, Obama encountered "the almost mathematical precision with which America's race and class problems joined," such that even the stalls of Columbia's bathrooms "remained scratched with blunt correspondence between niggers and kikes."[20] We can feel the pain and inner anger Obama feels when he describes his first experiences at Columbia, observing, "Despite a forty-year remove, the tumult of the sixties and the subsequent backlash continues to drive our political discourse."[21]

Reading Obama's books, we realize how little he has in common with the Reagan Democrats who gravitated to the Republican Party. Coming out of the turmoil of the 1960s and 1970s, Reagan Democrats in the 1980s were attracted to Ronald Reagan's brand of conservatism, while the McGovern Democrats moved even farther to the left. Obama's disdain of Reagan is obvious when he explains in *The Audacity of Hope* that he rejected Reagan for "his John Wayne, Father Knows Best pose, his policy by anecdote, and his gratuitous assaults on the poor."[22] Yet for many of the youthful voters Obama wants to attract, the 1960s and its radicalism are merely a distant history, from a time before they were born. For others of us, the radicalism of the 1960s and 1970s calls forth images of Malcolm X and William Ayers, extremists we continue to reject for their anti-American views, just as we rejected them four decades ago.

Chicago's South Side

Chicago's South Side is the home of Comiskey Park and the Chicago White Sox baseball team. The South Side is also where roving mobs of blacks and whites attacked one another in the race riot during the summer of 1919, the most violent of the post–World War I race riots that swept some twenty American cities that summer. Before the 1919 violence ended in Chicago, twenty-three blacks and fifteen whites had been killed and more than five hundred had been injured. Gunnar Myrdal, in his classic study, *An American Dilemma*, described the South Side as Chicago's "Black Belt," a neighborhood that was segregated as early as 1910.[23] Myrdal pointed out that the migration of African-Americans from the South to Chicago before World War I had created in the South Side a black ghetto not much different from the impoverished areas the blacks were fleeing. In the 1960s, Chicago's South Side came to symbolize the hardened ghetto segregation and poverty that derived from the income inequality and racial discrimination experienced from generations of northern white racism.

Reverend Martin Luther King, Jr., found the racism in Chicago more severe than he had expected. On August 5, 1966, King led a march through Marquette Park and Chicago Lawn, two predominantly white suburbs on Chicago's Southwest Side, near Chicago's Midway Airport. Getting out of a car to join the march, King was struck in the head and knocked down by a rock as big as a fist. With white hecklers continuing to taunt and assault the marchers, King picked himself up and kept going. Someone threw a knife at King, but it missed him, instead hitting a nearby white demonstrator in the shoulder. At another point in the march, some 1,200 police had to chase away a group of about three hundred whites who sat in the middle of the street to stop the march. At Marquette Park, an estimated four thousand white counterdemonstrators had gathered to assault the marchers. In the resulting melee, about thirty demonstrators marching with King were injured, until police intervened to drive back the hostile white crowd.

After the march, King told reporters, "I can assure you that the hatred and the hostility here [in Chicago] are really deeper than what I have seen in Alabama and Mississippi."[24] Andrew Young, then the executive director of King's Southern Christian Leadership Council, commented at the intensity of the Chicago violence. "Now, in the South, we faced mobs, but it would be a couple of hundred or even fifty or seventy-five. The violence in the South always came from a rabble element," Young said. "But these were women and children and husbands and wives coming out of their homes [and] becoming a mob—and in some ways it was more frightening."[25] The incident was well publicized at the time, awakening the nation's attention to Chicago's South Side as a focal point of the civil rights movement King led until his assassination in 1968. For two decades after King's death, the legacy of institutionalized South Side racism drew to Chicago a cadre of liberal community organizers, including Obama, who were committed to using the principles of change first developed in Chicago in the 1930s by Chicago-born, self-styled agitator Saul Alinsky.

Enter Jerry Kellman

"In 1983, I decided to become a community organizer," Obama proclaimed in his autobiography. His only explanation was, "I'll organize black folks. At the grass roots. For change."[26]

Though "change" is a theme Obama has carried into his presidential campaign, what does it mean? "Change" for what? What kind of "change," and why? These questions Obama typically leaves hanging, as if the meaning were obvious to all who share the ideology.

In trying to explain what he meant by "change," Obama said that organizing the African-American community could be for him "a redemption." Thinking back to "the sit-ins, the marches, the jailhouse songs" of the civil rights meetings, Obama imagined "the African-American community becoming more than just the place where you'd been born or the house where you'd been raised." Through organizing and shared sacrifice, Obama imagined he would finally find "membership" in a community, membership he could feel he had "earned."[27] "When classmates in college asked me just what it was that a community organizer did, I couldn't answer them directly," he wrote. "Instead, I'd pronounce on the need for change. Change in the White House, where Reagan and his minions were carrying on their dirty deeds. Change in the Congress, compliant and corrupt. Change in the mood of the country, manic and self-absorbed. Change won't come from the top, I would say. Change would come from a mobilized grass roots."[28]

In *Dreams from My Father*, Obama tells the story of how in 1985 he responded to a job advertisement he saw in the newspaper, that somehow "Marty Kaufman," Obama's fictional name for Jerry Kellman, answered. Obama said Kellman telephoned him and explained he'd started an organizing drive in Chicago and was looking to hire a trainee. The Calumet Community Religious Conference was trying "to convert the black churches of Chicago's South Side into agents of social change," and was looking for a community organizer to run the inner-city arm of the project, the Developing Communities Project, or DCP.[29] After Obama replied to the ad, so the story goes, Kellman showed up in New York and interviewed Obama, offering him a job on the spot.

This version, however, has the feel of being too lucky to be true. In *The Audacity of Hope*, Obama mentions in passing that in 1984 he had just graduated from college and was working as a community organizer out of the Harlem campus of the City College of New York.[30] This is a job Obama also mentions in passing in his autobiography, *Dreams from My Father*. Obama may have submitted dozens of unsolicited letters of application for employment to various community organization groups, as he maintained he did. Still, the meeting with Kellman suggests Obama was being recruited. In the 1980s, Kellman was a known figure in community organization and it is doubtful he would have driven from Chicago to New York just to meet a newly graduated college kid who wrote a letter looking for a job. Kellman happened to be visiting family in New York, so he was able to schedule an appointment to see if the reports coming out of New York City about Obama were right, that Obama's profile might just fit in with Kellman's organization.

In an article titled "The Agitator" in the *New Republic,* Ryan Lizza said Kellman paid a small fortune to run the ad in the *New York Times.* Kellman was in search of an African-American to help him break through the barriers he was facing in Chicago's African-American South Side. "Kellman and his colleagues couldn't break through," Lizza wrote. "Because he and his fellow organizers, Mike Kruglik and Gregory Galluzzo, where white (and two of the three were Jewish), the black pastors viewed them with suspicion and, in some cases, outright disdain."[31]

Obama explains in *Dreams from My Father* that he knew Kellman was Jewish, and was an experienced organizer since the 1960s, but he omits a critical detail: Kellman's organization was a product of Saul Alinsky's organization. Obama left this out for a good reason. Alinsky defined community organization tactics for several generations of American leftists, going back to his early efforts to organize Chicago's Back of the Yards meatpacking neighborhood in the 1930s. Alinsky died in 1972, more than a decade before Obama moved to Chicago to learn his methods. Still, Alinsky's impact on Obama is clear. We need look no further than Alinsky to find out where Obama got his mantra for "change." Long before Obama came on the scene, Alinsky became famous for making "change" his credo. For some three decades before Obama was born, Alinsky had been defining the political meaning of "change" for those radicals he was calling forth in his classic 1971 book, *Reveille for Radicals*.[32]

"Change," for Alinsky, invoked radical socialism and meant the redistribution of wealth. Obama means the same, but by hiding the reference he avoids having to be explicit about the radical goal behind the theme.

Alinsky advocated creating change through a set of carefully calculated power-politics tactics, where the end always justified the means. In *Rules for Radicals*, Alinsky sought to articulate his methodology of "community organization" for future generations of leftists. Alinsky taught practitioners of his methods the importance of raising the consciousness of the economically disadvantaged, who were typically also minorities. The goal was to stir the pain of economic suffering in order to create awareness in an economic underclass of its members' disadvantages. From there, the community organizer's job was to mobilize the discontent into political power.

Alinsky's goal was to set in motion a peaceful revolution, using the ballot box, not bombs or bullets, to wrench power from the hands of capitalist elites and business leaders currently in charge. Make no mistake about it: "change" was always Alinsky's code word for creating a socialist revolution, even if the methodology meant radicals would cut their hair, put on business suits, and run for political office.[33] Alinsky taught organizers to hide their true intentions in the words they spoke. Denying the truth or just plain lying were both acceptable tactics, as long as the cause was advanced. He taught organizers to ridicule opponents when the arguments of their opponent could not be refuted by logic, evidence, or argument. In the streets, Alinsky had learned the old communist adage that derision would cause community audiences to laugh at their opponents, rather than listen to what their opponents were saying.

Alinsky berated the street radicals of the civil rights movement, charging that the theatrics of their street protests and the physical danger inherent in calls to use violence undermined the cause. He famously said Yippie activists Jerry Rubin and Abbie Hoffman couldn't organize a luncheon, much less a revolution.[34] Alinsky also became uncomfortable as the methodology of the civil rights movement shifted from the nonviolent civil disobedience of Martin Luther King, first to the angry Stokely Carmichael cry for "Black Power," then to the antiwhite hatred of Malcolm X in his most extreme embrace of Islam as a spokesman for the Black Muslims. For Alinsky, the attraction that William Ayers and Bernardine Dohrn of the SDS Weather Underground felt for bombs was reminiscent of the attraction that World War I–era anarchists felt for bombs, and about as ineffective. In the final analysis, Alinsky taught community organization analytically, more as a social scientist would teach urban sociology.

Nevertheless, Alinsky disagreed with Malcolm X, Stokely Carmichael, and William Ayers only on tactics, not on radical ideology.

"Organization for action will now and in the decade ahead center upon America's white middle class," Alinsky wrote. "That is where the power is."[35] He taught the obvious: "When more than three-fourths of our people from both the point of view of economics and of their self-identification are middle class, it is obvious that their action or inaction will determine the direction of change."[36] Alinsky imagined that even if all low-income minorities could be organized together in one coalition, including blacks, Mexican-Americans, Puerto Ricans, and Appalachian poor whites, this coalition would fail because "it would not be powerful enough to get significant, basic, needed changes."[37] For Alinsky, the "pragmatics of power" meant radicals needed "to realize the value of their middle-class experience," so they could stop rejecting their middle-class identity to build "bridges of communication and unity over the gaps, generation, values."[38]

Correctly, Alinsky saw radicals such as himself and Obama as elitists by nature, in their assertion that the leftist social values they sought to pursue justified the use of tactics whose very nature was a lie. The last thing Alinsky wanted was for himself to be middle class. What he sought was to grab the power from the corporate and business elite he reviled. For Alinsky, the middle class was a pawn. As much as he disdained the middle class and wanted to overturn middle-class identity and values, Alinsky was smart enough to realize he could produce his desired "change" only by convincing the middle class to side with him in its own destruction.

Kellman was clearly a student of Alinsky. The school in which Obama enrolled when he decided to leave New York and head off to Chicago to work for Kellman was Saul Alinsky's school, whether Obama admitted it in his two books or not. The path he chose to follow was Alinsky's path—politics, not insurrection, even if in his own mind Obama was a revolutionary pursuing "change." Alinsky taught that politics, camouflaged as "community organizing," was the only effective way that the socialist elites could mobilize the have-nots to take power from the haves. In addition to receiving instruction from experienced Alinsky organizers in Chicago, including Kellman and his associate Mike Kruglik, whom Obama discusses in his autobiography, Obama went to school on Alinsky. Obama advanced to the point where he was able to teach in a classroom setting to new organizers associated with the Gamaliel Foundation and the

Industrial Areas Foundation, both of which "organize community groups, primarily religious groups, and trace their lineage to Saul Alinsky."[39]

Alinsky fashioned himself a modern-day Machiavelli, comfortable in the latter's teaching that "it is necessary for a prince, who wishes to maintain himself, to learn how not to be good, and to use this knowledge and not use it, according to the necessity of the case."[40] Alinsky wrote, "To me ethics is doing what is best for the most."[41] He could as easily have written, "To me ethics is doing what works." Teaching that "an organizer can communicate only within the areas of experience of his audience,"[42] Alinsky advised organizers to learn "the local legends, antidotes, values, idioms,"[43] avoiding rhetoric foreign to the local culture, including "worn-out words" like "white racist," "fascist pig," and other radical terms that tend to identify the speaker as a "nut." Instead, the Alinsky-trained organizer learned how to be "honest" by vocalizing discontent, to mobilize the community from within. The essential technique demanded learning how to listen carefully enough so the organizer could use the words and language of the community itself to move the community in the direction the organizer wanted to go.

One of Alinsky's prize pupils was Hillary Clinton, whose 1969 senior thesis at Wellesley College was "a 75-page salute to Alinsky."[44]

Alinsky acknowledged a second source of inspiration on an opening page of *Rules for Radicals*. In the last of three epigraphs, Alinsky quotes himself, saying, "Let us not forget at least an over-the-shoulder acknowledgment to the very first radical: from all our legends, mythology, and history (and who is to know where the mythology leaves off and history begins—or which is which), the first radical known to man who rebelled against the establishment and

did it so effectively that he at least won his own kingdom—
Lucifer."[45] Alinsky tells us he learned from Lucifer, the
Prince of Lies, and modeled his writing after Machiavelli,
the original architect of power politics. At the very least, no
politicians schooled in the Alinsky methodology can be assumed to mean what they are saying, not when their proclaimed agenda involves a battle cry under the banner of
"change." The call for "change" was the reveille Alinsky put
forth for radicals.[46] What Alinsky meant by "change" was
the type of radical socialist redistribution of wealth that a
committed communist could easily embrace.

Alinsky defined the job of an organizer as to "rub raw
the resentments of the people of a community."[47] When
he asked new students why they wanted to organize, he
shouted back at them a one-word answer: "You want to organize for *power*."[48]

The Community Organizer Enters Politics

In 1985, Kellman got the twenty-five thousand dollars he
needed to hire Obama from Jean Rudd at the Woods Fund, a
Chicago foundation that gives grants for community organizing.[49] Rudd had created the Woods Fund out of a charitable
trust established by Frank Woods, an attorney and nationally
prominent telephone company executive, in 1941.[50]

When Obama returned to Chicago at the end of 1991 after
graduating from Harvard Law School, he did not immediately
go to work for a law firm. Instead, in 1992, he was hired to
be the Chicago director of the national Project Vote! The goal
of Project Vote! was to register to vote as many disenfranchised
minorities as possible. As director of the project, Obama was
successful. He ended up registering thousands of previously

unregistered minority voters, most of whom were black Chicagoans living on the South Side. The volunteers' T-shirts proclaimed, "It's a power thing!"[51] This slogan was printed on the campaign posters that appeared everywhere in Chicago's South Side, subtly transitioning the angry Black Power of Stokely Carmichael and the 1960s into the empowerment campaign that in the 1990s was being argued nationally by Chicago-based Louis Farrakhan and the Black Muslims.

Then, in 1993, Obama joined the law firm of Davis, Miner, Barnhill and Galland,[52] the same law firm that was legal counsel to the Woods Fund.

In 1995, when Obama decided to run for the Illinois state senate, he returned to his old friend, Jean Rudd, to ask for help. "That's a switch," Rudd told him, surprised Obama wanted to leave community organizing. "Oh, no," Obama said, "I'm going to use the same skills as a community organizer." He was stepping onto the political stage with even larger ambitions to organize communities.

In a 1995 interview with the *Chicago Reader*, Obama asked, "What if a politician were to see his job as that of an organizer, as part teacher and part advocate, one who does not sell voters short but who educates them about the real choices before them? As an elected public official, for instance, I could bring church and community leaders together easier than I could as a community organizer or lawyer."[53] Representative Bobby Rush, the former Black Panther, who in 2000 defeated Obama for Congress, claims Obama exaggerates the limited success he had working in Chicago as a community organizer. Rush, for instance, has charged that activist Hazel Johnson discovered asbestos in the Altgeld Gardens housing project long before Obama latched on to the issue and made it a major part of the community organizing story he tells about himself in *Dreams from My Father*.[54]

When Obama tells audiences that his community organizing experience "taught me a lot about listening to people as opposed to coming in with a premeditated agenda,"[55] he is reciting pure Alinsky dogma. Listening, in the Alinsky lexicon, is just a tactic, but the tactic is powerful when listening is presented as genuine sympathy to understand the community's needs as the community understands those needs. Obama listens because he has been taught the only way to intensify discontent is to use the language of the community itself. The view is intrinsically an elitist view; always, the organizer knows best. It is the community that must be led, even if the only way to lead appears passive, by listening first. Becoming a politician, Obama was not planning to stop being a community organizer.

In an interview with the *Chicago Tribune*, Kellman provided insight into why Obama gravitated to politics.[56] Kellman explained to the *Tribune* that Obama told him his father had returned to his native Kenya "bursting with intellect and ambition, only to devolve into an embittered bureaucrat because he couldn't find a way to reconcile his ideals with political realities." Obama was determined not to end up like his father. "He talked about what happens to you if you're not practical in finding ways to do things effectively," Kellman said.

Kellman speculated Obama went to Harvard Law School to prepare himself for a life in politics.

Political Ties to Bill Ayers and Bernardine Dohrn

Far from it being a casual relationship, Obama began his political career in the home of Bill Ayers and Bernardine Dohrn.

In 1995, Obama saw his opening to run for elected office when Illinois state senator Alice Palmer decided to run for Congress the following year, in November 1996. Palmer went out of her way to name Obama as her handpicked successor. Palmer had her eye on the congressional seat being vacated by Mel Reynolds. In 1995, Reynolds was forced to resign from the U.S. House of Representatives after a state court convicted him of sexual misconduct with a sixteen-year-old campaign volunteer. Reynolds served two and a half years in prison for the crime and was subsequently sentenced to another six and a half years on federal corruption charges, including wire fraud and bank fraud. (President Bill Clinton commuted Reynolds's prison term, only hours before Clinton left office.)[57]

In 1986, Alice Palmer, as the editor of the *Black Press Review*, was the only African-American to cover the 27th Congress of the Communist Party of the Soviet Union meeting in Russia. On June 19, 1986, the *People's Daily World*, an overtly communist newspaper, wrote an article profiling Palmer's trip to Russia.[58] The article quoted Palmer as believing the Soviets could double their wealth and productive power by the end of the twentieth century. The article also quoted Palmer as saying the Soviet Union had "a comprehensive affirmative action program, which they have stuck to religiously—if I can use that word—since 1917." When Palmer visited the Soviet Union for the 27th Congress, Russia was about two years away from withdrawing its military from Afghanistan in failure and three years away from watching the Berlin Wall fall.

To get Obama's state senate race off to a good start, Palmer arranged a function for a few influential liberals in the district, at the Hyde Park home of Weather Underground activists Ayers and Dohrn. Palmer sought to introduce Obama to likely campaign supporters and contributors.[59] Dr. Quentin Young, a prominent Chicago physician who attended the informal get-together, remembered Palmer and Obama being there. Young told Politico.com that Obama and Ayers were "friends."[60] The *Boston Globe* reported that a Chicago-based blogger named Maria Warren, writing in her progressive liberal blog "Musings & Migraines," recalled seeing Obama give "a standard, innocuous little talk" in 1995 in the living room of Ayers and his wife.[61] Warren said Ayers and Dohrn were introducing Obama to the Hyde Park community as "the best thing since sliced bread."[62] Palmer would never have introduced Obama to the Hyde Park political community at the Ayers-Dohrn home unless she saw an affinity between Ayers and Dohrn's radical leftist history, her own history of far-leftist politics, and the politics of Barack Obama.

Obama's current press secretary, Bill Burton, has argued that Obama was an eight-year-old when Ayers and Dohrn were active in the Weather Underground and that "any attempt to connect Obama with events of almost 40 years ago is ridiculous."[63] Yet the record shows that connections between Obama and Ayers-Dohrn have actively continued since Obama launched his political career in their living room in 1995. Obama and Ayers served together on the Woods Fund board for three years, beginning in 1999, the year Obama joined it. Jean Rudd, who provided the Woods Fund money that Alinsky organizer Jerry Kellman needed to hire Obama, spoke very highly about Obama's role as a board member of the foundation. "He is among the most hard-nosed board members in wanting to see results," Rudd told the *Chicago Reader* in 1995. "He wants to see our grants make change happen—not just pay salaries."[64] Rudd was executive director of the Woods Fund when Obama was a board member with Ayers.

According to the Form 990-PF federal tax forms filed by the Woods Fund, Obama left the board in 2002 and Ayers is still a member of the foundation's board.[65]

Obama met his wife-to-be, Michelle, at the Chicago law firm Sidley Austin. Michelle was the attorney at the firm who was assigned to mentor Obama in the summer of 1989; Obama was an intern at the firm after his first year of Harvard Law School.[66] Bernardine Dohrn had also worked as a paralegal at Sidley Austin, from 1984 through 1988. Because of her felony conviction, Dohrn was not allowed to take the Illinois bar exam. It is widely speculated in Chicago that Dohrn got the job at Sidley Austin through the influence of her father-in-law, Thomas Ayers, former chief executive officer of Commonwealth Edison, who was one of the law firm's biggest clients.[67] Whether Barack Obama and Dohrn worked at the firm at the same time is unclear, but that Michelle and Dohrn worked at the firm together is well established.[68]

When Obama returned to Chicago after graduating from Harvard Law School, he, Thomas Ayers (Bill Ayers's father) and John Ayers (Bill Ayers's brother) served together on the Leadership Council of the Chicago Public Education Fund.[69]

In 1995, Bill Ayers co-founded the Chicago Annenberg Challenge with a $50 million grant program for the Chicago public schools. Ayers selected Obama to be the first chairman of the board of the Challenge, a position Obama held for eight years, until 2003, a period during which Ayers remained active with the Challenge.[70]

These connections make laughable the claim by Obama and campaign manager David Axelrod that Obama and Bill Ayers were just neighbors, who may have known each other casually because their children went to school together. Evidently Obama and Axelrod think all this inside-Chicago politics may be too difficult for anybody (except themselves) to track down and document. Given the attention bloggers have begun to devote to the Obama-Ayers connections, this assumption may turn out to be a particularly bad one in the Internet age. Or, as one blogger investigating Ayers asked, "Just how many bald-faced lies is Obama to be allowed without consequence?"[71]

As to Obama's suggestion that Ayers is just some professor he happens to know, bloggers wonder how Obama can think we are so gullible as to believe Obama was the only person in Chicago who did not know Ayers's bomb-throwing terrorist fame.

Still Extremists After All These Years

Bernardine Dohrn and Bill Ayers have aged and found jobs within educational institutions and foundations, but their politics are as far to the radical left as ever.

Dohrn and Ayers went underground after Dohrn was charged with instigating the riots during the 1968 Democratic National Convention in Chicago and after several of their Weathermen associates were killed when bombs they were building exploded in a Greenwich Village town house where they were being assembled. In 1970, Ayers, the wealthy son of the chairman of Commonwealth Edison, explained what the Weather Underground was about: "Kill all rich people. Break up their cars and apartments. Bring the revolution home, kill your parents, that's where it's really at." Dohrn was similar. Following the mass murders of Sharon Tate, who was eight and one half months pregnant when she was murdered, and others by Charles Manson's "family," Dohrn said: "Dig it. First they killed those pigs, then they ate dinner in the same room with them, then they even shoved a fork into a victim's stomach! Wild!"[72]

In his eleven-year reign of underground terror, Ayers participated in thirty bombings. In 1980, the pair, now married, surrendered to police, but the charges were dropped because the FBI used illegal wiretaps to investigate them. Only Dohrn was convicted, and only on a local charge of aggravated assault for which she pled guilty to two counts, received a $1,500 fine, and got no jail time. Both for their exploits in the SDS Weathermen and for their extended underground escapades, the pair became the Bonnie and Clyde of the 1960s. Dohrn today teaches law at Northwestern University and specializes in "juvenile justice reform." Bill Ayers served from 1999 to 2001 with Obama as a director of the Woods Fund. He became the vice chairman of the Woods board in 2003, overseeing the distribution of about $60 million a year. In 2002, the Woods Fund made a $60,000 grant to Northwestern University Law School's Children and Justice Center, where Dohrn works.[73] Ayers is currently a Distinguished Professor of Education and Senior University Scholar at the University of Illinois at Chicago, where, like Dohrn, he specializes in public school reform in Chicago.

Sol Stern, a contributing editor of Chicago's *City Journal*, has observed that while Ayers today "is widely regarded as a member in good standing of the city's civic establishment, not an unrepentant domestic terrorist," the impression of Ayers's good citizenship is incorrect. Stern argues that Dohrn and Ayers even today remain radicals, intent on inflicting harm on the nation's schoolchildren "by the political and educational movement in which Ayers plays a leading role today."[74] Guy Benson, a producer at radio station WYLL in Chicago, posted audio clips on the Internet from some "breathtaking videos featuring unrepentant terrorists William Ayers and Bernardine Dohrn."[75] The audio clips are from a speech Ayers gave at a November 2007 reunion of SDS members. Ayers can be clearly heard praising the SDS spirit of rebellion and quoting communist revolutionary heroes, including Chou En Lai, arguably Chairman Mao's right-hand man. At the same SDS reunion, Dohrn refers to the U.S. government as "the greatest purveyor of violence in the world," asserting that living in America constitutes living in "the belly of the beast" and "the heart of the monster."

These statements by Ayers and Dohrn are not from forty years ago, when Obama was eight years old. They are current, placing Obama in the dilemma that either he did not know Ayers and Dohrn are still radical leftists—in which case he is implausibly naïve—or Obama did know, which would confirm he joined with Ayers and Dohrn because Obama too continues to believe, albeit silently and secretly, in the Far Left's radical agenda.

Obama and Ayers Fund Pro-Palestinian Arab-American Group

In 2001, while Obama and Ayers were both on the Woods Fund board, the foundation made a $40,000 grant to the Arab American Action Network, followed up by an additional $35,000 grant in 2002.[76] The co-founder of the Arab American Action Network is Rashid Khalidi, who today is a Columbia University professor. According to an investigative report first developed by World Net Daily's Aaron Klein, Khalidi is a harsh critic of Israel. Klein began a controversy when he wrote Khalidi has made statements supportive of Palestinian terror and reportedly worked on behalf of the Palestine Liberation

Organization while it was involved in anti-Western terrorism and was labeled by the State Department as a terror group.[77] Ari Berman, writing in *The Nation*, objected that Khalidi said he never worked for the PLO.[78] Klein responded, distinguishing that Khalidi appears to have worked as a translator for the Palestinian press agency Wikalat al-Anba al-Filastinija, or WAFA, from 1976 to 1982, at the same time Khalidi's wife was a WAFA translator. [79] Klein acknowledged that Khalidi has denied working for the PLO.

When we investigate Obama's relationship with Khalidi, we find the grant was not made to someone Obama knew casually, just as Obama did not know Ayers and Dohrn casually.

Like Ayers and Dohrn, Professor Khalidi also held a political fund-raising event in his home for Obama.[80] The event was held in 2000, as Obama was embarking on his unsuccessful run for Congress against former Black Panther Bobby Rush. Obama and Michelle attended the event. In what was described as an intimate setting, the attendees had a chance to talk directly with Obama and his wife. Khalidi said he hosted the event for Obama because the two had become friends.

One of the attendees at the Khalidi fundraiser was Ali Abunimah, a Hyde Park Palestinian-American journalist sharply critical of Israel. Abunimah said Obama convinced him "he was very aware of the issues and critical of U.S. bias toward Israel and lack of sensitivity to Arabs. He was very supportive of U.S. pressure on Israel."[81] Abunimah also said "Obama was forthright in his criticism of U.S. policy and his call for an even-handed approach to the Palestinian-Israeli conflict." Abunimah is the founder of Electronic Intifada,[82] a journalistic website whose theme should be obvious from the name. He is also a vice president of the Arab American Action Network.

The *Los Angeles Times* described Obama as a "friend and frequent dinner companion" of Khalidi when the latter lived in Chicago.[83] According to the *Times*, when Khalidi, "an internationally known scholar, critic of Israel and advocate for Palestinian rights," was preparing to leave Chicago in 2003 to take a new position at Columbia, Obama attended his farewell party, "a night of music, dancing and a dash of politics." Obama told the *Times* that his many talks with Khalidi and his wife, Mona, had been "consistent reminders to me of my own blind spots and my own biases . . . It's for that reason that I'm hoping that, for many years to come, we continue that conversation—a conversation that is necessary not just around Mona and Rashid's dinner table, but around this entire world."

Khalidi left Chicago to become Edward Said Professor of Arab Studies at Columbia University and director of the Middle East Institute at Columbia's School of International and Public Affairs. Interestingly, Obama had met Said in Chicago, before Said died. At Columbia, Said held the prestigious position of University Professor until his death in September 2003.[84] Said also was known as an outspoken, anti-Israel advocate of a Palestinian state.[85] Journalist Ali Abunimah joined Obama at a May 1998 Arab community fund-raiser at which Edward Said was the keynote speaker. At ElectronicIntafada. net, Abunimah published two photographs from the event,[86] one showing then Illinois state senator Barack Obama and his wife sitting at a table having dinner with Said and his wife, as Obama engages in what appears to be animated conversation with the professor. The second photograph shows Obama and Michelle paying close attention to Said as the professor delivers the evening's keynote address.

Khalidi's books show he has continued in the tradition of Edward Said. In *The Iron Cage,* Khalidi presents a political apology for the creation of a Palestinian state in terms that demonize the United States. He characterizes the United States as supporting Israeli settlements on Palestinian land, in a pattern of "colonization, theft, and occupation" that makes the United States look like a "superpower bully" encouraging Israel "to impose its will on the weak and powerless." Khalidi's views are clearly anti-American. "Combined with its tragic and epically misguided adventure in Iraq, the Bush administration has brought the standing of the United States in the Middle East lower than ever before in American history," he writes. "It will soon be hard to recall that the United States was until relatively recently favorably regarded in the region."[87] As Obama has positioned himself to be the Democratic presidential candidate most opposed to the Iraq War, his campaign rhetoric and Khalidi's academic writing appear to be largely in agreement.

What evidence is there that the Arab American Action Network is a radical political group?

The Arab American Action Network, or AAAN, was established in 1995 as a nonprofit "grassroots, community-based organization working to improve the social, economic, and political conditions of Arab immigrants and Arab Americans in the Chicago Metropolitan area."[88] The group's home page says the AAAN is located in the "heart of the Palestinian Arab immigrant community, on the southwest side of Chicago." When Khalidi assumed his position at Columbia University, his wife began serving as president.

Klein reported in World Net Daily that speakers at AAAN dinners and events routinely have taken an anti-Israel line. The AAAN has become a strong advocate for illegal aliens, resolving in a statement on the group's website "to challenge government policies that violate the civil, political and human rights of the Arab American and Arab immigrant community." The group boasts about fighting the Department of Homeland Security in "detentions, deportations, and other attacks on immigrants."[89] The AAAN represented the Arab community in the May Day 2006 rally organized by the pro–illegal immigrant Movimiento 10 de Marzo to draw thousands into downtown Chicago to protest legislation sponsored by Republican congressman James Sensenbrenner of Wisconsin that would better secure our borders and tighten enforcement of immigration and employment laws.

The hostility of the AAAN to Israel was manifested in a project undertaken in collaboration with the American Friends Service Committee to solicit photographs, letters, and verbal accounts of local Palestinians' recollections about their sufferings around the formation of Israel in 1948.[90] Entitled "Al Nakba: 1948 as Experienced by Chicago Palestinians," the project was clearly politically biased against Israel. "Al Nakba," which translates to "The Catastrophe," is an Arabic name for Israeli independence that clearly telegraphs the politically charged, pro-Palestinian accusation that the creation of Israel was illegitimate.

Presidential Candidate Obama Distances Himself from Islamic Grantee

Is presidential candidate Barack Obama's decision to support Israel merely a matter of political convenience? Writing in March 2007 on Electronic Intifada, Ali Abunimah charged that Obama is engaged in a Middle East "make-over" designed to obscure the open advocacy Obama expressed for the Palestinian cause until he decided to run for the U.S. Senate. Obama "learned to love Israel," Abunimah wrote, not as a matter of personal belief, but as a political tactic designed to win Jewish votes and move to the more acceptable political center when running as a candidate for national office.[91]

"I first met Democratic presidential hopeful Senator Barack Obama almost ten years ago when, as my representative in the Illinois state senate, he came to speak at the University of Chicago," Abunimah wrote. "He impressed me as progressive, intelligent and charismatic. I distinctly remember thinking 'if only a man of this caliber could become president one day.'"

He wrote that the last time he spoke to Obama was in the winter of 2004, at a gathering in Chicago's Hyde Park neighborhood, when Obama was trailing in the polls, fighting to secure the Democratic nomination for the U.S. Senate. "As he came in from the cold and took off his coat, I went up to greet him," Abunimah wrote. "He responded warmly, and volunteered, 'Hey, I'm sorry I haven't said more about Palestine right now, but we are in a tough primary race. I'm hoping when things calm down I can be more up front.'"

Obama then referred to Abunimah's activism, including columns sharply critical of Israel and U.S. policy Abunimah was then publishing in the *Chicago Tribune*. "Keep up the good work!" Abunimah quoted Obama as telling him then, according to Abunimah, encouraging him in his pro-Palestinian writing.

Abunimah credited part of Obama's shift to a more pro-Israel stance to the influence of one of his "early backers," Penny Pritzker, whom Abunimah described as the "scion of the liberal but staunchly Zionist family that owns the Hyatt hotel chain." Pritzker, appointed in January 2007 to be the national finance chair of Obama's 2008 presidential campaign,[92] was ranked in September 2007 on the Forbes 400 as the 135th richest person in the United States.[93]

"If disappointing, given his historically close relations to Palestinian-Americans, Obama's about-face is not surprising," Abunimah wrote. "He is merely doing what he thinks is necessary to get elected and he will continue doing it as long as it keeps him in power."

The Betrayal of Alice Palmer

There is a bitter end to the story of Alice Palmer, the Illinois state senator who named Obama to be her successor in 1995. Palmer, we remember, decided to run for Congressman Mel Reynolds's seat. Palmer brought Obama out for the race with a party at the Hyde Park home of former Weather Underground radicals Bill Ayers and Bernardine Dohrn.

After Palmer stepped aside for Obama to take her seat, she suffered an unexpected electoral defeat. In the special November 1995 election held to pick the Democratic Party candidate to run for Reynolds's seat, she came in a distant third, behind Jesse Jackson, Jr., and Illinois state senate president Emil Jones, Jr., a power-wielder who would become Obama's mentor in the state legislature after Obama was elected to fill Palmer's seat in the 1996 race. Losing the special election for the congressional seat, Palmer reversed her decision and decided she did want to seek reelection to the Illinois legislature in 1996.

The year 1995 was a banner one for Obama. He had married Michelle in 1992 and the couple bought a Hyde Park condo in 1993, the first home Obama ever owned. In 1995, Obama became an author when his first book, his autobiography, *Dreams from My Father*, was published, to modest sales but good reviews. He was teaching constitutional law as a

University of Chicago adjunct professor and was about to run for the state senate. In 1995, Obama also participated in Farrakhan's Million Man March, a fact he has omitted from his 2008 presidential campaign biography.

In 1995, Obama had no intention of letting Palmer's defeat in the special election derail his political ambitions. Instead of stepping aside in deference to Palmer, Obama decided to fight her for the nomination. He hired a fellow Harvard Law School alumnus to be his gunslinger and challenged the legitimacy of the signatures on petitions to put Palmer's name on the ballot. Once he set on this strategy, Obama kept challenging petitions, until he succeeded in getting all four of his Democratic primary rivals forced off the ballot.

The *Chicago Tribune* wrote that "a close examination of Obama's first campaign clouds the image he has cultivated throughout his political career." The *Tribune* noted, "The man now running for president on a message of giving a voice to the voiceless first entered public office not by leveling the playing field, but by clearing it."[94] Obama stepped on the Chicago political stage with a pure power play even the most seasoned Daley-machine operative would have to appreciate, even if the strategy required Harvard-trained lawyers, instead of Al Capone–recruited thugs, to bring it to fruition.

Not surprisingly, in 2008, Alice Palmer showed up to campaign for Hillary Clinton in the Indiana primary.[95]

Bill Ayers Stands on the American Flag

Two photographs of Bill Ayers standing defiantly on the American flag surfaced as the Democratic presidential primary season began winding down with the North Carolina and Indiana contests. The photos were taken for an August 2001 interview with Ayers by *Chicago Magazine*'s Marcia Froelke Coburn. In the article, titled "No Regrets," Coburn wrote: "This—violence, death, and white-hot rhetoric—is his past and Ayers insists he has no regrets. 'I acted appropriately in the context of those times,' he says."[96] In both photos, Ayers is standing in a narrow alley. In the color photo used in the magazine article, Ayers has a somber expression on his face. He is wearing a blue blazer and open shirt with no tie; his hands are stuffed in the pockets of his jeans. The stars and stripes lies rumpled at his feet. In the second photo, a black-and-white apparently from the same photo shoot, but not used in the magazine, Ayers has his fists uplifted like a boxer, his knees are bent in a fighting pose, and he has a sly half-grin on his face.

Posting the second photo, blogger Anne Leary described the image as "Flag Stomping unrepentant terrorist Ayers. Obama's boss. As Barack talks family values in Indiana."[97] The reference to "Obama's boss" was to Obama's being a member of the Woods Fund board while Ayers was its chairman. Also prominent in disseminating the photos on the Internet was blogger Larry Johnson of NoQuarter. Posting the second photo of Ayers in the boxing pose, Johnson wrote, "Barack Obama may have been eight years old when William 'Billy' Ayers was planting bombs at the State Department and the U.S. Capitol, but the Senator was a grown man working in the employ of Mr. Ayers when this picture appeared in August 2001."[98]

The photographs and the *Chicago Magazine* article were both part of Ayers's publicity campaign for his book *Fugitive Days*.[99] Ironically, an interview with Ayers appeared in the *New York Times* on September 11, 2001, and thus was on the newsstands in New York City as the terrorists flew their hijacked airplanes into the World Trade Center. In the first lines of the interview, Ayers was quoted as saying, "I don't regret setting bombs. I feel we didn't do enough."[100]

Ayers obviously intended the photos to be inflammatory and he achieved his purpose. The American voting public looking at these images will predictably be outraged at his disrespect for the American flag. That Obama ever had anything to do with such an obvious America-hater is going to be difficult for the average person to understand. Try as the Obama campaign might to position the relationship as "guilt by association," the typical American voter understands the importance of character and Obama's relationship with Ayers was far deeper and longer than Obama would like to have been the case. Besides, Obama had to know who Ayers is and what he stands for, especially with Ayers making this splash on 9/11. Even today, Ayers appears to hold the same radical political beliefs he did in the Weather Underground, and Obama had to know that was also the case when he first met Ayers in 1995.

Today, with the Internet and twenty-four-hour cable news, Obama is certain to see this photo of Ayers displayed prominently, day after day, until he is forced to follow what has become his pattern of disowning previous friends from Chicago. Obama and his campaign manager Axelrod have already tried the approach of saying Obama did not know Ayers very well—that they were friends merely because Obama and Ayers lived in the same neighborhood and their kids went to school together.

We now know that is a misrepresentation, if not an outright lie.

Obama and Ayers were on the Woods Fund board for three years, approving grants together to radical groups like the Arab American Action Network. As the Democratic

Party presidential candidate, Obama will undoubtedly have to take the next step and say he is "deeply disappointed" to learn Ayers still adheres to the radical ideas that made him a cult leader in the Weather Underground. Finally, Obama will have to renounce Ayers and say he finds the image of Ayers standing on the American flag so deplorable that Obama rejects Ayers and his anti-American ideas.

None of this will explain why it took the national exposure of a presidential campaign for Obama to be forced to disavow Ayers. Why didn't Obama disavow Ayers in 2001 when the photographs of flag desecration appeared in *Chicago Magazine* and Ayers gave the 9/11 interview to the *New York Times* in which he regretted not carrying out even more radical leftist attacks?

Perhaps Obama said nothing in 2001 because he is a true student of Saul Alinsky.

One of Obama's Official Campaign Bloggers Is a Follower of Karl Marx

Obama's associations with radicals do not end with Ayers and Dohrn. Sam Graham-Felsen, one of the official bloggers for Barack Obama's 2008 presidential campaign,[101] was a self-proclaimed student of Karl Marx when he was an undergraduate at Harvard and proudly displayed a Russian Communist flag in his dorm room.

After leaving Harvard, Graham-Felsen published an article in an avowedly socialist magazine, expressing sympathy for the 2006 Paris street riots, which he observed in person, and working as a free-lance writer, he has posted dozens of comments and articles on the blog of the leftist publication *The Nation*.[102]

Behind the bar in their Quincy House suite at Harvard, Graham-Felsen, a graduate of the class of 2003, hung a Communist Party flag that he and a roommate brought back from Russia, according to an article published in the *Harvard Crimson* while he was a senior.[103] The *Crimson* article also noted that Graham-Felsen's bookcase in the Quincy House dorm included titles by Karl Marx and Howard Zinn, the socialist political science professor at Boston University known for his anti-American history texts and his extreme antiwar protest activity.

Graham-Felsen told the *Crimson* that he emulated his father, Michael D. Felsen, Harvard class of 1971, "who protested outside University Hall during the 1969 takeover." The *Crimson* noted, "Sam grew up with stories of his father's refusal to walk across the stage at his own commencement and his subsequent move to a commune. As a labor lawyer, he came to the Yard to advise members of the Progressive Student Labor Movement (PSLM) before their own three-week-long occupation of Massachusetts Hall in the spring of 2001."

Writing in a *Harvard Crimson* blog in his senior year, Graham-Felsen described meeting radical MIT professor and author Noam Chomsky as "a life changing experience" that left him feeling "as though I had been through the Matrix and back."[104] Graham-Felsen presumed to criticize Chomsky for his unwillingness "to compromise his beliefs for the sake of being accepted." He observed that "even if he [Chomsky] is waiting for Americans to rise up in mass movements, he's not going to spark widespread protest unless he can get more people to embrace his message." Graham-Felsen advised Chomsky to "tone his message down" so as "to convince Americans."

Writing in *Socialist Viewpoint* in the May/June 2006

issue, Graham-Felsen discussed a trip to Paris in which he participated in leftist street riots that involved a controversial employment law designed to facilitate the ability of French companies to fire workers under twenty-six years old. "I just returned from Paris," he wrote, "where I spent four days with the leaders of the student movement against the new employment law. I got a bird's-eye view of the whole operation, and I'd like to clarify a few things that the mainstream media has gotten completely wrong."[105]

According to *The Guardian*, the street violence in Paris during March 2006 lasted a week and involved hooded protesters who covered their faces with track-suit hoods and scarves, and came armed with baseball bats, wooden sticks, and metal bars.[106] The protesters rioted, smashing shop windows and setting cars afire. The only part of the story that went largely unreported by the mainstream media press was that much of the violence involved young Islamic immigrants from Africa, who lived in suburb tenements and were typically unemployed.

Graham-Felsen argued the street violence had nothing to do with "the movement," but involved kids who "just wanted to smash things and clash with the police.

"The story is that one million young people took to the streets to fight for their future," Graham-Felsen argued. "This is not a white, middle-class movement: The MSM, especially the *Times,* has painted these kids as uppity, white college students protecting their own interests. This is not the case at all. The kids from the suburbs—who are largely poor black and Arab kids—were out in full force."

The *Socialist Viewpoint* is a magazine published by the Socialist Workers Organization, a group that describes itself as "formed to advance the revolutionary Marxist political program in the United States. Our members are longtime active participants in the socialist and labor movements. We agree with Karl Marx that society is divided into social classes whose interests are irreconcilable."[107]

Even while he was contributing to *The Nation* as a free-lancer, Graham-Felsen was an enthusiastic supporter of Obama's presidential campaign. On October 18, 2006, in a posting on *The Nation*'s blog titled "Bonkers for Obama," Graham-Felsen called Obama "the political superstar of the moment—and perhaps ever—for Generation Y."[108] Writing in *The Nation* on February 1, 2007, he declared Obama "can now be considered the major antiwar candidate,"[109] after Obama gave a speech on the floor of the U.S. Senate calling for a removal of all combat brigades from Iraq by March 31, 2008, and calling the war in Iraq a "civil war."[110]

Conservative bloggers who have examined Graham-Felsen's record have been outspoken in their criticism. Graham-Felsen's far-leftist background was first explored by blogger "Common Ills." Common Ills posed this question about Graham-Felsen: "And exactly what is a Democratic candidate doing with a staffer who acts as the campaign's public face when the staffer is featured in Marxist publications?"[111]

Little Green Footballs has called Graham-Felsen "a hardcore Marxist."[112]

Blogger Warner Todd Huston observed that Graham-Felsen is "another Obama associate who seems to hate what most Americans love."[113]

How possibly can Obama argue his association with radicals such as Bill Ayers and Bernardine Dohrn was a long time ago, when he continues to recruit a Marxist sympathizer such as Sam Graham-Felsen to be an official blogger of his 2008 presidential campaign?

TONY REZKO AND
"THE CHICAGO WAY"

*And I was fighting against those ideas when you
were practicing law and representing your
contributor, Rezko, in his slum landlord
business in inner-city Chicago.*

—Senator Hillary Clinton, *speaking to Senator
Barack Obama, South Carolina Democratic
Primary Debate,* january 21, 2008[1]

Chicago is not Camelot.

—John Kass, *Chicago Tribune,* march 6, 2008[2]

The pattern of political corruption surrounding convicted
Chicago political fixer Tony Rezko and Barack Obama
is almost too complicated to follow for anyone whose bedtime
reading is not Machiavelli's *The Discourses.* Watching reruns of
the 1950s television show *The Untouchables* would help. But
living in Chicago, at least for a few years, and reading the local
newspapers would be the best preparation by far. The story
involves the type of bribes, payoff schemes, backroom deals,

and political favors only those who had grown up within a few miles of the Loop are prepared to understand. A small army of Chicago investigative reporters have dug into the story in the last two years, producing a mountain of incriminating evidence against Barack Obama that the mainstream media have failed to make known to the American public nationwide.

In a video archived on the *Chicago Tribune* website, reporter John Kass tries to explain "The Chicago Way" by interviewing Chicagoans. One explains that "The Chicago Way" involves power, access to government jobs, and taking care of your own—getting close to people in positions of power to gain access. Another explains the *C* in Chicago stands for "corruption." The image is one of access, influence, power, money, bribes, favors, and deals. Kass ends the video standing in front of a life-size replica of Gilbert Stuart's portrait of a standing George Washington, looking to the right, with his right hand extended. Kass takes a posture mimicking Washington in the painting, standing in front of the picture, facing the camera, with his right palm extended upward. He asks: "Your friend in government extends a hand. You don't leave that hand empty, do you? That's 'The Chicago Way.'"

Obama's Friend Tony Rezko

Tony Rezko, a Chicago slumlord, helped to bankroll Obama in five election runs—in Obama's successful 1996, 1998, and 2002 campaigns for the Illinois state senate, in 2000 for his unsuccessful run for the U.S. House, and in 2004 for his successful U.S. Senate campaign. As the 2008 Democratic presidential primaries were unfolding, Rezko stood trial, defending himself in criminal court against political corruption charges. On June 4, 2008, a federal jury found Rezko guilty on 16 out of

24 counts of political influence peddling. Obama's relationship with Rezko calls into question whether the lofty rhetoric of slogans like "Change We Can Believe In" belies a politics-as-usual reality whose truth is revealed by examining the shady financial deals that plague Obama's past with Rezko.

A full explanation of Chicago politics and Rezko's corrupt schemes would be a book in itself. While this book is not an investigative inquiry into Rezko's corruption, our question is, What can the Rezko scandals tell us about who Barack Obama truly is? The story is so complicated that tracking the key players virtually requires a flow chart so complex that most prosecutors would balk at explaining the connections to a jury. Perhaps the cover of that complexity is what Obama has been relying upon to give him enough wiggle room that the voting public will not hold him culpable. Unfortunately for Obama, since 2006 a dedicated group of Chicago investigative reporters have demanded answers, sensing that by pursuing Obama's relationship with Rezko, they would end up "exposing the corrupt backbone of Obama's political career."[3]

As Chicago reporter Evelyn Pringle tells us, Rezko was Obama's "political Godfather."[4] Rezko gave Obama his first political contribution, two thousand dollars, on July 31, 1995, when he learned Obama was going to run for Alice Palmer's seat in the Illinois state legislature. Pringle has claimed Rezko's financial assistance was critical to Obama launching his political career: "Without the fundraising of his political godfather, Rezko, Obama's rise to power would not have occurred."[5] Still, when the Rezko scandal first started coming to light, Obama did everything he could to deny he had anything to do with it. Pringle noted that for a year Obama minimized his relationship with Rezko, telling reporters he only had dinner or lunch with Rezko once or twice a year. But when *Chicago*

Sun-Times reporters finally confronted Obama on Friday, March 14, 2008, for an extended interview in the newspaper offices, the senator changed his tune.[6] Reporters presented Obama with information from John Thomas, an FBI mole, who often saw Obama coming and going at Rezko's offices. Three other sources told the newspaper that Obama and Rezko spoke on the phone daily. Obama was asked about this at the interview.

"I've known him for 17 years," Obama finally admitted. "There were stretches of time where I would see him once or twice a year. But, as I said, when he was involved in the finance committee for the U.S. Senate race, or the state senate races, or the U.S. Congressional races, then he was an active member." By saying Rezko was an "active member" of his campaigns, Obama acknowledged he relied upon Rezko to help him raise funds. Obama went on to admit that during the U.S. Senate race "there were stretches of like a couple of weeks—for example, prior to the fundraiser that he did for us—where I would probably be talking to him once a day to make sure that was going well." How close was Rezko to Obama? Pringle concluded harshly, "Without Rezko's fundraising, Obama would not have been elected to the Illinois senate, or the U.S. Senate, and he would not have sold the books he wrote about himself because like the Wizard of Oz, Obama is nobody special."[7]

"Tony Rezko" sounds like an Italian name you would expect to hear in Chicago. Antoin "Tony" Rezko, however, is not Italian. Rezko is Syrian, born in Aleppo, Syria's second largest city. He came to the United States after high school, drawn to Chicago to enroll in the Illinois Institute of Technology. He holds bachelor's and master's degrees from the institute in civil engineering and construction management.[8] As we will soon see, Rezko's money ties go back to the Middle East, back to one Islamic money mogul who could fairly be described as a "bag man" to Saddam Hussein at the height of his Oil for Food scam.

In that long interview with Obama in March 2008, the *Chicago Sun-Times* asked the senator if he was still friends with Rezko, even then, as Rezko's criminal trial was being held. "Yes," Obama answered, quickly adding a characteristic Obama qualification, "with the caveat that obviously, if it turns out the allegations are true, then he's not who I thought he was, and I'd be very disappointed with that." In the next chapter, we will see Obama attempt to distance himself from his pastor, Reverend Jeremiah Wright, in almost precisely the same words.

Wall Street Journal reporter John Fund, who has dug into the connections, concludes the potential damage to Obama's political career will be extensive, possibly even fatal, once the public understands the whole story. Quite simply, Fund believes Obama will have a hard time burying his relationship with Rezko when the public realizes Rezko has been Obama's "friend of two decades and his master campaign fund-raiser." Obama will have a hard time explaining that he didn't see Rezko was "a master fixer in Illinois politics," or that he didn't know Rezko was involved "with money laundering, attempted extortion, fraud and aiding bribery in an alleged multimillion dollar scheme shaking down companies seeking state contracts."[9]

Rezko's relationship with Obama was not a casual one. It actually traces back to Obama's decision to return to Chicago after he finished law school at Harvard in 1991.

Rezko Recruits Obama at Harvard

Although Obama has given various versions of the story, he met Rezko in Chicago, either while he was finishing law school at Harvard or when he had just graduated. Rezko wanted Obama to return to Chicago after he finished at Harvard so he could hire Obama in Rezmar, the name of Rezko's community development firm.

"I don't recall whether his office contacted me right before I graduated or when I was still in law school and visiting Chicago," Obama told the *Sun-Times*.[10] At the meeting with Obama, Rezko was accompanied by his two Rezmar business partners, Dan Mahru and David Brint. Rezko explained he knew Obama had worked at the Developing Communities Project in Chicago, before leaving for Harvard.

"They had started a real estate company called Rezmar," Obama told the *Chicago Tribune* in an extensive interview March 14, 2008, the same day as his question-and-answer session at the *Sun-Times*. "They [Rezko, Mahru, and Brint] contacted me while I was the president of the *Harvard Law Review* and asked if I was coming back to Chicago and was thinking about future employment, would I be interested in potentially getting involved in development."[11] With the *Tribune* staff, Obama once again hedged on when the meeting was held. "And so when I was back in Chicago, and I don't recall whether it was during the summer between, you know, my second and third year [in law school] or whether it was after I had graduated, or whether it was just visiting Michelle, I met with them."

Community organizing and community development are two different activities. In Obama's case, community organizing, as we saw in the last chapter, involved Obama working in a Saul Alinsky–type organization, with the goal of sharpening community dissatisfaction to organize community pressure for social changes, including redistribution of wealth. Community development, as Rezko practiced in

Chicago, involved building affordable housing projects in low-income areas. "They didn't talk to me about a specific job, but explained what they were doing in terms of development," Obama told the *Tribune*.[12] "Because I had been a community organizer, I think that's what part of what prompted their interest because they were doing a lot of affordable housing work and work with community development corporations." Obama then stated the conversation was "relatively brief," lasting "maybe 45 minutes." He said he "ultimately declined to go into development, but that was the first time I met Tony Rezko."

Obama had provided other details about his first meeting with Rezko to the *Chicago Tribune* in November 2006: "Rezko and two real estate partners called out of the blue to offer a job building inner-city homes," the *Tribune* reported. Obama said he declined the offer, "but I remained friendly with all three of them. All three of them remained great contributors of mine." The record shows Obama meant campaign contribution contributors.[13]

But this was not to be Obama's last association with Rezko. As we shall see, Rezko was persistent, ultimately convincing Obama to drop working for political organizing causes so he could supplement the dwindling advance he had received at Harvard to write a book with real income as a lawyer, working in the small Chicago law firm where the lead partner did much of Rezko's slumlord legal work for him.

Obama's Career Path

Most Obama biographies suggest he went directly from Harvard Law School to return to Chicago, where he decided to work for a small civil rights firm. Yet in 1991

Obama returned to Chicago not to join Rezmar, as Tony Rezko had suggested, or to go to work for a law firm, but to begin writing the book for which he had received a contract while at Harvard. The book, not finished and published until 1995, turned out to be Obama's autobiography, *Dreams from My Father*.

In 1992, Sandy Newman, a lawyer and civil rights activist who had founded Project Vote! as a national effort headed in Washington, hired Obama to head Project Vote! in Chicago.[14] Undoubtedly, Obama's advance for the book had worn thin and Project Vote! was work he was qualified to do, given his community organizing experience and his law degree. Project Vote!, as we noted in the previous chapter, was a national voter registration drive aimed at increasing minority voter registrations. In Chicago, Obama had his biggest impact registering African-American voters on Chicago's South Side. While he successful directed Project Vote! in Chicago, Obama certainly did not become wealthy doing it.

It wasn't until 1993, his book still unfinished, that Obama signed on with a small law firm, known at the time as Davis Miner Barnhill & Galland. The firm had a history in civil rights advocacy law, which most biographers again see as consistent with Obama's career record in public service activities. After successfully heading Project Vote!, Obama still should have had an opportunity to work at one of Chicago's prestigious law firms specializing in corporate law or municipal bond work, where he could have earned a six-figure salary.

In deciding to work for a small civil rights advocacy firm, Obama again appeared to be passing up an opportunity for substantial financial gain. Or was he?

Allison S. Davis, the lead partner in Davis Miner

Barnhill & Galland, was possibly a close business associate of Tony Rezko. Conveniently, the law firm represented Rezmar. Evidently, Rezko never lost interest in Obama. If Obama did not want to work directly for Rezko, then having Obama in Davis Miner Barnhill & Galland was possibly the next best thing for Rezko. Working as a lawyer, Obama could earn money he undoubtedly needed. Working at a small law firm with a civil rights advocacy reputation would allow Obama to argue that his social conscience was still dictating his career choices. Yet, while there, Obama could work for Rezko indirectly and benefit from Rezko's connections.

The likelihood is that Rezko played a role in getting Obama to join Davis Miner Barnhill & Galland.

Obama's career story leaving Harvard merits an even closer look.

How is it that the president of the *Harvard Law Review* ended up working at a small Chicago law firm that did the legal work for one of Chicago's most notorious slumlords?

At Harvard Law School, Obama was a star. The president of the *Harvard Law Review* typically would be offered an opportunity to clerk for one of the Supreme Court justices. If Obama's focus remained social change, what better place could he find to begin his career than clerking for a Supreme Court justice? From there, Obama would have available many different career paths, including a return to Chicago to begin a political career. Why not grab the Supreme Court credential and experience?

Moreover, as the first African-American president of the prestigious law review, Obama would have had his pick of top-name corporate law firms in New York or government practice law firms in Washington, D.C. The firms regularly recruiting at Harvard Law School would have competed for Obama's attention, offering him free first-class trips to visit the firms and be interviewed by the partners. Wined and dined by law firm recruiters in any city where Obama wanted to practice law, including Chicago, Obama could have written his own ticket. His future as an attorney was virtually ensured, as well as his ability to earn millions and live a life of comfort.

As we have seen, Obama learned his primary lessons before law school with the Developing Communities Project, where he was instructed in the Machiavellian power politics of Saul Alinsky's radical activism. Alinsky taught that power was everything and that image, words, and positioning were just methods to capture power, working from communities up. Whatever Obama and Rezko talked about in their first meeting, the record shows Obama ended up working for the lawyer Allison Davis, who was one of Rezko's business partners. The record also shows Obama, working as a lawyer within what was renamed Miner Barnhill & Galland after Davis left, took steps that helped Davis and Rezko in their business relationship.

This was the heart of Hillary Clinton's charge against Obama in the South Carolina debate: that as an attorney Obama had represented his campaign contributor in his questionable career as a slum landlord. The record of Obama's time at Davis Miner Barnhill & Galland is problematic for a candidate who likes to present himself as a champion of the poor, the minorities, and the disadvantaged among us.

Another Rezko partner, Dan Mahru, one of the other two who visited Obama while Obama was finishing law school, shows up in the record more than once. (It appears Rezko created the name "Rezmar" by taking the first three letters of his name, "Rez," and combining it with the sound of the first four letters of Mahru's name, "Mahr," shortened to "Mar.") On February 22, 2008, Rezko filed court documents claiming Mahru embezzled $1 million from the estate of his own mother, Gertrude Mahru, while he was executor of it.[15] Rezko further claimed that Mahru began cooperating with federal law enforcement authorities in December 2005, turning over evidence against Rezko as a confidential informant in a deal to avoid arrest. Mahru denied everything.

Slum Landlord "Friend of Obama" Takes Millions in Government Subsidies for Failed Projects

Rezmar was created in 1989—the year Richard M. Daley, Jr., won his first term as Chicago mayor. Its purpose was supposedly to purchase decrepit housing, renovate the units, and turn them into low-income apartments for the poor. Daley had campaigned on building more housing for the poor. To help Daley keep that promise, Rezko and his partner at the time, Daniel Mahru, applied for a $629,000 loan to fix up an abandoned apartment building at 46th and Drexel, even though neither man had prior construction experience. The *Chicago Sun-Times* reported that Rezko and Mahru got the loan four months after they applied, setting them on a fast track to be one of the Daley administration's favored developers. Over the next nine years, Rezmar got more than $100 million from the city, state, and federal government, plus bank loans, to rehabilitate thirty buildings in Chicago. Rezmar was paid at least $6.9 million to develop some 1,025 low-income apartments in the buildings.[16]

Instead, the *Sun-Times* investigation in 2007 found the following: six of the thirty Rezmar buildings were boarded up; seventeen had gone into foreclosure, most after Rezmar abandoned them; an eighteenth property was being foreclosed on by the state after Rezmar walked away from it (he left the building to corporate investors who got a state loan but failed to save the building); hundreds of apartments were vacant, most in need of major repairs. Eleven of the buildings were in the Illinois state senate district Obama represented.

The *Sun-Times* quoted Rezmar architect Phillip Kupritz as saying that every one of the Rezmar properties had failed.[17] Even when city attorneys repeatedly went to court to force Rezmar to make repairs on its buildings, and, in some cases, to get the heat turned on, Rezmar kept getting new rehabilitation loans. Rezko's low-income housing projects were a disgrace. He had rehabbed the apartments on the cheap and didn't put aside enough money for repairs once the cheap heaters and low-quality appliances gave out. After a few years, Rezko's low-income housing buildings were typically plagued by vacant units, drug dealers, squatters, a lack of heat in the winter, and general disrepair.

In every one of these low-income housing deals, lenders and investors lost money, but Rezmar still got paid, typically first. Rezko and his partner Mahru considered themselves not personally responsible for failed government or bank loans, and they still have not repaid the $50 million in federal tax credits they received to rehab the properties.[18]

Whatever happened, the money is gone. Today Rezko seems unable to account for what happened to the millions he had been lent or granted by the city, state, and federal governments, never mind the money from private investors and bank loans. Instead of doing what he promised, Rezko appeared notoriously irresponsible. In the process, Obama's reputation was tarnished, not only by his friendship with Rezko and the political contributions he took from him, but also by his involvement with the legal firm representing Rezko and, as we shall see, a shady deal in which Rezko helped the Obamas buy their dream home property.

Rezko, as we noted earlier, is a native of Syria who came to Chicago in the late 1970s to study engineering at the Illinois Institute of Technology. His big break came in 1984 when he went to work for Crucial Concessions, Inc., a food services company owned by Jabir Herbert Muhammad, whose father, Elijah Muhammad, founded the Nation of Islam. Herbert Muhammad was also the longtime manager of boxing champion Muhammad Ali. Crucial Concessions had city concessions to operate food services on city beaches and in many South Side parks. Over time, Rezko's food empire expanded through lucrative food contracts for Panda Express franchises and Subway sandwich shop concessions for the Illinois State Toll Highway Authority and O'Hare Airport. Rezko was running Crucial Concessions when he met Mahru in 1989. At the time Mahru was chief executive officer of Automatic Ice, Inc., a company that leased icemakers to bars, hotels, and restaurants. "I sold him ice" was the way Mahru typically explained how he met Rezko.[19]

Attorney Obama's Ties to Slum Landlord Rezko

Investigative reporter Tim Novak at the *Chicago Sun-Times* has identified fifteen building projects that Rezmar redeveloped while represented by the Chicago law firm Davis Miner Barnhill & Galland during the time Obama was a lawyer working at the firm.[20] All the projects were financial disasters. Typical of these are the three boarded-up apartment buildings on East 62nd Street on the South Side: Rezmar closed a deal with the Chicago Urban League in 1995 to rehab the buildings. Instead of getting rehabbed apartments as promised, the state of Illinois was forced to foreclose on a $2.6 million loan in 2006, when Rezmar quit making payments.

Rezko managed thirty projects in total, including the eleven that were in the Illinois state senate district Obama represented. Foreclosures followed by abandoned properties are the legacy of the Rezko low-income-housing empire. Despite giving the taxpayer and the poor the short end of the stick, Rezko made sure his earnings remained strong and that he had more than enough money to pay off the politicians who needed to remain happy. Rezko's cash flow on loan repayments dried up on every one of the fifteen building projects he managed. But the campaign contributions to Obama kept going even as the low-income housing projects failed.

Searching for a direct Obama-Rezko tie, Novak exposed the fact that Obama wrote letters to city and state officials supporting his political patron Rezko's successful bid to get more than $14 million from taxpayers to build apartments for senior citizens.[21] The deal included $855,000 in development fees for Rezko and Allison Davis, Obama's former boss at the law firm, who had now left the firm to work with Rezko in publicly funded housing projects. The development, Cottage View Terrace, opened in 2002, providing ninety-seven apartments for low-income senior citizens. From his office as state senator, Obama wrote letters to city and state officials supporting Rezko's bid to manage the low-income rehabs.

The letters appeared to contradict statements from Obama that he never did any favors for Rezko. Novak wrote, "Obama's letters, written nearly nine years ago, for the first time show the Democratic presidential hopeful did a political favor for Rezko—a longtime friend, campaign fund-raiser and client of the firm where Obama worked—who was indicted last fall on federal charges that accuse him of demanding kickbacks from companies seeking state business under Gov. Blagojevich."[22] In addition to the $855,000 in development fees Rezko and Davis made on the Cottage View Terrace project, the company owned by Davis stood to make another $900,000 through federal tax credits.

Yet Obama's campaign characteristically denied Obama had been involved in working at the law firm for Rezko or his rehab projects. "The senator, relatively inexperienced in this kind of work, was assigned to tasks appropriate for a junior lawyer," Robert Gibbs, a spokesman for Obama's presidential campaign, wrote in an e-mail to the *Sun-Times*. "These tasks would have included reviewing documents, collecting corporate organizational documents, and drafting corporate resolutions." To sum it up, Gibbs wrote, "Senator Obama does not remember having conversations with Tony Rezko about properties that he owned or specific issues related to those properties."[23]

Novak was not convinced. "Obama, who has worked as a lawyer and a legislator to improve living conditions for the poor, took campaign donations from Rezko even as Rezko's low-income housing empire was collapsing, leaving many African-American families in buildings riddled with problems—including squalid living conditions, vacant apartments, lack of heat, squatters and drug dealers."[24] Novak cited one particular Rezko-owned property, noting: "For more than five weeks during the brutal winter of 1997, tenants shivered without heat in a government-subsidized apartment building on Chicago's South Side."[25] While Rezko and Mahru could not find the money to get the heat back on, Rezmar came up with a thousand dollars to give to the political campaign of Barack Obama, the newly elected state senator whose district included the unheated building.

Novak further noted that eleven of Rezko's buildings were in Obama's state senate district.[26]

When questioned by the *Sun-Times* about an October 28, 1998, letter that Obama wrote as a state senator to city officials to urge them to approve the Cottage View Terrace apartments, Obama claimed Rezko had not solicited the letter and that it was "a form letter of the sort that I did all the time."[27] Obama said his office would find out if a particular project was worthy and proceed from there: "This was one of the many form letters, or letters of recommendation we would send out constantly for all sorts of projects."[28] At the time when Obama wrote the letter from his state senate office, he was also working for Davis Miner Barnhill & Galland, which was still representing Rezko.

Obama objected to the *Sun-Times*'s attempt to tie him to Rezko, arguing that "bootstrapping five or six hours of work that I did as an associate at a law firm" was not equivalent to his "helping a slumlord." The exchange occurred during the extensive question-and-answer session Obama granted in the newspaper's offices in March 2008 after the *Sun-Times* had been pounding him for weeks with headlines based on their investigative reports. The *Sun-Times* editorial staff bluntly asserted that Obama was trying to minimize his relationship with Rezko.

The *Sun-Times* stressed to Obama that their questions were never so much about the number of hours Obama worked on the Rezko case, but why he continued to work for a law firm that had Rezko as a client. The editors were especially perplexed since, again, when Obama wrote those letters on behalf of Rezko he was also serving as an Illinois state senator representing many of the poor people living in Rezko rehab projects. Rezko had apparently committed fraud, stealing or otherwise appropriating funds that were meant to provide quality low-income housing while residents were reduced to living in broken-down units without heat in the winter, in deteriorating projects plagued by vacancies, with squatters and drug dealers moving in. Though many of Rezko's projects were in Obama's district, Obama did nothing while Rezko used substandard or otherwise cheap materials in his rehabs and failed to save enough money to provide necessary repairs.

Obama had no answer, except to say, "I read the story. I understand the argument you're making."[29]

There is no record that Illinois state senator Obama ever so much as placed a speech in the record objecting to the public-housing practices perpetrated in his district by Tony Rezko, let alone calling for investigation of Rezko and his business practices.

Rezko Helps Obama Buy His Dream Home Property

When a prestige house across the street from Tony Rezko's came on the market, Rezko must have thought it was just perfect for Barack and Michelle Obama and their two daughters. Rezko found the house for Obama. Salon.com reported that Donna Schwan of MetroPro Realty, the real estate agent who listed the property, recalled the deal starting when Rezko expressed interest in the listing.[30] The house was evidently perfect, a ninety-six-year-old, multistory, 6,400-square-foot, brick Georgian Revival home with four fireplaces, six bedrooms, six bathrooms, glass-door bookcases fashioned from Honduran mahogany, and a wine cellar large enough to store a thousand bottles.[31] The house was situated on a large double corner lot, with the vacant lot adjoining the home at the street corner. With a foot-tall concrete barrier and a wrought-iron fence surrounding the property, there was no access to the vacant lot, except through Obama's driveway.

The neighborhood is Kenwood, a South Side oasis of pricey homes attractive to the University of Chicago professors who like to live close to work.[32] The property would be a nice step up for the Obama family from the small Hyde Park condo the couple had bought in 1993 for $277,500. The Obama family lived there for the eight years Obama was state senator. This new home would be suitable for the family of a U.S. senator.[33]

The problem was that the doctor who owned the property wanted to sell the vacant lot and the house at the same time, even though the two properties were separately listed. Also, while the sellers wanted to find a buyer as quickly as possible, they did not want to close the deal until June 2005. The list price just for the home was $1.95 million, outside the reach of the Obama family, even with Obama's reissued autobiography, *Dreams from My Father*, hitting bestseller lists, his U.S. Senate salary of $157,082, and Michelle's 2005 income of $317,000 at the University of Chicago Hospitals.[34]

Rezko came up with a solution. His wife, Rita, bought the vacant lot at full price, permitting Obama and Michelle to negotiate buying the house for $1.65 million, a discount of $300,000 from the asking price. Rezko's wife closed on the vacant lot the same day the Obamas closed on the house. She paid $625,000 for the lot, the full asking price.

"Both actions would be clear violations of Senate ethics rules barring the granting or asking of favors," wrote John

Fund in the *Wall Street Journal*.[35] The *Boston Globe* reported that Obama had asked for Rezko's advice in negotiating the deal—after all, Rezko was supposedly experienced with real estate, having negotiated so many low-income housing deals in Chicago—and Obama toured the house with Rezko before making an offer.[36] The *Globe* also reported real estate agent Schwan's recollection that the Obamas may not have made the highest bid, but that the willingness of the Obamas and Rita Rezko to close in June was decisive.[37] This detail shows the importance of Rezko to the ability of the Obamas to buy their dream house. Had Rita Rezko not been willing to buy the vacant lot in June, "the deal was off."[38]

The *Globe* also reported that one month after the house sale, Obama gave the son of a Rezko associate an internship in his Senate office in Washington.[39]

After the Obamas moved in, the senator and his wife decided they wanted to buy a slice of the vacant lot. The *Globe* reported that an independent appraisal of the entire vacant lot parcel put its worth at about $500,000, about $125,000 less than Rita had paid for it. The Obamas wanted to buy one-sixth of the vacant lot, to create a yard next to the house.[40] The strip the Obamas wanted to buy was appraised at only $40,500 because it was not suitable for building. Still, in January 2006, the Obamas paid Rita Rezko $104,500 for the one-sixth strip, a proportionate share of what Rita had paid for the entire vacant lot. Rita built a fence to separate off the rest of the vacant lot and the deal was closed. Obama hired an attorney and architect to design a wrought-iron fence for the new property line, including the one-sixth of the vacant lot bought from Rita. Rezko agreed to pay the $14,000 cost of building the fence and Obama agreed to pay his landscaper to mow Rita's lot for her.[41]

When Tony Rezko was indicted, Rita Rezko sold the vacant lot, evidently needing the funds. The *Chicago Tribune* looked at records in the Cook County registry of deeds showing Rita had sold the "garden lot" on December 28, 2006, to a company owned by former Rezko business attorney Michael J. Sreenan, which planned to develop housing on the lot.[42] Rita sold the remaining five-sixths of the vacant lot for $575,000, netting an estimated $54,500 from the sale. A spokesman for Obama said the senator was aware development was planned on the lot, but denied he knew any of the details.[43]

Following the sale of the lot and Obama's marathon sessions with the *Chicago Sun-Times* and *Tribune* on March 14, 2008, the blog Rezko Watch reported that Obama had provided a new list of Rezko-related campaign contributors whose money Obama had released to charity. On it was a $2,000 donation Michael Sreenan made to Obama on June 30, 2003.[44] According to Politico.com, Sreenan made five other contributions totaling $3,500 to Obama, on the same days other Rezko associates and employees contributed often matching sums.[45] For example, Sreenan's first contribution on record was a $1,000 check reported the same March 2000 day that five other Rezko employees contributed a like sum. Evidently, Obama donated all these Rezko contributions to charity.

Then, in an article titled "Obama is one lucky fellow," Rezko Watch found it was unlikely that Sreenan would actually construct any condos on the lot he had bought from Rita Rezko.[46] According to Rezko Watch, Alderman Toni Preckwinkle had rejected plans from a prospective buyer who wanted to build a single-family home on the lot adjoining the Obama home, as well as a developer's plans to put condos up there. Preckwinkle declared that any home built on that land would have to be compatible with the neighborhood's mansions. Preckwinkle, Rezko Watch noted, is not only the Democratic committeeman of the Fourth Ward but also a known Obama supporter. The *Chicago Sun-Times* has reported Rezko was conveniently the longtime head of Preckwinkle's campaign finance committee.[47] Six of Rezko's problem housing projects are in Preckwinkle's ward.

This too, *Chicago Tribune* reporter Jack Kass would most likely reassure us, is "The Chicago Way."

A "Bonehead" Deal

As we have noted, after taking heat for over a year in the local Chicago media over the Rezko scandal, Obama finally decided to face the music, coming into the offices of the *Chicago Sun-Times* and the *Chicago Tribune* on March 14, 2008, to give a lengthy opening statement and answer questions from the newspapers' editorial staff and investigative reporters.

The *Sun-Times* bluntly asked Obama, "Why didn't alarm bells go off when you agreed to buy a 10-foot-wide strip of property to buffer your home at the same time reports were coming out that he was being investigated for alleged illegal influence-peddling?" Obama answered, "Probably because I had known him for a long time and he had acted in an above-board manner with me and I considered him a friend. In retrospect it should have, so this was a mistake on my part." The newspaper pressed, reminding Obama that he had spoken a lot about judgment in his presidential campaign. Wasn't the decision to purchase the ten-foot-wide strip from Rezko a judgment issue? Obama repeated that the decision was a mistake, adding for emphasis, "I said it was a bonehead move. I think it is further evidence I am not perfect."[48] The "bonehead move" phrase stuck and was widely repeated in the media following the interview.

In his prepared statement, Obama told the *Sun-Times* that Michelle fell in love with the house. The next day, in his prepared statement to the *Tribune*, Obama explained, "Michelle calls me and says, 'I'm in, I love this house, but it's more than we were talking about paying for, but I really think it's a great house, you should go take a look at it.'"[49]

When the *Tribune* grilled Obama about whether he and Rezko had coordinated their bids so Obama could afford to buy the home at a discounted price, Obama admitted he and Rezko had toured the home together before making offers.

Still, Obama was determined to deny everything. He told the *Tribune* he had a written statement from the sellers saying that "at no time did they ever consider the lot in relation to the price of the house, that they did not offer a discount on the house, that there was no contingency with respect to our house purchase relative to the lot." The transcript of the question-and-answer session clearly shows the *Tribune* staff had a hard time believing Obama. Yet Obama persisted, denying he coordinated the purchase with Rezko. Obama insisted he believed Rezko bought the vacant lot because he believed Rezko thought it was a good business decision to develop it. Obama could offer no explanation of why Rita Rezko bought the vacant lot instead, and he complained that the sellers were private people who objected to the reporters intruding into their lives with hostile questions.

The *Tribune* asked directly, "The issue of judgment is one of the keystones of your campaign right now. How should Americans look at this series of events that you've just laid out?" Obama answered, "I think that the way they should view it is that I made a mistake in not seeing the potential conflicts of interest or appearances of impropriety." Nevertheless, "they should see somebody who was not engaged in any wrongdoing, who did not in any way betray the public trust, who has maintained consistently high ethical standards and who they can trust."

Tribune reporter David Jackson noted that the question-and-answer session was the first time Obama disclosed that he and Rezko had toured the Kenwood home together. "In his first accounts of the purchase, Obama did not divulge that tour," Jackson wrote. "He said Friday that he simply didn't feel the information was salient and insisted the tour didn't mean he and Rezko coordinated their purchases."[50]

"Obama: I trusted Rezko," was the headline on the story. But in March 2008, nearly three years after the Kenwood house sale closed, the issue had become whether Obama chose to close his eyes to Rezko's obvious improprieties simply because it was in Obama's personal financial interest not to examine his friend's business practices too closely.

Obama Backtracks on Rezko Campaign Contributions

By March 13, 2008, Obama was also backtracking fast on earlier low-ball estimates of just how much Rezko had contributed to his political campaigns, beginning with Obama's run for Alice Palmer's seat in the Illinois state senate in 1995.

The *Sun-Times* questioned Obama closely: "You told us in November 2006, that your best estimate was that Rezko raised somewhere between $50,000 and $60,000 during your political career. Since then, your campaign's given back $157,000 in Rezko-related contributions. Now the total is what?"

Obama explained that the original estimate was based on a figure his staff gave to him. He hedged that he had excluded listing some of the funds raised in 2003 at a fund-raising dinner Rezko gave for 150 people at his Mediterranean-style mansion in Chicago when Obama was running for the U.S. Senate. "The money that was given back includes money that was raised at the house when he had that fundraiser," Obama told the newspaper editors, "even though these are people who Tony didn't raise the money from, these would have been individuals who I had known separately who were supporters who basically got funneled into that fundraiser. But because they went to the fundraiser, we decided to return the money."[51]

The *Sun-Times* linked about $168,000 in Obama campaign contributions to Rezko.[52] The *Tribune* reported after their March 14, 2008, interview with Obama that the figure was much higher, estimating Rezko had raised as much as $250,000 for the first three offices Obama sought, up to and including his 2004 race for the U.S. Senate.[53]

Obama is always quick to deny any quid pro quo on Rezko campaign contributions. "At no time did he ever ask for any favors from me" is the refrain Obama recites every time he is asked about campaign contributions Rezko has given him personally or bundled for him. Still, every time new campaign contributions from Rezko are identified, Obama claims to have returned the money or to have donated it to charity.

Even if no illegality is ever identified, Obama's continued willingness to take campaign contributions from his "friend" Rezko, even after serious allegations about Rezko's low-income housing empire began to be raised, have the feel of impropriety. And it is ironic that his friend Rezko was exactly the kind of villain Obama was railing against when he first came to Chicago to work as a community organizer in the Alinsky-style Developing Communities Project.

Has Obama the politician made a hypocrite out of Obama the community organizer?

Or was Obama always the same person, when he first came to Chicago as a community organizer and now that he is running for president? A politician who first and foremost is interested in his own political and financial advancement, regardless of the moral consequences?

Rezko's Saddam Hussein Connection

Tony Rezko was indicted on October 5, 2006. On November 2, Rezko's legal counsel submitted documentation to assist the court in setting bond. In the letter to the court, Rezko claimed he currently had no income, negative cash flow, and no unencumbered assets.[54] Rezko said he had only $9,000 cash on hand and minimal funds in bank accounts, that he had been forced to rely on family and friends for financial assistance, and that the family's only source of income was his wife's annual salary of $37,000. If Rezko's financial situation was truly this strapped, how then did Rita Rezko come up with the $125,000 down payment and the collateral to secure the $500,000 loan needed to buy the vacant lot adjacent to Obama's Kenwood mansion?

The loan came from the Mutual Bank of Harvey, owned by Amrish Mahajan, an Indian who is also its president and chief executive officer. The *Chicago Tribune* reported that since 2002, Mutual Bank has lent more than $3.4 million to Rezko in three different real estate deals. In one questionable deal, the paper reported, Mahajan's bank lent $1.32 million to Rezko on several pieces of property that were deeded back and forth between Rezko partners before the loan was secured, a transaction raising questions about who owned the collateral for the loan. The Rezko partner taking out the loan was Abdel-hamid "Al" Chaib.[55] Chaib was subsequently indicted on federal fraud charges for allegedly participating in a scam to obtain the $3.4 million loan.

Al Chaib is another longtime Rezko friend and business associate who ran the Crucial Concessions food business established in 1976 by Jabir Herbert Muhammad, the son of Nation of Islam founder Elijah Muhammad. Federal prosecutors alleged that Chaib and Rezko planned to use some of the $3.4 million loan proceeds to buy a pizza franchise to add to their food services business.

When Chaib was indicted, Obama returned a $5,000 contribution Chaib had made in 2003 to Obama's 2004 U.S. Senate campaign. Previously, Obama had given to charities $34,500 he had received in campaign contributions from other people involved in the Chaib indictment.[56] Obama has also donated to charity a $1,000 campaign contribution from Amrish Mahajan.[57]

Obama Surrounded by Corruption, "The Chicago Way"

As remarkable as these connections seem, there are even more in Obama's Chicago history that have not been fully investigated. Take the case, for instance, of yet another Rezko business associate, Aiham Alsammarae, a dual Iraqi-

U.S. citizen. In a now-routine maneuver Obama is giving to charity the $2,300 he received online from Alsammarae in six presidential campaign contributions.

Who is Alsammarae? He was Iraqi minister of electricity from 2003 to 2005 but ended up being convicted in an Iraqi court of a fraudulent scheme to corner the Iraqi cellular telephone market in the aftermath of the U.S. invasion of Iraq in 2003. Although that conviction was overturned, Alsammarae was in prison facing other charges when in late 2006 a mysterious group of masked and heavily armed men broke him out of prison in Baghdad's Green Zone. Alsammarae fled from justice in Iraq, only to end up, of all places, in Chicago. There, he joined up with Rezko, who, strangely enough, turns out to be an old friend. Rezko and Alsammarae met in 1976 when the two were both attending the Illinois Institute of Technology.[58] As a testament to that friendship, Alsammarae posted his Oak Brook mansion in Chicago and two South Loop condominiums as bail to get Rezko out of jail following his criminal indictment.

When he was incarcerated in Iraq, Alsammarae contacted multiple elected officials in the United States to help him. Obama's Senate office has admitted Obama sought information from the U.S. State Department about Alsammarae on October 16, 2006, and got a reply from the U.S. consul in Iraq about a week later. Obama maintains his office provided the information to Alsammarae's daughter and took no further action.[59]

Obama also told the *Chicago Sun-Times* that he did not recall meeting Alsammarae, who was with Rezko at the Four Seasons dinner that Rezko had asked Obama to stop by at if he could fit a few minutes into his campaign schedule.

As the Democratic Party's presidential nominee, Barack Obama may find that his background with Rezko and other assorted colleagues in Chicago forms a deep mine of scandals to be examined, reexamined, and investigated anew. Just one photograph could create huge problems for Obama. Suddenly, a score of reporters would demand answers to whether Obama had granted any political favors in exchange for campaign contributions. New revelations about any of the donors discussed in this chapter could raise new questions. Why has Obama so firmly denied knowing much at all about these prominent Chicago wheelers and dealers from whom he has accepted campaign money?

"We have a sick political culture," Jay Stewart, the executive director of the Chicago Better Government Association, told ABC News, "and that's the environment that Barack Obama came from."[60] Obama has said he is disappointed by Tony Rezko and can return his campaign contributions or give the money to charity. But what Obama cannot erase is his record since 1995: he has overlooked Rezko's questionable activities to take money not just to finance his campaigns but to buy the mansion he feels his family deserves.

MEET REVEREND WRIGHT

*No, no, no. Not God Bless America, God damn
America.*

—REVEREND JEREMIAH WRIGHT,
"Confusing God and Government" sermon,
APRIL 13, 2003[1]

*In place of the white Jesus, we insisted that
"Jesus Christ is black, baby!"*

—JAMES H. CONE, *"Black Theology as
Liberation Theology"*[2]

On March 1, 2008, in an interview on Fox News's
Hannity & Colmes television show, Reverend Jeremiah
Wright got into a heated exchange with co-host Sean Hannity, charging that Hannity knew nothing about black-
liberation theology because he had not read the writings
of black theologians such as James H. Cone and Dwight
N. Hopkins. "How many books of Cone's have you read?"
Wright peppered Hannity with questions. "How many
books of Dwight Hopkins have you read?"[3]

This was an important exchange. Wright was insisting that the inflammatory remarks in his sermons at Trinity United Church of Christ, including the now-famous remark quoted above, derived from years of teachings that had coalesced into a comprehensive theology known as "black-liberation theology." In other words, Wright was arguing that as off-the-wall as statements from his sermons might sound when taken out of context, those statements were consistent with the teachings of prominent black-liberation theologians, including James Cone and Dwight Hopkins. Here Wright was correct in that we need to examine black-liberation theology itself in order to understand what he is preaching. Wright is not correct, however, when he suggests his sermons will be seen as less radical once we understand black-liberation theology.

Black-liberation theology is an inherently radical theology that owes its origin to radical black political thinkers, including Stokely Carmichael, Malcolm X, and Frantz Fanon. Deciding to be baptized in Trinity United Church of Christ, Barack Obama had to comprehend he was joining a church whose principles were based on the black-liberation theology Reverend Wright professes. If Obama was smart enough to get a Harvard law degree, he was smart enough to understand Trinity Church was and is a black-liberation theology church. When we read Wright's sermons in their entirety, and when we look at the black-liberation theology those sermons articulate, we see radical statements consistently flowing forth.

Thus Barack Obama's political problem in running for president in 2008 is that denouncing Reverend Wright is not enough. Obama will have to renounce black-liberation theology itself. However, Obama joined up with Wright and Trinity precisely because Wright's outspoken profession of black-liberation theology matched the radical political ideology Obama himself professed as a direct result of the lessons he had learned from his life experience. As we have seen in previous chapters, Obama's political consciousness developed in the footsteps of his father's anticolonial resentment against the British in Kenya. For this reason, Obama felt a personal identification with the revolutionary anticolonial writings of Frantz Fanon. In Chicago, Obama advanced his radical ideology by working for a community organization driven by the principles of socialist radical Saul Alinsky. In his autobiography, Obama openly tells us that when reading the black radicals and civil rights figures of the 1960s, including Martin Luther King, Jr., he found his greatest affinity with Malcolm X.

Obama may denounce Wright today because the reverend's radically outspoken statements and outlandish behavior are politically inconvenient to Obama's presidential run. Yet, again, Obama joined Trinity United Church of Christ not by accident but rather because the black-liberation theology spoke to who Obama was and what he believed was true. Yet, as we will see in this chapter, even when Father Pfleger's openly racist mocking of Hillary Clinton from the Trinity Church pulpit forced Obama to withdraw from the church for political reasons, Obama still resisted denouncing the church or its black-liberation theology.

Black-Liberation Theology

A core belief of black-liberation theology is that the historical Jesus Christ was black and, as such, he was oppressed by the ancient Romans, the white imperialists of their day who were then colonizing Israel. Black-liberation theologians see the biblical teachings of Jesus Christ as radical and revolutionary, delivering a social and political message that black people need to overthrow white imperial oppression in order to achieve liberation.

Black-liberation theology teaches that the African-Americans of today must worship a black Jesus and embrace his liberation teachings, this time to overthrow the oppression of the imperialist United States of America, a nation with a history of enslaving black people and colonizing them in modern ghettos of urban poverty.

Put simply, black-liberation theology reinterprets the biblical history and teachings of Jesus Christ to advance a revolutionary racial message.

James Cone, in his 1969 book *Black Theology and Black Power*,[4] attributes black-liberation theology to Stokely Carmichael and Charles V. Hamilton's own *Black Power: The Politics of Liberation in America*, published two years earlier.[5] Cone wrote that black power "means complete emancipation of black people from white oppression by whatever means black people deem necessary."[6] The methods "may include selective buying, boycotting, marching, or even rebellion." For Cone, black power meant "black freedom, black self-determination, wherein black people no longer view themselves as without human dignity but as men, human beings with the ability to carve out their own destiny." Cone comments that Stokely Carmichael was right in saying black power means "T.C.B.," or "Take Care of Business"—or, as Cone explained, "black folk taking care of black folks' business, not on the terms of the oppressor, but on those of the oppressed."

Cone argued there was a need for a black theology whose "sole purpose is to apply the freeing power of the gospel to black people under white oppression."[7] He added, "In more sophisticated terms this may be called a theology of revolution."[8] Cone taught that "Jesus' work is essentially one of liberation."[9]

Cone did not mean the historical Jesus was black in some figurative or symbolic way. Cone truly sought to establish that the historical Jesus of the Bible was black, not white. Jesus "was a Palestinian Jew whose racial ancestry may have been partly African but definitely not European," Cone wrote, rejecting the white Christian church's depiction of Jesus as a Caucasian. He argued that pictures of Jesus in Christian churches and homes "are nothing but an ideological distortion of the biblical portrait."[10] For Cone it was important to establish that the biblical Jesus was black because his liberation theology required that Jesus look "much more like oppressed blacks than white oppressors."[11]

Cone acknowledged that Frantz Fanon's *The Wretched of the Earth* drew his attention away from Europe, such that the consciousness of black-liberation theology came to center upon Africa.[12] He admits he was also influenced by theologians in South America and Latin America. In Brazil, he pointed out, there were more than 40 million blacks and in Latin America more than 70 million blacks. As such, Cone's black-liberation theology came to have a third-world revolutionary orientation. Cone combined the radical politics of anticolonialist Fanon with a vision of the Bible as liberation teachings of the historical Jesus, presenting Jesus as an African-Palestinian fighting the colonial oppression of ancient imperial Rome.

In *The Wretched of the Earth*, Fanon clearly taught a revolutionary socialist doctrine: "The colonized man finds his freedom in and through violence."[13] In his book on Martin Luther King, Jr., and Malcolm X, Cone discusses the 1960s birth of black-liberation theology, commenting, "During the time when the summer riots were a regular occurrence,

Black Power was on the lips of many young blacks, as they read Frantz Fanon's *Wretched of the Earth* and Malcolm's *Autobiography*."[14] While Cone admired Martin Luther King, Jr., believing King was becoming more radicalized just before he was assassinated, Cone ultimately rejected his nonviolent approach of Gandhi-like civil disobedience. Cone argued, "One cannot help but think that most whites 'loved' Martin Luther King, Jr., not because of his attempt to free his people, but because his approach was the least threatening to the white power structure."[15]

So, when Reverend Wright gives his sermons while dressed in African garb, he is consistent with the Afrocentric nature of black-liberation theology, just as he is when he rails against the United States as an imperial nation that engages in unjust foreign wars while oppressing its own black citizens. Wright has repeatedly defended himself by claiming that the provocative snippets repeatedly played on television are not representative of the speeches overall. Yet when we read the speeches, we come to understand that sound bites such as the infamous "God damn America" imprecation carry a black-liberation theme that the United States needs to be opposed to because we are an imperialist, colonizing nation; a white power elite oppresses black people as well as all third-world people of color.

In a Wright sermon titled "The Day of Jerusalem's Fall," given on September 16, 2001, only five days after 9/11,[16] Wright tries to turn the tables of 9/11 to portray the United States as the terrorist, not the hijackers. "We took this country by terror," Wright charges to the parishioners, "away from the Sioux, the Apache, the Arawak, the Comanche, the Arapahoe, the Navajo. Terrorism. We took Africans from their country to build our way of ease and kept them enslaved and living in fear. Terrorism." Wright continues, "We bombed Hiroshima, we bombed Nagasaki, and we nuked far more than the thousands in New York and the Pentagon and we never batted an eye." He then builds up to another line that has become a famous sound bite. He rails, "We have supported state terrorism against the Palestinians and black South Africans and now we are indignant because the stuff we have done overseas is now brought right back to our own front yards. America's chickens are coming home to roost."

Despite Wright's protestations to the contrary, the last thing Barack Obama should want is Wright's sermons played in their entirety to a national television audience, not unless Obama wants to explain why he remained a faithful member of the congregation and listened for some twenty years, with no apparent objection of any kind, to Wright's brand of virulent anti-American racial hatred that is central to black-liberation theology.

Malcolm X and "Chickens Coming Home to Roost"

The phrase "chickens coming home to roost" comes directly from Malcolm X. We might think that Malcolm X and Jeremiah Wright would have nothing in common, especially since Malcolm X was Islamic, a Black Muslim follower of Elijah Muhammad and the Nation of Islam, and Reverend Wright is a proponent of Christian black-liberation theology. But the two share a great deal in the belief "The enemy of my enemy is my friend." Black Muslims are as radically anti-American as the followers of black-liberation theology, sharing many ideas, principles, and phrases. Reading quotations from Malcolm X and Reverend Wright without being told who is the author of each, we might have difficulty telling them apart since the thoughts and the language of the two men are so much alike.

Malcolm X believed in Elijah Muhammad's teaching that white America must suffer a doomsday calamity and feel the full fury of God's wrath for unjustly inflicting a host of social and political ills on blacks, including slavery, segregation, poverty, and racial inequality. When John F. Kennedy was assassinated, Malcolm X, the featured speaker for a Black Muslim rally in New York City, answered a reporter's question by likening the assassination to "chickens coming home to roost." Reverend Wright adapted the phrase to imply that the terrorist attacks of 9/11 were divine retribution for white America's continuing racial injustice.

As a Black Muslim, Malcolm X embraced the idea that white people were devils and he rejected the United States as an oppressive society controlled by a white establishment. "No. I am not an American," Malcolm X told the congregation of the Cory Methodist Church in Cleveland on April 3, 1964. "I am not standing here speaking to you as an American, or a patriot, or a flag-saluter, or a flag-waver—no, not I! I'm speaking as a victim of this American system. And I see America through the eyes of the victim. I don't see any American dream; I see an American nightmare!"[17] As James Cone wrote, "Malcolm viewed the Nation [of Islam] as the 'divine solution' to the black people's sociopolitical oppression in America, countering Christianity's anti-black and pro-white ideology that fed the oppression of blacks."[18] As a Black Muslim, Malcolm X preached against integration with whites, seeing the whole idea of integration as just one more white ploy to keep blacks placated by holding out a false hope of equality that white people had no intention of ever fulfilling.

Malcolm X's critique of Christianity can be seen as establishing the intellectual basis for the formation of black-liberation theology and the substitution of black-liberation theology as the true alternative to an oppressive, white-dominated, false Christianity. "The greatest miracle Christianity has achieved in America is that the black man in white Christian hands has not grown violent," Malcolm X told radio audiences. "It is a miracle that 22 million black people have not *risen up* against their oppressors—in which they would have been justified by all moral criteria, and even by the democratic tradition!"[19]

As religion scholar C. Eric Lincoln explained in his classic study of the Black Muslims, the religion taught that the Original Man was the black man, with a history that was "coextensive with the creation of the earth."[20] The African-American was seen as a descendant of the Original Man of the Asian Black Nation and the tribe of Shabazz. The Black Muslims were the first to argue Jesus Christ was black and that the Black Man by nature is divine. Malcolm X preached, "Brothers and sisters, the white man has brainwashed us black people to fasten our gaze upon a blond-haired, blue-eyed Jesus! We're worshiping a Jesus that doesn't even look like us!" He drove home the point, arguing, "The blond-haired, blue-eyed white man has taught you and me to worship a white Jesus, and to shout and sing and pray to this God that's his God, the white man's God." This, Malcolm X insisted, was part of an elaborate social control plan in which the white establishment used white religion to promise blacks "to wait until death, for some dreamy heaven-in-the-hereafter, when we're dead, while this white man has his milk and honey in the streets paved with golden dollars here on earth!"[21]

Wright openly acknowledges his affinity for Black Muslims. "Louis Farrakhan is not my enemy," Wright told the National Press Club on April 28, 2008, defending himself against charges from the political right and increasing criticism from Barack Obama for his extreme statements. "He did not put me in chains. He did not put me in slavery. And he didn't make me this color."[22]

As we saw earlier, Obama said in his autobiography that Malcolm X and Frantz Fanon both had an impact on his intellectual development, aiding him in a search for identity that Obama resolved by embracing his African-American roots. It's clear that as a product of the radical racial politics of the 1960s and as the son of a Kenyan seeking to advance independence in Africa, Obama was intellectually and emotionally prepared to encounter and accept black-liberation theology.

It is easy to shift from a Malcolm X speech at the height of his Black Muslim days to a sermon from Reverend Wright at Trinity United Church of Christ. "The United States government has failed the vast majority of her citizens of African-American descent," Wright told the Trinity congregation, concluding a sermon titled "Confusing God and Government," which contained Wright's now-famous "God damn America" phrase. "Think about this, think about this. For every one Oprah, a billionaire, you've got five million blacks who are out of work," Wright continued. "For every one Colin Powell, a millionaire, you've got ten million blacks who cannot read. For every one Condoleezza Rice, you've got one million in prison."[23]

Thus Malcolm X and Wright both blamed whites, portraying blacks as victims of a white elite power structure. Their solutions were also similar, revolutionary in nature, requiring the wrath of God to be visited on earth, even though the God that Malcolm X had in mind was Allah and the God that Wright has in mind is Jesus Christ.

Wright neglects to mention that he should be placed in the privileged class. A Fox News investigation uncovered documents in March 2008 indicating that in retirement from his thirty-six years of ministry in Chicago, Wright was to move into a luxury home in a predominantly white, up-scale suburb of Chicago.[24] The newly constructed home was to be a 10,340-square-foot, four-bedroom mansion. According to Fox News, Trinity United Church of Christ had secured a $1.6 million mortgage for the home purchase and attached a $10 million line of credit to the house, for reasons unspecified in the paperwork.

Obama Decides to Be a Christian

Jerry Kellman, the Chicago-trained professional organizer who recruited Obama to Chicago to work in the Developing Communities Project, was known for using "[Saul] Alinsky's technique of extensively interviewing pastors and active church members to identify salient community issues, concerned residents and respected community leaders."[25] By the 1980s, Alinsky gravitated toward using community churches as focal points for his organizational efforts, knowing local churches had strong community ties, could provide the community organization with experienced, respected leaders, and offered a wide range of material resources that included office space, access to meeting rooms, and office machinery.[26] In explaining his success in organizing the Back of the Yards, Alinsky said, "The first thing I always do, is to move into the community as an observer, to talk with people and listen and learn their grievances and their attitudes." Moreover, the area was 95 percent Roman Catholic and so he recognized that "if I could win the support of the Church, we'd be off and running."[27]

After Kellman hired him, Obama followed Alinsky's rules by moving into the Hyde Park–Kenwood area he had been assigned to organize. Obama was not immediately drawn to seek out the African-American churches to assist him. In *The Audacity of Hope*, Obama explains at length that he "was not raised in a religious household."[28] His mother approached religion as the anthropologist she was. "For my mother, organized religion too often dressed up closed-mindedness in the garb of piety, cruelty and oppression in the cloak of righteousness," he wrote.[29] In his household, "the Bible, the Koran, and the Bhagavad Gita sat on the shelf alongside books of Greek and Norse and African mythology." As always, Obama insisted that "although my father had been raised a Muslim, by the time he met my mother he was a confirmed atheist, thinking religion to be so much superstition, like the mumbo-jumbo of witch doctors that he had witnessed in the Kenyan villages of his youth."[30]

Why did he decide to join Reverend Jeremiah Wright's controversial Trinity Church? Obama explained that his community organizing experience in Chicago forced him to realize "the fact that I had no community or shared traditions in which to ground my most deeply held beliefs."[31] Still, he openly admits, in terms Alinsky and Kellman would have easily understood, "I was drawn to the power of the African American religious tradition to spur social change."

The question then is this: Was Obama's decision to seek out an African-American church driven by his pragmatic need as a community organizer to have a base from which to relate to the community, or was it driven by a conversion experience, an epiphany in which Obama truly embraced Christianity out of faith and a change in heart and mind from his previously described indifference?

From his first conversation with Kellman, Obama was made to understand that he could not ignore the African-American church if he were to succeed as a community organizer. "Most of our work is with churches,"[32] Obama reported Kellman saying at their first meeting. "If poor and working-class people want to build real power, they have to have some sort of institutional base."[33] But even here Kellman displayed Alinsky-like pragmatism. "Churches won't work with you, though, just out of the goodness of their hearts," Kellman instructed Obama, in what Obama described as his job interview. "They'll talk a good game—a sermon on Sunday, maybe, or a special offering for the homeless. But if push comes to shove, they won't really move unless you can show them how it will help them pay their heating bill."[34]

Obama himself acknowledged the Alinsky-taught power of the church as a vehicle for community organization. Writing in 1990, Obama speculated, "Should a mere 50 prominent black churches, out of the thousands that exist in cities like Chicago, decide to collaborate with a trained organizing staff, enormous positive changes could be wrought in the education, housing, employment and spirit of inner-city black communities, changes that would send powerful ripples throughout the city."[35]

During his time with the Developing Communities Project, Obama did not join a church. It was not until near the end of this period of his life in Chicago, when he had already received his acceptance to attend Harvard Law School. Obama recalls the concerns raised by various pastors that he did not have his identity rooted in a church. "Had I heard the Good News?" they would ask him. "Do you know where your *faith* is coming from?"[36] A Reverend Philips was more direct. "It might help your mission if you had a church home," he admonished community organizer Obama. "It doesn't matter where, really. What you're asking from pastors requires us to set aside some of our more priestly concerns in favor of prophecy. That requires a good deal of faith on our part. It makes us want to know where you're getting yours from. Faith, that is."[37]

Why Did Obama Join Trinity?

New Republic senior editor Noam Scheiber considered this question and rejected a cynical answer, that Obama was a black politician who needed a home in a black church to gain credibility with his less educated, less affluent constituents. He also rejected a psychological explanation, namely that Obama, as a product of a racially mixed marriage, in which the black father was largely absent, sought in Wright the father and the identity he never had. Scheiber argued that neither explanation answers the important question of "why *this* particular church, *this* particular pastor."[38] Instead, Scheiber pointed to *Chicago Tribune* reporter David Mendell's biography of Obama, in which Mendell writes that Obama first noticed the church because Wright had placed a "Free Africa" sign out front to protest apartheid in South Africa. In Mendell's view, Wright had the needed combination of being less socially conservative and better educated than most of the ministers around Chicago. So, in choosing Wright, Mendell concluded, Obama found a counselor and monitor who could help Obama grapple with "the complex vagaries of Chicago's black political scene," as Obama "sought to understand the power of Christianity in the lives of black Americans."[39]

One shouldn't reject outright any of these explanations, including the cynical and psychological ones. To these we can add Obama's exposure to the Alinsky method, which taught the importance of churches in community organizing. Obama knew he needed a Chicago church if he were to advance in Chicago politics. Wright's involvement with black-liberation theology had to appeal to Obama's leftist thinking, influenced as it had been by radical thinkers including Frank Marshall Davis, Malcolm X, Frantz Fanon, and Saul Alinsky.

Now add one more factor: before Obama's baptism at Trinity, when he was nearly thirty years old, there is no other life incident evidencing he is a Christian. Obama had to know that running for political office, even state office, would be much more difficult to do if voters suspected he was a Muslim. While there is no evidence Obama has ever practiced Islam, other than people remembering he attended mosque with his stepfather in Indonesia, the most likely conclusion was that his faith was unimportant to him, or that he was an agnostic, maybe even an atheist. Yet once Obama became a member of Trinity, he had proof he was a Christian, as he professed to be.

None of us can look into his heart or read his soul. The best evidence we have to judge by is first, the record of what Obama has done, and second, what he has said about what he has done.

Obama also gives us a tantalizing clue. In introducing Reverend Wright in *Dreams from My Father*, Obama says in passing that Wright had dabbled with liquor, Islam, and black nationalism in the 1960s.[40] In the version of his sermon "Audacity to Hope," from which Obama got the title of his second book, Wright himself admits he was a Black Muslim for a time. "I was influenced by Martin King, yes, but there was this other guy named Malcolm, and I tried one brief time being a Muslim: 'As salaam alaikum,' ['Peace be with you']," Wright said in the sermon, "Anything but Christian."[41] If we wanted proof that Wright was ever a Black Muslim, this sermon gives us proof in Wright's own words. One wonders if Obama did not recognize himself in the reverend and his experiences, including Islam.

Black nationalism is a direct reference to Louis Farrakhan and the Black Muslims he leads. Although the Nation of Islam was founded in Detroit, the center of the movement had shifted to Chicago, another reason the Windy City and especially the South Side had become a focal point of black militant activity by the early 1970s. Obama, coming to the South Side as a community organizer, entered a site of turmoil between more militant black forces—led by the black power movement, the black-liberation theology movement, and the Black Muslims—and the dwindling residue of Martin Luther King's civil rights movement, characterized as it was by nonviolent action and civil disobedience. As a community organizer schooled in the methodology of Saul Alinsky, Obama would have felt this tension but still have been strongly attracted to the more aggressive approach.

In *The Audacity of Hope,* Obama reveals that a key factor in his decision to join Trinity was, somewhat oddly, that he did not necessarily have to be a believer. He wrote that "faith doesn't mean you don't have doubts, or that you relinquish your hold on this world."[42] He walked down the aisle of Trinity United Church of Christ and decided to be baptized only after he realized "that religious commitment did not require me to suspend critical thinking, disengage from the battle for economic and social justice, or otherwise retreat from the world I knew and loved." In clear and direct terms, Obama said his decision to become a Christian "came about as a choice and not an epiphany."[43]

This too, Alinsky—or Alinsky's admitted teacher, Machiavelli—would have understood: a calculated decision to position yourself favorably in the eyes of those you want to lead, whether you believe in the decision or not. It could easily have been added to Alinsky's *Rules for Radicals*. Or, as Machiavelli taught, "For the great majority of mankind are satisfied with appearance, as though they were realities and are often more influenced by the things that seem than by those that are."[44]

Obama's political career, in which he intended to apply the principles he had learned as a Saul Alinsky community organizer, ultimately demanded he associate himself with one African-American Christian church or another. The church Obama chose was a radical one, deeply identified with black-liberation theology—Trinity United Church of Christ, led by pastor Jeremiah Wright.

Ironically, Kellman's life turned out differently. After both he and Obama moved on from the Developing Communities Project, Kellman had a religious conversion experience that caused him to drop his Jewish faith and enroll in a Christian divinity school. After his life-changing experience, Kellman decided to leave community organizing. Or, perhaps more precisely, he decided to become religious and continue his community organizing from within the church, instead of trying to use the church from the outside.

Kellman took a job as the director of spiritual formation for several parishes in the Catholic Archdiocese of Chicago. When interviewed in 2007, Kellman was strong in expressing his own faith in Christ, but his understanding of Obama's faith appeared much more pragmatic. "With his strong bond in the African-American community in Chicago, Barack has been able to express his beliefs in a community drenched in religion," Kellman said. "We find God together as a people and Barack brings that faith perspective in finding God in the community. His church, Trinity United Church of Christ, has a strong sense of community as a whole."[45] In sharp contrast, Kellman says in the interview that he had a conversion experience, that he had a need to grieve and he was in denial until he accepted Jesus into his life. Kellman says nothing like this when he is asked why Obama decided to be a Christian.

Kellman's explanation of Obama's conversion was pure Alinsky—community social change is the end, faith is the means. Clearly, for Kellman and Obama, the ultimate political goal has always remained the same—to redistribute power and wealth from the haves to the have-nots, as openly articulated by Alinsky at the very beginning of *Rules for Radicals*. Kellman now pursues the goal through the church, while Obama pursues the goal through politics.

Obama Joins Farrakhan on the "Million Man March"

In a 1995 interview with the *Chicago Reader*, Obama acknowledged that he took time off that year from his first political campaign, for the Illinois state senate, to participate in Louis Farrakhan's Black Muslim–organized Million Man March in Washington, D.C.[46]

As pointed out by theologian Mattias Gardell in his study of Louis Farrakhan and the Nation of Islam, the black-liberation movement established numerous organizations for converting theory into practice, and co-opted demands that had characterized the classic black nationalists of the older liberation tradition. These included "demands for reparations, black self-determination, the construction of an independent black economy and education." These demands "were again voiced from the rostrums of the black churches" under black-liberation theology, as they were proclaimed by Louis Farrakhan as head of the Nation of Islam.[47]

Gardell also points out that the black-liberation theology movement caused a fissure in the black community, a distancing from more traditionally Christian black churches as represented by Reverend Jesse Jackson, who stands firmly in the tradition of Martin Luther King, Jr., and Booker T. Washington. The strength of Farrakhan and the Nation of Islam comes from "the prisons, the permanent poor, the urban youth, and—a category conspicuously absent in the church—black urban males."[48] Gardell correctly notes that the "vitality of black Islam is an integral part of contemporary black youth culture," evidenced in hip-hop culture, rap, and the symbolism of black urban gangs. Gardell, writing in the late 1990s, estimated there were fifty thousand gang members in Chicago, with ties to other black urban gang members throughout the United States.[49]

Farrakhan regularly tells black youth they are playing into the hands of the Devil with narcotics and drugs. "A climate is being created in America to kill all black people," Farrakhan has preached. "After you live in America and see evils that are going down, no black people are paranoid. We know that there is a plan being made ready to be used against our rise."[50] It's not a stretch to conclude that Reverend Wright's railing against the United States is in harmony with Farrakhan's.

In the 1983 black march on Washington, Farrakhan was permitted only a short speech, one of the shortest speeches on record for such events. In the 1993 march he was excluded altogether. In both instances, the objections came from Jewish groups that argued successfully that Farrakhan was an anti-Semite.[51] Unfortunately, there is justification for this concern. In a televised interview with Reuters on October 4, 1995, ten days before that year's scheduled march, Farrakhan said, "Many of the Jews who owned the homes, the apartments in the black community, we considered them bloodsuckers because they took from our community and built their community but didn't offer anything back to our community."[52] In a speech the previous year, Farrakhan had proclaimed, "The Jews don't like Farrakhan, so they call me Hitler. Well, that's a good name. Hitler was a very great man."[53]

In reaction to the rejection in the 1983 and 1993 marches, Farrakhan had decided he would organize his own 1995 Million Man March on Washington, as a Nation of Islam event. In direct contrast to the African-American marches on Washington that had been organized since 1963, when Martin Luther King, Jr., gave his famous "I Have a Dream" speech, the 1995 Million Man March was a Black Muslim event in which Farrakhan was positioned to be the star. The event was billed as a Day of Atonement and Reconciliation. In speaking to one of the largest African-American marches on the capital ever conducted, Farrakhan called for a voter registration drive aimed at registering eight million African-Americans to vote.[54]

When the 1995 *Chicago Reader* article surfaced in 2008, Obama supporters predictably tried to distance him from the Million Man March, arguing Obama had attended the event as an observer, not as a participant.[55] Still, Obama's reaction at the time was enthusiastic. "What I saw was a powerful demonstration of an impulse and need for African-American men to come together to recognize each other and affirm our rightful place in the society," he told the *Chicago Reader*. "There was a profound sense that African-American men were ready to make a commitment to bring about change in our communities and lives."

His only objections came from the perspective of a community organizer who had clearly embraced globalism and multiculturalism. "Any solution to our unemployment catastrophe must arise from us working creatively within a multicultural, interdependent, and international economy." Still, Obama was careful to make sure the interviewer did not take his comments as critical of the Million Man March. "This doesn't suggest that the need to look inward emphasized by the march isn't important, and that these African-American tribal affinities aren't legitimate," he added. "Historically, African-Americans have turned inward and towards Black Nationalism whenever they have a sense, as we do now, that the mainstream has rebuffed us, and that white Americans couldn't care less about the profound problems African-Americans are facing."[56]

A blogger known as Gateway Pundits[57] found an interesting detail in a biography of Louis Farrakhan posted on Biography.com: "In 1995, along with other prominent black leaders such as Al Sharpton and Barack Obama, Farrakhan helped lead the Million Man March on Washington."[58] Obama's supporters, who clearly want to move Obama as far away from Farrakhan as possible, will be certain to disavow that Obama had any leadership role in Farrakhan's 1995 march.

Reverend Jeremiah Wright was also there and coauthored a book on the Million Man March, in which he published a six-part sermon expressing what the march had meant to him. "It was a once in a lifetime, amazing experience," Wright wrote. "All who saw it were amazed. All who heard it were amazed, and all who experienced it were amazed. It was a feeling like no other feeling ever. It was a deeply spiritual feeling."[59]

In calling one million black men to Washington, D.C., in October 1995, Farrakhan said, "Once we get him [the black male] hooked up, once we get him wired up, once we get him fired up, then hand-in-hand, side-by-side as co-creators, he and 'sister girlfriend' can be inspired to make this world what God meant for it to be before white supremacy messed it up and got us mixed up, working *against* each other rather than *with* and *for* each other. Look at what God did! It was an amazing moment."[60]

Wright Went with Farrakhan to Visit Qaddafi in Libya in 1984

In 1984, Wright accompanied Farrakhan to Libya, where they met with Muammar Qaddafi. Referring to the relationship between Libya and the Nation of Islam, Mattias Gardell has commented, "Qaddafi has for many years been the Nation's most prominent supporter in the Islamic heartland and regularly has assisted the Nation of Islam whenever the need has arisen."[61] Farrakhan finds great affinity with the revolutionary Islamic socialism professed by Qaddafi. Gardell notes, "The mutual sympathy and appreciation between the Nation of Islam and the Libyan leadership began as a continuation of the friendly relationship that, to the annoyance of the CIA, was established between Elijah Muhammad and Qaddafi's first mentor, Gamal abd al-Nassar." In 1972, in a second tour of the Muslim world, Elijah Muhammad and a personal delegation that included boxer Muhammad Ali visited Libya as honored guests of state and met with Qaddafi.[62]

In the previous chapter, we established that Tony Rezko, the Chicago fixer who assisted Obama in buying his Georgian Revival home, got his start after studying engineering at the Illinois Institute of Technology, when he met Jabir Herbert Muhammad, the son of Elijah Muhammad. At that time,

Herbert was managing the boxing career of Muhammad Ali. Herbert Muhammad brought Rezko into his food services business, Crucial Concessions, Inc., which then had a contract with the Chicago park districts to sell food on the beaches and in many South Side Chicago parks. As his relationship with Herbert deepened, Rezko began putting together endorsement deals for Muhammad Ali. Later, he became the executive director of the Muhammad Ali Foundation, a group described as being devoted to the spread of Islam.[63]

In 1967, Muhammad Ali became a hero in the Black Muslim movement after he refused to serve in the U.S. military in Vietnam, a decision that cost him his boxing championship title and risked a jail sentence of up to five years in prison. In the 1970s, Muhammad Ali played a prominent role, along with Nation of Islam leaders, including Farrakhan, in negotiating financial aid for the Nation from Qaddafi.[64] In 1972, Libya provided an interest-free loan of $3 million, permitting the Nation of Islam to purchase what became their national center on Chicago's South Side.[65] Since then, Farrakhan has been able to call on Qaddafi to use Libya's oil revenue to assist the Nation through various financial hard times.

Gardell quotes Farrakhan as saying, "We've come back by the grace of God and the help of Brother Muammar Qaddafi. This is why we will always love him, admire him and respect him and stand up and speak on his behalf."[66]

What exactly Wright and Farrakhan accomplished in their 1984 visit to see Qaddafi in Libya has never been disclosed. Judging by the history of the relationship between the Nation of Islam and Qaddafi, we can safely speculate that at a minimum the meeting further affirmed the anti-American views that Black Muslims and black-liberation theology hold in common with Libya.

Wright himself has acknowledged the explosive nature of his visit to Libya, commenting that Obama's "Jewish support will dry up quicker than a snowball in hell" once his enemies learn of the 1984 trip he made with Farrakhan.[67]

Wright Remains Close to Farrakhan

In 2007, the *Trumpet Newsmagazine*, published by Trinity United Church of Christ, gave Louis Farrakhan an Empowerment Award. *Washington Post* columnist Richard Cohen objected, charging that for most Americans "Farrakhan epitomizes racism, particularly in the form of anti-Semitism," not the type of greatness an "Empowerment Award" would imply. Cohen wrote that over the years Farrakhan "has compiled an awesome record of offensive statements, even denigrating the Holocaust by falsely attributing it to Jewish cooperation with Hitler—'They helped him get the Third Reich on the road.' His history is a rancid stew of lies." Cohen dismissed as "a distinction without much of a difference" the point that the award was given by a magazine published by Wright's church and not by the church itself. He also disagreed that Obama, once told about the award, had no obligation to speak out and express his outrage. "Any praise of Farrakhan heightens the prestige of the leader of the Nation of Islam," Cohen wrote.[68]

Clearly, Obama supporters know how potentially radioactive the award to Farrakhan is to the Obama presidential candidacy. ABC News's Jake Tapper observed in March 2008 that all links to the *Trumpet Newsmagazine* had been removed from the website of the Trinity United Church of Christ.[69] Extensive Internet searches confirm that the church's website, including archived pages, appears to have been thoroughly scrubbed to erase any trace of the Farrakhan "Empowerment Award" fiasco.

Yet Wright's continued support of Farrakhan is apparent. On April 25, 2008, in a PBS interview with Bill Moyers, Wright admitted he has had a "long complicated relationship" with Farrakhan, adding this boast: "Louis Farrakhan is like E. F. Hutton. When Louis Farrakhan speaks, black America listens. They may not agree with him, but they're listening."[70]

Three days later, at the National Press Club in Washington, D.C., Wright repeated his praise, asking, "How many other African-Americans or European-Americans do you know that can get one million people together on the mall? He is one of the most important voices in the 20th and 21st century." Later, he told the press club and the national TV audience, "I am not going to put down Louis Farrakhan any more than Mandela would put down Fidel Castro."[71]

Reverend Wright's bodyguards that day were Black Muslims provided by Louis Farrakhan and the Nation of Islam.[72]

Obama Mismanages the Wright Controversy

When the controversy broke out over Reverend Wright's inflammatory sermons, Barack Obama's first strategy to control the damage was to deny he had been in church when Wright gave them. On March 14, 2008, Obama made this claim on the Huffington Post website: "The statements that Rev. Wright made that are the cause of this controversy were not statements I personally heard him preach while I

sat in the pews of Trinity or heard him utter in private conversation."[73] The denial tactic was in keeping with Obama's
first instinct when confronting controversy. Predictably, if
the controversy continued, Obama would move through his
repertoire of responses, moving step by step to disassociate
himself from Wright, trying to avoid having to repudiate
someone with whom he had maintained a long-term relationship prior to the criticism.

Denying he had been in church when the sermons
were given quickly turned out not to be a credible response. As we have demonstrated, the antiwhite, anti-
American statements Wright made in his sermons derive
directly from key tenets of black-liberation theology and
its roots in black power and Malcolm X. The Trinity
United Church of Christ website, before it was purged
of the more radical material, contained magazine issues,
church bulletin issues, and archived speeches from Wright
that proved the objectionable sermons were in keeping
with the general tone of the black-liberation theology that
guides the congregation and dominates Reverend Wright's
thinking.

Few could believe Obama sat in Trinity United Church
of Christ and was unaware of what black-liberation theology taught or the antiwhite, anti-American tenor of
Wright's speeches. Just to make clear no one missed the
Afrocentric nature of the church's teachings, Wright regularly gave his videotaped Sunday sermons in African costume, including colorful dashikis. Even the DVD videos
of Wright's past sermons that the church sold through its
website make clear that Wright delighted in being outlandish and that his statements attacking whites and con-
demning the United States were not exceptions, but rather
his rule.

Obama's denial spurred investigators to prove the contrary. On March 16, two days after Obama's denial appeared on the Huffington Post, new evidence emerged. NewsMax's Ronald Kessler reported that Obama had been in Trinity United Church of Christ on July 22, when Kessler was present.[74] Kessler claimed he and Obama both heard Wright preach a sermon that day in which the preacher blamed the "white arrogance" of America's Caucasian majority for the world's suffering, especially the oppression of blacks. The Obama campaign promptly posted a new denial, claiming Obama did not attend church services in Chicago on July 22.[75]

What the sequence proved was that Obama was in for a prolonged series of investigations and denials if he insisted on maintaining his story that he never personally heard Wright preach anything politically objectionable.

As the controversy continued, Obama shifted gears. On March 18, he delivered a major speech in Philadelphia, titled "A More Perfect Union."[76] Obama's strategy was to take the focus off Wright by locating the angry preacher in a dialogue on race that goes back to slavery but that we now have the opportunity to elevate to a new level and transcend. In a central part of the speech, Obama retracted his claim he had never heard Wright make the type of outlandish statements that were causing outrage. "Did I know him to be an occasionally fierce critic of American domestic and foreign policy? Of course," Obama told the national audience watching on cable television. "Did I ever hear him make remarks that could be considered controversial while I sat in church? Yes. Did I strongly disagree with many of his political views? Absolutely—just as I'm sure many of you have heard remarks from your pastors, priests, or rabbis with which you strongly disagreed."

The way Obama chose to condemn Wright made clear, even if indirectly, that he knew full well what Wright had been preaching. Obama said Wright's remarks "expressed a profoundly distorted view of this country—a view that sees white racism as endemic, and elevates what is wrong with America above all that we know is right about America; a view that sees conflicts in the Middle East as rooted primarily in the actions of stalwart allies like Israel, instead of emanating from the perverse and hateful ideologies of radical Islam."

How could Obama know these were the subjects of Wright's sermons unless he had heard them?

The problem Obama faces when he first denies anything about a controversy is that, later, when he has to admit he did know something he had earlier denied knowing, we can only conclude Obama's first instinct was to lie, or at least misconstrue the truth so as to engage in a cover-up. Both strategies, when finally exposed, backfire.

If Obama would lie that he had been in church to hear Wright's outrageous speeches, what else would he lie about? Perhaps Obama is lying about, or covering up, the full extent of his relationship with Bill Ayers? How about Tony Rezko? Is Obama lying there, too?

In refusing to disavow Wright in the Philadelphia speech, Obama interestingly attacked his grandmother, as we have observed earlier. "I can no more disown him," Obama said, referring to Wright, "than I can disown the black community. I can no more disown him than I can my white grandmother— a woman who helped raise me, a woman who sacrificed again and again for me, a woman who loves me as much as she loves anything in this world, but a woman who once confessed her fear of black men who passed by her on the street, and who on more than one occasion has uttered racial or ethnic stereotypes that made me cringe." Strangely, Obama seemed to be admitting that he himself harbored the same type of racial resentments Wright had been expressing for the twenty years Obama was a member of the congregation.

Obama Condemns Wright, but Still Stays in Trinity

On April 28, 2008, when Wright gave a speech and answered questions before a national cable news audience, Obama was forced to ramp up the denial. In a press conference the next day, Obama repeated his previous positions, including his claim he had not before heard Wright's outrageous statements, clearly contradicting his Philadelphia speech. "His comments were not only divisive and destructive," Obama said, beginning the press conference, "but I believe they end up giving comfort to those who prey on hate, and I believe that they do not portray accurately the perspective of the black church."[77]

To explain why he was denouncing Wright now, whereas he had not done so when the controversy began, Obama tried to argue that Wright's performance at the National Press Club was more outlandish than ever. "The person I saw yesterday was not the person I met twenty years ago," Obama said. "But when he states and amplifies such ridiculous propositions as the U.S. government somehow being involved in AIDS, when he suggests that Minister Farrakhan somehow represents one of the greatest voices of the 20th and 21st centuries, when he equates the United States wartime efforts with terrorism, then there are no excuses." Obama tried to say Wright's press club appearance was the last straw, that his statements "rightly offend all Americans. And they should be denounced. And that's what I'm doing very clearly and unequivocally here today."

As he concluded his prepared comments, Obama made

some remarks that suggested his real objection to Wright was not what Wright said, but that Wright was disrespecting him by trying to dominate the spotlight when Obama was trying to run for president. He objected that "this campaign has never been about me. It's never been about Senator Clinton or John McCain. It's not about Reverend Wright." Then he added, "And the fact that Reverend Wright would think that somehow it was appropriate to command the stage for three or four consecutive days in the midst of this major debate is something that not only makes me angry, but saddens me."

Finally, on April 28, appearing with Chris Wallace on Fox News Sunday, Obama commented on Wright, admitting, "I think that people were legitimately offended by some of the comments that he made in the past. The fact he's my former pastor I think makes it a legitimate political issue. So I understand that."[78]

With this interview, Obama came full circle, from his initial denials he knew anything about Wright's more outlandish statements to finally admitting that his twenty-year membership in Wright's congregation was a legitimate political issue. Still, Obama resisted making the ultimate decision to leave Trinity United Church of Christ. Obama's incremental approach to distancing himself from a variety of politically inconvenient associations in Chicago, including Wright, allows the issue to remain open, with the continuing liability the issue will rise once again, only to plague Obama in the general election to come.

By remaining a member of Trinity, Obama miscalculated that the church would give him no future problems. At his April 28 press conference, Obama said Wright's replacement, Reverend Otis Moss III, was a "wonderful young pastor" who promised a change in direction. But within a week, Moss gave a sermon at Trinity Church in which he referred to rap singer Ice Cube and his song titled "The wrong n-gga to f— wit." That song includes the lyrics "F— America, with the triple K," referring to the KKK. Ice Cube also uses the spelling "AmeriKKKa" to emphasize the point.[79] We assume Moss is a believer in black-liberation theology, since otherwise Wright would never have selected him to be his successor.

Father Pfleger, a Radical Catholic Priest, Enters the Scene

We soon discovered the ranks of Obama supporters include a white priest of a mostly black church who has links to Nation of Islam chief Louis Farrakhan and an apparently low level of tolerance for the Second Amendment. The supporter is Father Michael Pfleger, a white Roman Catholic priest who is the pastor of the predominantly African-American Saint Sabina Church on Chicago's South Side.

Pfleger was listed on Obama's 2008 presidential campaign website as one of the "people of faith" who endorse Obama's campaign. There is a photo of Pfleger and a testimonial in which he compares Obama to RFK: "I haven't heard anyone since Robert F. Kennedy who is causing such an emotional awakening to the political possibilities."[80]

According to the *Chicago Tribune*, Pfleger gave Obama political contributions of $1,500 between 1995 and 2001, including $200 in April 2001, about three months after Obama announced $225,000 in grants to Saint Sabina programs.[81] The newspaper quoted Pfleger as saying he made those donations personally, not on behalf of the church or to win grants. Another newspaper article, this one published in July 2007 in the *Christian Science Monitor*, quoted Pfleger as saying he has known Obama for over twenty years, since 1985, when Obama moved to Chicago "for a job organizing impoverished South Side residents in campaigns for jobs, schools, and housing."[82]

Pfleger's open support of Farrakhan is also easily documented. According to a Chicago television news report on May 25, 2007, Farrakhan returned to Saint Sabina following serious surgery for cancer to give a fiery hourlong speech to a packed congregation. "The 73-year-old Farrakhan's return to the church he visited many times before, seemingly as animated and energetic as ever, fulfilled a promise he'd made to its pastor, Father Michael Pfleger," said the story, written by local CBS reporter Jay Levine.[83] The CBS story included a video clip of Farrakhan's speech to the church; Pfleger can be seen accompanying Farrakhan into the church and sitting behind Farrakhan as the latter gives his speech from the pulpit.

Several examples of Pfleger's radical street protest politics are also fully documented and available for easy reference on the Internet. On May 29, 2007, Pfleger joined Jesse Jackson and his organization, Operation Push, in a protest in front of Chuck's Gun Shop in the Chicago suburb of Riverdale, threatening Second Amendment rights. According to TheCapitalFaxBlog.com, a well-read Chicago blog, Pfleger twice threatened to "snuff out" the shop's owner and threatened the same for legislators who oppose gun-control legislation. The blog said the comments went "way over the top," describing Pfleger's comments as a "threat."[84] For his comments in the antigun rally, Pfleger received a rebuke from the Archdiocese of Chicago's Cardinal Francis George, who said in a statement, "Publicly delivering a threat against anyone's life betrays the civil order and is morally outrageous, especially if this threat came from a priest."[85]

A video on YouTube.com of another protest speech by Pfleger shows his nighttime candlelit speech at Jackson

Square in New Orleans, Louisiana, on August 29, 2007, calling on President Bush to resign for having immorally invaded Iraq and abandoning the African-American community of New Orleans after Hurricane Katrina.[86]

Pfleger's resulting reputation is one of being an activist priest who involves himself directly in radical protest situations, giving speeches that suggest extreme, even violent political action. His endorsement on Obama's website described Obama as a kindred spirit, an activist in the tradition of RFK.

On January 16, 2007, on WBBM, a news talk radio station in Chicago, Pfleger expressed concern that Obama's high profile could make him a target for people not able to accept an African-American in power.[87] "I think Barack Obama is in a class of his own," Pfleger said. "I think he is the best thing that has come across the political scene since Bobby Kennedy." Pfleger continued with this theme. "When anybody comes along with that much hope, whether it's a Bobby Kennedy or whether it's a Martin Luther King Jr., they do become vulnerable," he said. "They become vulnerable because they tell the country and the world that we can be better and we don't have to accept what is. And unfortunately, we live in a world where not everybody wants it to be different."

That is why, he said, people should be concerned about Obama and his safety. "Do not touch this man," he said on air, "for if you do, you will answer to all of us."

Wright Charges United States Created AIDS Virus to Kill Blacks

One of Wright's more incendiary charges is that the United States made the AIDS virus intentionally, as part of a plan to kill African-American citizens.

On April 28, 2008, after delivering his speech at the National Press Club, Wright was asked about a claim he made in one of his sermons that the government had lied about inventing the HIV virus as a means of genocide against people of color.

Wright immediately referenced two books: Leonard Horowitz's *Emerging Viruses: AIDS and Ebola*[88] and Harriet Washington's *Medical Apartheid*.[89] Both books argue that the U.S. government has manufactured viruses to kill or experiment upon people of color. Wright also referenced the Tuskegee experiment, discussed below, as further "proof" of his argument, charging that "based on what has happened to Africans in this country, I believe our government is capable of doing anything."

Wright used an argument that we supplied Saddam Hussein with weapons of mass destruction. "In fact, one of the responses to what Saddam Hussein had in terms of biological warfare was a non-question, because all we had to do was check the sales records," he said. "We sold him those biological weapons he was using against his own people. So any time a government can put together biological warfare to kill people, and then get angry when those people use what we sold them, yes, I believe we are capable."

Reverend Wright is fairly deficient on proof. Yes, the Tuskegee Institute medical experiment was a disgrace. In 1933, the U.S. Public Health Service in Macon County, Alabama, decided to study African-Americans who already had syphilis. The scandal was that African-Americans in the test were denied informed consent and were not told medical treatments were intentionally withheld from them. However, there is no evidence that the U.S. government contaminated African-Americans in the Tuskegee experiment with syphilis.

Wright's charge that the U.S. government created the AIDS virus and infected African-Americans with AIDS in order to commit genocide is a highly inflammatory but totally unsubstantiated allegation.

Cliff Kincaid, editor of the Accuracy in Media Report, and president of America's Survival, Inc., has traced the AIDS allegation to a Soviet-era disinformation campaign concocted by the KGB to divert attention from their own biological weapons program.[90] Kincaid references an Associated Press report published in the *New York Times* in 1987, in which three Soviet scientists disavowed charges in the Soviet-sponsored press that the AIDS virus was artificially cultivated at a secret American military base.[91]

Kincaid's research further reveals that the AIDS claim was picked up by the Nation of Islam's newspaper, the *Final Call*, which quoted Horowitz's book to echo Farrakhan's concern that AIDS was a genocidal population control plan launched against blacks by whites.[92] Once again Wright and Farrakhan were in agreement.

On February 25, 2008, Farrakhan publicly endorsed Obama for president, telling a crowd of twenty thousand at the Nation of Islam annual convention in Chicago's McCormick Place, "We are witnessing the phenomenal rise of a man of color in a country that has persecuted us because of our color." Farrakhan spoke of Obama as if he had nearly mystical powers, saying, "If you look at Barack Obama's audiences and look at the effect of his words, those people are being transformed from what they were. This young man is the hope of the entire world that America will change and be made better."[93]

Obama's campaign quickly made clear that the senator had not sought Farrakhan's endorsement.

Still, Obama's association with Farrakhan goes back to

his participation in the Million Man March. And Farrakhan and Wright appear to be largely in agreement ideologically, even though Farrakhan believes in Allah and Wright professes belief in Christ. Moreover, Farrakhan appears to have a close association with many of the non-Muslim clergy close to Obama, including Father Pfleger.

Concern over these issues may not have swayed Democratic voters in the primaries, since many Democrats voting in the primaries were as radically to the left as Obama, or possibly even further. In the general election, when the broad base of voters across the political spectrum is truly engaged, these controversies may take on a whole new life.

Millions of American voters who did not care what candidate the Democratic Party advanced for president in 2008 will suddenly start to care when it comes time for them to get serious about their vote in the general election.

Father Pfleger Gives a Sermon Mocking Hillary Clinton

On Thursday, May 29, 2008, World Net Daily's Aaron Klein broke a story that Father Pfleger had given a sermon the previous Sunday at Trinity Church in which Pfleger implied Hillary Clinton was a white supremacist who believed she would win the Democratic presidential nomination because of "white entitlement." World Net Daily embedded a video of Pfleger's speech into the headline story.[94]

Beginning the 3-minute-and-45-second video, Reverend Moss welcomes Pfleger to the congregation, saying, "He is a friend of Trinity; he is a brother beloved; he is a preacher par excellence; he is a prophetic, powerful pulpiteer; he is our friend; he is our brother."

Pfleger then takes the handheld microphone at the pulpit and begins his sermon softly and dramatically. "You must be honest enough to expose white entitlement and supremacy wherever it raises its head. I've said before and I really don't want to make this political, because you know I'm very unpolitical."

Here, Pfleger was interrupted by appreciative laughter from the congregation.

"But, Reverend Moss, when Hillary was crying and people said that was put on, I really don't believe it was put on. I really believe that she just always thought, 'This is mine.'"

Pfleger was referring to the incident that occurred during the New Hampshire primary, when Hillary Clinton's emotions erupted into tears in a scene captured by news cameras.

The congregation responded with applause.

Pfleger resumed, quoting Hillary in some invented quotations. "'I'm Bill's wife. I'm white and this is mine. I just got to get up and step into the plate.' And then out of nowhere came, 'Hey, I'm Barack Obama.'"

As Pfleger built his story, his voice grew in loudness and intensity. He began moving around in the pulpit, his voice amplified by the handheld microphone. The congregation's reaction in the background sounded increasingly excited, responding enthusiastically to his words and expressions.

"And she said, 'Oh, damn. Where did you come from?'" Pfleger continued, inventing more dialogue for Hillary. "'I'm white. I'm entitled. There's a black man stealing my show.'"

By the time Pfleger finished this section, he was gesturing profoundly, his voice was more intense, almost shouting, and his expressions were animated.

He paused and began acting out loud sobs, mocking

Hillary crying by wiping fake tears from his eyes with a handkerchief.

The congregation applauded loudly, appearing to love the scene Pfleger was enacting before them. The video camera panned the church to show the congregation on their feet, applauding.

"She wasn't the only one crying," Pfleger continued. "There was a whole lot of white people crying."

The tape ends with Moss shaking Pfleger's hand and congratulating him. "We thank God for the message and we thank God for the messenger," Moss said as he took the microphone from Pfleger and assumed the pulpit himself. "We thank God for Father Michael Pfleger. We thank God for Father Mike."

Within hours of Aaron Klein's article's appearing on World Net Daily, Sean Hannity was featuring the audio from Pfleger's sermon on his nationally syndicated radio talk show. That evening the Fox News *Hannity & Colmes* television show devoted a segment to showing the video. By the next day, Friday, May 30, the story had swept the Internet and was being featured by Rush Limbaugh on his nationally syndicated radio talk show.

The video was particularly damaging not just for Pfleger's obviously racist remarks, but for the clear enthusiasm with which Reverend Moss and the Trinity congregation embraced his sermon. The video left no doubt that black rage was not a problem confined to Reverend Wright, but was at the core of black-liberation theology and would continue to find expression under the leadership of Reverend Moss.

Obama issued a typical first response, saying he was "deeply disappointed" in Father Pfleger's "divisive, backward-looking rhetoric."[95] This was not good enough for Clinton's spokesman Howard Wolfson, who said, in turn, "We remain disappointed that Senator Obama did not specifically reject Father Pfleger's despicable comments about Senator Clinton."[96]

For Obama, the damage control had only begun.

Obama Leaves Trinity Church

On Saturday night, May 31, 2008, campaigning in Aberdeen, South Dakota, Obama held a surprise news conference and announced he was leaving Trinity after "the recent episode with Father Pfleger."[97]

In his prepared statement, Obama made it clear his decision was based primarily on considerations of political expediency. "We don't want to have to answer for everything that's stated in a church," Obama said directly. When questioned whether he was renouncing the church, Obama stopped short of doing so. "I am not denouncing the church," he answered. "I am not interested in people who want me to denounce the church, because it's not worthy of denouncing." What Obama meant by saying the church was not worthy of denouncing was unclear. What was clear was that Obama was still trying to justify his twenty-year membership at Trinity.

Obama implied that he was being treated unfairly in that the segments of sermons played in the media were "caricatures of the church," complaining that anyone would "accept those caricatures despite my insistence that's not what the church is about." Still, he had to admit, "Well, look, there's no doubt that had Reverend Wright's controversial statements not surfaced, then this would not have been a prominent issue." He also persisted in distancing himself from Wright, "And I have said before, I think that some of the statements that he [Wright] made were indefensible and deeply offensive."

Clearly, Obama hoped that by leaving the church, he would end the controversy. At a minimum, he wanted to be able to wash his hands of any subsequent incidents coming from Trinity's pulpit. Yet, by not denouncing Wright, Pfleger, and Trinity Church itself, Obama remains open to continuing criticism as further incidents develop. Fundamentally, Obama knows he chose Trinity in full awareness of how radical the church's theology truly is. But Obama is in a dilemma. If he denounces black-liberation theology, he will appear to be a sellout to many of his more radical African-American supporters.

Moreover, by leaving Trinity Church only after the Pfleger episode added fuel to the fire, Obama displayed himself once again to be a typical politician whose decisions derive from political expediency. Dumped is the church where Obama was baptized and married, and his children were baptized, simply because the national media exposure of the theology preached in the church proved a political embarrassment to Obama's presidential campaign. Poll numbers, not principle or deeply felt religious belief, explained entirely Obama's "Saturday Night Massacre," in which he dumped Father Pfleger, Reverend Moss, and Trinity United Church of Christ, just as he had dumped Reverend Wright a few weeks earlier.

Obama needed a Christian church in order to succeed in Chicago politics. He selected Trinity because it best matched his personal and political feelings. Then he dumped the entire relationship when it got in the way of his presidential ambitions.

PART THREE

THE CANDIDATE
IS THE MESSAGE

Sir, you have to give me his [Obama's] legislative accomplishments. You support him for president. You are on national television. Name his legislative accomplishments, sir. Can you name anything he has accomplished, sir?

—CHRIS MATTHEWS, MSNBC, FEBRUARY 19, 2008[1]

The idea wasn't to have him bowl. The idea was to have him go to a bowling alley.

—DAVID AXELROD, APRIL 3, 2008[2]

David Axelrod, Obama's chief strategist, has crafted a campaign centered on Obama's personality. But how solid is this veneer? Will charisma be sufficient to put Obama in the White House, or will John McCain force Obama and his surrogates to come forth to debate the issues?

If the 2008 presidential campaign becomes a campaign of issues, Obama may find that field as challenging as a bowling alley, given the limited experience he has had in the national political arena. Can Obama win on the issues?

These are the key concerns we will examine in this last section of the book.

What Accomplishments?

In a remarkable segment on MSNBC's *Decision '08* show on February 19, 2008, Chris Matthews badgered Texas state senator Kirk Watson to name one specific legislative accomplishment Watson could attribute to Barack Obama as a U.S. senator.

Watson dodged the question, asserting that Obama's goal was really to bring hope to the American people. "He has been about building coalitions, like we've not seen in a long time, and being able to throw away some of these contrived labels that tend to divide us, and bring us together," Watson argued. "And you're seeing that kind of excitement, tonight in Houston, Texas, earlier today in San Antonio, you saw how he is able to bring a large group of people together that is excited and working to make sure he gets elected president."

That prompted Matthews to ask Watson pointedly if he was "a big Barack supporter." When Watson affirmed he was, Matthews launched into an even more petulant demand that Watson list some of Obama's accomplishments as U.S. senator. Watson offered a weak response: "Well, you know, what I can talk about is more what he is offering the American people right now . . ." Matthews reminded Watson he was on national television and again demanded he list at least one Obama accomplishment in the U.S. Senate. Watson, clearly embarrassed, finally had to admit, "No, I'm not going to be able to do that tonight." The sequence ended with Watson trying to shift the ground of the discussion by asserting, "I think one of the things Senator Obama does is inspires."

Matthews had moved in like a shark going for a kill, rudely harassing Watson. Yet, in the process, he succeeded in exposing Obama as "an empty suit," long on rhetoric and short on established political deeds. Matthews, a Democratic Party cheerleader at heart, later turned on Hillary. The sequence with Watson probably would never have happened after Matthews himself succumbed to Obama-mania.

Obama Can't Bowl

On March 29, 2008, preceding the Democratic primary in Pennsylvania, another incident reinforced the impression that Obama was truly an Ivy League elitist out of place among middle Americans. Obama made a routine campaign stop in Altoona, a middle-class industrial town in central Pennsylvania with about fifty thousand residents that has struggled as globalism has outsourced jobs overseas. The stop was like hundreds of others the senator had made in months of primary campaigning. This one, however, was at a bowling alley.

For some reason, Obama decided to take off his suit jacket, roll up his shirtsleeves, rent some bowling shoes, and bowl. He was dreadful. Writing for the *Chicago Tribune*, Eric Zorn estimated Obama had a score of 53, extrapolated from his seven-frame total of 37.[3] Zorn commented Obama's score was "pathetic," especially when the throwing motion involved in bowling is "both simple and intuitive," such that "a strong, coordinated adult ought to be at least mediocre—scoring at least 80—in his first game." What's worse, the television news cameras were there to record the event. Throughout the rest of the day, televisions from coast to coast showed Obama rolling one gutter ball after another.

When the media caught up with David Axelrod, he was clearly perturbed, explaining the idea was never to have Obama bowl. "Apparently some advance person decided it would be a good idea to have him roll a game," Axelrod groused to the *Tribune*.

The Candidate Is the Message

Axelrod would have been well advised to grab his copy of Marshall McLuhan's classic book, *Understanding Media*, so he could reread the section on politicians and television.

Writing in 1964, McLuhan commented on an appearance Richard Nixon made on the Jack Paar show on March 8, 1963. Paar, realizing Nixon was both a pianist and a composer, brought a piano onstage and invited Nixon to play, with excellent effect. As McLuhan concluded, "Instead of the slick, glib, legal Nixon, we saw the doggedly creative and modest performer." McLuhan perceived that the media of television was perfect to allow a piano-playing Nixon to come across to the viewing public as softer, more human, and therefore more accessible to the average person. "A few timely touches like this would have quite altered the result of the Kennedy-Nixon campaign," McLuhan correctly concluded.[4]

McLuhan advised, "TV is a medium that rejects the sharp personality and favors the presentation of processes rather than of products." This, Axelrod knew. For Axelrod, Obama's inexperience and lack of accomplishments were not a problem, precisely because Axelrod never planned to run a "product campaign" in which Obama would be packaged as a series of policy issues. Axelrod's entire political career is based on avoiding issues, just so he can package candidates as "processes," with catchy phrases like "Yes, We Can," or lofty slogans like promising "Change We Can Believe In."

The bowling incident was brief, but the error was major, especially for Axelrod, a "campaign strategist" with a reputation for constructing campaigns where the image is everything. If McLuhan became famous for saying "the medium is the message," Axelrod's strategizing in Obama's 2008 run for the White House could easily be branded with the slogan "The Candidate Is the Message." That is how Axelrod strives to craft his campaigns. As we will see, an Axelrod campaign is a campaign of personality, not a campaign of issues.

Who Is Barack Obama?

If the candidate is the message, then who is Obama and how does Axelrod plan to communicate that message to voters in the general election?

In a nation where the majority of the voters remain center-right politically, Obama can expect an uphill battle on the issues, which is the fight McCain plans to wage in the general election contest. Axelrod knows this, which is why he wants to run what in the movie industry would be called a "high-concept" campaign. In the next chapter we will see whether David Axelrod's political messaging skills and Barack Obama's natural political talents are up to the challenge of winning a presidential campaign whose foundation includes a cult of personality.

If McCain succeeds in shifting the 2008 presidential context to a campaign of issues, can Obama successfully move to the political center? An adage of American presidential politics has been that candidates must move to the political center to win. But if Obama tries to move to the center, will he risk losing the base of left-leaning Democratic Party activists who promoted him over Hillary Clinton in the 2008 primaries?

In the final two chapters of this book, we will find out what Obama's past accomplishments and his votes as an Illinois state senator and U.S. senator tell us about his positions on key issues. Then, we will ask how Axelrod and Obama plan to deliver their message of "change," both in domestic and foreign policy specifics, around these issues. Can Obama win a majority of the voters in the general election if the campaign turns into a debate about public policy alternatives?

Rather than focus on every possible question of public policy likely to be debated in the 2008 presidential campaign, we are going to focus on those key areas where Obama's past positions are likely to be "show stoppers" for important segments of the general election voters whom Obama can't afford to lose.

THE CULT OF PERSONALITY

We all know Obama's style, his regal, visionary bearing, his above-the-fray persona, his inspired—and, give him his due, inspiring—performances, his "Audacity of Hope," and his hypnotic, upbeat, unifying message. He is skilled. If we were voting for a chief motivational speaker or a political "American Idol," even I'd be on board.

—Abraham Katsman, *Jerusalem Post*,
April 3, 2008[1]

How has Obama positioned himself to pull off winning the presidency in 2008? To begin the analysis, we are going to focus on the campaign modus operandi of his chief strategist, David Axelrod. Axelrod's strategy is to win elections by promoting the personality of the candidate, not issues. In other words, Axelrod selects clients around whom he believes he can promote a cult of personality, with an emphasis long on lofty themes pointing to the future and short on content. Axelrod's claim to fame in Bill Clinton's successful 1996 presidential reelection was that he coined the phrase "Bridge to the Twenty-First Century."[2] Whether even Bill Clinton had any clear idea what that meant in terms of specific public policy objectives is still debatable.

Meet David Axelrod, Obama's Image Master

David Axelrod was born to Jewish parents on New York City's Lower East Side in 1955, making him six years older than Obama.

His mother, Myril Axelrod, was a writer for *PM*, a leftist tabloid newspaper published in New York City from 1940 to 1948. *PM* was founded by Ralph McAllister Ingersoll, described in his obituary as the John L. Lewis of journalism, and who "thought that he could use the Communists to achieve his ambitions as a liberal newspaper editor and publisher."[3] Among the communist sympathizers hired by *PM* was I. F. Stone, who became the newspaper's Washington correspondent. In the 1990s, Stone's reputation was posthumously rocked (he died in 1989) when a retired KGB agent said he had been a paid agent of the Soviet Union.[4] While probably never on the Soviet payroll as a spy, Stone was often accused of being a "fellow traveler" who willingly assisted Soviet KGB agents in the United States for free.[5] Leftist writer Earl Conrad, who wrote for *PM*, also wrote for another leftist newspaper, the *Negro Story*, as did Frank Marshall Davis. This was the same Davis we discussed earlier, the communist journalist and poet who ended up in Hawaii, a mentor to young Barack Obama in his rebellious years of marijuana, cocaine, and liquor in the 1970s. Frank Marshall Davis in his autobiography discusses Marshall Field III, the Chicago department store king who funded both *PM* and the Lincoln School in Chicago, where Davis taught.[6]

Even this quick history shows that Axelrod and Obama both have roots in the leftist political environment of the 1940s, one dominated by literary intellectuals who were comfortable with self-proclaimed communists in their midst. Axelrod and Obama were also both indirectly affected by the McCarthyism that tore apart the lives of sensitive souls such as Frank Marshall Davis.

In other words, Axelrod and Obama understood this socialist milieu, not because they lived it themselves, but because they were raised or mentored by people who did experience it. Both Axelrod and Obama grew up to be liberals committed to the emergence of African-Americans, not only within the Democratic Party, but within America, even at the highest levels of power.

It remains to be seen whether Axelrod and Obama are showing up at the right moment historically to run for president, or if they are foreshadowing an emergence of African-Americans in national U.S. politics that is sure to come. To a large degree this will depend on whether Obama's image as managed by Axelrod can be made to appear sufficiently mainstream that his truly radical political views do not disqualify him from holding the presidency, and the power he and Axelrod both aspire to attain.

As we have noted before, American voters may be ready to elect an African-American to the White House, but it is much less likely they will be equally ready for a politically radical African-American to succeed.

In 1977, after graduating from college, Axelrod decided he would stay in Chicago, where he took a job as a young reporter on the city desk of the *Chicago Tribune*. In 1984 he worked as communications director for the campaign of U.S. senator Paul Simon and in 1985 formed Axelrod & Associates to work as a political consultant. In 1987, he worked on the successful reelection campaign of Chicago mayor Harold Washington. For a few years, Axelrod focused on mayoral campaigns, always working for Democrats, specializing "in packaging black candidates for white voters."[7] In 2004, he worked on the failed presidential campaign of John Edwards. Then, in 2006, he consulted with Eliot Spitzer in his New York gubernatorial campaign.

In addition to his political consulting firm, Axelrod is also a partner in AKP&D Message & Media, a Chicago-based media/public relations firm that works for corporate clients, including Cablevision and AT&T.[8] The firm sets up front organizations for corporations that want to run "public interest" ads without having the ads identified as paid for by the corporations. The practice is known in the industry as "astro-turfing," the simulation of grassroots support for a public interest concern when the grassroots support probably does not exist at all. The trick is intentionally to mask the truth that the corporation itself has sponsored the front organization paying for the "public interest" ad.

BusinessWeek cited as an example a television commercial Axelrod's firm created for ComEd, or Commonwealth Edison, the largest electric utility in Illinois. The ad warned that a ComEd bankruptcy and blackouts could occur unless a rate hike was approved. The ad was sponsored by CORE, which described itself as "a coalition of individuals, businesses and organizations." After a complaint was filed with state regulators, ComEd was forced to admit it had bankrolled the entire $15 million effort.[9] From this, we can conclude Axelrod's enthusiasm for public relations packaging is not heavily dependent upon moral standards, including truth.

Interestingly, Obama, Axelrod, and Obama's grandfather all have something in common: all three suffered suicides in their immediate families.

- Axelrod's father, a psychologist, was divorced from Axelrod's mother when he shot and killed himself in a Manhattan studio apartment. At the time, Axelrod was nineteen years old, a junior at the University of Chicago.

- Obama's father killed himself driving drunk in Nairobi, having failed to advance his career in the Kenyan government bureaucracy where he had worked as a Harvard-trained economist. To be precise, Obama Senior was killed in a car accident, but his pattern of drinking and driving had resulted in a number of very serious car accidents, such that the behavior was at least arguably suicidal. At the time, Obama was a student at Columbia University, living in New York City. Obama begins his autobiography, *Dreams from My Father,* with a scene where he gets a phone call in his New York City apartment from his half-sister Auma in Kenya, who tells him their father is dead.

- In 1926, Ruth Armour Dunham, the mother of Obama's grandfather, Stanley Armour Dunham, shot herself, committing suicide at the age of twenty-six. Obama's grandfather was eight years old at the time and he was the one who discovered his mother's body. Ruth Dunham evidently had fallen into despair after her husband abandoned the family.

We have seen that in his autobiography Obama himself makes it clear he is seeking to resolve his search for identity in his consciousness as an African-American. As we just saw, Axelrod has developed his political consulting career with a specialty in "packaging" African-American candidates to be acceptable to white voters.

All these factors predisposed Axelrod and Obama to understand each other when they met and to be matched perfectly to work together.

JFK, Axelrod's Predictable Hero

Axelrod tells interviewers his political heroes are John and Robert Kennedy. Axelrod likes to tell reporters an apocryphal story about when he saw JFK campaigning in Stuyvesant Town, when Axelrod was five years old. As the tale goes, it was October 27, 1960, twelve days before the presidential election, and JFK was holding a series of rallies throughout New York City. Young Axelrod was lifted on top of a mailbox to witness a scene that he tells reporters is "indelibly etched in his memory," a phrase reminiscent of how Senator John Kerry has described his recollection that President Nixon ordered him into Cambodia in December 1968, one month before Nixon had taken the oath of office.

Axelrod is then quoted as saying, "I remember the excitement. I remember the sense that something really important was happening. I remember being intrigued that all this was being caused by the presence of this guy."[10] Whether Axelrod truly realized all this at five years old, we have no way of knowing. What is clear, however, is that the adult Axelrod has projected onto the experience a conclusion that personality in politics is paramount.

Obviously, the five-year-old Axelrod did not know that JFK was running as a foreign policy hawk, charging Republican president Eisenhower with having allowed our Soviet communist enemies to develop a "missile gap" that put the United States in military jeopardy.

Axelrod has also told the *New York Times* that his model

for the Obama presidential campaign of 2008 is the successful 2006 gubernatorial campaign of Deval Patrick in Massachusetts.[11] Axelrod was responsible for framing Patrick's political message for the campaign. The *Times* noted the many ways in which the Patrick and Obama campaigns are similar: "the optimism, the constant presence of the candidate's biography, the combination of a crusading message of reform with the candidate's natural pragmatism, the insistence that normal political categories did not apply, even the same, unofficial slogan, shouted from the crowds—'Yes, We Can!'"[12] What Axelrod fails to note in interviews is that voter satisfaction with Governor Deval Patrick in Massachusetts has reached lows not seen in the commonwealth since Governor Michael Dukakis in the 1980s.

In the *Nation*, leftist journalist Christopher Hayes argues that Axelrod's campaign message for Obama in 2008 can be reduced to one word—"hope."[13] Hayes writes that Axelrod wants to avoid the rancor of the culture wars, preferring to express themes that suggest the possibility of "a new kind of politics" to be found in "a politics of consensus," avoiding the "wedge issues" that typically characterize a whole series of divisions, including black-white, pro-choice–pro-life, and red state–blue state. Hayes acknowledges the technique is adapted for a client like Obama, who, despite his Harvard Law pedigree, has a biography that can be cast into an "up-by-the-bootstraps" drama, with overtones of having overcome racial prejudice. Besides, one might add, Obama has the looks and rhetorical skills to play the showman in an Axelrod campaign emphasizing personality.

In an interview with the *New York Times*, Axelrod explained, "But I think that in a sense Barack is the personification of his own message for this country, that we can get past the things that divide us and focus on the things that unite us. He is his own vision."[14] We get the point.

Axelrod—No Karl Rove

Axelrod's official title is "chief strategist," not campaign manager. But if Axelrod aspires to be Obama's Karl Rove, he's missing an important dimension: in Texas, when George W. Bush was running for governor, Rove was known for his commanding knowledge of voters and voting statistics. Rove, in direct contrast to Axelrod, is a numbers guy, not an image maker. Even in the 2008 campaign, when Rove appears on television as a Fox News contributor, his knowledge of each state, in many cases down to the county, or in some cases even down to the ward and precinct level, is remarkable. Rove spends his time comprehending how policy issues impact voters. Rove is a quantitative analyst who counts votes, whereas Axelrod can be seen as a qualitative thinker who paints impressions with words, hoping the images will translate into votes.

What Rove knows, and Axelrod may yet find out, is that general election campaigns are about issues. We hold campaigns because voters do change their votes, because of issues and how they are debated. In the Democratic primary campaign, Obama had a clear weakness facing Hillary Clinton in a one-on-one debate. Why? The answer is simple. Axelrod has focused 100 percent of Obama's campaign on a cult of personality, in an attempt to transcend issues.

At a deeper level of this subject is a crucial truism about politics: regardless of what words are used in campaigns, politics never transcends issues, at least not since Aristotle first wrote his books on politics. We are political animals first and foremost, as Aristotle taught. In politics we are not reducible to New Age McLuhanesque consumers of subliminal messages shaped by the clever manipulation of media, even if these images influence us. At the end of every rhetorically uplifting speech Obama gives about the future of hope, millions of listeners are still left pondering, "Now, what exactly did he say?" If the politician is the message, as Axelrod and Obama have proclaimed, they can't forever avoid telling us what precisely that message is.

Obama "Conversions"

A new tongue-in-cheek Internet blog, titled "Obama Messiah Blogspot," opens with the question "Is Barack Obama the Messiah?"[15] A quote is provided from a speech Obama gave in Lebanon, New Hampshire, in January 2008: "A light will shine through that window, a beam of light will come down upon you, you will experience an Epiphany . . . and you will suddenly realize that you must go to the polls and vote for Obama."

The creator of the website, Christopher Blosser, says, "My hope is the media will work through its childish infatuation with Obama." Thus he suggests a serious purpose behind his satiric website.[16] Blosser, a web designer by profession, describes himself as a political independent that leans somewhat conservative. "While less than satisfied with John McCain, I'd honestly prefer him to either of the alternatives," Blosser admitted.

"Overall, the site is intended to be parody," he acknowledged. "But at the same time I hope the website will provoke some of Obama's more ardent disciples among the masses and, sadly, the media, to reevaluate their behavior."

Under the heading of "Conversions," the website lists numerous well-known figures who have represented Obama in larger-than-life terms. For example, New Age luminary Deepak Chopra claimed in a January 5, 2007, op-ed piece on the Huffington Post that "the X factor which sets Barack Obama aside as a unique candidate is his hard-won self-awareness."[17] In keeping with title of the piece, "Obama and the Call: 'I Am America,'" Chopra spared no transcendent language: "If we are lucky, we will wake up and begin the journey back to self-awareness as people," he wrote. "That happens only rarely, and now it has happened to a junior senator from Illinois." Clearly Chopra was swept up by what has come to be called "Obama-mania." Chopra then projected Obama forward into the presidency. "If Barack Obama makes it all the way to the White House, it will represent a quantum leap in American consciousness and a promise to restore America's position in the world," he asserted.

The site includes a video clip in which MSNBC anchor Chris Matthews claims he felt a "thrill going up my leg" when listening to an Obama speech.[18] Matthews bubbled on, claiming Obama "speaks about America in a way that has nothing to do with politics. It has to do with the feeling we have about our country. And that is an objective assessment." Oprah Winfrey, listening to a speech Obama gave to a Des Moines, Iowa, audience on December 8, 2007, told reporters, "When you listen to Barack Obama, when you really hear him, you witness a very rare thing. You witness a politician who has an ear for eloquence and a tongue dipped in the unvarnished truth."[19]

Conservative critics have pondered whether the messiah phenomenon will help or hurt Obama. Writing in the *American Thinker*, J. R. Dunn noted the tendency liberals have to see their leaders as "in no way limited to anything as mundane as running a country." Instead, liberals see their leaders "as transcendent beings, someone more than human, someone with a touch of the divine."[20] This explains, Dunn argued, why liberals are so attracted to tyrants on the international scene. He claims Stalin is the classic historical example that proves his point. The film *Mission to Moscow*, a film FDR requested be made during World War II to bolster U.S. support for Russia as an ally against Hitler,[21] was "a dose of political hagiography at its most nauseating." Examining how liberals tend to put FDR and JFK on a godlike pedestal, Dunn commented that for the American left, "leaders don't handle tasks, they lead movements, they embody the spirit of the age. They transform. Leaders, to put it simply, are führers."

Internet blogger Jon Swift, writing critically about the "Obama Messiah" movement, mused that "there comes a time in the life of every adolescent girl, and even Chris Matthews, when they peel the yellowing photos of Scott Baio they cut out of *Tiger Beat* off their bedroom walls and toss them in the garbage bin."[22] Not impressed by Matthews's gushing, Swift observed that he "sounded like a schoolgirl at a Justin Timberlake concert who doesn't quite understand the strange sensations she is feeling." Yet, appreciative of how fleeting fame is in politics, Swift wondered, "Barack Obama will be 47 in August. Will Chris Matthews and Obama's other devoted disciples still have his picture on their bedroom walls then?"

Obama the Cult Figure

Blosser is concerned Obama will turn out to be just another politician, especially if Obama is elected president. "On a basic level, my concern is that Obama will ride the wave of emotion and mob enthusiasm to office," Blosser said. "With the challenges and inevitable compromises that come with the job, illusions are going to fade and dreams are going to crumble." Blosser expressed concern that voters are projecting onto Obama expectations that will be impossible to fulfill. "People talk as if this man will bring the troops home and end the war within his first year of office," he noted. "That's a pretty naïve hope, considering the global jihadists threat.

"Obama's campaign seems to be predicated on the assumption that he has somehow transcended 'power politics,' that he is in fact the anti-politician," Blosser stressed. "Call me a cynic, but I have the hunch when you peel off the hope-saturated facade and get down to the hard business of running this country, you will find Obama is a politician, much like any other.

"How that will affect the masses will, of course, depend on the degree to which they were taken in," he added, noting the potential for letdown Obama has created by raising expectations. "The Left has typically decried the mixing of faith and politics among the Right, and yet there are those who have embraced Obama with a fervor that can be aptly described as 'religious.'" Blosser stated his goal was "to chronicle what I thought was the curious, yet troubling, phenomenon of the 'cult of personality' and elements of 'secular messianism'" that he has seen surrounding Obama's campaign. "On one hand, every political race has some degree of enthusiasm," he admitted. "That is to be expected. But what I've chronicled on the website is something else entirely."

Blosser hopes his underlying serious concern will be evident to those discerning enough to look below the surface of the website's contrived adoration. "I'm concerned about the degree this man, or anybody, could be carried into office by mob passion and idolatrous hysteria," he admitted. "I'm concerned about political 'rallies' that are consciously orchestrated along the lines of a rock concert," he continued. "I'm concerned when a candidate breaks out a hankie and blows his nose—and the crowd breaks into applause.

"I'm concerned when ambiguous talk of 'unity' and 'change' and 'yes, we can!' carry the day with precious little discussion of how this man actually intends to bridge the gulf between ideological and philosophical convictions." Blosser has not been swept away by Obama's rhetoric. "To suggest that 'there are no red states or blue states' sounds good, but I wonder if the intention is not simply to pave over sincere moral convictions held between the two parties with flowery rhetoric," he said seriously.

"It's very questionable how many of the twenty thousand screaming, crying, chanting, and in some cases fainting fans in any one political rally actually read and are aware of his positions," he pondered, "and how many simply attend 'for the Obama experience,' or to 'witness history in the making,' and might end up voting for him for that reason alone."

When we were first researching and writing at World Net Daily about the Obama the Messiah website, a large number of e-mails were received from readers objecting that Obama was not the Messiah but rather the biblical Antichrist prefigured in Saint John's Apocalypse. This book does not make the argument that Obama is either the incarnation or reincarnation of the Messiah or the Antichrist. The point here is to demonstrate how Axelrod's politics of personality has elevated Obama to new, quasireligious heights, with followers and detractors alike susceptible to being influenced either positively or negatively by a cult of personality.

Obama Themes Are Borrowed

Evidence is accumulating that Barack Obama borrowed some of the catchiest phrases in his campaign speeches and ads from a variety of literary, film, political, and popular sources, all without giving credit or attribution to the original source.

A major contributing cause of Obama's liberal borrowing of previously used political language is David Axelrod, who has borrowed freely from client Deval Patrick. Axelrod appears to have tried out much of Obama's 2008 campaign language in the Patrick gubernatorial campaign in 2006 in Massachusetts.

As we have seen, Axelrod's objective in being the chief strategist of a political campaign is to craft lofty phrases around which to build his personality and image campaigns, and coming up with successful lofty phrases is not easy, especially if you are limited to slogans that are so unique they have never been used before. Axelrod and Obama's task is made much easier if he and Obama are free to range over all previous political speeches, political books and articles, and pop culture, including movies, music, and poetry, to grab statements they like, regardless of where they came from, to use as their own.

This solution, however, ignores one important problem: most serious writers object to their phrases being borrowed without attribution. Yet, just as Axelrod's commercial company has readily engaged in "astro-turfing" to create a deception of public interest advertising for his paid commercial accounts, Axelrod the chief strategist of a political campaign evidently has no objection to stealing other people's words when it comes to advancing his current paid political candidate. The downside risk Axelrod runs in both his commercial and political public-relations/media businesses, however, is that Axelrod might get caught and the unethical practice revealed, to the detriment of both him and the client.

On February 18, 2008, the *Washington Post* reported a Clinton campaign charge that a speech by Obama in Wisconsin included a passage nearly identical to one in a speech delivered two years earlier by Deval Patrick.[23] "In many respects, he [Obama] is asking the public to judge him on the strength of his rhetoric," said Howard Wolfson, a top Clinton advisor, according to the *Washington Post* article. "When we learn he has taken an important section of his speech from another elected official, it raises very fundamental questions about his campaign."

The controversy was fueled by a YouTube.com video showing side-by-side segments from Patrick's and Obama's speeches, making the similarity between them obvious."[24] Particularly striking was how both candidates focused on the theme "Just Words," followed by a string of famous quotations that obviously were not just words, but statements of important political moments and causes. ABC noticed the same thing,[25] citing a speech Patrick gave in 2006 answering the question, "Just words?" with a string of famous phrases that included "'We have nothing to fear but fear itself,' . . . just words? 'Ask what you can do for your country,' just words? 'I have a dream,' just words?" Obviously these statements of Franklin Roosevelt, John Kennedy, and Martin Luther King, Jr., were not "just words" with no political impact, but rather had defined political moments for a generation or more of listeners.

ABC matched Patrick's 2006 speech against a speech Obama gave in Wisconsin during the 2008 campaign. Obama's language almost identically matched the substance and structure of what Patrick had said in Massachusetts. Obama's phrasing was "Don't tell me words don't matter. 'I have a dream.' Just words? 'We hold these truths to be self-evident, that all men are created equal.' Just words? 'We have nothing to fear but fear itself.' Just words? Just speeches?"

Appearing on ABC on February 19, Patrick defused the controversy by claiming a charge of plagiarism was not fair.[26] "It's an elaborate charge and an extravagant one," Patrick said. But it was undeniable that Obama had copied Patrick exactly. Axelrod most likely liked how the speech worked with his client in Massachusetts and so decided to try it once again with Obama, perhaps thinking no one would notice.

That same day, a second video clip was posted on You-Tube.com showing Obama copying from yet another Patrick speech, nearly word for word, again without attribution to Patrick.[27] Patrick said, "I am not asking anybody to take a chance on me. I am asking you to take a chance on your own aspirations." Obama's speech contained nearly identical language: "I'm not just asking you to take a chance on me. I'm also asking you to take a chance on your own aspirations."

As the controversy built, Obama engaged in one of his typical efforts to distance himself, claiming he had not intentionally done anything wrong.[28] At a press conference in Youngstown, Ohio, Obama admitted he should have given credit to his friend Governor Patrick, saying, "I was on the stump, and he [Deval Patrick] had suggested that we use these lines. I thought they were good lines. I'm sure I should have [given him credit], [but I] didn't this time." Trying to make the controversy go away, Obama issued a nondenial denial: "Deval and I do trade ideas all the time, and, you know, he's occasionally used lines of mine. I, at a fundraising dinner in Wisconsin, used some words of his." Obama's surrogates pointed to video clips showing Obama onstage with Patrick at campaign appearances in 2006. His supporters were arguing that since Obama had worked for Patrick's campaign in 2006, and was frequently onstage with him to hear Patrick give speeches, it was reasonable to assume some Patrick speech phrases would stick in his mind.

Perhaps Obama and Axelrod expected us to think, "No harm, no foul." What's a little word-swapping among friends? Yet Democratic senator Joe Biden of Delaware was forced to drop out of the 1988 presidential campaign when astute observers found he had borrowed generously from relatively obscure speeches given by British Labor Party leader Neal Kinnock, a politician little known in the United States. Biden's rival in that election, Massachusetts governor Michael Dukakis, had secretly distributed to news media an "attack video" juxtaposing the Biden and Kinnock speeches,[29] much as the YouTube.com videos of Patrick and Obama were posted in 2008.

Obama Borrows Lines from Movies

There are other cases where Obama presented language he borrowed from other sources as unique or new. Unfortunately, Axelrod and Obama are not so clever that they can avoid being exposed within a matter of days or hours by a good Internet detective with access to YouTube.

"Bamboozled" is the title of an Internet article[30] in which blogger Seymour Glass demonstrated that Obama borrowed language from Spike Lee's script of his 1992 feature film, X.[31] Glass pointed out that in many primary states, including South Carolina, Maryland, Delaware, and Texas, Obama has repeatedly used the words "bamboozled" and "hoodwinked" in framing his argument that the truth has been hidden from voters. Unfortunately, the language is not unique to Obama. Glass traced the use of "bamboozled" and "hoodwinked" back to dialogue Lee wrote for actor Denzel Washington, who played the character of Malcolm X in Lee's movie. To make the point that Obama got the words from Spike Lee and not Malcolm X, Glass pointed out that in real-life speeches, Malcolm X never uttered the words "bamboozled" or "hoodwinked."

A video clip on YouTube.com compares Obama's speeches with Washington's speeches as Malcolm X in the movie. The comparison makes painfully clear exactly how "bamboozled" and "hoodwinked" are used almost identically in both. The result is that Obama looks like a word thief and Axelrod looks like a fool for thinking nobody would track down Spike Lee's dialogue in the film.[32]

Jay Freeman, writing in the *Boston Globe*, traces "bamboozled" and "hoodwinked" back to Charles Cavendish Fulke Greville's memoir in 1885. Greville had written of an associate, "Palmerston never intended anything but to hoodwink his colleagues, bamboozle the French, and gain time." Freeman also found another prior usage in H. L. Mencken, who wrote in 1928, "He does not merely tell how politicians hoodwink, bamboozle and prey upon the boobs; he shows precisely how."[33]

Freeman's point was to show the two words have been commonly connected, such that X was not the only source that Obama could have copied. Freeman might also have been implying that the two words are naturally associated in this type of political context. Copying Denzel Washington in Spike Lee's film is a risk Obama and Axelrod might have wanted to avoid, especially when the character Washington was playing was Malcolm X. Does Axelrod really want to make the subconscious suggestion that Obama is today's version of the radical extremist that Malcolm X was in the 1960s?

The YouTube video also examines Obama's assertion, "We are the ones we have been waiting for." The video clip skillfully links this phrase to four previous uses: (1) a music album by the Visionaries[34] by the same title; (2) a book by Alice Walker,[35] a poet who also used the title; (3) a December 12, 2007, column by *New York Times* writer Thomas Friedman, who cited the phrase as a tagline used by three engineering undergraduates who helped launch something known as the "Vehicle Design Summit"; and (4) a campaign speech Democratic representative Dennis Kucinich gave in April 2004 when he was running for president.

The video includes a speech Oprah Winfrey gave at a December 9, 2007, Obama rally in Columbia, South Carolina. Oprah introduced Obama by asking, "Is he the one?" She then answered the rhetorical question: "South Carolina, I do believe he is the one to bring us the audacity of hope," tying the answer to the title of Obama's second book, a title Obama borrowed from a Reverend Wright sermon.

The video demonstrates that Oprah's use of the phrase "He is the one" traces back to the Warner Brothers 1999 movie *The Matrix*.[36] For many born in the 1970s and '80s, the *Matrix* films have almost become a pop culture substitute for religion. The phrase "He is the one" designates Neo, the character played by Keanu Reeves, a gifted computer programmer with superhero powers who takes on the challenge of destroying the entrapment of "the Matrix" to break free from its liberty-confining code of domination over human beings. Use of the phrase to identify Obama with "The One" interestingly extends the messiah theme to reach a new generation of voters coming of age in the music-video iPod generation.

Another example of Obama's borrowing is his use of the catchy "Sí, se puede," which translates into English as "Yes, we can." This slogan traces back to César Chávez and his efforts to organize Hispanic farm workers in the United Farm Workers in the 1960s. "Sí, se puede" more recently became a slogan widely used by the pro–illegal immigration forces in the May Day rallies launched in major cities across the United States over the past few years. That the phrase "Yes, we can" became firmly identified as a signature phrase with the Obama campaign is witnessed by the "Yes We Can" Barack Obama music video produced by DipDive.com.[37] The DipDive video has now been viewed on YouTube.com over six million times.[38]

Other Obama phrases, such as "I choose hope over fear . . ." or "I'm not just asking you to take a chance on me, I'm asking you to take a chance on your own aspirations . . ." go back to other Axelrod campaigns, including John Edwards's unsuccessful race for the White House in 2004.

As we pointed out earlier, even the use of "Change" as a political slogan dates back to socialist Saul Alinsky and his desire to cause a radical redistribution of income from the haves to the have-nots in America. Does Axelrod really want his candidate identified with Saul Alinsky? This is a risk Obama takes in making "Change" his campaign catchword.

By now, Internet bloggers have so clearly exposed Obama's pattern of borrowing that every time he introduces a new catchy phrase into his campaign lexicon, they stand ready to search past political speeches, books, albums, and movies to find out where it came from.

Michelle, the Angry Obama

Axelrod has one other challenge in his attempt to frame Obama as a candidate who can transcend race—Barack's wife, Michelle.

On February 18, 2008, at a rally in Madison, Wisconsin, Michelle Obama made a political gaffe, implying to the audience she had not been proud of America until her African-American husband had ascended to be a front-running candidate for president.

"What we have learned over this year is that hope is making a comeback," Michelle began, echoing the title of Barack's second book and themes of hope Axelrod was crafting for the campaign. "It is making a comeback," she continued. "And let me tell you something—for the first time in my adult lifetime, I am really proud of my country. And not just because Barack has done well, but because I think people are hungry for change. And I have been desperate to see our country moving in that direction and not just feeling so alone in my frustration and disappointment."

Mostly Michelle was on theme, except for her comment this was the "first time" she felt proud of America and her suggestion that up until now her feelings about America were characterized by frustration and disappointment. Then, she concluded, "I've seen people who are hungry to be unified around some basic common themes, and it has made me proud." The implication is that she had not been proud of America until her African-American husband introduced "change."[39]

The Wisconsin rally was covered by C-SPAN and within minutes news of Michelle's statement was breaking on the wire services,[40] with the video posted to YouTube.[41] Michelle's statement was being packaged to say she felt proud of her country "for the first time," implying she had never before been proud of America. Within hours of the speech, a firestorm of criticism broke out on talk radio and cable news television. Then, as was typical for the Internet age, bloggers found a second speech in which Michelle had said approximately the same thing. Both clips were packaged and shown together by Bill O'Reilly on the Fox News show *The O'Reilly Factor*.[42]

At a press conference, John McCain took the opportunity to take a swipe at Obama, commenting, "I just wanted to make the statement that I have and always will be proud of my country."[43] Without mentioning his military service and Obama's lack thereof, McCain reminded the country he was a real hero, a former Vietnam War POW who had demonstrated beyond any need for further proof how proud he was of the U.S.A.

The Obama camp quickly went into damage control. Campaign spokesperson Jen Psaki issued a statement saying, "What she meant is that she's really proud at this moment because for the first time in a long time, thousands of Americans who've never participated in politics before are coming out in record numbers to build a grassroots movement for change."[44]

"Statements like this are made and people try to take it out of context and make a great big deal out of it, and that isn't at all what she meant," Obama himself said, trying to dig out from the hole. "What she meant was, this is the first time that she's been proud of the politics of America. Because she's pretty cynical about the political process, and with good reason, and she's not alone. But she has seen large numbers of people get involved in the process, and she's encouraged."[45]

Still, the damage had been done.

Michelle Obama's Campaign Liability

Researchers immediately began combing through Michelle Obama's 1985 thesis at Princeton University, which she wrote to fulfill her requirements for a bachelor's degree in sociology. In the thesis, titled "Princeton-Educated Blacks and the Black Community,"[46] Michelle tells us that her experiences at Princeton made her "far more aware of my 'Blackness' than ever before." She went on to write, "I have found that at Princeton no matter how liberal and open-minded some of my White professors and classmates try to be toward me, I sometimes feel like a visitor on campus; as if I really don't belong." Moreover, she wrote, "Regardless of the circumstances under which I interact with Whites at Princeton, it often seems as if, to them, I will always be Black first and a student second."

Christopher Hitchens noted on Salon.com[47] that Michelle announces in her Princeton thesis that she has been influenced by the definition of "black separatism" given by Stokely Carmichael and Charles Hamilton in their 1967 book *Black Power: The Politics of Liberation in America*. This prompted Hitchens to comment, "I remember poor Stokely Carmichael quite well. After a hideous series of political and personal fiascos, he fled to Africa, renamed himself Kwame Toure after two of West Africa's most repellently failed dictators, and then came briefly back to the United States before electing to die in exile."

Hitchens also recalled he saw Stokely Carmichael last "as the warm-up speaker for Louis Farrakhan in Madison Square Garden in 1985, on the evening when Farrakhan made himself famous by warning Jews, 'You can't say "Never Again" to God, because when he puts you in the ovens, you're there forever.'" Forget about transcending race. From the heart of the Left, Michelle's "finally proud of America" speeches and her college thesis at Princeton had allowed a notable critic to link her with black radical extremists such as Stokely Carmichael and Louis Farrakhan. Hitchens questioned whether Michelle was fulfilling Bill Clinton's 1992 offer about Hillary that voters would get "two for one" by voting for him.

This was the last thing Axelrod and Barack Obama needed: a wife of the presidential candidate who made herself look like a black racist.

The American people know almost nothing about Michelle, but the first time she came to attention she appeared as an angry black woman who was not proud of America. The tag stuck, just as Reverend Jeremiah Wright's statement "God damn America" stuck. Now, Barack Obama was surrounded by two people close to him—his pastor and his wife—who came off as bitter people filled with black rage against white people and hatred for the United States. Both now had ties that went back to Stokely Carmichael: Wright through black-liberation theology and its roots in black power thinking, Michelle through her Princeton thesis, in which she begins her analysis with a concern that the separatism embraced by black power thinking defined the racial experience a black student could expect, even at an Ivy League school.

Moreover, when Michelle's thesis came to light and the public realized she had been educated at Princeton, she began to look as elitist as Obama and largely for the same reason. Michelle might have been raised by a middle-class black working family on Chicago's South Side, but while being educated at an Ivy League school she indulged in the luxury of experiencing alienation, instead of being grateful for the opportunity. Nor was the impression diminished when the public learned that Michelle, like Barack, also got her law degree at Harvard, in 1988.

The impression that Michelle Obama is a loose cannon filled with rage was reinforced by a profile in the London paper the *Observer*. Reporter Lauren Collins asked Michelle if she was offended by Bill Clinton's use of the phrase "fairy-tale" to describe her husband's argument we should pull out of Iraq. Michelle responded immediately with "No," but then added in what Collins described as an affected, funny voice, "I want to rip his eyes out!" As she said this, Collins reported, Michelle clawed at the air for effect. Then one of her advisors gave Michelle a nervous look, so she covered herself, adding quickly, "Kidding! See, this is what gets me into trouble."[48]

Obama, Secret Smoker

A once-rare photograph now widely circulated on the Internet shows Barack Obama smoking a cigarette. The lit cigarette, which looks like a Marlboro, is smoked more than halfway down. The butt hangs by the filter from his lips. Gone is the smiling Obama image we are encouraged to identify with hope. Instead of showing the camera his famous movie-star smile, Obama is caught looking down, frowning. The corners of his mouth are pursed in what looks like an expression of annoyance. The collar of his white suit is open; he is wearing a suit without a tie. But he is not relaxed. Obama appears tired, or maybe even angry.

That Obama smokes cigarettes should be a trivial concern, especially if he were open about it. But he's not. The photo circulating on the Internet is remarkable because so few unaltered photos of Obama smoking exist. When cameras are around, Obama typically does not smoke.

Obama's smoking habit was discussed at length by *Chicago Tribune* reporter David Mendell in his 2007 biography, *Obama: From Promise to Power*. When Obama was running for the U.S. Senate in 2004, Mendell noticed he was getting less face time with him. At first Mendell attributed this to Obama's need for personal privacy, but then he realized there was another reason. "Obama was a secret smoker," Mendell wrote, "and he did not want to light up a Marlboro in front of a reporter."

Mendell appreciated immediately how smoking would affect Obama's public image. "The public portrait of Obama now bordered on saintly, especially for a politician," he wrote. "Learning that he smoked might tarnish this picture. So Obama went to great lengths to conceal the habit."[49] Later, one of Obama's aides confirmed Mendell's observations, explaining to the reporter that Obama preferred to travel in the car to campaign appearances alone with his campaign aides because "he wanted to have that cigarette, and he couldn't have it when you were with him or he had to sneak it."[50]

A person who has to hide his or her smoking appears to be living in a lie. Moreover, New Age guys do not smoke; New Age guys who smoke out of sight cannot be trusted. A New Age politician dreaming of change and hoping for the future is not an image consistent with a guy who has to smoke cigarettes on campaign breaks just to make it through the day. Maybe that's why Obama takes such care to maintain the pretense he is a nonsmoker. The smoker image conflicts with the campaign personality Axelrod is trying to craft, so much so that Obama hid the habit from a reporter who had become like a friend to him.

If Obama takes pains to hide his smoking from us, what else does he take pains to hide?

In other words, Obama's secret smoking may not be a trivial issue after all. Looked at from a certain perspective the habit is a crack in the wall, a flaw that calls into question whether the persona Axelrod has crafted for Obama is who Obama really is, or simply the person Axelrod wants us to see. Axelrod's goal with Obama is to mask from white voters the radical intellectual background that has shaped his politics. When we hear the Axelrod-packaged language Obama speaks, what we are supposed to hear is a universal message of hope. We are not supposed to remember the angry politics of race defined by the black-liberation theology Obama has professed since he was baptized and married by Reverend Wright at Trinity United Church of Christ on Chicago's South Side. Nor are we supposed to associate calls for "Change" with the redistribution of income that Saul Alinsky had in mind when he advocated using "Change" as a radical socialist call to action.

Defeating Obama will require removing the mask Axelrod has placed before Obama's face, so that important segments of the electorate can fully appreciate how radical, and politically unacceptable to them, his policy views truly are.

A FAR-LEFT DOMESTIC POLICY

Sen. Barack Obama, D-Ill., was the most liberal senator in 2007, according to the National Journal's *27th annual vote ratings. The insurgent political candidate shifted further to the left last year in the run-up to the primaries, after finishing as the 16th- and 10th-most-liberal during his first two years in the Senate.*

—BRIAN FRIEL, RICHARD E. COHEN, AND
KIRK VICTOR, *National Journal*,
JANUARY 31, 2008[1]

You know, the truth is that right after 9/11 I had a [flag] pin [on my lapel]. Shortly after 9/11, particularly because as we're talking about the Iraq War, that became a substitute for I think true patriotism, which is speaking out on issues that are of importance to our national security, I decided I won't wear that pin on my chest.

—SENATOR BARACK OBAMA, *on ABC News*,
OCTOBER 4, 2007[2]

Obama's life history and ideological beliefs predispose him to support a wide range of public policy positions on the far left. Despite his proclaiming himself a unifier, Obama's public policy views run the risk of dividing the electorate. Can Obama win the presidency in 2008 when important voter segments in the center-right majority learn that specifics of his domestic policy program threaten ideas and values they hold dear? Clearly, Obama will make his best effort to present his potentially divisive views with such rhetorical eloquence that their underlying extremism is clouded. Yet when we look to his voting record to determine his history, we can cut through the rhetorical haze to uncover exactly what issues Obama intends to support.

This chapter focuses on specific issues in Obama's domestic policy agenda, including his strong pro-abortion line, his antagonism to the Second Amendment and his desire to introduce gun-control measures, his program to increase the capital gains tax, his commitment to implement a government-sponsored program of national health care, and his support of a global tax imposed on Americans to reduce poverty in other countries.

In the next chapter, we will focus on Obama's key foreign policy initiatives that will also be dismaying to the country's center-right majority.

The goal in both chapters is not to provide a comprehensive analysis of Obama's platform across the board, but to highlight specific policy issues that will be decisive. Obama's extremist views will turn off voter segments Obama needs to win.

If John McCain is able to focus the general election debate around the type of domestic policy issues we discuss here, he will succeed in framing Obama as unacceptable to values voters, Second Amendment advocates, fiscal conservatives, and opponents of government welfare and income distribution programs, as well as opponents of globalism.

Radical Pro-Abortion Views

A late-term abortion is planned when the fetus is fully developed, sometimes even into the ninth month of pregnancy. The doctor induces birth in order to abort the baby in the process of birth, but before the baby is born naturally. The goal of a late-term induced labor is to prevent the baby from living outside the mother's womb, even though the baby is ready to do so. Late-term induced-labor abortions sometimes fail: instead of the doctor aborting the baby as planned, the infant survives.

Obama has consistently refused to support legislation that would define an infant who survives a late-term induced-labor abortion as a human being with the right to live. He insists that no restriction must ever be placed on the right of a mother to decide to abort her child.

More than once, Obama heard Illinois nurse Jill Stanek testify before the Illinois Senate Judiciary Committee, relating the following story of an aborted Down syndrome baby who survived a late-term induced-labor abortion and was abandoned in the hospital's Soiled Utility Room because the baby's parents did not want to hold him.[3] "I couldn't bear the thought of this child lying alone in a Soiled Utility Room," Stanek testified before Obama's committee in the Illinois Senate. "So, I cradled and rocked him for the 45 minutes that he lived." Stanek reported Obama was "unfazed" by the testimony.[4]

On March 30, 2001, Obama was the only Illinois senator who rose to speak against a bill that would have protected babies who survive late-term labor-induced abortions.

A transcript of the Illinois Senate session has been archived on the Internet, complete with Obama's comments as he made them that day on the Senate floor. Obama rose to object that if the bill passed, and a nine-month-old fetus survived a late-term labor-induced abortion was deemed to be a person who had a right to live, then the law would "forbid abortions to take place." Obama further explained the equal protection clause of the Fourteenth Amendment does not allow somebody to kill a child, so if the law deemed a child who survived a late-term labor-induced abortion had a right to live, "then this would be an anti-abortion statute."

Not wanting to be the only Illinois state senator to vote against the bill, a move that Obama realized would be politically unpopular with his constituency, he took the easy way out and voted "Present."[5] In the Illinois Senate, voting "Present" is the equivalent of voting "No," because a bill must have a majority counting only "Yes" votes to pass.

In 1997, Obama voted in the Illinois Senate against SB 230, a bill designed to prevent partial-birth abortions. In a partial-birth abortion, the baby is delivered feetfirst, so the head remains in the mother's womb, allowing the courts to maintain that the baby has not yet been born. The doctor then uses surgical instruments to crack the back of the baby's skull, permitting a suction tube to be inserted, so the baby's brain can be removed from the body. In the U.S. Senate, Obama has consistently voted to expand embryonic stem cell research. He has voted against requiring minors who get out-of-state abortions to notify their parents. The National Abortion Rights Action League, which prefers to represent itself more euphemistically under its acronym, NARAL, gives Obama a 100 percent score on his pro-choice voting record in the U.S. Senate for 2005, 2006, and 2007.[6]

Obama, who voted against the appointments of John Roberts and Samuel Alito to the Supreme Court, told Planned Parenthood in a speech on July 17, 2007, "We're at a crossroads right now in America—and we have to move this country forward. This election is not just about playing defense, it's also about playing offense. It's not just about defending what is, it's about creating what might be in this country. And that's what we've got to work on together."

Here, translating this lofty language into specifics, Obama was calling for more Supreme Court justices like Ruth Bader Ginsberg. "We need more programs in our communities like the National Black Church Initiative, which empowers our young people by teaching them about reproductive health, sex education and teen pregnancy within the context of the African-American faith tradition," Obama said, citing his church, Trinity United Church of Christ, as an example.[7] The right of a woman to demand an abortion is for Obama a political issue of major importance. "With one more vacancy on the Court," he told Planned Parenthood, "we could be looking at a majority hostile to a woman's fundamental right to choose for the first time since *Roe v. Wade* and that is what is at stake in this election."[8]

This was Obama's argument to the group why he needed to be elected president, to prevent opponents of *Roe v. Wade* from being appointed as Supreme Court justices.

At a rally in Jamestown, Pennsylvania, on March 29, 2008, Obama referenced his two daughters, ages nine and six, commenting, "I am going to teach them first of all about values and morals. But if they make a mistake, I don't want them punished with a baby." Only a pro-abortion radical would conceptualize an unwanted pregnancy as being "punished with a baby."[9] Even California's Democratic senator Barbara Boxer, another far-left advocate of abortion, tempered her views and voted for the 2002 Born-Alive Infants Protection Act, when an amendment specified the bill would not otherwise infringe on abortion rights. Obama's history offers no prospect of compromise on the issue of abortion, since he views a woman's right to choose as absolute.

Obama also chooses conveniently to ignore the great harm abortions have done to African-American communities. Approximately 79 percent of Planned Parenthood clinics are placed in target minority neighborhoods. While African-Americans make up only about 13 percent of the U.S. population, their abortions account for 35 percent of the total.[10] Since *Roe v. Wade* was passed in 1973, there have been 13 million African-American abortions in a U.S. black population estimated at some 37 million.[11] The staggering number of African-American abortions since *Roe v. Wade* in 1973 would suggest the "abortion on demand insistence of the political left is permitting genocide to be waged against blacks in America."[12]

Obama's radical pro-abortion views will turn off a large segment of Christian voters, who will resolve to oppose vocally his presidential candidacy and vote against him on this one issue alone. One of John McCain's strong points in appealing to values voters will be his pro-life voting record in the U.S. Senate. NARAL calls McCain an "anti-choice" senator, noting that through 2006, McCain cast 117 votes in the U.S. Senate on abortion and other reproductive rights issues, 113 of which NARAL categorized as "anti-choice."[13] In the general election campaign, McCain will be sure to wear this negative NARAL designation as a badge of courage, knowing a large segment of Christian voters will turn against Obama once they understand his radical pro-abortion agenda, including his expressed determination to appoint to the Supreme Court only justices who agree with him.

A History of Opposition to the Second Amendment

A gun case that unfolded while Obama was in the Illinois state senate reveals his hostility toward the Second Amendment, which he tries to mask by saying he is in favor of hunting and other sport uses of firearms.

Hale DeMar, a fifty-two-year-old Wilmette resident, was arrested and charged with misdemeanor violations for shooting, in the shoulder and leg, a burglar who broke into his home not once, but twice. DeMar, well known in Chicago as the owner of the Oak Tree Restaurant, on the Magnificent Mile along Michigan Avenue, bought the gun legally in the 1980s from Chuck's Gun Shop in Riverdale. On December 28, 2003, DeMar woke up in the middle of the night to find his home had been invaded by a criminal who stole various household items including a television, a ring of keys, and DeMar's BMW sport utility vehicle. The next night the thief returned and used DeMar's keys to get back into the house. This time, the thief set off the alarm system, automatically notifying the security company. Concerned his children were in danger, DeMar got his handgun from the safe where he kept it and shot the thief, who then fled the house by crashing through the front window. The burglar, a thirty-one-year-old with a criminal record, then drove DeMar's SUV to the hospital, where he was arrested.

On January 8, 2004, Wilmette police chief George Carpenter arrested DeMar for violating the town's handgun ban, in effect since 1989. "Wilmette homes are much safer without a handgun," Carpenter told the *Chicago Sun-Times,* defending his decision to enforce the North Shore suburb's ordinance.[14] Additionally, Carpenter charged DeMar with failing to renew his Illinois firearm owner's identification card, which had expired in 1988. DeMar faced some hefty fines and possibly even jail time under the violations.

A few days later, appearing before the Wilmette Village Board to defend why he arrested DeMar under the town's handgun ban, Chief Carpenter explained, "Handguns create a hazard in the home." Against a background of booing from local residents attending the packed meeting, Carpenter argued his case. "My experience is that handguns are more likely to be used or threatened to be used in quarrel or domestic situations or in suicide attempts," he explained. Town residents testifying disagreed, describing gun ownership as "a God-given right" and "the most sacred civil right." According to a *Chicago Sun-Times* reporter present at the hearing, at one point a man in the audience stood up and yelled, "Give me liberty or give me death!" using Patrick Henry's famous line.[15]

"Until you are shocked by a piercing alarm in the middle of the night and met in your kitchen by a masked invader as your children shudder in their beds, until you confront that very real nightmare, please don't suggest that some village trustee knows better," DeMar said in his own defense. "If my actions have spared only one family from the distress and trauma that this habitual criminal has caused hundreds of others, then I have served my civic duty and taken one evil creature off our streets, something that our impotent criminal justice system had failed to do, despite some thirty-odd arrests, plea bargains and suspended sentences."[16]

In February 2004, Cook County prosecutors dropped

all charges against DeMar, having thought better about the public outcry that had developed throughout the state over the case. In March 2004, the Illinois Senate passed Senate Bill 2165, a law introduced in response to DeMar's case, with provisions designed to assert a right of citizens to protect themselves against home invasions, such that self-defense requirements would be viewed to take precedence over local ordinances against handgun possession. The measure passed the Illinois Senate by a vote of 38–20.

Barack Obama was one of the twenty state senators voting against the measure.

After passing the Illinois House by an overwhelming majority of 86–25, the measure went to the desk of Governor Rod Blagojevich, who vetoed it. On November 9, 2004, the Illinois Senate voted 40–18 to override Blagojevich's veto.

Again Obama acted against the bill, voting with the eighteen who wanted to sustain the governor's veto.

On November 17, 2004, the Illinois House voted overwhelmingly, 85–30, to override the governor's veto and Senate Bill 2165 became law. According to the *Chicago Sun-Times*, the override vote in the Illinois legislature demonstrated that "legislatures are responding—albeit with very small steps in Illinois—to constituents who demand that their right of self-defense be held sacrosanct."[17]

Obama was one of the few state senators who did not get the point.

Commenting on the DeMar case, Wayne LaPierre, the executive vice president of the National Rifle Association, said that when Obama says he believes in the Second Amendment because he likes to "protect sportsmen," Obama does not understand that the Second Amendment was intended to allow U.S. citizens to defend themselves, not just to shoot pheasants. "Obama's alleged support of the Second Amendment is utterly cynical and false," LaPierre wrote. "Barack Obama is not for the right to keep and bear arms; he's out to destroy it."[18]

Before the Pennsylvania primary, on April 11, 2008, when Obama was recorded at a private fund-raiser in San Francisco as claiming people in small towns in the Midwest "cling to guns and God," LaPierre was quick to respond. "It was and sounded like an arrogant statement from an out-of-touch elitist." Thinking back to the DeMar case, LaPierre said, "Senator Obama opposes people having guns in their homes for self-defense while he and his family enjoy armed professional security around the clock."[19]

As a state senator in Illinois, Obama supported various gun-control measures, including a ban on the sale and transfer of all forms of semiautomatic firearms, a bill limiting handgun purchases to one a month, and a bill requiring manufacturers to place child-safety locks on firearms.

Kenneth Vogel, writing in Politico.com, pointed out that before Obama became a national political figure, he sat on the board of the Chicago-based Joyce Foundation, which gave out at least nine grants totaling $2.7 million to groups advocating gun-control measures.[20] Among the grants approved while Obama was on the board was $20,000 for a group called the Violence Policy Center, which used the money to publish a book titled *Every Handgun Is Aimed at You: The Case for Banning Handguns.*[21] Josh Sugarmann, the director of the Violence Policy Center and the author of the book, wrote in its introduction, "A single consumer product holds our nation hostage: the handgun."[22]

For his eight years with the Joyce Foundation, Obama was paid more than $70,000 in director's fees, according to Vogel's article in Politico.com.

Obama apparently learned nothing from the DeMar case. On February 15, 2008, the Associated Press reported that Obama had voiced support for the District of Columbia ban on handguns, while the case was pending in the Supreme Court.[23] In a sit-down interview with the *Chicago Sun-Times* on April 25, 2008, Obama repeated his support of local officials who enact gun bans in their areas.[24]

Agreeing with the National Rifle Association, the Gun Owners of America have also tagged Obama as "a committed anti-gunner."[25]

So we can now add a second large segment of voters unlikely to support Obama: advocates of the Second Amendment who believe in the right to keep and bear arms, not as a state-organized militia, but as peace-loving citizens interested in upholding their right to self-defense.

Income Redistribution

On September 18, 2007, when Obama laid out his tax fairness plan for the middle class, he proposed adjusting the capital gains rate "to something closer to—but no greater than—the rates Ronald Reagan set in 1986."[26] The reference to raising the capital gains rate to the Ronald Reagan level was clever, suggesting that there was nothing Obama wanted to do that Ronald Reagan, a great hero to the Republican Party and the Wall Street community, hadn't already done. The problem is that the capital gains rate has *dropped* since the days of Ronald Reagan. Stated less rhetorically and more straightforwardly, Obama was proposing to *raise* the long-term capital gains tax rate from 15 percent to 28 percent, nearly doubling it.

Characteristically, Obama typified the capital gains tax

as being one of the $1 trillion in "corporate loopholes and tax havens" he feels are somehow unfair and should be captured as tax revenue. His goal, he said, is to cause "a shift in our tax values that disproportionately benefits the wealthiest Americans." In introducing his plan to increase capital gains, Obama played to the "tax the rich" themes that critics in the business world have associated for decades with the plans of Democratic Party politicians to redistribute wealth to their large client base of welfare-dependent poor.

James Pethokoukis, a reporter for *U.S. News & World Report*, renamed Obama's plan from the senator's proposed "Tax Fairness for the Middle Class" to what it really is— "Ways in Which Government Can Collect More Taxes to Pay for New Spending."[27] Pethokoukis saw Obama's proposal as symptomatic of the Democratic primary candidates "scrambling to figure out ways to plausibly pay for new health care, education, and infrastructure spending if elected."

Pethokoukis then pointed to the result of most Democratic plans to increase corporate taxes: the government ends up collecting less capital gains tax revenue, not more. Why? The answer is fairly simple: under higher capital gains tax rates, investors realize their gains before the higher capital gains rates kick in. Moreover, as long as the higher rates remain in effect, investors and corporate boards make decisions to reduce the amount of capital gains that have to be realized. One clear way to accomplish this goal is for investors and corporations to cut back on investments. Discourage investments and fewer capital gains taxes will be paid. As a result, higher capital gains tax rates tend to produce less capital gains tax revenue, not more. The economics of this principle have been proved repeatedly in the two decades since Reagan was president.

Ed Morrissey, posting on the Michelle Malkin blog, HotAir.com, took Obama to task[28] for missing this point altogether in his presidential primary debate with Hillary Clinton in Philadelphia on April 16, 2008.[29] During the debate, ABC News moderator Charles Gibson pointed out statistics from changes in the capital gains tax, including reductions in the capital gains tax put in place by President Clinton, showing that reductions in capital gains tax rates produce more tax revenue and that the opposite happens, tax revenue goes down, when capital gains tax rates are increased.

As Morrissey pointed out, Obama shifted ground in giving his answer, arguing that "fairness" was the real reason he wanted to raise capital gains taxes. "Well, Charlie," Obama began his answer, "what I've said is that I would look at raising the capital-gains tax for purposes of fairness. We saw an article today which showed that the top 50 hedge fund managers made $29 billion last year—$29 billion for 50 individuals. And part of what has happened is that those who are able to work the stock market and amass huge fortunes on capital gains are paying a lower tax rate than their secretaries. That's not fair."

"The higher priority for Obama isn't to raise revenue; it's to ensure *fairness*," Morrissey properly pointed out. "In order to do that, he will have the government take a bigger share of the gains and redistribute them through social programs to others. The pretense of having more money acts as a veneer for good, old-fashioned redistributionism."

In our analysis of Obama's experience as a Chicago community organizer trained in Saul Alinsky's radical socialist methodologies, we warned that "Change," a slogan first introduced by Alinsky, was nothing more than a code word for the typical income redistribution those on the left have sought since the days of Karl Marx. Here, in Obama's proposal for increasing the capital gains tax, we find proof of the point.

"Obama's blindness on capital gains reveals a hard-Left mindset," Morrissey wrote. "He sees investors always profiting and never losing, while the people who work at jobs created by successful investment as victims of this exchange rather than the beneficiaries of it." Yet the secretary in Obama's example earns an income because investors have risked capital to create her job. When investment is discouraged, the economy as a whole falters, creating fewer jobs for secretaries, as well as all other workers. "The surest way to start an economic disaster is to increase penalties for investment," Morrissey correctly concludes.

This Obama proposal is certain to look like amateurism at best to successful investors, experienced corporate executives, and economists. To the extent Obama manages to convince these more economically sophisticated voters his economic naïveté truly reflects his genuine lack of experience—both in politics and in business—Obama will lose another core group of voters he may not be able to afford losing.

Clinton Attacks Obama on Universal Health Care

Republican Party opposition research experts can take their lead on universal health care from the strong attacks Hillary Clinton launched on Barack Obama's proposal during the hard-fought Democratic Party primary campaign.

In 1993, eight days after Bill Clinton was inaugurated, Hillary was appointed to head the President's Task Force on National Health Care Reform, in what became a center-piece of Bill Clinton's first term in office. Hillary launched the concept of a universal health-care card with a health-care identification number reminiscent of the Social Security number. Hillary's goal was to rewrite the complex health-care rules that regulate some 14 percent of the U.S. economy and to report her final proposal to Congress within one hundred days.[30] In a Democratic primary debate in South Carolina on April 26, 2007, Clinton claimed that opposition from the insurance and pharmaceutical companies ended up killing her program. "I tried to achieve universal health care back in '93 or '94, and I still have the scars from that experience," she commented.[31] Still, she indicated she believed the country was now ready for universal health care.

During the South Carolina debate, Obama described what has become the trademark of his proposal: an extension of the private health insurance system that would include everyone who wanted to purchase health insurance. "Number one, I think we should have a national pool that people can buy into if they don't have health insurance," he said, "similar to the ones that most of us who are in Congress enjoy right now." Obama made clear that his objections to lack of universal health care were based primarily on "fairness," just as were his objections to a low capital gains tax rate. "It doesn't make sense to me that my bosses, the taxpayers, may not have health insurance that I enjoy," he continued. "And we can provide subsidies for those who can't afford the group rates that are available."[32]

Whenever Obama mentions health care, he also takes a shot at health-care profits, suggesting they are "too high." In presenting his plan for universal health care to the Families USA Conference on January 25, 2007, Obama contended,

"Another, more controversial area we need to look at is how much of our health-care spending is going toward the record-breaking profits earned by the drug and health-care industry. It's perfectly understandable for a corporation to try and make a profit, but when those profits are soaring higher and higher each year while millions lose their coverage and premiums skyrocket, we have a responsibility to ask why."[33]

In a Democratic primary debate held in Cleveland on February 26, 2008, Hillary said her main objection to Obama's plan was that universal health care would not work unless participation was mandatory. She argued Obama's plan was tantamount to making Social Security or Medicare voluntary. She objected, "The difference between Senator Obama and myself is that I know, from the work I've done on health care for many years, that if everyone's not in the system we will continue to let the insurance companies do what's called cherry picking—pick those who get insurance and leave others out."[34] She argued that Obama's plan would end up leaving about 15 million people without coverage because they would not opt into buying health insurance. She countered, "You know, for example, it's been unfortunate that Senator Obama has consistently said that I would force people to have health care whether they could afford it or not. You know, health-care reform and achieving universal health care is a passion of mine. It is something I believe in with all my heart."

Obama disputed Hillary's contention that 15 million people would be left out of his plan, arguing he would mandate every person buy health insurance under his plan, one way or the other. "I have endured over the course of this campaign repeatedly negative mailings from Senator Clinton in Iowa, in Nevada and in other places suggesting that I want to leave 15 million people out," Obama responded.

"According to Senator Clinton, that is accurate. I dispute it, and I think it is inaccurate." In explaining why he felt Clinton's charge was inaccurate, Obama sharpened the contrast, saying: "The reason she thinks that there are more people covered under her plan than mine is because of a mandate. That is not a mandate for the government to provide coverage to everybody; it is a mandate that every individual purchase health care."

Obama has attacked Clinton by demonizing mandates, but he has not explained how his program would work *without* mandates. In the end we are left with an Obama plan that simply assumes everyone will buy the universal health insurance he forces insurance companies to provide, as long as the government subsidizes those who cannot afford the premiums. This has been the crux of the debate between Clinton and Obama on health care. Clinton continues to argue universal health care will not be universal unless participation is mandated.

Fundamentally, Hillary is charging Obama's proposal is impractical, reflecting his naïve assumption his program will become "universal" simply because all consumers will make the decision he wants them to make. As liberal economist and columnist Paul Krugman has concluded, writing in the *New York Times*, "If Mr. Obama gets to the White House and tries to achieve universal coverage, he'll find that it can't be done without mandates—but if he tries to institute mandates, the enemies of reform will use his own words against him."[35]

Obama has placed himself in a dilemma: Clinton's universal health program might fail simply because the cost is uncontainable, resulting in a tax burden Americans could not afford, at least not without destroying the economy by crippling the consumer spending it relies upon for growth.

Clinton's program might result in a bureaucracy that would soon destroy the health system itself, leaving Americans with long lines and endless delays that would end up denying the very health care she wants to provide.

We will probably never get a chance to find out whether Obama's program would suffer from these difficulties. In his determination to distinguish his health program from Hillary's, Obama has gone down a path that has a dead end. Hillary is right: universal health care requires a mandate to participate, just as Social Security and Medicare do. Obama's plan has rhetorical appeal, but examined critically, the plan fails to accomplish the universal coverage that has been the goal for all Democrats since Harry Truman. As Krugman concluded, once we combine the economic analysis and the political reality we are left with the following conclusion: "If Mrs. Clinton gets the Democratic nomination, there is some chance—nobody knows how big—that we'll get universal care in the next administration. If Mr. Obama gets the nomination, it just won't happen."

Under detailed analysis, Obama's rhetoric on universal health care fails to produce a practical plan with a realistic chance of accomplishing his stated goal of being universal at all. Moreover, to defeat Obama, Republican critics only have to repeat, in television commercial after television commercial, Clinton's objection that Obama's plan has no chance whatsoever of working. The ad can conclude: "Obama's Universal Health Insurance Plan? Hillary says, 'IT WON'T WORK!'"

The Clinton-Obama debate has vastly simplified Mc-Cain's task: he can argue that he cannot be expected to figure out the Democratic Party universal health-care plan when even Clinton and Obama cannot agree on what it is. He can then repeat the reliable Republican objections that universal health care would be another bottomless Democratic pit, nothing more than a social welfare giveaway that would destroy the private health-care system.

Conservative surrogates supporting McCain will then be positioned to argue that Obama's plan amounts to merely another instance of income redistribution from the haves to the have-nots, with insurance and pharmaceutical company profits subject to confiscation. The McCain campaign can thus support private enterprise solutions to expand health insurance coverage, as a policy alternative likely to appeal to right-center voters seeking to rein in government spending and bureaucracies.

Obama's Global Poverty Act

As the Democratic primaries were winding down in May 2008, Obama quietly steered his Global Poverty Act, known as S. 2433, through the Senate. Obama likes to characterize S. 2433 as requiring "the president to develop and implement a comprehensive policy to cut extreme global poverty in half by 2015 through aid, trade debt relief, and coordination with the international community, businesses and NGOs (non-governmental organizations)."[36] Obama clearly hopes he will be in his second term as president by then, so reduction of global poverty by half can be traced back to his co-sponsorship of this visionary piece of legislation.

Critics on the right, who were anything but enthusiastic, sarcastically renamed the bill the "Global Poverty Tax." Getting past the typical lofty language of the press release quoted above, Cliff Kincaid, writing in Accuracy in Media, noted the legislation "would commit the

U.S. to spending 0.7 percent of Gross Domestic Product on foreign aid, which amounts to a phenomenal total of $845 billion over and above what the U.S. already spends."[37] Of course, the bill would be paid by the U.S. taxpayer, in what amounts to a redistribution-of-income plan, not from the U.S. haves to the U.S. have-nots, but from the U.S. haves to the world have-nots. Evidently Obama's "Audacity of Hope" extends to giving the U.S. taxpayer the added burden of halving poverty worldwide. Forget about expanding productive business activity to the third world; Obama would end global poverty by largesse.

Moreover, the global poverty reduction goal was mandated by the United Nations General Assembly in its Millennium Declaration of 2000.[38] The declaration specifies, "No individual and no nation must be denied the opportunity to benefit from development," with no particular expectation that each individual or every nation would contribute to economic development. Conservative stalwart Phyllis Schlafly saw Obama's bill as imposing a UN tax on the United States with no concern that "U.S. handouts go into the hands of corrupt dictators who hate us and vote against us in the UN, and that only 30 percent of American foreign aid ever reaches the poor." Schlafly also sees the Global Poverty Act as advancing an undeclared but determined objective of Obama to place the United States under international controls, seriously compromising U.S. sovereignty. Calling the bill anti-American in intent, Schlafly wrote, "The Global Poverty Act would be a giant step toward the Millennium Goals of global governance and international taxes on Americans."[39]

The Millennium Project is monitored by Jeffrey D. Sachs, an economist who directs the "Earth Institute" at Columbia University. In 2005, Sachs presented then–

UN secretary-general Kofi Annan with a three-thousand-page report specifying a series of lofty development goals the United States was committed to bring about through the United Nations as part of the Millennium Development Plan.[40]

Reviewing Sachs's book *The End of Poverty*[41] in the *Washington Post*, New York University economics professor William Easterly severely criticized Sachs for being naïve, describing him as "simply the world's greatest economic reformer,"[41] who had no compunction about enlisting U2 lead singer Bono to pen the book's introduction.[42] Calling Sachs a "utopian," Easterly ridiculed him, explaining that Sachs's plan "covers just about everything in mind-numbing technical jargon, from planting nitrogen-fixing leguminous trees to replenishing soil fertility, to antiretroviral therapy for AIDS, to specially programmed cell phones that provide real-time data to health planners, to rainwater harvesting, to battery-charging stations, and so on." Easterly further noted that under Sachs's scheme "the UN secretary general personally run[s] the overall plan, coordinating the actions of thousands of officials in six UN agencies, UN country teams, the World Bank and the International Monetary Fund." Easterly expressed surprise at how unaware Sachs was of the extent to which his plan resembled other well-intentioned but ill-fated grand plans to eliminate poverty that were championed through international organizations in the 1950s and 1960s.

In the end, Sachs's and Obama's scheme amounts to little more than resentment against the United States for the extent of economic development and standard of living enjoyed in this country. Conservative commentator Lee Cary shared the observation, writing in the *American Thinker* about Obama's Global Poverty Act, that "those who feel like victims want the guilty exposed and loathed."[43] In this context, Cary noted the Obama campaign was airing radio ads in Texas in which Obama claimed that "some CEOs make more in 10 minutes than some American workers make in a year," arguing that this was somehow unfair. Cary noted that Obama did not include in this derision his endorser, television talk show host Oprah Winfrey. Calling Obama the "Global Candidate," Cary concluded his goal was to "cite multinational corporations as the leading exploiters of the world's poor, with Wall Street's favorites leading the pack."

When we examine where Obama has gotten most of the funds to run his 2008 presidential campaign, we find that hypocrisy is evidently not a fault Obama minds having. According to watchdog OpenSecrets.org, Wall Street investment firms and U.S. law firms representing multinational U.S. corporations in their global operations lead the list of Obama bundling contributors.[44] At the top of Obama's contributor list is Goldman Sachs, followed by UBS, JPMorgan Chase, Citigroup, Lehman Brothers, and Morgan Stanley. Among the law firms leading the list of Obama 2008 campaign contributors are New York–based Skadden, Arps; Los Angeles–based Latham & Watkins; Chicago-based Kirkland & Ellis and Sidley Austin, the law firm where Michelle Obama was an associate and met her future husband.

America's middle-class voters, already feeling the economic squeeze from globalization and the outsourcing of U.S. jobs to India and China, would probably not appreciate Obama's plan to increase taxes on U.S. citizens to pay for world poverty through the United Nations. Their resentment could be expected to grow after realizing Obama himself liberally takes campaign contributions from the very investment bankers and law firms benefiting from globalization and outsourcing. In this context, Obama's railing against the rich appears little more than a leftist resentment traceable to his days in Hawaii and in college, smoking marijuana and drinking liquor while listening to the likes of aging communist poet Frank Marshall Davis rail against capitalism.

Obama Fails to Hold Hand over Heart During National Anthem

A photograph published by *Time* magazine during the Iowa Democratic primary showed Obama standing onstage in Indianola, Iowa, on September 17, 2007, during what the magazine identified as a "[Senator] Tom Harkin Steak Fry." The magazine reported the national anthem was being played. Surprisingly, Obama was the only one in the photo who did not have his right hand over his heart. Behind Obama, also standing, were New Mexico governor Bill Richardson and Hillary Clinton, both with their right hands over their hearts. Standing behind Clinton was an identified Iowa Democratic Party official, also with her right hand over her heart. A large American flag formed the backdrop to what appears to be the speakers platform on which they were standing. All four appeared to be looking offstage, at what must have been a flag to their left side, outside the frame of the photograph.

An ABC News video of the event made clear "The Star-Spangled Banner" was being played while Obama stood there, his hands folded together casually in front of him.[45] As the national anthem ended, the ABC camera panned, showing the entire speakers' platform. To the right of the podium were Iowa's Democratic senator Tom Harkin and three other Democrats, who were then still running for president: former North Carolina senator John Edwards, Connecticut senator Christopher Dodd, and Delaware senator Joseph Biden. Everyone on the speakers' platform had their right hand over their heart as the national anthem was being played, except Obama.

The story was first picked up by Mark Finkelstein on the blog NewsBuster.org. Finkelstein cited federal law, subtly making the point Obama lacked respect. According to U.S. Code, Title 36, Chapter 10, Section 171, "During rendition of the national anthem when the flag is displayed, all present except those in uniform should stand at attention facing the flag with the right hand over the heart. Men not in uniform should remove their headdress with their right hand and hold it at the left shoulder, the hand being over the heart." Finkelstein commented, "Does he [Obama] perhaps believe that, like wearing the flag pin, the hand on the heart isn't 'true patriotism'?"[46]

Obama explained, "I was taught by my grandfather that you put your hand over your heart during the pledge, but during the Star Spangled Banner you sing!"[47]

With one photo, the impression swept the country that somehow Obama did not share the pride in the United States that most Americans feel. The image was a prelude to the firestorm over Obama's San Francisco comments about Midwestern voters who "cling to their religions and guns" when economic times get tough. Was Obama so intellectually elite that his patriotism derived from the existentialism of French writers Jean-Paul Sartre or Albert Camus, who refused to affirm, "My country, right or wrong"? As we saw in the quotes at the beginning of this chapter, Obama told ABC News he refused to wear a flag lapel pin because he wanted to maintain the purism of his opposition to the Iraq War. Was his failure to hold his hand over his heart another expression of his antiwar sentiments?

Leftists in the Democratic Party seem untroubled by these images, just as they were in 1971 when John Kerry published his radical antiwar book, *The New Soldier*,[48] with text that disparaged the U.S. military in Vietnam and photographs of bearded leftist street protesters in intentionally disrespectful military uniforms. That book chronicled the events of a three-day protest against the Vietnam War in Washington, D.C., during an event called "Dewey Canyon III," when Kerry was a spokesman for the Vietnam Veterans Against the War. By the time Kerry ran for president in 2004, *The New Soldier* had become a rare book. For decades, Kerry and his supporters had evidently been buying copies of it to remove it from the market, likely aware of the explosive impact the book could have if copies of the original were allowed to circulate widely during his presidential run. Yet in 1971, when the book was published, in both hardcover and paperback, in multiple printings, Kerry was prominently displayed as the lead author on the front cover.

The symbolism captured by the camera, even in an otherwise fleeting moment, can have a major impact, especially if it solidifies for viewers an impression they have held, perhaps until then almost subconsciously, about a candidate. Obama and his supporters may think it is not important to wear a flag lapel pin or to hold his right hand over his heart while the national anthem is played, but try explaining that to veterans and thousands of American families who have lost loved ones in this country's foreign wars, as well as those currently serving in the military and their families.

When the United States has its armed forces in the field of battle, a politician running for president raises many unnecessary questions by refusing to make simple expressions of devotion to the country he aspires to lead. To not do so risks alienating important voter segments, ones that Obama can ill afford to lose, especially when his opponent is John McCain, a former Vietnam War prisoner. Even Obama will have to honor his rival as a legitimate war hero.

OBAMA'S ANTIWAR, ANTI-ISRAEL FOREIGN POLICY

What I do oppose is a dumb war.

> —ILLINOIS STATE SENATOR BARACK OBAMA,
> *antiwar rally, Chicago,* OCTOBER 2, 2002[1]

Some seem to believe we should negotiate with terrorists and radicals, as if some ingenious argument will persuade them they have been wrong all along. We have heard this foolish delusion before. As Nazi tanks crossed into Poland in 1939, an American senator declared: "Lord, if I could only have talked to Hitler, all this might have been avoided." We have an obligation to call this what it is—the false comfort of appeasement, which has been repeatedly discredited by history.

> —PRESIDENT GEORGE W. BUSH,
> *addressing the Israeli Knesset, Jerusalem,*
> MAY 15, 2008[2]

Barack Obama's foreign policy views also derive from his fundamentally leftist orientation. He has opposed the war in Iraq. He has argued we should rapidly become a nation without nuclear weapons in what he imagines could become a "no-nukes" world. He has pledged to reduce the size of the military and stop spending money on expensive new military systems, so we can redirect the savings to social welfare spending. He has been endorsed by a Hamas advisor and accepted the resignation of a Middle Eastern advisor who had been privately meeting with Hamas. He has suggested we should talk with enemies of the United States, including the radical Ahmadinejad regime in Iran, which has threatened to eradicate Israel from the face of the earth. Meanwhile, he has appointed several top foreign policy advisors who deserve their anti-Israel reputations.

As Obama campaigned for the 2008 Democratic presidential nomination, Hillary Clinton repeatedly attacked his foreign policy positions as reflecting his inexperience in international affairs. Moreover, Clinton charged that Obama's votes in the Senate, especially on issues of Iraq War funding, were inconsistent with the antiwar sentiments he expressed in his speeches. Arguing that her foreign policy positions reflected a more mature understanding of what was possible in international affairs, Clinton insisted Obama would have to move more to the political center, as she had, if he were to have any chance of winning the general election contest. At one point President Bill Clinton, campaigning for his wife, shouted out in frustration there was no difference between Obama's and Hillary's voting records on Iraq. "Give me a break," Bill Clinton pleaded with the audience. "This whole thing is the biggest fairy tale I have ever seen."[3]

This chapter will lay out the case that Obama is vulnerable to the charge that his inexperience makes him naïve in foreign policy. His antiwar positions on Iraq and his determination to push nuclear disarmament make him appear soft on defense, just as his willingness to meet with enemy nations makes him look like an appeaser. If Obama is seen as anti-Israel, he will have a very hard time winning the general election, especially since he will need to directly encounter and dismiss an unspoken feeling many voters harbor that his experience growing up with an Islamic father and an Islamic stepfather have predisposed him to side with the Muslim states in the Middle East.

Fundamentally, Obama cannot afford for voters to conclude that his foreign policy is closer to that of Jimmy Carter than of Ronald Reagan.

A Fairy Tale?

Obama's claim that he opposed the Iraq War from the beginning is based on a speech he gave on October 2, 2002, at a modest antiwar rally of about one thousand people in downtown Chicago's Federal Plaza, before a giant abstract Calder statue of a red flamingo. At the time he gave the speech Obama was an obscure Illinois state senator. Surprisingly, in this day of handheld camcorders, Obama's speech was not recorded by anyone. Not even an audiotape of the speech has ever been found. Bill Glauber, the *Chicago Tribune* reporter who covered the protest event, intentionally didn't report on Obama's speech, focusing instead on Reverend Jesse Jackson, the featured speaker.[4] Obama was a mere warm-up act.

Yet, for Obama true believers, this obscure speech has become a defining moment, allowing Obama to claim repeatedly that he is the only candidate running for president in 2008 who opposed the Iraq War before the Senate had even passed a resolution authorizing President Bush to use military force to remove Saddam Hussein from power. "On the most important national-security question since the Cold War, I am the only candidate who opposed the war in Iraq from the beginning," Obama has frequently said in stump speeches. NPR correspondent Don Gonyea has reported that to recover from having no actual recording of the speech at the time it was given, the Obama campaign has gone so far as to re-create portions of the speech for a television ad, with Obama rereading the text in a sound studio, with crowd noises and reactions added to make it seem like the real thing.[5]

Hillary Clinton repeatedly dismissed Obama's claim, saying, "I have the experience. John McCain has the experience. All Barack Obama has is just a speech."[6] In the back-and-forth of the primaries, Obama responded, "My objections to the war in Iraq were not simply a speech. I was in the midst of a U.S. Senate campaign. It was a high-stakes campaign. I was one of the most vocal opponents of the war." Yet NPR's Gonyea has been quick to correct Obama, pointing out that he gave his famous antiwar speech in October 2002 but didn't officially declare his candidacy for the U.S. Senate until January 2003.[7]

The *Sun-Times* reported that during his 2004 race for the U.S. Senate, Obama filled out a questionnaire answering "no" to this question: Would you have voted for the $87 billion supplemental appropriation for Iraq and Afghanistan? Yet, after being elected to the Senate, Obama voted for a series of funding measures, as did Hillary Clinton.[8] Obama's Senate voting record on the Iraq War was the basis for the Bill Clinton accusation that Obama's opposition to the war was a "fairy tale."

Jamie Rubin, a Hillary Clinton spokesman, pointed out that Hillary Clinton's and Barack Obama's voting records in the Senate on the war are virtually identical: "There is nothing unique about his Iraq war position except a speech he made that he never followed through on."[9] Attempting to defend himself, Obama then told reporters in a conference call, "I have been very clear even as a candidate that, once we were in, that we were going to have some responsibility to make it work as best we could, and more importantly that our troops had the best resources they needed to get home safely."[10]

In the end, Hillary scored the point: Obama had to shift ground in order to explain a voting record more centrist on the Iraq War than the words of his unrecorded but highly touted antiwar speech would suggest. The issue was not decisive for Clinton in the primary battle with Obama, but McCain can be expected to revisit the contradiction by showing Obama voted for the war despite his antiwar rhetoric. Obama can be expected to invoke more explanations, attempting to sound patriotic in his unwillingness to abandon U.S. troops in Iraq and Afghanistan now that they are there, but he will still be explaining himself. A presidential candidate in a close general election campaign who is forced to spend time explaining contradictions between his words and actions is, by definition, losing ground.

Since becoming a U.S. senator in 2004, Obama has not introduced a single resolution or bill calling on President Bush to end the war in Iraq or Afghanistan, only a January 2007 bill to de-escalate. In the Democratic debate held in Las Vegas on January 15, 2008, NBC moderator Tim Russert pointedly asked Obama if he would guarantee all U.S. troops would be out of Iraq by January 2013, at the end of his first presidential term in office. Obama refused to issue that guarantee.[11]

Instead, Obama gave a nuanced answer, explaining, "I will end the war as we understand it in combat missions. But we are going to have to protect our embassy. We're going to have to protect civilians. We're engaged in humanitarian activity there. We are going to have some presence that allows us to strike if Al Qaeda is creating bases inside of Iraq.

So I cannot guarantee that we're not going to have a strategic interest that I have to carry out as commander in chief to maintain some troop presence there, but it is not going to be engaged in a war and it will not be this sort of permanent bases and permanent military occupation that George Bush seems to be intent on."[12] The sound bite in that answer is "I cannot guarantee." The rest provides a great deal more wiggle room than Vietnam antiwar protesters of the John Kerry and George McGovern era would have tolerated.

Besides, why exactly is the war in Iraq "dumb," in Obama's view? That the war is "dumb" might be a facile phrase an obscure state senator could issue as the warm-up act in a downtown rally, but the presidential candidate Obama will have to take a clear "Get Out Now" position to explain himself, or risk sounding like a flip-flopper, a charge about John Kerry's position on the war that plagued his 2004 presidential campaign.

Obama repeatedly calls President Bush's policy in Iraq a failure. Yet the surge did succeed in reducing the violence in Iraq. Will Obama still run against the war if the reports coming from Iraq and Afghanistan continue to validate the Bush administration's military policy in the region?

If McCain wanted to stay the course until he could declare victory and stage an orderly withdrawal, why would Obama object? Would Obama do anything different?

McCain has been consistent. He was one of the few U.S. senators to support the surge, and the surge has worked. Obama is stuck with an antiwar policy he may come to regret.

No Nukes!

No Nukes was the name of a 1980 triple live album produced by MUSE, or Musicians United for Safe Energy, from a concert held in New York's Madison Square Garden in September 1979. It is also a key Barack Obama 2008 campaign promise—a world without nuclear weapons. Critics charge that Obama's "No Nukes" policy also bears another resemblance to the bestselling rock album: both sounded good, but neither had any realistic chance of accomplishing the policy goal they proclaimed.

On October 2, 2007, in a much-ballyhooed speech given at Chicago's DePaul University, Obama declared "A New Beginning," announcing, "America seeks a world in which there are no nuclear weapons."[13] The idea sounded right for a New Age candidate promising to transcend all differences and resolve, by new thinking, such complex conundrums as nuclear weapons, which have terrorized the world ever since we dropped the first bomb on Hiroshima in 1945 as a step to end World War II.

We should probably be relieved that in the next sentence Obama made clear he did *not* intend to pursue unilateral disarmament. How then does he intend to pull off the magic of making nuclear weapons go away? He promised to work with Russia "to take U.S. and Russian ballistic missiles off hair-trigger alert." Okay, we can all agree that is a good idea, but how will we do that? Perhaps we should ask the Russians to promise they will think hard about launching a nuclear war before sending the missiles flying.

Next, Obama announced, "We'll start by seeking a global ban on the production of fissile material for weapons." But what happens if China and North Korea simply ignore the global ban or, worse, agree to the global ban with no resolve to keep their promise?

Finally, Obama stated we would set a goal to expand the U.S.-Russian ban on intermediate-range missiles so the agreement is global. Again, this is unlikely to impress Iran's president Mahmoud Ahmadinejad or Ayatollah Ali Khamenei, who seem determined to develop a new class of missiles beyond the Shahab-3, most likely with the purpose of visiting a nuclear weapon upon Israel.

Obama next argued, "As we do this, we'll be in a better position to lead the world in enforcing the rules of the road if we firmly abide by those rules." This is truly the crux of Obama's argument: because we do not demonstrate moral leadership, other nations have no choice but to proliferate nuclear weapons. At the base of the argument, Obama is saying a world with nuclear weapons is our fault. "It's time to stop giving countries like Iran and North Korea an excuse," he said. "It's time for America to lead."

A bit earlier in the speech, Obama took a not very well disguised swipe at what he likes to call George W. Bush's "cowboy diplomacy." Returning to his theme of talking with our enemies, Obama again tried to justify his position: "When I said that as president I would lead direct diplomacy with our adversaries, I was called naïve and irresponsible. But how are we going to turn the page on the failed Bush-Cheney policy of not talking to our adversaries if we don't have a president who will lead that diplomacy?" What happens if our nuclear-powered adversaries are unimpressed? "When I'm president," Obama promised, "we'll strengthen the Nuclear Non-Proliferation Treaty so that nations that don't comply will automatically face strong international sanctions."

Iran is a signatory to the Nuclear Non-Proliferation Treaty. For years the UN International Atomic Energy Agency (IAEA) has issued report after report documenting Iran's refusal to bring their nuclear program into the inspection and compliance requirements the agency has clearly demanded be met. President George W. Bush has worked through his second term in office to negotiate with Iran, first through the EU-3 of France, Germany, and Great Britain, then through the IAEA itself. We have imposed sanctions on Iran through the UN Security Council. But despite all this effort, Iran continues to enrich uranium, ignoring repeated offers from Russia and the United States to supply Iran with all the enriched uranium Iran would need to run a peaceful nuclear program. Despite all this diplomatic pressure, China continues to buy massive quantities of oil and natural gas from Iran, while Russia sells Iran advanced surface-to-air missile systems that Iran uses to harden its multiple nuclear facilities against air and missile attack. Meanwhile, Germany and France, two additional permanent members of the Security Council, continue to allow corporations within their countries to negotiate contracts with Iran, and even to provide assistance to Iran with their nuclear technology.

Every president since Harry Truman has entered office with a resolve to end nuclear proliferation. No president got closer to the goal than Ronald Reagan. At the 1986 summit in Reykjavík, Iceland, Mikhail Gorbachev, then president of the Soviet Union, offered major concessions on reducing nuclear weapons, with only one proviso: the United States had to agree to abandon the space-based missile defense program known as "Star Wars."[14] Reagan refused.

Obama would probably fault Reagan for lack of leadership. Yet, holding firm on the Strategic Defense Initiative, or SDI, Reagan began a military buildup that ultimately forced the Soviet Union to spend itself into bankruptcy and ruin.

Obama's DePaul speech on nuclear weapons bears a lot in common with his later Philadelphia speech on race, "A More Perfect Union," which he gave responding to the attacks over his pastor Reverend Jeremiah Wright's angry anti-American sermons. In both speeches, Obama proposed we needed to take an issue—nuclear proliferation or racial injustice—to a "higher level." His suggestion was that we needed to reframe the questions so we could have a new national debate that would lead to breakthrough ideas and new solutions. This approach would certainly get a top grade, even at Harvard. Yet, what are the new ideas? Countries have nuclear weapons because their enemies have nuclear weapons. It's similar to how since the Supreme Court decided *Brown v. Board of Education* in 1954, we have had a series of laws and court decisions that have essentially made racial discrimination a crime. Yet, we still experience racial prejudice, and the effects of racial inequality are clearly visible in the impoverished ghettos that plague nearly every major city in the nation. We entered a new level of dialogue with *Brown v. Board of Education*, but the underlying reality of racial problems continues. Talk and dialogue over half a century have not been enough to solve either problem— racial discrimination or nuclear weapons. What specifically does Obama want us to do that hasn't already been done?

When Rand Corporation military strategist Herman Kahn wrote his groundbreaking book, *On Escalation,* in 1965, Obama was four years old. Kahn formulated the concept of MAD, or "mutually assured destruction," in the recognition that the only rational solution to another nation's pursuing nuclear weapons aggressively was to pursue nuclear weapons aggressively ourselves. Does Obama truly believe Zbigniew Brzezinski, one of his top foreign policy advisors, is more brilliant than Herman Kahn? Brzezinski advised President Jimmy Carter, and the two of them were clueless during the 444-day American hostage crisis in Iran. Does Obama truly believe Israel will wait indefinitely for Ahmadinejad to build a nuclear weapon that can be dropped on

Tel Aviv? Israel struck Iraq in 1981 when Saddam Hussein was building a nuclear reactor at Osirak. In September 2007, Israel attacked Syria, destroying what is widely believed to be a nuclear reactor being built by Syria with the assistance of North Korea.

Obama's resolve to create a "no-nukes" world is admirable. Yet even Obama realizes unilateral nuclear disarmament is foolhardy. Short of unilateral nuclear disarmament, what sentence does Obama think he can form that will convince China, Russia, North Korea, and Iran that they are making a mistake to pursue nuclear weapons?

Obama's Anti-Israel "No-Nukes" Advisor

A contributor to Obama's "no-nukes" policy is Joseph Cirincione, the president of the Ploughshares Fund. Writing in the *New York Review of Books*, Cirincione has blamed the late Caspar Weinberger and a group of analysts that have come to be known as the "neocons," including Richard Perle and Paul Wolfowitz, for wrongly dismissing Gorbachev's disarmament proposals at Reykjavík as mere tricks. Cirincione believes momentum is building for a nuclear-free world from the efforts of former secretaries of state George Shultz and Henry Kissinger. He argued, "For the first time since the initial efforts of the Truman administration in the 1940s, a movement to eliminate nuclear weapons has developed not from the political left but from the 'realist' center of the security elite."[15] Cirincione acknowledges that nuclear disarmament proposals from the political left have historically been doomed to failure, yet he places himself squarely on the left anyway, joining with Obama in calling Iraq a "disastrous conflict" that has shown "how misguided the Bush Doctrine was."[16]

Just as Cirincione was inclined to believe Gorbachev at Reykjavik, he seems perpetually inclined to dismiss threats we face from enemies. He embraced the November 2007 National Intelligence Estimate (NIE) that claimed Iran ended its work on a nuclear weapons program in 2003,[17] ignoring critiques of the NIE process.[18] Meanwhile, the International Atomic Energy Agency continues to insist Iran maintains a secret nuclear weapons program in contravention of the agency's inspection requirements. An IAEA report issued on February 22, 2008, repeated concerns about undisclosed aspects of Iran's nuclear program and emphasized that Iran has added new-generation centrifuges to the uranium enrichment plant at Natanz, a plant Iran insists on operating despite IAEA decisions to the contrary.[19] In numerous writings Cirincione has argued the Bush administration is running a scare campaign over Iran's nuclear program similar to the concerns over Iraqi weapons of mass destruction the administration cited in the ramp-up to the Iraq War.

Cirincione has been outspoken in his criticism of Israel's attack in Syria. Quoted in September 2007, on the blog of *Foreign Policy* magazine, Cirincione claimed the White House was trying to push a North Korea–Syria connection as a political story. "The mainstream media seams to have learned nothing from the run-up to the war in Iraq," he said.[20] "Once again, this appears to be the work of a small group of officials leaking cherry-picked, unvetted 'intelligence' to key reporters in order to promote a pre-existing political agenda." Seeing Israel as the real culprit, he continued, "If this sounds like the run-up to the war in Iraq, it should. This time it appears aimed at derailing the U.S.–North Korean agreement that administration hardliners think is appeasement. Some Israelis want to thwart any dialogue between U.S. and Syria."

In a September 2007 interview with National Public Radio, Cirincione argued, "certain hard-line Israelis" were using the air strike to prevent U.S.-Syrian or Israeli-Syrian dialogue. "This is the most overblown story I've seen since before the buildup to the war in Iraq," he repeated. "There's precious little information available, but it hasn't stopped people with political agendas from spinning at such an absurd level as if these claims are facts."[21]

Even after the United States released photographs in April 2008 showing what appears to be the inside of the nuclear reactor, and a Syrian official standing with a well-known engineer for the North Korean government with Syrian license plates in the background,[22] Cirincione still refused to believe U.S. intelligence assessments that Israel destroyed in Syria a North Korean–built nuclear reactor that Syria had not disclosed to the IAEA. Cirincione told the *Guardian* in London, "We should learn first from the past and be very cautious about any intelligence from the U.S. about other country's weapons."[23] This is a major Cirincione theme that Obama seems to have bought—that a major reason for the nuclear arms race is not objective assessments of foreign nuclear threats, but a tendency by U.S. intelligence to overestimate the nuclear weapons capabilities of our enemies.

Aaron Klein, World Net Daily's Jerusalem correspondent, wrote an exposé of Cirincione on May 1, 2008. He found that Cirincione's writings show a fundamental anti-Israel resentment that guides much of his thinking about nuclear weapons and the Middle East. In Klein's words, Cirincione believes "Israel should give up its nuclear weapons to ensure Iran halts its illicit nuclear program."[24] Klein essentially concludes that Cirincione blames Israel for Iran's secret pursuit of nuclear weapons, sees Iran as taking a defensive posture against Israel, and absolves the Ahmadine-jad regime of any truly aggressive, hostile intent to vanquish the Jewish state. Klein turned up many instances of Cirincione describing Syria's nuclear capabilities as "minuscule" in an attempt to justify his position that Israel's air strike was an overreaction. Cirincione has been quoted as saying, "The world does well to remember most Middle East weapons programs began as a response to Israel's nuclear weapons."[25]

Ed Lasky, writing in the *American Thinker*, agrees with Klein. "Cirincione blames Israel for nuclear proliferation," Lasky wrote, "and seemingly wants to pressure Israel to shut down its nuclear program and strip itself of any nuclear weapons it may or may not have in its inventory." Lasky noted Cirincione was "another in a disconcertingly long line of Obama advisors, who seemingly have an anti-Israel bias and who would be very willing to apply American pressure on our tiny ally to disarm itself in the face of its mortal enemies."[26] If Obama's "new idea" on nuclear weapons means Israel should first disarm, the idea is certain to be a nonstarter. If Obama's policy is rooted in Cirincione's anti-Israel thinking, Obama will soon be seen as doing no more service to Israel than Jimmy Carter did when he decided to tell the world Israel has 150 nukes, classified information Carter had no authorization to disclose.

Obama's Anti-Israel Campaign Co-Chairman

Another Obama advisor with decidedly anti-Israel views is General Merrill "Tony" McPeak, retired U.S. Air Force chief of staff under President Clinton, who is currently a senior foreign policy advisor to Obama and co-chairman of

Obama's presidential campaign committee.

Since the 1970s, McPeak has repeatedly stated that Israel runs U.S. foreign policy. McPeak has implied U.S. politicians are afraid of Jewish voters in New York City and Miami and that American Jews are the "problem" impeding a solution to the Israeli-Palestinian conflict. McPeak has also compared the Hamas and Hezbollah terrorist organizations to what he has described as religious radicals in Oregon. McPeak claims born-again Christians supported the war in Iraq because they wanted Israel to win, as part of a grand strategy to prepare the world for the second coming of Jesus Christ. In 2004, McPeak supported Howard Dean, before backing John Kerry.

Robert Goldberg, vice president of the Center for Medicine in the Public Interest, first exposed McPeak's anti-Israel views in an article Goldberg authored in the *American Spectator* in March 2008.[27] McPeak had just filmed a television commercial for Obama accusing Bill Clinton of using McCarthy-like techniques to unfairly question Obama's patriotism. Goldberg began by pointing to a 1976 article McPeak penned in the Council on Foreign Relations magazine *Foreign Affairs*,[28] in which McPeak questioned Israel's insistence on holding on to the Golan Heights and parts of the West Bank.

In a 2003 interview with the *Oregonian*,[29] McPeak advanced the theory that an Israeli lobby controls U.S. policy in the Middle East, with the result that we have inflamed Islamic public opinion against us, thereby jeopardizing U.S. national security. "We don't have a playbook for the Middle East," McPeak told the *Oregonian*. "You know, for instance, obviously part of that long-term strategy would be getting the Israelis and the Palestinians together at ... . something other than a peace process. Process is not a substitute for achievement or settlement. And even so, the process has gone off the tracks." The *Oregonian* asked McPeak if the problem in solving the Israeli-Palestinian conflict was the White House or the State Department. McPeak surprisingly answered, "New York City. Miami. We have a large vote—vote here in favor of Israel. And no politician wants to run against it." McPeak went on to say, "I think that everybody understands that a settlement of the Arab-Israeli problem would require the Israelis to stop settling the West Bank and the Gaza Strip, and maybe even withdraw some of the settlements they've already been put there. And nobody wants to take on that problem. It's just too tough politically. So that means we can't . . . you can't develop a Middle East strategy. It's impossible."

Goldberg quoted McPeak as claiming, "Let's say that one of your abiding concerns is the security of Israel as opposed to a purely American self-interest, then it would make sense to build a dozen or so bases in Iraq. Let's say you are a born-again Christian and you think that Armageddon and the rapture are about to happen any minute and what you want to do is retrace steps you think are laid out in Revelations, then it makes sense. So there are a number of scenarios here that could lead you in this direction. This is radical . . ." Goldberg also quoted McPeak's comment, "The secret of the neoconservative movement is that it's not conservative, it's radical. Guys like me, who are conservatives, are upset about these neocons calling themselves conservative when they're radical."

For Goldberg the conclusion was clear: "Guys like McPeak are upset because they think Jews have too much influence." McPeak's argument is that American foreign policy is the result of a Jewish lobby in New York and Miami, evangelical Christians, and neocons—all of whom he demonizes. "McPeak's comments are worse than McCarthyism," Goldberg charged. "They reflect the views of Reverend Wright and other Obama advisors who believe that Israel is just a problem to be solved, not an ally to support.

"Obama has a Jewish problem and McPeak's bigoted views are emblematic of what they are," Goldberg stressed. "Obama can issue all the boilerplate statements supporting Israel's right to defend itself he wants. But until he accepts responsibility for allowing people like McPeak so close to his quest for the presidency, Obama's sincerity and judgment will remain open questions."

Hamas Endorses Obama

On April 13, 2006, Aaron Klein of World Net Daily and talk radio host John Batchelor interviewed Ahmed Yousef, the chief political advisor to the prime minister of Hamas, on ABC radio. Yousef endorsed Barack Obama for president, saying, "We like Mr. Obama, and we hope that he will win the elections."[30]

Yousef picked up the phrasing of Obama's campaign slogan calling for change: "I hope Mr. Obama and the Democrats will change the political discourse." He went on to say that Obama "is like John Kennedy, a great man with a great principle. And he has a vision to change America to make it in a position to lead the world community, but not with humiliation and arrogance." Yousef, the Hamas figure responsible for coordinating meetings with foreign officials, had told Klein a week earlier that Jimmy Carter's visit to the Middle East to meet with Hamas would help end the group's international isolation. "If he comes and meets Hamas, this will also enhance the image and understanding between America and the Muslim world," Yousef explained by phone from Gaza. "Carter's visit is a good step and a positive step in the right direction. It would engage the world community."[31]

"I think it's very clear that it's understandable why they [Hamas] would not want me to be president of the United States," McCain told Fox, responding to the news that Hamas had endorsed Obama. "So, if Senator Obama is favored by Hamas, I think people can make judgments accordingly." He added, "I think that the people should understand that I will be Hamas's worst nightmare." McCain's campaign spokesman, Brian Rogers, told Fox News the Hamas endorsement of Obama "is a legitimate issue for the American people to think about." He further suggested that Hamas's support stemmed from Obama's willingness to hold diplomatic talks with nations such as Iran. Rogers called Obama's foreign policy a "radical departure" from current standards of dealing with "rogue regimes."[32]

Obama spokesman Hari Sevugan fired back a testy statement charging McCain had broken his word to run a respectful campaign. "This type of politics of division and distraction not only lead to a campaign not worthy of the American people but also has failed to help our families for too long," Sevugan said, insisting Obama had already rejected Hamas's legitimacy. Sevugan also insisted Obama would not negotiate with Hamas unless the group renounced terrorism, recognized Israel's right to exist, and held to other agreements.

The Obama camp's reaction prompted Philip Klein, a reporter for the *American Spectator*, to write, "Throughout the campaign, Obama and his staffers have dismissed any scrutiny of his views on Israel with a blend of outrage and sarcasm, as if his record of support for Israel is so extensive, so undeniable, that anybody who raises doubts about his actual views is launching an inquisition." Still, Klein observed, "as is the case with most issues, Obama is such a blank slate, has such a thin public record, that voters are forced to parse his statements, sift through his past, and examine those he chooses to associate with to get a better sense of his underlying philosophy."[33]

An exchange of barbs ensued between the Obama and McCain campaigns. On May 8, 2008, Obama spoke at a Washington reception marking the sixtieth anniversary of Israeli independence, where he affirmed that his commitment to Israel was "unshakable."[34] Obama also counterattacked McCain, denouncing McCain's comments about Hamas as a "smear tactic." The same day, in an interview with CNN's Wolf Blitzer, Obama said McCain's comments about Hamas endorsing Obama showed McCain was "losing his bearings as he pursues this nomination."[35] This prompted McCain spokesman and senior advisor Mark Salter to point out that Obama chose the words "losing his bearings" intentionally, "a not particularly clever way of raising John McCain's age as an issue." Salter further charged that Obama was "trying desperately to delegitimize the discussion of issues that raise legitimate questions about his judgment and preparedness to be President of the United States."[36]

The next day, McCain could well feel vindicated on the issue, when an Obama Middle East advisor, Robert Malley, was forced to sever ties with the Obama campaign. The *Times* of London confirmed Malley had been holding a series of previously undisclosed, private meetings with the Palestinian terrorist group Hamas.[37] Malley told the *Times* he had been in regular contact with Hamas, which controls Gaza and is listed by the U.S. State Department as a terrorist organization. Malley said his talks were related to his work for the International Crisis Group, a conflict resolution think tank where Malley works. Malley also claimed that his talks with Hamas had no connection with his position on Obama's Middle East advisory council. "I've never hidden the fact that in my job with the International Crisis Group I meet all kinds of people," Malley told the *Times*.[38]

This was another story Aaron Klein cracked, first writing an exposé in World Net Daily on January 29, 2008.[39] Klein focused on opinion articles that Malley had coauthored with Hussein Agha, a former advisor to the late Palestinian Authority president Yasser Arafat, urging Israeli dialogue with Hamas and blasting Israel for numerous policies Malley says harm the Palestinian cause. Klein further highlighted a piece Malley wrote in the *New York Times* when the Camp David talks broke down at the end of the Clinton administration. Malley had characteristically blamed the United States for the failure of the talks. Klein also pointed out Malley was on record saying the United States should "not discourage third-party unofficial contacts with Hamas in an attempt to moderate it." Yet, Klein noted, Hamas has been responsible "for scores of deadly shootings, suicide bombings and rocket attacks aimed at Jewish population centers. The past few weeks alone, Hamas militants took credit for firing more than 200 rockets into Israel." Klein also noted that Hamas's official charter still calls for the murder of Jews and the destruction of Israel.

Thus the disclosures forced Malley's resignation from Obama's Middle East advisory council. To explain Malley's departure, Ben LaBolt, yet another Obama spokesman, used a familiar Obama technique when confronted with the politically inconvenient views of close associates. LaBolt simply denied Malley played any formal role in the campaign.

Randy Scheunemann, McCain's foreign policy chief, responded, "Perhaps because of his inexperience Senator

Obama surrounds himself with advisers that contradict his stated policy." Obama's camp made no effort to refute or explain the extensive pro-Hamas and anti-Israel pieces that Malley wrote over a period of years.

On May 12, 2008, Jeffrey Goldberg published an interview on Atlantic.com with Obama in which he asked about the Ahmed Yousef endorsement. "I think what is going on there is the same reason why there are some suspicions of me in the Jewish community," Obama said. He then commented, "We don't do nuance well in politics and especially don't do it well on Middle Eastern policy." Then Obama admitted, "It's conceivable that there are those in the Arab world who say to themselves, 'This is a guy who spent some time in the Muslim world, has a middle name of Hussein, and appears more worldly and has called for talks with people, and so he's not going to be engaging in the same sort of cowboy diplomacy as George Bush,' and that's something they're hopeful about."[40] What Obama said, in effect, was that the Hamas endorsement made sense to him.

Two days later, Hamas sources, speaking on condition of anonymity, told Aaron Klein that the terror group was strongly considering issuing an official statement claiming it does not endorse any U.S. presidential candidates and that the remarks made by Yousef were "misunderstood."[41] Clearly, Hamas wanted Obama to win so badly, the organization was contemplating doing whatever it could to end the controversy, even if it required backtracking on its endorsement.

Regardless of whether Hamas formally decides to withdraw their endorsement of Obama or not, the damage to the Obama campaign had been done. In the initial interview with Yousef, Klein pointed out that Obama had called Hamas a "terrorist organization" that should remain isolated until it renounces violence and recognizes Israel. Klein also brought to Yousef's attention the fact that Obama had told reporters he opposed Carter's meeting with Hamas. Yousef chalked up Obama's statements to political posturing: "I understand American politics and this is the season for elections and everybody tries to sound like he's a friend of the Israelis," Yousef responded to Klein. In other words, Yousef was saying he and his fellow terrorists accepted that Obama would say whatever he had to say just to get elected.

Obama Promises to Talk with Our Enemies, Without Preconditions

Obama's promise to talk with avowed enemies of the United States can be traced back to the CNN/YouTube primary debate held in Charleston, South Carolina, on July 23, 2007. A prerecorded question from a viewer asked, "In the spirit of bold leadership, would you be willing to meet separately, without precondition, during the first year of your administration, in Washington or anywhere else, with the leaders of Iran, Syria, Venezuela, Cuba and North Korea, in order to bridge the gap that divides our countries?"[42]

Obama answered first, affirming instantly, "I would. And the reason is this, that the notion that somehow not talking to countries is punishment to them—which has been the guiding principle of this administration—is ridiculous." Clearly, Obama used the question to take yet another swipe at the Bush administration. Yet, in saying he would meet without preconditions, Obama had committed himself to a position in which he looked inexperienced. As the issue developed, Obama has tried to take this statement back, qualifying that he would not put the United States in a position of being humiliated by an ill-advised meeting with a hostile head of state.

In follow-up questions, Obama agreed he would meet with a real rogues' gallery without preconditions: Mahmoud Ahmadinejad, Bashar al-Assad, Hugo Chávez, Fidel Castro, and Kim Jong Il. The video clip of Obama's answer can be played over and over in opposition television commercials in the general election, forcing Obama to either support this position or explain later qualifications in a nuanced answer unlikely to make points with voters.

Hillary Clinton was the first to criticize Obama, right then and there. "Well, I will not promise to meet with the leaders of these countries during my first year," she said. "I will promise a very vigorous diplomatic effort because I think it is not that you promise a meeting at that high a level before you know what the intentions are." She indicated she wanted to return to pursue diplomacy aggressively, but she cautioned, "But certainly, we're not going to just have our president meet with Fidel Castro and Hugo Chávez and, you know, the president of North Korea, Iran and Syria until we know better what the way forward would be."

CNN's Anderson Cooper, the debate moderator, then asked John Edwards if he would meet with Hugo Chávez, Castro, and Kim Jong Il. Edwards responded reflexively saying "yes," though he immediately added, "I think actually Senator Clinton's right, though. Before that meeting takes place, we need to do the work, the diplomacy, to make sure that the meeting's not going to be used for propaganda purposes, will not be used to just beat down the United States of America in the world community."

Obama should know that diplomacy has not always been a successful foreign policy ploy for Democratic presidents. Many attribute the building of the Berlin Wall and the Cuban Missile Crisis to miscalculations Soviet premier Nikita

Khrushchev made, judging President John F. Kennedy as weak, after Kennedy's poor performance at the summit meeting in Vienna on June 4, 1961. Kennedy had just come off the failure of the Bay of Pigs invasion and most observers felt Khrushchev held the edge in his one-on-one talks with JFK.

During Bill Clinton's administration, Secretary of State Madeleine Albright pursued a policy of meeting and working with our enemies, often to the administration's and the nation's detriment. On Saint Patrick's Day in 2000, Albright addressed the Iranian government in a speech to the American Iranian Council. Albright actually apologized for U.S. involvement in the 1953 overthrow of Iranian prime minister Mohammed Mossadegh. She engaged in historical revisionism, arguing that Iranians were right to resent the United States because our intervention included sustaining the Shah's regime. She then took steps toward normalizing relations with Iran, allowing the import of carpets and food products, including dried fruits, nuts, and caviar. The response from Iran was considerably less than Albright hoped for. The following month, Ayatollah Khamenei launched an even more repressive crackdown on dissidents within Iran.[43]

Yet liberal Democratic senators running for president for some reason think they will look like leaders if they campaign on their willingness to meet with dictators. In 2004, during the first presidential debate held between President Bush and Senator John Kerry, the Democratic challenger suggested diplomacy could resolve our concerns over North Korea's and Iran's nuclear programs, almost exactly prefiguring the stance Obama articulated four years later. With regard to Iran, Senator Kerry went so far as to argue, "I think the United States should have offered the opportunity to provide the nuclear fuel, to test them, see whether or not they were actually looking for it for peaceful purposes."[44]

Kerry was advocating a repeat of the failed Clinton administration approach with North Korea, when we supplied the repressive communist nation with nuclear technology and fuel on the presumption we would be able to control their nuclear program to keep it peaceful. Clinton even dispatched Jimmy Carter to North Korea to negotiate, resulting in the "Agreed Framework" of 1994, in which North Korea agreed not to pursue nuclear weapons. In the end, Kim Jong Il kept all the economic aid and the nuclear technology Bill Clinton shipped to North Korea and developed nuclear weapons anyway. The Democratic Party appears to have amnesia over the total failure of the Clinton-Albright-Carter team to produce results with either Iran or North Korea, despite all the diplomacy they tried and all the face-to-face meetings they held.

Bush Blasts Appeasement

On May 15, 2008, President Bush addressed the Israeli Knesset in Jerusalem, on the occasion of the sixtieth anniversary of Israel. His speech included the statement about appeasement that appears at the beginning of this chapter. Without mentioning anyone by name, Bush recalled the statement of a U.S. senator at the time of World War II who felt he could have stopped Hitler from invading Poland in 1939, if only he had had the chance to talk with Hitler in advance.

Senator Obama decided the comment was aimed at him and took offense. The White House expressed surprise at his reaction. Ed Gillespie, an advisor traveling with President Bush in the Middle East, told the press the White House actually had a rebuke to Jimmy Carter in mind when the speech to the Knesset was drafted.[45] But CNN reported that White House aides privately indicated the criticism was aimed at various Democrats, including Obama and former president Carter.[46] The month before, Carter had held unauthorized private meetings in Damascus with exiled Hamas leader Khaled Meshaal, despite Bush administration requests that he forgo the meeting. Obama could have avoided the entire controversy simply by ignoring Bush's remarks; instead he chose to jump on the remarks, a decision that put appeasement front and center in the presidential contest.

Obama's seemingly disproportionate response revealed his campaign's sensitivity on foreign policy issues. Obama decided to blast Bush, saying his comments on appeasement were "exactly the appalling attack that's divided our country and alienates us from the rest of the world."[47] Obama defended himself, insisting he would pursue diplomacy aggressively, and that the difference in his policy would be the willingness by an Obama administration to negotiate directly with our enemies, not through surrogates such as the EU-3 or the IAEA.

But the more Obama explained his position, the less distinct his approach began to seem. Responding to questions from news reporters, Obama admitted he would first work through administration operatives before he as president would meet with an enemy head of state. Obama also hedged, saying he would have preconditions, trying to sidestep an appearance he would negotiate with Hamas, for instance, unless Hamas dropped its insistence that the state of Israel must be destroyed. The more Obama retreated into government-to-government negotiations preceding head-of-state summits and the more he hedged that there would have to be conditions before meetings could be held with terrorist states, the less sharp was the distinction he was advocating.

In the final analysis, what would Obama say to Iran in a face-to-face meeting with Ahmadinejad that has not already been communicated? Iran understands the United States wants Iran to stop enriching uranium. For four years since 2004, the Bush administration has worked to obtain UN Security Council sanctions on Iran in order to get the Islamic republic to stop enriching uranium. How could Iran possibly miss the point? Iran also understands we want them to stop funding terrorist organizations, including Hezbollah in Lebanon and Hamas in the Gaza Strip. We have been equally clear about Iran meddling in Iraq. Virtually since the beginning of the Iraq War, the Bush administration has been using a wide variety of diplomatic forums to show evidence to the world that Iran has been funding terrorists in Iraq and supplying them with Iranian-made weapons, including advanced design improvised explosive devices.

The Bush administration has managed to communicate all this very clearly, without a single face-to-face encounter between Bush and Ahmadinejad.

Obama may have best explained his underlying thinking during an interview with Tim Russert on NBC's *Meet the Press* on May 4, 2008. Answering Russert's question about how Obama planned to deal with Iran, Obama first took his usual swipe at Bush, repeating his often used line about "cowboy diplomacy." Then, Obama said, "When Iran is able to go to the United Nations complaining about the statements made and get some sympathy, that's a sign that we are taking the wrong approach."[48]

Somehow, Obama, along with Clinton and Kerry before him, believes we have foreign policy problems because we are the bad guy. That explains why Madeleine Albright thought she could make progress with Iran by apologizing. Chamberlain tried appeasing Hitler in Munich in 1938. President Bush has a point: diplomacy does not typically work with insane dictators.

Iran has refused to stop enriching uranium regardless of what approach the United States, Israel, the EU-3, and the United Nations have collectively taken. Iran has not stopped enriching uranium, because Iran does not *want* to stop enriching uranium.

The truth is that President Ahmadinejad represents a very radical, terrorist-supporting regime and Iran has a stated public policy to destroy Israel. Very possibly, even Democratic contenders for the presidency might want to consider taking Ahmadinejad at his word. While Bush was addressing the Knesset, Ahmadinejad was telling the French press, "Those who think they can revive the stinking corpse of the usurping and fake Israeli regime by throwing a birthday party are seriously mistaken. Today the reason for the Zionist regime's existence is questioned and this regime is on its way to annihilation."[49] Ahmadinejad has always spoken clearly about his hatred for Israel and he has never needed a face-to-face meeting with any counterpart head of state to do so.

In the end, Obama was cornered. He had to explain why he was not an appeaser, in a policy debate that made him appear eager to be sympathetic to a leader like Ahmadinejad—who appears at best to be a madman obsessed with Jew-hatred. This is the exact foreign policy posture Obama should avoid if he wants to have any realistic chance of being elected president in November 2008.

An Obama Foreign Policy

Obama's foreign policy appears predicated on an overconfidence that the power of his personality and his willingness to negotiate will somehow transform international politics to the point where we can pursue nuclear weapons disarmament, reduce our military, and withdraw from Iraq without adverse consequences, even for Israel. Obama talks as if he can transcend international politics-as-usual simply by employing some of the listening skills he learned in Saul Alinsky's radical community-organizing methodology.

As noble as these Obama goals are, Obama risks looking naïve and inexperienced not to realize that both Democratic and Republican presidential administrations have pursued goals such as worldwide nuclear disarmament since the Kennedy administration, with only minimal progress. To be credible, Obama will have to articulate specific methods by which he intends to achieve these goals. Iran, certain to be a major issue in the 2008 contest, is a good example. Since the Carter administration, U.S. presidents, again both Democratic and Republican alike, have failed to make progress stopping the Iranian revolution from spreading across the region. What exactly will Obama do differently when the Carter and Clinton administrations demonstrated how intractable the mullahs are, even in the face of sincere efforts to negotiate?

Moreover, American presidents who have distinguished themselves in foreign policy have done so from a position of strength. FDR won World War II by *fighting* Nazi Germany and Imperial Japan, not by negotiating with them. Demanding "unconditional surrender" positioned FDR for victory, not a willingness to meet with Adolf Hitler and Hideki Tojo in unconditional talks. Ronald Reagan won the Cold War by pursuing Star Wars and revitalizing the U.S. military, not by conceding to Gorbachev in Iceland.

Military strength, not an enthusiasm for listening to dictators, has been the backbone of U.S. foreign policy since the end of World War II. Or, as Scott Johnson has observed on Power Line, "Obama's foreign policy 'realism' is of the peculiarly unrealistic kind that verges on fantasy and delusion."[50]

When Obama backs away from a debate position where he stated clearly he would negotiate with U.S. enemies without preconditions, he risks proposing a foreign policy that could appear nuanced at best and confused at worst. Neither is likely to impress undecided voters. Would Obama not negotiate with Hamas or Hezbollah because both are sworn to destroy Israel? Or would Obama seek direct talks with Ahmadinejad, with the idea that he can go directly to the terrorist sponsor to solve the problem?

Ahmadinejad has sent President Bush letters that amount to little more than ideological bombast. Does Obama want to travel to Tehran or a neutral site such as Geneva to hear more of the madman's lectures?

Foreign policy is Obama's Achilles' heel. McCain will succeed by pressing Obama on specifics, demanding Obama stop blaming George W. Bush for international problems that go back at least to the Clinton administration, if not farther into history. Obama appears to have at best only an intellectual understanding of foreign affairs. He has had limited international travel in his life, with Kenya being the foreign country he has visited the most often. As the Kenyan angle is investigated and Obama's interference to support Raila Odinga is understood, Obama may be seen to be inclined to pursue personal objectives in international relations, not necessarily objectives that derive from wide experience or a consistent concept of U.S. national security interests.

Obama will undoubtedly campaign in the general election saying he wants to maintain a strong military, just as he will say he is fully committed to the survival of Israel.

Obama's problem is that neither position may be credible in the face of video clips that show him saying he wants to reduce the military, cut nuclear weapons, and pull out of Iraq.

Nor are Israel or supporters of Israel likely to be impressed if Obama insists on surrounding himself with top advisors such as Robert Malley, Joseph Cirincione, and General Tony McPeak.

~ CONCLUSION ~

Defeating Obama

Tonight, with the wind at our backs, with friends at our sides, and with courage in our hearts, the race to the finish line begins. And we're going to win this race.

—MICHAEL DUKAKIS, *acceptance speech, Democratic National Convention, ATLANTA, JULY 21, 1988*[1]

We cannot win with eggheads and African-Americans. OK, that is the Dukakis Coalition, which carried ten states and gave us four years of the first George Bush.

—PAUL BEGALA, *remarks on CNN, MAY 6, 2008*[2]

Politics, in a sense, has always been a con game," wrote Joe McGinniss in his classic book, *The Selling of the President 1968.*[3] McGinnis pointed out that U.S. presidential candidates ever since Dwight Eisenhower in 1952 have routinely hired advertising agencies. Image packaging has become so much a part of presidential politics that top political operatives of both parties have been forced to realize that "you sell your candidates and your programs the way a business sells its products."[4]

A generation before McGinnis, the importance of imaging was fully appreciated by Edward Bernays, the man who created the modern public-relations business. "Present-day politics places emphasis on personality," Bernays wrote in 1928, the year Republican Herbert Hoover defeated Democratic challenger Al Smith. "An entire party, a platform, an international policy is sold to the public, or is not sold, on the basis of the intangible element of personality. A charming candidate is the Alchemist's secret that can transmute a prosaic platform into the gold of votes."

Yet Bernays fundamentally disagreed with McGinnis: "Not personality, but the ability of the candidate to carry out the party's program adequately, and the program itself should be emphasized in a sound campaign," Bernays continued. "Even Henry Ford, the most picturesque personality in business in America to-day, has become known through his product, not his product through him."[5] In other words, for Bernays in 1928, a con game was not enough to win. Public relations and image advertising were necessary, Bernays argued, but not sufficient conditions for guaranteeing electoral success. For Bernays, policy issues and the substance of a party's program were of such paramount importance that the candidate should never be allowed to become the message.

In 2008, David Axelrod and Barack Obama decided to run a presidential campaign on a cult of personality. Will they succeed, especially given Obama's leftist political record?

In U.S. presidential general elections, the winner is determined more by issues than by personality. Here

John McCain has an advantage. McCain's strength involves policy issues, especially with a general electorate that in the United States is still today more center-right politically than it is far left. Moreover, campaigns run on personality are inherently difficult to pull off. The problem Axelrod and Obama have is that maintaining the facade of a cult of personality is a bit like a tightrope act: one misstep and the tightrope walker can fall ingloriously.

By pressing issues, McCain can force Obama to enter the specifics of policy arguments, pointing out contradictions every time Obama tries to move from his leftist voting record to the political center. Does Obama really want to campaign on the extreme positions he took to win the primaries? For instance, does Obama really want to insist he will meet with heads of state of nations hostile to the United States, face-to-face without preconditions? The more Obama hedges and qualifies to say he will or will not meet with Hugo Chávez, or Fidel Castro, or Mahmoud Ahmadinejad, the more confusing his policy becomes. Obama succeeded in the Democratic primaries by positioning left of Hillary Clinton, but this very advantage could easily turn around to defeat him in a general-election campaign, in which voters typically reject extreme policy positions.

Then too, the facade of personality Obama has constructed in his two books is a complex story that includes an African father, a youthful search for identity that included drug use, and an angry Christian black-liberation theology pastor whose sermons offend with outrageous statements of anti-American rage and anti-Israel hate. Cracks in this facade are tough to repair in general-election news cycles where stories that normally would take weeks to develop can be fully played out in a matter of minutes. With Obama's complex life story, Axelrod has a lot to defend, as Hillary Clinton effectively pointed out.

Is Obama Another Dukakis?

Paul Begala, a top Democratic consultant, raised the concern that Obama may be another Dukakis, a candidate without a deep enough political base to win a general election presidential campaign. As Begala pointed out in the quotation at the beginning of this chapter, Obama cannot win with a coalition of eggheads and African-Americans. Begala argued that with a similar coalition, Michael Dukakis won only ten states in his 1988 presidential contest with George H. W. Bush.

Twenty years ago, when Massachusetts governor Michael Dukakis accepted the Democratic Party nomination for president, he was confident of victory. Understanding why Dukakis lost to George H. W. Bush in 1988 provides clues as to how Barack Obama can be defeated by John McCain in 2008.

In his acceptance speech at the Democratic National Convention in Atlanta on July 21, 1988, Dukakis made reference to his Greek ancestry, telling the enthusiastic delegates that he was a product of the American dream, "a dream that brought my father to this country 76 years ago; that brought my mother and her family here one year later—poor, unable to speak English; but with a burning desire to succeed in their new land of opportunity." He referred to his cousin, Olympia Dukakis, who had just won an Oscar for her supporting role in the hit movie *Moonstruck*.

In 1988, the country was ready for a Democratic president, after eight years of Republican rule under Ronald Reagan.

What was decisive in defeating Dukakis was not his Greek heritage. That was seen as a positive by many voters, as was his success in advancing from an immigrant family to be the Democratic Party's candidate for president. What was decisive was where Dukakis stood on the issues.

Bush effectively portrayed Dukakis as being soft on crime, an impression forcefully communicated by a television commercial explaining how Dukakis had given a furlough to Willie Horton, a convicted murderer, who then committed a rape and assault in Maryland. Then, in responding to a question in a debate with Bush, Dukakis hedged when asked how he would respond if his wife were raped and murdered.

Bush also succeeded in portraying Dukakis as weak on national defense, pointing out Dukakis's opposition to President Reagan's "Star Wars" space-defense initiative. Again, Bush was aided by a Dukakis misstep. Dukakis never recovered from his famous "tank moment," when he was photographed wearing a tank helmet, sitting in the turret of an M1 Abrams tank during a visit to the General Dynamics plant in Michigan where the tank was made. The photograph was taken and released by the Dukakis campaign, not by the Bush campaign or opposition researchers. But Dukakis looked silly in the tank helmet, and the image graphically reinforced Bush's argument that Dukakis lacked what it took to be commander in chief.

Obama faces challenges similar to those Dukakis faced in 1988: both candidates won the Democratic Party nomination even though they were largely unknown to American voters. Both candidates maintained leftist positions on key domestic and foreign policy issues. And Obama, like Dukakis, is vulnerable to negative information about his past that can burst any cult-of-personality bubble that public-relations experts, such as Axelrod, can try to create around a political persona.

A Far-Left Obama Nation

Obama's liability is not his race, but his liberal stance on the issues.

Once they get beyond the intriguing story of his personal biography, voters will be left asking: *What policies will Obama implement once he is in the White House?*

Put directly, voters in 2008 will have one key question in mind: *Will we be better off after four years of Barack Obama in the White House or four years of John McCain?*

Contrasted to McCain's extensive history in the U.S. Senate and his status as a legitimate POW hero of Vietnam, Obama was elected to the U.S. Senate only in 2004, and his lack of any military experience will cause voters to wonder if we know enough about Obama to predict what he will do as president. Looking at the limited record available, McCain will be able to portray Obama as one of the most liberal candidates ever to run as the Democratic Party's nominee, more liberal on domestic politics than Michael Dukakis, more liberal on foreign policy than George McGovern.

McCain will do well to position clear choices between his center-right policies and Obama's leftist policies. Running against Obama, McCain should position himself as pro-military and strong on national defense. McCain should advocate continuing the Bush tax cuts and exploring private enterprise solutions to our nation's health needs. McCain is pro-life and a strong advocate of the Second Amendment.

Even though a large number of Americans still have

questions about why the United States entered the war in Iraq, few American voters will want to abandon our military in the field of battle, or withdraw precipitously, especially not after the surge of additional troops has stabilized the level of terrorism in Iraq. The Middle East remains a powder keg and the United States has worked for the entire second term of George W. Bush to negotiate with Iran through the EU-3 of France, Germany, and Great Britain, as well as through the UN's International Atomic Energy Agency and the Security Council. What difference does Barack Obama believe he will accomplish with direct head-of-state talks while the radical Mahmoud Ahmadinejad gives speech after speech attacking Israel and while Iran refuses to stop enriching uranium?

Obama will have problems in domestic politics as well: as the U.S. and world economies slow down, raising taxes will most certainly further depress the economy. Given Obama's belief that a woman's right to choose is absolute in questions of abortion, key Christian pro-life voter segments will resolve to work hard for his defeat. So will proponents of the Second Amendment, once Obama's support of local gun-control ordinances is fully understood. Obama's determination to impose a UN-motivated tax on U.S. citizens to combat global poverty will fuel concerns that Obama is at heart a globalist, ready to succumb to a wide variety of international government initiatives that could compromise the sovereignty of the United States.

In the general-election campaign, Obama will have to explain his connections to a long list of leftists, from communist poet and journalist Frank Marshall Davis, his mentor while in high school, to Weather Underground figures Bill Ayers and Bernardine Dohrn, to his twenty-year membership in Trinity United Church of Christ, listening to anti-American tirades from his pastor, Reverend Jeremiah Wright.

Hillary and the Race Card

Through the 2008 Democratic primaries, Hillary Clinton waged a hard-fought but divisive presidential campaign, in which she first laid out many of the kind of opposition-research attacks against Obama that Democrats usually expect to be launched by Republican Party officials or surrogates supporting the Republican presidential nominee. In an important sense, Hillary Clinton's primary campaign attacks against Barack Obama legitimized many of the lines of inquiry explored in the first two sections of this book. Hillary's race-based arguments also pricked the bubble of "beyond race" that is key to Axelrod's personality positioning of his candidate.

On May 7, 2008, the day after Hillary lost the North Carolina primary by double digits and won the Indiana primary narrowly, she put race squarely on the table. Clinton did so by telling *USA Today*, "I have a much broader base to build a winning coalition on." Hillary cited an Associated Press article that found that "Sen. Obama's support among working, hard-working Americans, white Americans, is weakening again, and that whites in both states who had not completed college" were supporting her, not Obama. What Hillary said next clearly argued white voters versus black voters, dropping any pretext that could easily have been covered by using a more general term, such as "middle-American" or "working-class voters" to make her point: "There is a pattern emerging here," she said, defining her base as white voters, as opposed to the African-Americans she was defining as Obama's base.

Hillary, not McCain or any Republican Party surrogate, took the giant step to frame Barack Obama as an African-American candidate. From that moment on, Axelrod's positioning of Obama as a red state/blue state candidate who transcends racial lines of division was lost forever. In her last attempt to save her faltering candidacy, Hillary let the race genie out of the bottle, making sure the subliminal message stuck in the minds of U.S. voters that Obama was an African-American running for the White House. Hillary needed to advance her argument that Obama was running a hopeless race for the White House, without any chance of attracting the middle-class white voters he would need for victory.

In other words, Hillary argued that Obama was an African-American who had not transcended race at all, at least not so far as the statistical analysis of voter cross-tabulations could prove. Axelrod's "Messiah," in other words, had clay African-American feet, or so Hillary Clinton charged, with a numbers analysis of primary voters that was impossible to ignore. After Hillary's attack, the issue with Reverend Wright concerned not only his anti-American tirades, but also his black rage, as expressed in the black-liberation theology he espoused, and in Louis Farrakhan, whom Wright strongly championed.

Begala Versus Brazile on Race

Begala's May 9 appearance on CNN involved an exchange with Donna Brazile, manager of Al Gore's presidential campaign in 2000. Brazile took exception to the race issue being used to categorize Obama supporters. "I was one of the first Democrats who were going to the white working-class neighborhoods, encouraging white Democrats not to forget their roots," Brazile shot back at Begala. "I have drunk more beers with 'Joe Six Pack,' 'Jane Six Pack' and everybody else than most white Democrats that you're talking about.[6]

"So stop the divisions," Brazile reprimanded Begala. "Stop trying to split us into these groups, Paul, because you and I both know we have been in more campaigns. We know how Democrats win and to simply suggest that Hillary's coalition is better than Obama's, Obama's is better than Hillary's—no. We have a big party, Paul."

And again, she protested, "Just don't divide me and tell me I cannot stand in Hillary's camp because I'm black, and I can't stand in Obama's camp because I'm female. I'm both."

But, as Begala knew, the divisions had already been created. Ironically, Hillary had been so successful in framing Obama's core support as the vast majority of African-American voters that she sealed out her own chance of ever being the Democratic Party nominee in 2008. The Democratic Party could not nominate Hillary, because that would now mean alienating the very African-American voters the Democratic Party is counting on for victory.

If large numbers of African-American voters became so disillusioned that they stayed home on Election Day, November 4, 2008, the Democratic Party would lose congressional state and local campaigns across the country. A great number of the Democratic Party superdelegates are local and state politicians themselves. Even if these superdelegates became convinced Hillary had the better chance of beating McCain in the general election, they would still vote to give the nomination to Obama. Superdelegates facing election or reelection campaigns of their own were counting on African-American voters in their precincts, districts, and states to come to the polls to vote for them.

As the primary season headed toward June 2008, Hillary's only chances of winning the nomination demanded she use one of two strategies guaranteed to alienate African-American voters: She could insist on getting new primaries to be held in the contested states of Michigan and Florida, or she could pressure superdelegates in the hope of convincing a sufficient number to swing her way. Either of these options would certainly look to African-American Democratic voters as though a backroom deal had been made between Hillary and the Democratic Party white hierarchy to deny the African-American candidate the presidential nomination.

Ironically, by advancing a racial argument to support her faltering candidacy, Hillary assured the *worst* possible result: should the party hierarchy take the extraordinary steps she was recommending, African-Americans would be almost certain to sit out the 2008 election. Securing her party's presidential nomination through a superdelegate deal, Hillary risked asking the party to take steps that could tear apart the Democratic Party, perhaps permanently.

Like it or not, in 2008, Democrats who had courted African-American voters since LBJ's Great Society suddenly found themselves held hostage by that very African-American constituency, now demanding Barack Obama be given the chance to win the top prize.

Unfortunately, Begala Was Right

Since Franklin Delano Roosevelt, only one Democratic contender for the presidency has gotten more than 50 percent of the white vote—Lyndon B. Johnson, in 1964, when he won a landslide against Republican conservative Barry Goldwater by capitalizing on the overwhelming wave of national sympathy the country felt in the wake of the assassination of John Kennedy. Since FDR, Democrats have won the presidency by getting an overwhelming majority of the African-American votes and trying to win more than 40 percent of the white votes. As we mentioned earlier, LBJ in 1964 and Jimmy Carter in 1976 were the only two Democratic presidential candidates to win over 50 percent of the popular vote since FDR in 1944.

Analyzing voting statistics from this perspective, we see why superdelegates who have to run for office or who are party officials dependent upon Democrats winning state and local offices cannot afford to alienate African-American voters where they live. Even if the Democrats lose the presidency in November 2008, the party has excellent prospects of gaining seats in both the U.S. House and Senate—unless the party alienates African-American voters who simply decide to sit out the election.

After the bitterness of the Democratic Party's divisive primary contest in 2008, most attacks on Obama in the general-election campaign will be able to be justified simply by pointing to similar attacks on Obama that Hillary made first. The longer Hillary stayed in the primary race, the more she attacked Obama, including by making race an issue. Once Hillary raised race as an issue, it became harder to dismiss than if it had never been raised in the first place.

If Obama loses in November 2008, Hillary Clinton will get much of the blame, including for fixing in voters' minds the image of Obama as an African-American candidate.

Political strategist Dick Morris went so far as to argue that Hillary stayed in the race long in order to make *sure* Obama would lose the general election. Morris argued McCain in 2012 would be seventy-six years old and vulnerable to defeat, whereas Obama would be positioned to run for a second term in the White House. "The best or the worst" Hillary could do after losing the North Carolina primary, Morris cynically wrote, was "to bloody Barack Obama enough to make him lose in the fall, allowing her to come back in 2012."[7]

Axelrod's Worst Dream Comes True

In plotting Obama's run for the White House, campaign strategist David Axelrod had planned to present Obama as a candidate above the politics of division, a unifier beyond race. Working with Obama as a largely unknown candidate on the national stage, Axelrod planned to emphasize Obama's charisma. In debating on CNN with Begala, Donna Brazile had just defined Axelrod's nightmare: a 2008 general-election contest divided along lines of race and class, in which his candidate was identified as an African-American elitist running against a Republican Party independent who was a legitimate war hero, with significantly more political experience and history.

This, as we have discussed, was the beginning of John McCain's campaign against Obama.

On May 6, 2008, Obama's acceptance speech in the North Carolina primary was pure Axelrod, as Obama told a national television audience, "We intend to march forward as one Democratic Party, united by a common vision for this country." Obama hit on every Axelrod theme as he proclaimed, "We need change in America and that's why we will be united in November." He even returned to a stalwart red state/blue state Axelrod comparison when he argued, "The attempts to play on our fears and to exploit our differences, to turn us against each other for political gain, to slice and dice this country into red states and blue states, blue collar and white collar, white, black, brown, young, old, rich, poor . . . [applause] . . . this is the race we expect, no matter whether it's myself or Senator Clinton who is the nominee."[8]

Two days later, Obama returned to Washington, D.C., from North Carolina, to take a "victory lap" around the Capitol. Obama showed up on the floor of the House of Representatives, where he made the grand tour, speaking to superdelegates as well as Clinton supporters and Majority Leader Steny Hoyer, a Democrat from Maryland, who was at that time neutral in the race.[9] Followed by an army of television cameras as he marched on foot from the Senate side of the Capitol, Obama smiled broadly and strode confidently, demonstrating to the nation that his "Obamamania" rock-star charisma was still intact.

Yet, the question Hillary Clinton had posed still hung in the air: Shouldn't the Democratic Party be nominating her for president in 2008, especially since she had proved in the primaries she was the better candidate to beat John McCain in the general election? That was the core of Hillary's final pleas to the superdelegates, as she begged them to consider that Obama could not win the big states, primarily because working-class white voters were sure to reject his candidacy. Even as her candidacy was running out of money, Hillary's plea was, in effect, that the Democratic Party had a historic opportunity to nominate for the first time ever a woman or an African-American for their presidential candidate. Why not select her, she insisted, the one most likely to win? The choice to nominate the first woman for president would still be historic, even if the African-American candidate did not win the nomination this time around.

Unfortunately for Hillary, the race card has the potential to boomerang. Now, if Obama does lose in the 2008 general election, the Democratic Party will be certain to blame Hillary for having tarnished Axelrod's effort to frame Obama as the one Democratic Party candidate who could transcend race in 2008.

Could Latino Voters Swing for McCain?

Obama will no doubt pick up the vast majority of African-American voters, but African-Americans still make up only about 13 percent of the U.S. population. Moreover, Latinos are beginning to overtake African-Americans as this country's largest minority, both in absolute numbers and proportionately. While Latino voters lean toward the Democratic Party, their willingness to vote for Barack Obama is by no means assured. Latino voters in the 2008 presidential election are not going to vote along racial lines. What they want is a candidate who will support their interests, either in obtaining U.S. citizenship and employment, or in opposing Castro, a key issue to Cuban-Americans.

The Democratic Party courted Hispanic voters nationwide, championing comprehensive immigration reform through none other than Senator Ted Kennedy, arguably the patriarch of the party. Of all the Republican candidates running for president in 2008, John McCain was always the one with a chance of winning the largest percentage of Latino voters. Early in the Republican Party primaries, McCain appeared to be nearly out of the race, largely because his support for comprehensive immigration reform had disenchanted conservative Republicans. Yet, ironically, it is McCain's position on comprehensive immigration reform that ends up making him an attractive candidate to Hispanic voters. In his willingness to partner with Ted

Kennedy, not once but twice, in an effort to get comprehensive immigration reform through the U.S. Senate, McCain managed to convince Hispanic voters he is sympathetic to their concerns. In the general-election campaign, McCain is calculating he will need the Latino vote in certain key states where Latinos are the swing constituency. He is betting, probably correctly, that Republican conservatives will ultimately vote for him, even if he never was their first choice.

In 2000, Al Gore took 65 percent of the Latino vote, which turned out to be an important reason the election was so close. In 2004, George W. Bush gained ground with Latino voters by winning 44 percent of their votes. Winning this large a percentage of Hispanic voters helped Bush distance himself from his Democratic opponent. Had Bush won only the 35 percent of the Hispanic vote that he won in 2000, he may well have lost to John Kerry, in an election that ultimately was determined by as few as some fifty thousand voters in Ohio.

If Obama loses more than 50 percent of the Hispanic vote, even states such as California may be in play.

McCain has an additional advantage with the Hispanic population in Florida. Since the 1960s, southern Florida has had a strong anti-Castro Cuban population, which has lobbied strongly to remove the communist dictator from power and liberate Cuba. McCain is perceived as a staunch opponent of Fidel Castro, whereas Obama's ill-advised comment in the CNN/YouTube debate indicated that he as president would be willing to engage in face-to-face negotiations with Castro, and we assume with Castro's successor as well, even if the successor is as communist and anti-American as Castro is.

McCain and the Republican Party are calculating that once the issue of immigration is hurdled, Hispanic voters are center-right voters, believing in hard work over welfare, and inclined to be strongly Christian, pro-life, and pro-family voters.

Why Democrats Nominate Leftists for President

The fatal flaw in the Democratic Party presidential nominating process, stretching back to the late 1960s, is that the base of the party has been moving farther left than the general electorate.

In a winner-take-all primary system such as the one the Republican Party uses, little-known contenders have a hard time gaining traction. Yet, since the Democrats split delegates proportionately in primaries depending upon total votes for each candidate, little-known candidates can rise to the top. In 2008, Obama gained an insurmountable advantage simply by racking up a series of impressive wins in selected smaller states where he had an advantage.

The other quirk of primaries is one that both parties suffer: voters in primaries tend to be party activists who are not typically representative of general-election voters. Political junkies follow candidates nearly all the time, even in years where there is no election. Most voters, however, find it difficult to take the time to vote, even in important general elections, and they find it almost impossible to take time to vote in primaries. In each presidential election year since 1968, Democratic activists on the far left have set the political agenda for the party's primaries.

Because Democratic activists dominate primary voting, the winners of the primaries tend to reflect those who vote. As a result, Democratic presidential primaries since the late 1960s have favored leftist candidates who are favorites of the party's activist hard core, but are little known to the general public.

The question in 2008 will be if the Democrats have succeeded in nominating another Mike Dukakis or, even worse, a George McGovern. Neither Dukakis nor McGovern could assemble a winning voter coalition. McGovern, with his antiwar campaign, managed to win only Massachusetts. Yet both left their Democratic Party national nominating conventions confident their leftist message would bring electoral victory in the fall.

In a fundamental sense, Begala was right. Even winning 90 percent or more of the African-American voters and a large percentage of college-educated white voters would not be enough to produce a Democratic victory in 2008. The working-class and minority coalition put together by FDR has broken up, maybe forever. For a post–World War II generation of Democrats, Adlai Stevenson epitomized the intellectual, or "egghead" alternative to the war hero, yet Stevenson lost the presidential contest to General Dwight D. Eisenhower, not once, but twice, in both 1952 and 1956. The last vestige of the FDR coalition began dissipating the day LBJ decided not to run for reelection in 1968, amid a continuing Vietnam War that was increasingly unpopular with both the Far Left and with minorities, including, importantly, African-Americans.

For the most part, African-Americans have remained Democratic, but only because Democratic candidates continue to support massive welfare programs, many of which FDR started, and LBJ expanded under the banner of the Great Society. The FDR coalition of minorities and blue-collar, middle-class union workers is unlikely to ever come back together. The problem is that working-class white voters became "Reagan Democrats," largely in their opposition to the Democratic Party's enthusiasm for the welfare state, their disdain of taxes, and their disapproval of leftist anti-war Democrats they saw as opposing the U.S. military even when U.S. armed forces were overseas, in the field of battle.

In a nation where the majority of the voters remain center-right politically, Obama can expect an uphill battle on the issues, and that will be the fight McCain plans to bring in the general election contest.

Axelrod knows this, which is why he wants to run what in the movie industry would be called a "high-concept" campaign. Can Obama move to the center, a necessity in presidential politics, without losing his base of left-leaning activists in the Democratic Party? When Obama finally denounced Reverend Wright and left Trinity United Church of Christ, he faced strong criticism from radical elements in the African-American community. Almost immediately after Obama's "More Perfect Union" speech in Philadelphia, when he began distancing himself from Wright, charges were posted on Internet chat rooms by radicals upset that Obama was just another "Uncle Tom" because he dared say anything negative about Wright.

Unfortunately, winning a general presidential election is a completely different phenomenon from winning the Democratic Party presidential primaries. The Axelrod positioning that helped Obama win the primaries may turn around and hurt Obama in the general election. This is a phenomenon the Democrats should have learned from studying how Dukakis and McGovern went down to resounding defeats, as well as how Kerry boxed himself in for the general election by basing so much of his primary contest on Vietnam.

"Hope" is a great theme for winning a Democratic primary campaign, but how far will "Yes, We Can!" take Obama when the policy questions on the table involve what exactly he plans to do about issues such as taxes, abortion, globalism, and national defense?

Debatable Issues

There are many issues around which Obama can be attacked and defeated.

Obama and the Democratic Party have been buoyed by poll results showing growing dissatisfaction with George W. Bush. A *Washington Post*–ABC News poll reported on May 13, 2008, showed Americans are gloomier about the direction of the country than they have been at any point in fifteen years, with eight out of ten now saying the country is headed in the wrong direction.[10] Yet, despite the poll showing Bush's approval rating had dropped to an all-time low, the poll also showed McCain remaining competitive in a hypothetical general-election match-up with Obama. Results such as these should give the Obama camp pause before locking into a general election strategy where the main goal is to say repeatedly, "Bush-McCain, Bush-McCain, Bush-McCain."

McCain has a deserved reputation as a maverick, so much so that he has had a difficult time in 2008 convincing conservatives that he is one of them.

McCain most likely will position his campaign close to George W. Bush, but only on issues of foreign policy. If the 2008 election comes down to a question of which candidate is the best commander in chief, McCain wins and Obama loses. Despite the unpopularity of the Iraq War, most Americans want to see the United States stay long enough to obtain lasting results. In 1972, the Democrats lost forty-nine states nominating Senator George McGovern on an antiwar platform, despite the widespread street protests against the war that began in 1966. Obama would be well advised to concede war-hero status to McCain, especially with McCain enjoying the strong support of Colonel Bud Day, a POW Medal of Honor recipient who is probably the nation's most decorated living service member and war hero.

Claiming that electing McCain will essentially produce a third George W. Bush term simply will not be credible after McCain has sufficient time to differentiate himself both from Bush and from conservatives on a wide range of issues, including even global warming and carbon taxes. McCain is much more of a centrist, especially on domestic issues, than he is a conservative Republican. Truthfully, Hillary Clinton's positions on many issues resemble McCain's very closely, a key reason Clinton may well have been the harder candidate to beat. Even McCain said he would have preferred to run against Clinton, probably since their closeness in the Senate suggested a more amicable general election than the predictable battle against Obama.

Cracks in the Cult of Personality

By entrusting his strategy to David Axelrod, Obama signed on to a campaign where his life story and personality would be put forward to voters as the substance of the theme.

The liability here is that few have life stories without blemish, and Obama's life story may not be as heroic as Axelrod would like to portray. By definition, cults of personality create larger-than-life stories of their central figure, but the facade is vulnerable to careful investigation. One crack in a key feature of the life story invites more scrutiny, and inevitably, more cracks. That Obama's father was a polygamist and an alcoholic may or may not tell us much about Obama. But that Obama does not present the true story about his father outright in his autobiography, in an easy-to-follow fashion, leaves the reader to discover the revelation, much as Obama claims he himself did. Voters who are led to see Obama's father as first presented by Obama himself may suffer disappointment and decide to reevaluate Obama himself when the truth is known.

His father was not the crusading young goatherd who ventured forth to get a U.S. education, ultimately at Harvard, so that he could return to Kenya to lend his skills as an economist to the development of the newly independent state. In reality, the father turns out to be a socialist who failed because of continuing tribal politics in which the father came out on the losing side. Then, when Obama ventures forth to Kenya to conduct his own personal "roots" journey, he gets connected with a politician named Raila Odinga, who is presented by Obama as an incidental player in the drama. Yet, when we learn that Raila Odinga's father played a role in the tribal politics that led to Obama's father's demise, we begin to contemplate whether Obama is playing a grudge match in Kenya, supporting Odinga in order to rectify perceived insults and injuries done to both their fathers.

Obama brought Kenya into the story himself, devoting the entire third section of his autobiography to the African nation. Axelrod has projected Obama's rise as a triumph of internationalism, so how then are we to be faulted for looking closely at the details? Widely disseminated reports that Odinga has signed a memorandum of understanding with leading Islamic figures in Kenya raises eyebrows, especially when Kenyan television news confirms that the document is authentic. Next, another document surfaces suggesting "Friends of Obama" and prominent Islamic figures in Kenya have each contributed more than $1 million to Odinga's campaign. The issue might pass, especially when Obama supporters question the documents supporting these claims, but the controversy built when Odinga lost the election and appeared to encourage an outbreak of tribal and religious violence in which Christian churches are destroyed while no mosques are damaged. When Odinga finally ascended to share power by being appointed prime minister, we were relieved that the civil violence subsided as a consequence, but disturbed to learn that Obama has been a player in the unfolding drama, in an ongoing relationship with Odinga by long-distance telephone.

Now, we return to Axelrod's fiction of Obama's life as articulated in his autobiography. Is Kenya part of Obama's past or his present? What exactly is the role of the clearly Islamic family in the predominantly Christian Luo tribe? Did Odinga sign a memorandum of understanding to expand Islam in Kenya simply because he wanted the votes? Or is he secretly in sympathy with Islam, perhaps not even a Christian at all? These are the questions Kenyans themselves are asking: Has Odinga allowed himself, for simply pragmatic reasons, to benefit from postelection violence in Kenya in which Islamic radicals are an active force? Or has Odinga joined with radical Islamicists in Kenya simply because they oppose the current Kenyan regime and the dominant tribe controlling that regime, as does Odinga himself?

Obama, having endorsed Odinga for president and having stayed in contact with him by telephone throughout the postelection violence, would have to answer questions of his own:

• Why did Obama meddle in the presidential politics of a foreign nation?

- Why did he support Odinga after he signed the memorandum of understanding with the radical Islamicists in Kenya?
- The postelection violence in Kenya killed over a thousand people and displaced another three hundred thousand or more. Scores of Christian churches were burned in a wave of tribal and anti-Christian religious violence that, again, left no mosques damaged. If Obama continues to support Odinga as prime minister, is he thereby accepting or condoning the postelection violence that brought Odinga to power, and a radical agenda from the left that would expand Islam in Kenya? Obama could have an increasingly difficult time convincing U.S. voters he is anything but pro-Islam.

As we have already noted, Obama's many top advisors who have decidedly anti-Israel histories will be a serious detriment in attracting the Jewish voters Obama needs to win. Now that the Tony Rezko trial has ended in multiple convictions, Rezko's use of Middle Eastern money to help the Obamas buy their dream home property could surface at any time and cause the Obama campaign serious problems.

Examining Obama's past, we find many ties to pro-Islam, Palestinian-supporting causes and people that will need to be explained to U.S. voters in the general presidential election. As we have discussed at length, Reverend Wright's anti-Israel rhetoric helps explain his closeness to radically anti-Israel Louis Farrakhan. So far Obama has minimized his own participation in Farrakhan's 1995 Million Man March on Washington, but his association with William Ayers is a problem both because of Ayers's domestic terrorist activities as a leader of the Weather Underground and because of Obama's connection to the use of grants from Ayers's Woods Fund to support the Arab-American Action Network and Rashid Khalidi, a radically pro-Palestinian professor. Ali Abunimah, the founder of a radically pro-Palestinian website titled Electronic Intifada, has written extensively that before he stepped onto the national scene as a U.S. senator, Obama was decidedly pro-Palestinian in his views.

Similarly, when voters come to understand the roots of black-liberation theology in the radical black rage writings of authors such as Stokely Carmichael, who penned *Black Power* in 1967, Obama will be seen to have accepted Reverend Wright's more anti-American views because those views are central to the theology itself. Whether or not voters believe black-liberation theology demands viewing Jesus Christ as a black whose revolutionary teachings were aimed at overthrowing the imperialist power of the day—the ancient Romans who were then "colonizing" Israel—the religion does profess this view.

That Obama was baptized and married into Christianity at Trinity United Church of Christ and yet did not comprehend the radical nature of black-liberation theology is simply not credible, especially when we consider that Obama has sufficient intelligence to have obtained a law degree at Harvard.

Obama knew what Reverend Wright was preaching; indeed, he joined that church *because of* it. Even if Trinity United gave Obama identification with an African-American Christian church that helped him advance in the leftist politics of Chicago, this same association will continue to plague Obama in the general election, especially if Obama continues to insist he did not know the full extent of Reverend Jeremiah Wright's radically anti-American black rage.

A campaign of personality requires by its very nature

putting a mask on a candidate. Jack Kennedy knew this and took pains not to be portrayed as a war hero. When JFK was asked what he did in World War II to become a war hero, he typically answered dismissively that the Japanese sank his boat. John Kerry, in direct contrast to JFK, whom he emulated, sailed into Boston Harbor for the Democratic National Convention in 2004 surrounded by a group of supporting Swift Boat veterans and looking like George Washington crossing the Delaware. Then Kerry accepted the nomination by saluting and proclaiming he was "reporting for duty," recalling the title of the campaign biography *Tour of Duty* written for Kerry by Douglas Brinkley.[11] Neither JFK nor John Kerry, the second JFK, needed to present himself as a war hero to qualify to be commander in chief. Abraham Lincoln campaigned for president with a modest comment about his limited experience in the little-known Black Hawk War, yet, Lincoln defeated the South in the Civil War.

Kerry's mistake was to put on the mask of the war hero in the first place.

Axelrod has masked as a "Messiah-like" candidate a virtual unknown on the national political scene. Obama has already gone through a round of troubles caused by his former pastor. Those troubles are likely to continue as Jeremiah Wright gets more opportunities for interviews during the general election. Should Wright decide to author a book of his own prior to the general election, or simply accept payment for a prominent magazine interview or two, Obama could see those troubles resurface with a vengeance. Wright has turned hard against Oprah Winfrey, who once attended his church, and he shows no great sympathy for Obama, after Obama asked him to wait in the basement while he gave his speech announcing his candidacy for the president.

We find a similar problem with Obama's lofty language about "hope" and "change." As we have seen, under close analysis these cries have such extensive antecedents they appear borrowed. As we have seen, *The Audacity of Hope,* the title of Obama's second book, was first used by Reverend Wright as the title of a sermon. "Change" is the battle cry championed by radical socialist organizer Saul Alinsky, who devoted a section of his book *Rules for Radicals* to the topic "The Ideology of Change." Obama has borrowed phrases freely even from movies, taking "bamboozled" from Spike Lee's movie about Malcolm X and the phrase "He is the One" from the *Matrix* movie series. When we look closer at Obama's intellectual legacy, we find him telling us the writers who impressed him growing into intellectual maturity included Malcolm X and Frantz Fanon, both masters of black rage.

Nor is Obama helped when we examine his self-proclaimed mentor in Hawaii, communist journalist-poet Frank Marshall Davis. We might excuse this as youthful rebellion, until we find Obama being introduced into Chicago politics by African-American socialist Alice Palmer, with a coming-out party held first at the home of Weather Underground heroes William Ayers and Bernardine Dohrn. Then we cap the analysis off by seeing the continuity to current Obama public-policy positions, running for president with positions that include a woman's unqualified right to an abortion, a community's unqualified right to impose gun control on gun owners, an expansion of social-welfare programs that includes universal health care, nuclear-weapons disarmament, and a pledge to withdraw soon (if not now) from Iraq and to reduce military spending.

Behind the Axelrod-Obama "hope" and "change" rhetoric, we find the verbal mask has covered over the development of a liberal Democratic politician who, in truth, harbors radical views that are extreme even for most Democrats.

Defeating Obama

Democrats in many ways feel 2008 is their year. With President Bush's ratings low, an unpopular war continuing in Iraq, and an economy threatening to go into recession, the Republican Party should be expected to lose the presidency to Barack Obama. By all rights, the Democratic Party entered the 2008 presidential year enthusiastically. The Obama campaign has reason to believe they could sweep to victory and claim the White House on the promise of "change" and the prospect of "hope."

However, Democrats should remember a key adage of American politics: *Voters rarely allow the same political party to control the presidency as well as the U.S. Senate and the House of Representatives.* The Democrats already control Congress, and all indications are that they will increase majorities in both the House and Senate in 2008. Ironically, for this very reason, voters may be reluctant to put a Democrat in the White House. Opinion polls have consistently shown that the House and Senate, under Democratic leadership, rival President Bush for obtaining historically low ratings.

As we have emphasized throughout, John McCain's best chances against Obama lie in running an issues-based attack on Obama's vaguely stated liberal programs, probing them for their realistic chance of achieving the effect Obama claims and forcing Obama to defend specifics. Axelrod and Obama are good at deflecting general attacks as "smears." Almost as a knee-jerk reaction, Axelrod's first instinct is to cry foul whenever anyone objects to something about

Obama's past history or political record on issues, as thin as that record is. Hillary Clinton failed to dent Obama's armor simply by charging he lacks experience. For that argument, or any argument, to make an impact on Obama, McCain will have to explain to voters what specifically in Obama's proposals will not work because experience demonstrates otherwise.

Obama will be beaten by detailed arguments that are well researched and fact-based.

This is why, for example, we took pains here to make it clear Obama did *not* attend a madrassa when he was educated as a child in Indonesia. CNN was able to go to Indonesia and document fairly easily that there was no madrassa at the public school Obama attended. A madrassa, to be precise, is a particular kind of Islamic religious school.

We were, however, able to prove that Obama had at least one year of instruction in Islam at the public school he attended in Indonesia, and we were able to prove that, in part, by reference to Obama's own words. That is very different from attending a madrassa. We also refrained from claiming Obama is a Muslim because of that limited experience. We have carefully stated that Obama is the best authority on his religious beliefs and we will take him at his word.

Those of us who oppose Obama would make a mistake to claim he is secretly Islamic or that Obama professes Christianity only as a front. None of us are able to read another person's soul. When Obama tells us he has never believed in Islam and that today he professes Christianity, we must take him at his word. Yet, if voters perceive that Obama tilts in his current politics toward Islam, that conclusion alone will be detrimental to Obama's chances in the general election.

Our argument is that Obama's experience with Islam predisposes him to Islam in a way that is reflective of his political associates, his political advisors, and his specific policies regarding the Middle East. This is a very different argument than to claim Obama is a Muslim, something no one can prove one way or the other, except for Obama himself.

John McCain should give the country clear choices, such as a foreign policy backed by a strong military, with a willingness to negotiate with adversaries according to the normal rules of international diplomacy. He should put Obama on the defensive, forcing Obama to retract his promise to negotiate with adversaries without preconditions. McCain can then press Obama for what his exact timetable is for withdrawal from Iraq and what steps Obama would take if Iran or Al Qaeda attempt to take advantage of the Obama-directed rapid withdrawal by ramping up terrorism in Iraq—or elsewhere.

If Axelrod and Obama persist in objecting that every attack on their positions is a "smear," the Obama campaign will quickly appear unable to defend itself in a debate of issues on the merits. Deflecting attacks by crying foul is a technique that should have limited appeal, especially if repeated often. A petulant Obama objecting to every attack as "Swift-boating" and calling every critic a "racist" will quickly sound overly defensive, as if the campaign is protesting too much.

Besides, soon every American likely to vote in the 2008 presidential election can be expected to have heard, at least once, Obama's call for "change" and "hope." After that, what's the follow-up act?

Exactly what kind of change does Obama have in mind?

What specifically are we hoping is going to happen?

In the heat of a general-election presidential campaign, Axelrod and Obama are going to experience a level of scrutiny neither has ever seen before, whether they like it or not. Attacking critics or complaining that all questions raised about Obama involve attempts to "smear" Obama will not work in the general-election campaign, not when voters demand credible answers to legitimate questions raised.

The way to beat Obama is to follow Hillary Clinton's lead: Hillary truly did win the primaries in key, large states the Democrats will have to carry if Obama is to win. Hillary's only mistake was not to take Obama seriously from the very beginning. Obama's advantage is charisma, an advantage not to be taken lightly. Obama beat some very impressive opponents in the Democratic primaries, many of whom were more experienced than he. Yet, policy differences between the contending Democrats were typically small, often detectable only to experts. In recent election years, the Democratic presidential primaries have not been about sharp policy differences distinguishing the candidates from one another.

Still, when it came down to one-on-one, Obama did very poorly in the debates against Hillary Clinton, largely because in that format one can't count on style points and a smile to win the day. To win, McCain will have to take Obama seriously from the very beginning and he will have to go after Obama hard on the issues, without letting up.

The Democrats can be counted on to come out of their Denver nominating convention as confident of victory as they were in 1988, if not more confident. However, with approximately the same coalition of voters Obama has today, Dukakis won only ten states and the District of Columbia, despite having a seventeen-point lead in the polls in the weeks immediately following the Democratic convention.

Dukakis was beaten by a Willie Horton television commercial and a photograph of himself in a tank wearing a silly helmet, but all this was not until after Vice President George H. W. Bush had made sure that contrasts between his strong anticrime and pro-military national defense policies were on the table as top debate issues in the 1988 presidential contest.

In the final analysis, the best way to defeat Obama may be simply to give him a microphone, but only after McCain has attacked Obama hard on the issues, drawing specific contrasts on important policy questions where McCain feels he has solid ground and superior arguments.

If he sticks to the issues, McCain will defeat Barack Obama.

— NOTES —

PREFACE TO THE PAPERBACK EDITION

1 See: (1) Jack Cashill, "Who Wrote Dreams and Why It Matters," American Thinker, May 24, 2009, at http://www .americanthinker.com/2009/05/who_wrote_dreams_and_why _it_ma_1.html. (2) Jack Cashill, "Did Bill Ayers Write Obama's 'Dreams'?" Cashill.com, Part 1 at http://www .cashill.com/natl_general/did_bill_ayers_write_1.htm; Part 2, "Decon-structing the Text," at http://www.cashill.com/ natl_general/did_bill_ayers_write_2.htm; Part 3, "Why It Matters," at http://www.cashill.com/natl_general/did_bill_ ayers_write_3.htm. (3) "Who Wrote 'Dreams from My Father'?" World Net Daily, at http://www.wnd.com/index .php?fa=PAGE.view&pageId=79392. (4) Ron Radosh, "An Old Claim Arises Once More: Did Barack Obama Write 'Dreams from My Father'?" PajamasMedia.com, Sept. 23, 2009, at http://pajamasmedia.com/ronradosh/2009/09/23/ an-old-claim-arises-once-more-did-barack-obama-write-dreams -of-my-father/.

2 "President Obama's 'Czars,'" Politico.com, Aug. 8, 2009, at http://www.politico.com/news/stories/0909/26779.html.

3 Scott Wilson and Garance Franke-Ruta, "White House Adviser Van Jones Resigns Amid Controversy Over Past Activism," Washington Post, Sept. 6, 2009, at http://voices.washington post.com/44/2009/09/06/van_jones_resigns.html.

4 Aaron Klein, "Sunstein picked for sharing Obama's radi-cal views?" World Net Daily, Sept. 22, 2009, at http://www .wnd.com/index.php?fa=PAGE.view&pageId=110601.

5 Ibid.

6 Aaron Klein, "Sunstein: Take organs from 'helpless patients,'" World Net Daily, Oct. 12, 2009, at http://www.wnd.com/ index.php?fa=PAGE.view&pageId=112757.

7   Joseph Abrams, "Obama's Science Czar Considered Forced Abortions, Sterilization as Population Growth Solutions," Fox News, Jul 21, 2009, at http://www.foxnews.com/politics/2009/07/21/obamas-science-czar-considered-forced-abortions-sterilization-population-growth/; and Jerome R. Corsi, "Holdren says Constitution backs compulsory abortion," World Net Daily, Sept. 22, 2009, at http://www.wnd.com/index.php?fa=PAGE.view&pageId=110720.

8   Mark Lloyd, "The Structural Imbalance of Talk Radio," Center for American Progress, June 21, 2007, at http://www.americanprogress.org/issues/2007/06/pdf/talk_radio.pdf; and Kathy Shaidle, "FCC's new 'Diversity Czar' revives Fairness Doctrine Fears," Examiner.com, Aug. 17, 2009, at http://www.examiner.com/x-722-Conservative-Politics-Examiner-y2009m8d17-FCCs-new-Diversity-Czar-revives-Fairness-Doctrine-fears.

9   John D. McKinnon, "Deficit of $1.4 Trillion Limits Democrats," Wall Street Journal, Oct. 17, 2009, at http://online.wsj.com/article/SB125572226287190597.html.

10 "Obama to raise 10-year deficit to $9 trillion," Reuters, Aug. 21, 2009, at http://www.reuters.com/article/newsOne/idUSTRE57K4XE20090821.

11 Ross Colvin, "Obama says new data shows economy recovering," Reuters, Nov. 1, 2009, at http://www.reuters.com/article/businessNews/idUSTRE59U0N220091101.

12 Jeanne Sahadi, "47% will pay no federal income tax," CNNMoney.com, Oct. 3, 2009, at http://money.cnn.com/2009/09/30/pf/taxes/who_pays_taxes/?postversion=2009093012.

13 Stephen Lebaton, "Treasury to Set Executives' Pay at 7 Ailing Firms," New York Times, June 10, 2009, at http://www.nytimes.com/2009/06/11/business/11pay.html.

14 "World Currency," in "The Works of Robert A. Mundell," archived on Robert Mundell's website, RobertMundell.net, at http://www.robertmundell.net/Menu/Main.asp?Type=5&Cat=09&ThemeName=World%20Currency.

15 "Global plan for recovery and reform: Communiqué from

the London Summit," April 2, 2009, archived on the web-site of the London Summit 2009, at http://www.london summit.gov.uk/en/summit-aims/summit-communique/.

16 President Barack Obama, "Remarks by the President on a New Beginning: Cairo University, Cairo, Egypt," White House, June 4, 2009, at http://www.whitehouse.gov/the_press_office/Remarks-by-the-President-at-Cairo-University-6–04–09/.

17 "White House Escalates War of Words with Fox News," Fox News.com, Oct. 12, 2009, at http://www.foxnews.com/politics/2009/10/12/white-house-escalates-war-words-fox-news/.

18 Jeff Greenfield, "President Obama's Feud with Fox News," CBSNews.com, Oct. 23, 2009, at http://www.cbsnews.com/stories/2009/10/23/eveningnews/main5415921.shtml.

19 "Administration Loses Bid to Exclude Fox News from Pay Czar Interview," FoxNews.com, "Politics" blog, Oct. 23, 2009, cached at http://74.125.93.132/search?q=cache:zV9Ur ZtG7_AJ:www.foxnews.com/politics/2009/10/23/white-house-loses-bid-exclude-fox-news-pay-czar-interview/+Administra tion+Loses+Bid+to+Exclude+Fox+News+From+Pay+Czar+In terview&cd=1&hl=en&ct=clnk&gl=us.

20 "Obama at 100 Days: Strong Job Approval, Even Higher Personal Ratings," Pew Research Center for the People & the Press, April 23, 2009, at http://people-press.org/report/509/obama-at-100-days.

21 "Jimmy Carter 1976 Election Ad: Change!" LittleGreenFoot balls.com, June 2, 2008 at http://littlegreenfootballs.com/article/30162_Jimmy_Carter_1976_Election_Ad-_Change.

22 "Partisan Gap in Obama Job Approval Widest in Modern Era," Pew Research Center Publications, April 2, 2009, at http://pewresearch.org/pubs/1178/polarized-partisan-gap-in-obama-approval-historic.

23 "Obama Approval Index Month-by-Month," Rasmussen Reports, Nov. 1, 2009, at http://www.rasmussenreports.com/public_content/politics/obama_administration/obama_approval_index_month_by_month.

24 Jeffrey Jones, "Obama Quarterly Approval Average Slips Nine

Points to 53%," Gallup.com, Oct. 21, 2009, at http://www
.gallup.com/poll/123806/obama-quarterly-approval-average-
slips-nine-points.aspx.

25 John Avlon, "Commentary: Obama losing independent voters," CNN, CNNPolitics.com, Aug. 27, 2009, at http://www
.cnn.com/2009/POLITICS/08/27/avlon.obama.independents/
index.html.

PREFACE

1 John E. O'Neill and Jerome R. Corsi, *Unfit for Command:
Swift Boat Veterans Speak Out Against John Kerry* (Washington, D.C.: Regnery, 2004).

2 For archived articles by Jerome Corsi on the World Net
Daily website, see http://www.worldnetdaily.com/?pageId=4
3&authorId=82&tId=7.

3 J. Kenneth Blackwell and Jerome R. Corsi, *Rebuilding Amer-
ica: A Prescription for Creating Strong Families, Building the
Wealth of Working People, and Ending Welfare* (Nashville,
Tenn.: WND, 2006).

4 Louis H. Masotti and Jerome R. Corsi, "Legal Assistance
for the Poor: An Analysis and Evaluation of Two Programs,"
Journal of Urban Law 44 (Spring 1967), pp. 483–502; and
Jerome R. Corsi, "Detroit 1967: Racial Violence or Class
Warfare," *Journal of Urban Law* 45 (Spring/Summer 1968),
pp. 641–71.

5 Louis H. Masotti, Jeffrey K. Hadden, Kenneth F. Seminatore,
Jerome R. Corsi, *A Time to Burn? An Evaluation of the Present
Crisis in Race Relations* (Chicago: Rand McNally, 1969).

6 The Edward Howard & Co. home page is http://www
.edwardhoward.com/about.htm.

7 Louis H. Masotti and Jerome R. Corsi, *Shoot-Out in Cleveland: Black Militants and the Police: July 23, 1968,* Staff
Report to the National Commission on the Causes and Prevention of Violence (Washington, D.C.: U.S. Government
Printing Office, 1969).

8 Louis H. Masotti and Jerome R. Corsi, *Shoot-Out in Cleve-*

land: Black Militants and the Police: July 23, 1968 (New York: Bantam, 1969) and (New York: Praeger, 1969).

9 David G. Hubbard, *The Skyjacker: His Flights of Fancy*, rev. ed. (New York: Collier, 1973), and *Winning Back the Sky: A Tactical Analysis of Terrorism* (Dallas: Saybrook, 1986).

10 Jerome R. Corsi, "Terrorism as a Desperate Game: Fear, Bargaining, and Communication in the Terrorist Event," *Journal of Conflict Resolution* 25, no. 1 (March 1981), pp. 47–85.

11 Jerome R. Corsi, *Atomic Iran: How the Terrorist Regime Bought the Bomb and American Politicians* (Nashville, Tenn.: WND Books, 2005), and Michael D. Evans with Jerome R. Corsi, *Showdown with Nuclear Iran: Radical Islam's Messianic Mission to Destroy Israel and Cripple the United States* (Nashville, Tenn.: Nelson Current, 2006).

INTRODUCTION

1 "In 52 Seconds Why Barack Obama Cannot Win a General Election," You Tube.com video, posted by "jcjcd," on February 18, 2008, with 1,404,124 views as of April 17, 2008, at http://www.youtube.com/watch?v=dl32Y7wDVDs.

2 This section draws on the following printed articles: John Fund, "Not So Fast: Why Barack Obama may not run," *Wall Street Journal*, December 18, 2006, at http://www.opinionjournal.com/diary/?id=110009401; John Fund, "Obama and Chicago Mores," *Wall Street Journal*, March 3, 2008, at http://online.wsj.com/public/article_print/SB120450564143806509.html; John Fund, "Obama's Flaws Multiply," *Wall Street Journal*, April 15, 2008, at http://online.wsj.com/public/article_print/SB120821921853714665.html. Additional comments were drawn from speeches Fund gave in March and April 2008.

3 Mayhill Fowler, "Obama: No Surprise That Hard-Pressed Pennsylvanians Turn Bitter," *Huffington Post*, April 11, 2008, http://www.huffingtonpost.com/mayhill-fowler/obama-no-surprise-that-ha_b_96188.html.

4 William Kristol, "The Mask Slips," *New York Times*, April 14,

2008, at http://www.nytimes.com/2008/04/14/opinion/14kris tol.html?_r=2&ei=5088&en=31f1f15e03188cec&ex=13659 12000&oref=slogin&partner;eqrssnyt&emc=rss&pagewanted= print&oref=slogin.

5   George Will, "Candidate on a High Horse," Real Clear Politics, April 15, 2008, at http://www.realclearpolitics.com/ articles/2008/04/obamas_condescension.html.

6   Interview Archive, "Former Bush Adviser Karl Rove on Barack Obama's 'Bitter' Comments and Rev. Wright," Fox News, April 15, 2008, at http://www.foxnews.com/ story/0,2933,351331,00.html.

7   "Who is Mayhill Fowler," TPM Café, April 15, 2008, at http://tpmcafe.talkingpointsmemo.com/talk/2008/04/who-is-mayhill-fowler.php.

8   Phillip Matier and Andrew Ross, "Undercover blogger taped Obama's blunt remarks," SF Gate, April 14, 2008, at http:// www.sfgate.com/cgi=bin/article.cgi?f=/c/a/2008/04/13/BA16 1046G7.DTL&tsp=1.

9   June Hill, blog, "Junehill, Owl and a Green Dog, Too," at http://junehill.blogspot.com/2007_03_01_archive.html.

PART ONE: ROOTS

1   Erik H. Erikson, *Young Man Luther: A Study in Psychoanalysis and History* (New York: Norton, 1958), p. 16.

2   Barack Obama, *Dreams from My Father: A Story of Race and Inheritance* (New York: Crown, 2004 [1995]), pp. 3–5. The book, when initially issued in 1995, sold poorly, such that many copies were sold as publisher's remainders. The 1995 edition, as a result, is difficult to find. All quotes are to the 2004 reissue. Obama's autobiographical book is hereafter referred to as *Dreams*.

3   Ibid., Introduction, p. xiv.

4   Erik H. Erikson, *Ghandi's Truth: On the Origins of Militant Nonviolence* (New York: Norton, 1969), p. 57.

5   Obama, *Dreams*, Introduction, p. xv.

6   Ibid.

7 Ibid., pp. xv–xvi.

Chapter 1. MYTHS FROM HIS FATHER

1 Sean Wilentz, "The Delusional Style in American Pun-
ditry," *New Republic*, December 19, 2007, at http://www
.tnr.com/politics/story.html?id=1f22d28c-ced2-4761-b350-
77f3513928ac.

2 Andy Martin, "Washington Post backs Andy Martin on
Barack Obama's lies," ContrarianCommentary.com, March 30,
2008, at http://www.pr-inside.com/washington-post-backs-
andy-martin-on-r509563.htm.

3 Sharon Churcher, "A drunk and a bigot—what the U.S. Presidential hopeful HASN'T said about his father. . . ," *Daily
Mail*, January 27, 2007, at http://www.dailymail.co.uk/pages/
live/articles/news/news.html?in_article_id=431908&in_page
_id=1770.

4 Sharon Churcher, telephone interview with Jerome Corsi,
March 24, 2008.

5 Rob Crilly, telephone interview with Jerome Corsi, March
24, 2008. Crilly is a freelance journalist writing about Africa
for the *Times* (London), the *Irish Times*, the *Daily Mail* (London), the *Scotsman*, and the *Christian Science Monitor* from
his base in Nairobi. Crilly's Internet blog, From the Front-
line: Championing Independent Journalism, can be found at
http://www.fromthefrontline.co.uk/blogs/index.php?blog=14.

6 Obama, *Dreams*, pp. 3–5.

7 All quotes in this paragraph from Obama, *Dreams*, p. 9.

8 Ibid.

9 Ibid.

10 Ibid., pp. 9–10.

11 Ibid., p. 10.

12 Ibid., p. 10.

13 Steve Sailer, "Obama's Identity Crisis," *American Conservative*, March 26, 2007, at http://www.amconmag.com/
2007/2007_03_12/feature.html.

14 Obama, *Dreams*, p. 124.

15 Ibid., p. 126.

16 Ibid., p. 104.

17 Ibid., p. 335.

18 Ibid., p. 336.

19 Author's telephone interview with Sayid Obama in Kisumu, Kenya, April 6, 2008.

20 Obama, *Dreams*, p. 337.

21 Ibid., p. 344.

22 Ibid., p. 335.

23 Ibid., pp. 420–22.

24 Ibid., page 424.

25 Michael Dobbs, "Obama Overstates Kennedys' Role in Helping His Father," *Washington Post*, March 30, 2008, p. A01, at http://www.washingtonpost.com/wp-dyn/content/article/2008/03/29/AR2008032902031.html.

26 Barack Obama, "Selma Speech, Text as Delivered," Brown Chapel A.M.E. Church, Selma, Alabama, March 4, 2007, at http://blogs.suntimes.com/sweet/2007/03/obamas_selma_speech_text_as_de.html.

27 A video of the Obama speech at Selma on March 4, 2007, has been archived on YouTube.com at http://www.youtube.com/watch?v=DdYByptC8mY.

28 "Background Memorandum Prepared by Senator Kennedy's Office, August 1960: The Facts on Grants to American Students Airlift," archived on the Internet at http://www.jfklink.com/speeches/jfk/misc60/jfk010860_africangrant.html.

29 Philip Ochieng, "From Home Squared to the US Senate: How Barack Obama Was Found and Lost," The East African published in the *Daily Mail*, Nairobi, Kenya, November 1, 2004, at http://www.nationmedia.com/EastAfrican/01112004/Features/PA2-11.html.

Chapter 2. STRANGERS IN STRANGE LANDS

1 Barack Obama Podcast, "Meet Barack's Half-Sister Maya," a video posted on Barack Obama's 2008 presidential campaign website, August 9, 2007, at http://uncutvideo.aol.com/videos/efed81d71a332ce3d9d5d60d4262debf.

2   Kristen Scharnberg and Kim Barker, "The not-so-simple story of Barack Obama's youth: Shaped by different worlds, an outsider found ways to fit in," *Chicago Tribune*, March 25, 2007, at http://www.chicagotribune.com/news/politics/chi-070325obama-youth-story,1,4006113.story.

3   Tim Jones, "Part 2: Obama's mom: Not just a girl from Kansas: Strong personalities shaped a future senator," *Chicago Tribune*, March 27, 2007, at http://www.chicagotribune.com/news/politics/chi-0703270151mar27,0,5157609.story?page=1. All the quotations in this section come from this source.

4   The first version, that Stanley Ann Dunham Obama divorced Obama Senior, is the version commonly found. The version that Obama Senior divorced Stanley Ann under sharia law is told in sources such as the following: Majalah Bulanan Komunitas Indonesia Di Edmonton, "Barack Hussein Obama Was Muslim for 31 Years," March 20, 2008, at http://www.indonesiaedmonton.org/berita/2008/03/20/barack-hussein-obama-was-muslim-for-31-years/.

5   Obama, *Dreams,* p. 126.

6   Obama, *Dreams,* p. 22. Obama quote in next paragraph is from this same page.

7   Amanda Ripley, "The Story of Obama's Mother," *Time*, April 9, 2008, at http://www.time.com/time/nation/article/0,8599,1729524,00.html.

8   Obama, *Dreams*, p. 12.

9   Ibid., p. 21.

10 Scott Fornek, "Stanley Armour Dunham: 'Gramps had entered the space age,'" *Chicago Sun-Times*, September 9, 2007, at http://www.suntimes.com/news/politics/obama/familytree/545442,BSX-News-wotreedd09.article.

11 Obama, *Dreams*, pp. 30–31.

12 For instance, see Jonathan Martin, "Obama's mother known here as 'uncommon,'" *Seattle Times*, April 8, 2008, at http://seattletimes.nwsource.com/html/politics/2004334057_obama08m.html.

13 Obama, *Dreams*, p. 50.

14 Ibid., pp. 44–45.

15 Ibid., p. 43.

16 Ibid., pp. 42–43.

17 Ibid., p. 47.

18 An American Expat in Southeast Asia, "Tracking Down Obama in Indonesia," January 20, 2007, at http://laotze .blogspot.com/2007/01/tracking-down-obama-in-indonesia-barack.html.

19 Obama, *Dreams*, p. 54.

20 Ibid., p. 75.

21 Ibid., p. 76.

22 Ibid., p. 26.

23 Ibid., p. 27.

24 Barack Obama, "Obama Has Never Been a Muslim, and Is a Committed Christian," November 12, 2007, at http:// www.barackobama.com/factcheck/2007/11/12/obama_has_ never_been_a_muslim_1.php. Also discussed in: Aaron Klein, "Obama was 'quite religious' in Islam," World Net Daily, April 3, 2008, at http://www.worldnetdaily.com/ index.php?fa=PAGE.view&pageId=60559.

25 Letter from Ambassador Sudjadnan Parnohadiningrat to Senator Barack Obama, January 25, 2007, referenced on the Barack Obama 2008 presidential campaign website in a section titled "Indonesian Embassy Says that Besuki School Attended by Barack Obama Has Never Been an Islamic Madrassa Type of School," at http://www.barackobama .com/factcheck/2007/11/12/obama_has_never_been_a_mus lim_1.php#no-muslim-school.

26 "Barack Obama is Not and Never Has Been a Muslim," Barack Obama 2008 presidential campaign website, at http:// www.barackobama.com/factcheck/2007/11/12/obama_has_ never_been_a_muslim_1.php#obama-on-emails.

27 "Hillary's team has questions about Obama's Muslim background," *Insight*, January 16, 2007, at http://www.insight mag.com/Media/MediaManager/Obama_2.htm.

28 "CNN debunks false report about Obama," CNN, January 23, 2007, at http://www.cnn.com/2007/POLITICS/01/22/obama .madrassa/.

29 All quotations in this paragraph and the previous paragraph come from Obama, *Dreams*, p. 154.

30 Quoted in "Obama Flak: 'We Will Not Be Swift-Boated,'" NewsMax, January 25, 2007, at http://archive.newsmax .com/archives/ic/2007/1/25/73337.shtml.

31 An American Expat in Southeast Asia, "Tracking Down Obama in Indonesia—Part 3," January 24, 2007, at http:// laotze.blogspot.com/2007/01/tracking-down-obama-in-indo nesia-part-3.html.

32 Obama, *Dreams*, p. 36.

33 Ibid., p. 46.

34 Ibid., pp. 46–47.

35 Scharnberg and Barker, "The not-so-simple story."

36 Ahmad Dani, "Jejak Barack Obama: Rumah Dempo yang Hilang," Detik News, April 7, 2006, at http://jkt1.detiknews .com/index.php/detik.read/tahun/2006/bulan/07/tgl/04/time/ 095455/idnews/628704/idkanal/10.This is also the source for the information in the next paragraph.

37 Obama, *Dreams*, p. 33.

38 Paul Watson, "Islam an unknown factor in Obama bid," *Los Angeles Times*, March 16, 2007, at http://www.latimes .com/news/nationworld/nation/bal-te.obama16mar16,1,718 1735,full.story?coll=la-headlines-nation. Indonesian tele-vision spells the name Zulfan Adi with an "a" not Zulfin Adi with an "i" as here in the *Los Angeles Times*. We choose to follow the Indonesian television spelling, believing it is more likely correct.

39 "Jejak Obama: Sekolah di SD Asisi dan SD Menteng," Detik TV, Jakarta, Indonesia, posted April 2, 2008, at http:// tv.detik.com/index.php?fa=content.main&id=TURndd01q QTBOVGM0SXpJd01EZ3ZNRE12.

40 "Jejak Barack Obama: Dari Menteng Dalam ke Dempo," Detik TV, Jakarta, Indonesia, posted April 2, 2008, at http:// tv.detik.com/index.php?fa=content.main&id=TURnd01qQ TBOamc1SXpJd01EZ3ZNRE12.

41 "Jejak Obama: Kamar Tidur yang Tak Berubah," Detik TV, Jakarta, Indonesia, posted April 2, 2008, at http://tv.detik .com/index.php?fa=content.main&id=TURnd01qQTBOak V5SXpJd01EZ3ZNRE12.

42 Obama, *Dreams*, p. 37.

43 "Senator As Rasa Indonesia: Bocah Negro Gemuk Itu Rajin Ke Mushala," *Banjarmasin Post*, July 9, 2006, at http://www.indonesia.com/bpost/072006/9/depan/utama4.htm.

44 Arifin Asydhad, "Bersarung ke Musala, Lucu Deh!" Detiki Net, June 7, 2006, at http://jktl.detikinet.com/index.php/detik.read/tahun/2006/bulan/07/tgl/06/time/092146/idnews/630128/idkanal/10.

45 "Musala Tempat Bermain Obama," Detik TV, posted February 5, 2008, at http://tv.detik.com/index.php?fa=content.main&id=TURnd01qQTFPVGMxSXpJd01EZ3ZNRE12.

46 An American Expat in Southeast Asia, "Obama on Indonesian Television—Part 1," February 19, 2008, at http://laotzeblogspot.com/2008/02/obama-on-indonesian-television-part-1.html.

47 "Aktif Pramuka, Cuek Dijuluki si Lentik Barry: Menelusuri Jejak Capres AS Barack Obama di SD Menteng, Jakarta," *Kaltim Post* Cyber News, January 27, 2007, at http://www.kaltimpost.web.id/berita/index.asp?Berita=Utama&id=195481. The article is translated by "An American Expat in Southeast Asia" at the Laotze blog, "Tracking Down Obama in Indonesia—Part 5," January 28, 2007, at http://laotze.blogspot.com/2007/01/tracking-down-obama-in-indonesia-part-5.html.

48 Interview with Emil Satar, *Poskota*, January 22, 2007, at http://www.poskota.co.id/news_baca.asp?id=29295&ik=6. The *Poskota* article is referenced and translated by the Laotze blog in "Obama Hoisted on his own Petard," January 25, 2007, at http://laotze.blogspot.com/2007/01/obama-hoisted-on-his-own-petard-one.html.

49 Jodi Kantor, "A Candidate, His Minister and the Search for Faith," *New York Times*, April 30, 2007, at http://www.nytimes.com/2007/04/30/us/politics/30obama.html?_r=1&n==Top/News/Politics/Series/The%20Long%20Run&oref=slogin.

50 Lambert Kelabora, "Religious Instruction Policy in Indonesia," *Asian Survey* 16, no. 3 (March 1976), pp. 230–48, at p. 247. Archived at http://www.jstor.org/pss/2643542.

51 Ibid.

52 Ibid., emphasis in original.

53 Lambert Kelabora, "Assumptions Underlying Religious Instruction in Indonesia," *Comparative Education* 15, no. 3, Special Number (4): Disparities and Alternatives in Education, October 1979, pp. 325–39, at p. 325. Archived on the Internet at http://www.jstor.org/pss/3098905.

54 Kim Barker, "Obama madrassa myth debunked," *Chicago Tribune*, March 25, 2007, at http://www.chicagotribune .com/news/politics/chi-070325obama-islam-story,0,7180545 .story.

55 Nicholas D. Kristof, "Obama: Man of the World," *New York Times*, March 6, 2007. Parentheses in the quotation are in the original source.

56 Ibid.

57 Obama, *Dreams*, p. 50.

58 Ibid., p. 51.

59 Ibid.

60 Ibid., p. 123.

61 Ibid., p. 124.

62 Ibid. The quote in the next paragraph is from. the same page.

63 Ibid., p. 51.

64 Ibid., p. 52.

65 Ibid.

66 Richard Cohen, "Obama's Back Story," *Washington Post*, March 27, 2007, at http://www.washingtonpost.com/wp-dyn/content/article/2007/03/26/AR2007032601583.html.

67 Kristen Scharnberg and Kim Barker, "The not-so-simple story of Barack Obama's youth," *Chicago Tribune*, March 25, 2007, at http://www.chicagotribune.com/news/politics/ chi-070325obama-youth-story,1,4006113.story.

68 Evelyn Nakano Glenn, "Yearning for Lightness: Transnational Circuits in the Marketing and Consumption of Skin Lighteners," *Gender & Society*, April 3, 2008, at http://gas .sagepub.com/cgi/rapidpdf/0891243208316089v1.pdf.

69 Obama, *Dreams*, p. 29.

70 Hillary Clinton, 2008 Presidential Campaign Press Re-

lease, "Sen. Obama Rewrites History, Claims He Hasn't Been Planning a White House Run," December 2, 2007, at http://www.hillaryclinton.com/news/release/view/?id=4470.

71 Jennifer Steinhauer, "Charisma and a Search for Self in Obama's Hawaii Childhood," *New York Times*, March 17, 2007, at http://www.nytimes.com/2007/03/17/us/politics/17 hawaii.html?pagewanted=1&ei=5090&en=2547387fee9fa83 a&ex=1331784000&adxnnl=1&partner=rssuserland&emc= rss&adxnnlx=1208103087-c9NgVxfGvjHha8LOKvvB5A.

Chapter 3. BLACK RAGE, DRUGS, AND A COMMUNIST MENTOR

1 Frantz Fanon, *Black Skin, White Masks* (New York: Grove, 1967), p. 117.

2 Shelby Steele, *A Bound Man: Why We Are Excited About Obama and Why He Can't Win* (New York: Free Press, 2008), p. 25.

3 Obama, *Dreams*, p. 60.

4 Ibid., p. 59.

5 Dan Nakaso, "Obama's tutu a Hawaii banking female pioneer," *Honolulu Advertiser*, April 8, 2008, at http://the .honoluluadvertiser.com/article/2008/Mar/30/ln/hawaii803 300356.html.

6 Obama, *Dreams*, p. 60.

7 Sudhin Thanawala, Associated Press, "Obama worked to fit in at elite school," *Boston Globe*, March 26, 2008, at http:// www.boston.com/news/nation/articles/2008/03/26/obama_ worked_to_fit_in_at_elite_school.

8 Kristen Scharnberg and Kim Barker, "The not-so-simple story of Barack Obama's youth," *Chicago Tribune*, March 25, 2007, at http://www.chicagotribune.com/news/politics/chi-070325obama-youth-story,1,4006113.story.

9 Ibid.

10 Obama, *Dreams*, pp. 67–68.

11 Ibid., p. 63.

12 Ibid., p. 72.

13 Scharnberg and Barker, "The not-so-simple story."

14 Jackie Calmes, "From Obama's Past: An Old Classmate, A Surprising Call," *Wall Street Journal,* March 23, 2007, at http://online.wsj.com/public/article/SB1174616208511463 60-oaQpgJQXqks0usbmVr_JaYNRJCg_20070330.html.

15 Jake Tapper, "Life of Obama's Childhood Friend Takes Drastically Different Path," ABC News, March 30, 2007, at http://abcnews.go.com/GMA/story?id=2989722&page=1.

16 Obama, *Dreams,* p. 93.

17 Ibid.

18 Ibid.

19 Ibid., pp. 93–94.

20 Ann Coulter, "Obama's Dimestore 'Mein Kampf,'" *Human Events,* April 2, 2008, at http://www.humanevents.com/article/php?id=25831.

21 Obama, *Dreams,* p. 84.

22 Coulter, "Obama's Dimestore 'Mein Kampf.'"

23 Obama, *Dreams,* page 84.

24 Ibid., p. 85.

25 Punahou School website, at http://www.punahou.edu/page .cfm?p=15.

26 Obama, *Dreams,* p. 85.

27 Ibid., pp. 85–86.

28 Ibid., p. 81.

29 Fanon, *Black Skin, White Masks,* p. 17.

30 Obama, *Dreams,* p. 72.

31 Ibid., p. 74.

32 Fanon, p. 69.

33 Ibid., p. 111.

34 Obama, *Dreams,* p. 100.

35 Alistair Horne, *A Savage War of Peace: Algeria 1954–1962* (New York: New York Review of Books, 2006 [1977]), p. 139.

36 Gunnar Myrdal, *An American Dilemma: The Negro Problem and Modern Democracy* (New York: Harper & Bros., 1944).

37 Kenneth B. Clark, *Dark Ghetto: Dilemmas of Social Power* (New York: Harper & Row, 1965).

38 Obama, *Dreams,* p. 85.

39 Fanon, p. 18.

40 Ibid.

41 Obama, *Dreams*, p. 76.

42 Trevor Loudon, "Barack Obama's Marxist Mentor," NewZeal
    .Blogspot.com, March 29, 2007, at http://newzeal.blogspot
    .com/2007/03/barack-obamas-marxist-mentor.html.
    See also Cliff Kincaid, "Obama's Communist Mentor,"
    Accuracy in Media, AIM.org, February 18, 2008, at http://
    www.aim.org/aim-column/obamas-communist-mentor/.

43 Gerald Horne, "Rethinking the History and Future of the
    Communist Party," *Political Affairs*, March 28, 2007, at
    http://www.politicalaffairs.net/article/articleview/5047/1/32/.

44 Ibid.

45 "Scope of Soviet Activity in the United States," Hearings
    before the Subcommittee to Investigate the Administra-
    tion of the Internal Security Act and Other Internal Secu-
    rity Laws of the Committee on the Judiciary, United States
    Congress (Washington, D.C.: U.S. Government Printing
    Office, 1957), Part 41, December 5 and 6, 1956, pp. 2518–
    19.

46 "Scope of Soviet Activity in the United States," Hearings
    before the Subcommittee to Investigate the Administration
    of the Internal Security Act and Other Internal Security
    Laws of the Committee on the Judiciary, United States
    Congress (Washington, D.C.: U.S. Government Printing
    Office, 1957), Part 41-A, Appendix III, and the 1955
    Report of the Commission on Subversive Activities of the
    Territory of Hawaii, pp. 2782–83.

47 "Scope of Soviet Activity in the United States," at p. 2783,
    note 40.

48 Richard Wright, *Native Son* (New York: Harper & Bros.,
    1940).

49 John Edgar Tidwell, *Frank Marshall Davis: Black Moods:
    Collected Poems* (Urbana and Chicago: University of Illinois
    Press, 2002), p. xxvii.

50 Frank Marshall Davis, *Livin' the Blues: Memoirs of a Black
    Journalist and Poet*, ed. by John Edgar Tidwell (Madison:
    University of Wisconsin Press, 1992), p. 276.

51 Ibid.

52   Ibid., p. 272.

53   Ibid., p. 277.

54   Ibid.

55   Ibid., p. 278.

56   Ibid.

57   Kincaid, "Obama's Communist Mentor."

58   Obama, *Dreams*, pp. 76–77.

59   Ibid., p. 88. Italics in original.

60   Ibid., pp. 88–89.

61   Barack Obama, "A More Perfect Union," speech delivered at Philadelphia, March 18, 2008, text and video archived at http://my.barackobama.com/page/content/hisownwords/.

62   Steve Sailer, "Obama throws his own 85-year-old grand-mother under the wheels of the BS Express," posted on Steve Sailer's iSteve blog, March 18, 2008, at http://isteve.blogspot.com/2008/03/obama-throws-his-own-living-grannie.html.

63   Obama, *Dreams*, p. 86.

64   Malcolm X, with the assistance of Alex Haley, *The Autobiography of Malcolm X* (New York: Grove, 1965), pp. 203–4. All quotations in this paragraph are from this source and these pages.

65   Obama, *Dreams*, p. 86.

Chapter 4. KENYA, ODINGA, COMMUNISM, AND ISLAM

1   Obama, *Dreams,* p. 220.

2   Reader comment posted by "fwslusser," April 16, 2008, on "The Stump," in response to Noam Scheiber, "Obama—Busted!" posted April 15, 2008, on the *New Republic* website, at http://blogs.tnr.com/tnr/blogs/the_stump/archive/2008/04/15/obama-busted.aspx#comments.

3   "Clinton Staffers Circulate 'Dressed' Obama," Drudge Report, February 25, 2008, at http://www.drudgereport.com/flashoa.htm.

4   "U.S. Senator Barack Obama is dressed as a Somali Elder by Sheikh Mahmed Hassan, during his visit to Wajir, a rural area in northeastern Kenya, near the borders with Somalia

and Ethiopia," Han-Geeska Africa On Line, September 1, 2006, at http://www.geeskaafrika.com/ethiopia_31aug06.htm.

5   "Obama draws crowd on slum tour," BBC News, August 27, 2006, at http://news.bbc.co.uk/2/hi/africa/5290844.stm.

6   *Senator Obama Goes to Africa*, documentary film by Bob Hercules and Keith Walker, available at http://firstrunfeatures.com/barackobamadvd.html. Hercules and Walker previously collaborated to produce a documentary titled *Saul Alinsky and His Legacy*. See Capitol Hill Arts Center, at http://www.capitolhillarts.com/livewire/2008/04/21/senator-obama-goes-to-africa.

7   News broadcast from CBS2Chicago.com, "The Obama and Odinga Connection," posted on YouTube.com on May 5, 2008, at http://www.youtube.com/watch?v=bpvLV3d1Eq4.

8   Lynn Sweet, "Obama: Tells Kenyan President Chicago TV crews had to pay bribes to get equipment out of Nairobi airport," *Chicago Sun-Times*, August 25, 2006, at http://blogs.suntimes.com/sweet/2006/08/obama_tells_kenyan_president_c.html.

9   "Death in the Afternoon," *Time*, July 11, 1969, at http://www.time.com/time/magazine/article/0,9171,900985,00.html.

10 Babafemi A. Badejo, *Raila Odinga: An Enigma in Kenyan Politics* (Lagos and Nairobi: Yintab, 2006), p. 52.

11 Ibid., p. 51.

12 Ibid., p. 53.

13 Ibid., pp. 4–5.

14 Obama, *Dreams*, pp. 214–15.

15 "Odinga says Obama is his cousin," BBC News, January 8, 2008, at http://news.bbc.co.uk/2/hi/africa/7176683.stm.

16 Thomas Mukoya and Leon Malherbe, "Some Kenyans forget crisis to root for Obama," January 8, 2008, at http://africa.reuters.com/wire/news/usnL08727241.html.

17 Alisha Ryu, "Despite Power-Sharing Accord, Ethnic Division in Kenya Runs Deep," Voice of America, March 19, 2008, at http://www.voanews.com/english/2008-03-19-kenyaland.cfm.

18 Adrian Blomfield, "Rape, the mob's latest weapon in Kenya," *Telegraph*, January 7, 2008, at http://www.telegraph.co.uk/news/main.jhtml?xml=/news/2008/01/04/wkenya204.xml.

19 Mike Dorning, "Obama Calls Kenyan Leaders," *Chicago Tribune*, January 8, 2008, at http://weblogs.chicagotribune.com/news/politics/blog/2008/01/obama_calls_kenyan_leaders.html.

20 Joe Klein, "Obama's Other Life," in Swampland, January 7, 2008, at http://www.time-blog.com/swampland/2008/01/obamas_other_life.html.

21 All quotations in this paragraph come from Maina Waruru, "Why are we wary of Obama victory?" *Africa News,* March 26, 2008, at http://www.africanews.com/site/list_message/12153#m12153.

22 Ibid. All quotes in this paragraph are from the same source.

23 "Memorandum of Understanding Between Hon. Raila Amolo Odinga Representing The Orange Democratic Movement (ODM) and National Muslim Leaders Forum (NAMLEF)," signed by Raila Odinga and NAMLEF on August 27, 2007. Posted on the website of the Evangelical Alliance of Kenya at http://eakenya.org/newsevents/article.htm?id=8.

24 Jack Wheeler, the author of a conservative subscription newsletter titled "To the Point," has written several insightful articles about Raila Odinga and his rise in Kenyan politics, at http://www.tothepointnews.com/.

25 Bernard Namunane, "Kenya: Revealed—Raila's Real MOU with Muslims," *Nation*, November 28, 2007, at http://allafrica.com/stories/200711280012.html.

26 "Raila pact with Muslims made public," YouTube.com, posted November 27, 2007, at http://www.youtube.com/watch?v=nqzf-4SWrZE.

27 "MOU between RAILA & NAMLEF," posted on True Kenyan.com, at http://www.truekenyan.com/?p=123.

28 Ibid.

29 Barak H. Obama, "Problems Facing Our Socialism," *East Africa Journal*, July 1965, pp. 26–33. Greg Ransom,

creator of the blog PrestoPundit, first wrote about Obama's paper in "Barack Obama Hid His Father's Socialist and Anti-Western Convictions from his Readers," posted on PrestoPundit, April 7, 2008, at http://gregransom.com/pres topundit/2008/04/gregs-guide-to-barack-obamas-d.html. Ransom faxed a copy of the paper to the author. Barack Obama's first name was published as "Barak" by the *East Africa Journal*. A copy of the paper was subsequently published by Politico.com, with a PDF file of the original paper available for download at http://www.politico.com/news/stories/0408/9610.html and http://www.politico.com/static/PPM41_eastafrica.html.

30 David William Cohen and E. S. Atieno Odhiambo, *The Risks of Knowledge: Investigations into the Death of the Hon. Minister John Robert Ouko in Kenya, 1990* (Athens: Ohio University Press, 2004), p. 10.

31 Ibid.

32 Associated Press, "Kenyan rivals sign power-sharing deal," *USA Today*, February 28, 2008, at http://www.usatoday.com/news/world/2008-02-28-kenya-elections_N.htm?loc=interstitialskip.

33 C. Bryson Hull, "Kenyan coalition will buy peace for now," Reuters, April 16, 2008, at http://africa.reuters.com/wire/news/usnL16457022.html.

34 David J. Jonsson, "The Clash of Ideologies in Africa: Kenya," *New Media Journal*, February 9, 2008, at http://www.newmediajournal.us/guest/jonsson/2008/02092008.htm.

35 "Your Agent for Change," Raila Odinga 2007 presidential campaign website, Kenya, Africa, at http://www.raila07.com/.

36 Quotations in this paragraph are drawn from "Odinga denies 'ethnic cleansing,'" BBC News, January 16, 2008, at http://news.bbc.co.uk/2/hi/africa/7192958.stm.

37 Obama, *Dreams*, p. 220.

38 "Raila gets Clinton advisor for campaigns," YouTube.com, posted November 13, 2007, at http://www.youtube.com/watch?v=vyprn8P8FaU.

39 C. Bryson Hull, "US strategist to help Kenya presidential

challenger," Reuters Africa, November 14, 2007, at http://africa.reuters.com/top/news/usn BAN447825.html.

40 Dana Hughes, "Bridges Burned in U.S., Political King Makes Hit in Africa," ABC News, November 20, 2007, at http://blogs.abcnews.com/theblotter/2007/11/bridges-burned.html.

41 The story about the ODM internal funding memo appears to have been broken first on the following Kenyan Internet blog: "Exclusive: The People Behind ODM Funding," Abunuwasi.com, December 19, 2007, at http://www.abunu wasi.com/?q=detail&id=%201629. The list was then published in its entirety on "PNU!! Show Kenyans your funding source. The Full List of 72 Organizations and Individuals Funding ODM," December 19, 2007, at http://wanjuguna.blogspot.com/2007/12/pnushow-kenyans-your-funding-source.html. See also "Over 50 Reasons for Raila to be the President—by Kadinya," posted on blog ButDoI-Say? on January 17, 2008, at http://butdoisay.wordpress.com/2008/01/17/over-50-reasons-for-raila-to-be-the-president-by-kadinya/.

42 "Exclusive: The People Behind ODM Funding," posted on JahaWatch, December 17, 2007, at http://jukwaa.proboards 58.com/index.cgi?board=general&action=print&thread=1452. For the complete document, see "ODM document," January 20, 2008, posted at http://www.network54.com/Forum/204096/thread/1200846405/last-1200846405/ODM+.

PART TWO: THE MAKING OF A RADICAL POLITICIAN

1 Bill Ayers, *Fugitive Days: A Memoir* (Boston: Beacon, 2001), p. 256.

2 Ben Smith, "Ax on Ayers," February 26, 2008, at http://www.politico.com/blogs/bensmith/0208/Ax_on_Ayers.html.

3 Noted by *Guardian* journalist Daniel Nasaw in "Obama and Bill Ayers," posted on DeadlineUSA, a *Guardian* blog, February 26, 2008, at http://blogs.guardian.co.uk/usa/2008/02/obama_and_bill_ayers.html.

Chapter 5. THE IDEOLOGY OF "CHANGE"

1   Saul D. Alinsky, *Rules for Radicals: A Pragmatic Primer for Realistic Radicals* (New York: Vintage, 1971), p. 3.

2   Obama, *Dreams,* pp. 144–45.

3   Ryan Lizza, "The Agitator: Barack Obama's Unlikely Political Education," *New Republic*, March 19, 2007, at http://www.bustedhalo.com/features/BarackObamaandJerryKellman.htm.

4   Barack Obama, "Why Organize? Problems and Problems in the Inner City," in Peg Knoepfle, ed., *After Alinsky: Community Organizing in Illinois* (Springfield, Ill.: Institute for Policy Affairs, 1990), pp. 35–40. Archived at http://www.edwoj.com/Alinsky/AlinskyObamaChapter1990.htm.

5   Kenneth T. Walsh, "On the Streets of Chicago, a Candidate Comes of Age," *U.S. News & World Report*, August 26, 2007, at http://www.usnews.com/usnews/news/articles/070826/3obama.htm. This quotation is also included in Bob Sector and John McCormick, "Part 3: Portrait of a Pragmatist," *Chicago Tribune*, March 30, 2007, at http://www.chicagotribune.com/news/politics/obama/chi-0703300121mar30,0,5699271.story?page=2.

6   David Moberg, "Obama's Third Way," Shelterforce Online, National Housing Institute, No. 149, Spring 2007, at http://www.nhi.org/online/issues/149/obama.html.

7   Alinsky, *Rules for Radicals*, p. 10.

8   Barack Obama, *The Audacity of Hope: Thoughts on Reclaiming the American Dream* (New York: Crown, 2006).

9   Ibid., p. 29.

10 Ibid. Quotations in previous sentence from this page as well.

11 Ibid., p. 30. Quotations in previous paragraph from this page as well.

12 Ibid.

13 Ibid.

14 Obama, *Dreams,* p. 96.

15 Ibid., p. 93

16 Ibid.

17 Ibid., p. 100.

18 Ibid., p. 103.

19 Ibid., p. 115.

20 Ibid., p. 121.

21 Obama, *Audacity of Hope*, p. 32.

22 Ibid., p. 31.

23 Gunnar Myrdal, *An American Dilemma: The Negro Problem and Modern Democracy* (New York: Harper & Row, 1944), p. 1127.

24 Reverend Martin Luther King, Jr., speaking with a reporter during a Chicago protest, in NBC News for History, *King: Go Beyond the Dream to Discover the Man*, documentary shown on the History Channel, Executive Producer Knute Walker, Narrator Tom Brokaw, Copyright 2008, A&E Networks.

25 The account of the August 5, 1966, march is drawn from James R. Ralph, Jr., *Northern Protest: Martin Luther King, Jr., Chicago and the Civil Rights Movement* (Cambridge, Mass.: Harvard University Press, 1993), p. 123.

26 Obama, *Dreams*, p. 133.

27 Ibid., pp. 134–35.

28 Ibid., p. 133.

29 Lizza, "The Agitator."

30 Obama, *Audacity of Hope*, p. 43.

31 Lizza, "The Agitator."

32 Saul D. Alinsky, *Reveille for Radicals* (New York: Vintage, 1946).

33 David Horowitz and Richard Poe present an excellent analysis of Saul Alinsky's influence on political radicals in *The Shadow Party: How George Soros, Hillary Clinton, and Sixties Radicals Seized Control of the Democratic Party* (Nashville, Tenn.: Nelson Current, 2006), pp. 56–60.

34 Marshall Rosenthal, "Bringing It All Back Home," *Rolling Stone*, March 4, 1971, pp. 2–6, at p. 3.

35 Alinsky, *Rules for Radicals*, p. 184.

36 Ibid.

37 Ibid.

38 Ibid., pp. 185–86.

39 Moberg, "Obama's Third Way."

40 Niccolò Machiavelli, *The Prince*, chapter 15, "Of the Things for Which Men, and Especially Princes, Are Praised or Blaimed," in *The Prince and the Discourses* (New York: Modern Library, 1940), p. 56.

41 Alinsky, *Rules for Radicals*, p. 33.

42 Ibid., p. 69.

43 Ibid., p. 70.

44 Horowitz and Poe, *The Shadow Party*, p. 56.

45 Alinsky, *Rules for Radicals*, epigraph.

46 Alinsky, *Reveille for Radicals*.

47 Alinsky, *Rules for Radicals*, p. 116.

48 This was a frequent Saul Alinsky line in speeches and lectures. For a textual basis for the comment, see *Rules for Radicals*, p. 113: "Power is the reason for being of organizations."

49 Lizza, "The Agitator."

50 David Horowitz, "Woods Fund of Chicago," DiscoverTheNetworks.org, http://www.discoverthenetworks.org/funderprofile.asp?fndid=5340&category=79.

51 Background for this section is drawn from David Jackson and Ray Long, "Obama knows his way around a ballot," *Chicago Tribune*, April 3, 2007, at http://www.chicagotribune.com/news/local/chi-070403obama-ballot,1,4762574,print.story.

52 The Chicago firm Obama joined when he graduated from Harvard Law School is now known as Miner, Barnhill & Galland. See http://www.lawmbg.com/index.cfm/PageID/2782.

53 Hank De Zutter, "What Makes Obama Run?" *Chicago Reader*, December 9, 1995, at http://www.chicagoreader.com/features/stories/archive/barackobama/.

54 Letta Tayler and Keith Herbert, "Obama forged path as Chicago community organizer," *Los Angeles Times*, March 2, 2008, at http://www.latimes.com/news/nationworld/nation/ny-usobam025598601mar02,1,6933215,full.story.

55 Walsh, "On the Streets of Chicago."

56 Sector and McCormick, "Part 3: Portrait of a Pragmatist."

57 "Ex-Chicago Congressman Mel Reynolds Returns After Clinton Commutes Prison Sentence," *Jet*, February 12, 2001, at http://findarticles.com/p/articles/mi_m1355/is_9_99/ai_70696215.

58 "Life Under Socialism: An Afro-American journalist in the USSR," *People's Daily World*, June 19, 1986, p. 18-A. The author is indebted to researcher Max Friedman for finding this newspaper article.

59 "The Friends of Barack Obama, Part 1," PowerLineBlog.com, April 22, 2008, at http://www.powerlineblog.com/archives2/2008/04/020358.php.

60 Ben Smith, "Obama once visited '60s radicals," Politico.com, February 22, 2008, at http://dyn.politico.com/printstory.cfm?uuid=3FC289D8-3048-5C12-009AD5180C22FF0B.

61 Mentioned in Joanna Weiss, "How Obama and the radical became news," *Boston Globe*, April 18, 2002, at http://www.boston.com/news/nation/articles/2008/04/18/how_obama_and_the_radical_became_news/?page=2.

62 Maria Warren, "Get to know Barack Obama," posted on the blog Musings & Migranes, January 27, 2005, at http://warrenpeacemuse.blogspot.com/2005/01/get-to-know-barack-obama-when-i-first.html.

63 Bill Burton is quoted in Smith, "Obama once visited '60s radicals."

64 De Zutter, "What Makes Obama Run?"

65 Woods Fund of Chicago, Form 990, filed on Guidestar.com, at http://www.guidestar.org/pqShowGsReport.do?partner=grantexplorer&npoId=486440.

66 "Did Bernardine Dohrn Mentor Michelle [Robinson] Obama at Chicago Law Firm?" at http://www.crosstabs.org/blogs/daveinboca/2008/apr/25/did_bernardine_dohrn_mentor_michelle_robinson_obama_at_chicago_law_firm.

67 Larry Johnson, "Why Is Obama Hiding the Truth About William Ayers? Follow the Money," posted on NoQuarter USA.com, April 26, 2008, at http://noquarterusa.net/blog/2008/04/26/why-is-obama-hiding-the-truth-about-william-ayers-follow-the-money/.

68 Steve Diamond, "Who 'sent' Obama?" posted on Global labor.blogspot.com, April 22, 2008, at http://globallabor .blogspot.com/2008/04/who-sent-obama.html.

69 Tom Maguire, "Obama and Ayers Worked Together Once?" posted on JustOneMinute.com, April 27, 2008, at http:// justoneminute.typepad.com/main/2008/04/obama-and-ayers. html. This paragraph also draws on comments added to this post by readers.

70 Johnson, "Why Is Obama Hiding the Truth?"

71 Jim Addison, "Obama's Ayers evasions don't hold up," Wiz BangPolitics.com, April 28, 2008, at http://wizbangpolitics .com/2008/04/28/obamas-ayers-evasions-dont-hold-up.php.

72 This and the following paragraph rely heavily on Joseph Farah, "Meet Mr. and Mrs. William Ayers," World Net Daily, April 25, 2008, at http://www.worldnetdaily.com/ index.php?fa=PAGE.view&pageId=62481.

73 Horowitz, "The Woods Fund of Chicago." The $60,000 Woods Fund grant to Northwestern University Law School's Children and Justice Center is also documented in the foundation's Form 990 submitted to the IRS for 2002, archived at http://www.guidestar.org/pqShowGsReport.do?partner= grantexplorer&npoId=486440.

74 Sol Stern, "Obama's Real Bill Ayers Problem," *City Journal*, April 23, 2008, at http://www.city-journal.org/2008/eon 0423ss.html. See also Sol Stern, "The Ed Schools' Latest— and Worst—Humbug," *City Journal*, Summer 2006, at http://www.city-journal.org/html/16_3_ed_school.html.

75 "The Friends of Barack Obama, Part 2," PowerLine.com, April 23, 2008, at http://www.powerlineblog.com/archives2 /2008/04/020362.php.

76 Documented by the Form 990 IRS federal tax reports filed by the Woods Fund of Chicago in 2001 and 2002, archived at http://www.guidestar.org/pqShowGsReport.do? partner-grantexplorer&npoId=486440.

77 Aaron Klein, "Obama worked with terrorist," World Net Daily, February 24, 2008, at http://www.worldnetdaily.com/ index.php?fa=PAGE.view&pageId=57231. See also "Rashid

Khalidi," DiscoverTheNetwork.org, at http://www.discover thenetworks.org/individualProfile.asp?indid=1347.

78 Ari Berman, "Smearing Obama," *The Nation,* March 13, 2008, at http://www.thenation.com/doc/20080331/berman.

79 Aaron Klein, "Smeared by Obama-hacks," World Net Daily, March 14, 2008, at http://www.worldnetdaily.com/index .php?fa=PAKE.view&pageId=58854.

80 Jim Kouri, "Obama Connection to Terrorists Revealed by Talk Show Host," reporting on an interview conducted by talk show host Laurie Roth, New Media Alliance, March 22, 2008, at http://www.thenma.org/blogs/index.php/kouri /2008/03/22/obama_connection_to_terrorists_revealed.

81 Larry Cohler-Esses, "Obama Pivots Away From Dovish Past," *Jewish Week*, March 8, 2007, at http://www.thejewish-week.com/viewArticle/c37_a7525/News/National.html.

82 See "Ali Abunimah, EI Founder, Journalist," Electronic Intifada.net, at http://electronicintifada.net/v2/article2242 .shtml#ali.

83 Peter Wallsten, "Allies of Palestinian see a friend in Barack Obama," *Los Angeles Times*, April 10, 2008, at http://www .latimes.com/news/politics/la-na-obama mideast10apr10,0,5 826085.story.

84 Suzanne Trimel, "Faculty Profile: Edward Said," *Columbia University Record*, April 24, 1998, at http://www.columbia .edu/cu/record/23/22/22.html.

85 Gil Ronen, "Arab-American Activist Says Obama Hiding Anti-Israel Stance," *Arutz Sheva*, IsraelNationalNews.com, March 23, 2008, at http://www.israelnationalnews.com/ News/News.aspx/125656.

86 Ali Abunimah, "How Barack Obama learned to love Israel," Electronic Intifada, March 4, 2007, at http://electronicinti fada.net/v2/article6619.shtml.

87 Rashid Khalidi, *The Iron Cage: The Story of the Palestinian Struggle for Statehood* (Boston: Beacon Press, 2006), p. 216.

88 Arab American Action Network, at http://www.aaan.org/.

89 Ibid., at http://www.aaan.org/programs.html#coa.

90 "Arab American Action Network (AAAN)," DiscoverThe

Network.org, at http://www.discoverthenetworks.org/group Profile.asp?grpid=6462.

91 Abunimah, "How Barack Obama learned to love Israel."

92 "Penny Pritzker as National Finance Chair for Barack Obama," reported January 31, 2007, at http://blog.4president.org/ 2008/2007/01/penny_pritzker_.html.

93 "#135 Penny Pritzker," Forbes.com, September 20, 2007, at http://www.forbes.com/lists/2007/54/richlist07_Penny-Pritzker_CDNP.html.

94 David Jackson and Ray Long, "Obama knows his way around a ballot," *Chicago Tribune,* April 3, 2007, at http:// www.chicagotribune.com/news/local/chi-070403obama-bal lot,1,57567.story.

95 "Once Obama's mentor, Alice Palmer now campaigns for Clinton," *Los Angeles Times,* April 26, 2008, at http://latimesblogs. latimes.com/washington/2008/04/once-obamas-men.html.

96 Marcia Froelke Coburn, "No Regrets," *Chicago Magazine,* August 2001, reported in "One-degree of separation: Ayers: 'No regrets,'" Rezko Watch, May 5, 2008, at http://rezkowatch .blogspot.com/2008/05/one-degree-of-separation-ayers-no.html.

97 Anne Leare, "Wright Wrong Again," BackyardConservative. blogspot.com, May 4, 2008, at http://backyardconservative .blogspot.com/2008/05/wright-wrong-again.html.

98 Larry Johnson, "Stomp on This?" NoQuarter, May 3, 2008, at http://noquarterusa.net/blog/2008/05/03/stomp-on-this/.

99 Bill Ayers, *Fugitive Days: A Memoir* (Boston: Beacon, 2001).

100 Dinita Smith, "No Regrets for a Love of Explosives: In a Memoir of Sorts, a War Protestor Talks of Life with the Weathermen," *New York Times,* September 11, 2001, at http://query .nytimes.com/gst/fullpage.html?res=9F02E1DE1438F932A25 75AC0A9679C8B63&sec=&spon=&pagewanted=all.

101 Sam Graham-Felsen's Blog, on Barack Obama's 2008 presidential campaign website at http://my.barackobama.com/ page/community/blog/samgrahamfelsen.

102 Search on *The Nation* for comments and articles by freelance writer Sam Graham-Felsen at http://www.thenation.com/ search/index.mhtml?search=graham-felsen&page=1.

103   Daniela J. Lamas, "The Four-Year Path to a Quincy Suite," *Harvard Crimson*, June 5, 2003, at http://www.thecrimson.com/article.aspx?ref=348237.

104   Sam Graham-Felsen, "Chomsky's Choice," *Harvard Crimson*, November 4, 2003, at http://www.thecrimson.com/article.aspx?ref=349802.

105   Sam Graham-Felsen, "What's Really Happening in France?" *Socialist Viewpoint*, May/June 2006, at http://www.socialistviewpoint.org/mayjun_06/mayjun_06_03.html.

106   Angelique Chrisafis, "Riot police seal off Paris streets as protests escalate," *The Guardian*, March 24, 2006, at http://www.guardian.co.uk/world/2006/mar/24/highereducation.internationaleducationnews.

107   "Who We Are," *Socialist Viewpoint*, at http://www.socialistviewpoint.org/who_we_are.html.

108   Sam Graham-Felsen, "Bonkers for Obama," *The Nation*, October 18, 2006, at http://www.thenation.com/blogs/notion?pid=130647.

109   Sam Graham-Felsen, "Obama Steps Up on Iraq," *The Nation*, February 1, 2007, at http://www.thenation.com/blogs/notion?pid=162299.

110   Shailagh Murray, "Obama Bill Sets Date for Troop Withdrawal," *Washington Post*, January 31, 2007, at http://www.washingtonpost.com/wp-dyn/content/article/2007/01/30/AR2007013001586.html.

111   Common Ills, "Sam Graham-Felsen stands for what?" CommonIlls.blogspot.com, April 22, 2008, at http://thecommonills.blogspot.com/2008/04/sam-graham-felsen-stands-for-what.html.

112   "Obama's Official Blogger: A Hardcore Marxist," Little Green-Footballs, April 23, 2008, at http://littlegreenfootballs.com/article/29708_Obamas_Official_Blogger_A_Hardcore_Marxist#rss.

113   Warner Todd Huston, "Another Unsavory Obama Associate, Official Blogger a Communist?" Red State, April 24, 2008, at http://www.redstate.com/blogs/publiusforum/2008/apr/24/another_unsavory_obama_associate_official_blogger_a_communist.

Chapter 6. TONY REZKO AND "THE CHICAGO WAY"

1 "The Democratic Debate in South Carolina," January 21, 2008, transcript prepared by CNN, at http://www.nytimes.com/2008/01/21/us/politics/21demdebate-transcript.html.

2 John Kass, "The Chicago Way," March 6, 2008. Also see the John Kass video, "Yes way. Chicago's conduct code is a priceless legacy." Both at http://www.chicagotribune.com/news/opinion/chi-kass06mar06,0,3632128.column.

3 Evelyn Pringle, "Barack Obama—The Wizard of Oz," Counter Currents.org, March 28, 2008, at http://www.countercurrents.org/pringle280308.htm.

4 Ibid.

5 Evelyn Pringle, "Barack Obama: Operation Board Games for Slumlords," CounterCurrents.org, April 7, 2008, at http://www.countercurrents.org/pringle070408.htm.

6 *Sun-Times* Staff, "Complete transcript of the *Sun-Times* interview with Barack Obama," March 15, 2008, at http://www.suntimes.com/news/politics/obama/844597,transcript031508.article.

7 Pringle, "Barack Obama—The Wizard of Oz."

8 Ray Hanania, "Arabs in Chicago discover political clout and controversy," Arab American Media Services, June 8, 2005, at http://www.hanania.com/profiles/Rezko06-08-05.htm. See also James L. Merriner, "Mr. Inside Out," *Chicago Magazine*, November 2007, at http://www.chicagomag.com/Chicago-Magazine/November-2007/Mr-Inside-Out/index.php?cp=2&si=1.

9 John Fund, "Obama and Chicago Mores," *Wall Street Journal*, March 3, 2008, at http://online.wsj.com/public/article_print/SB120450564143806509.html.

10 *Sun-Times* Staff, "Complete transcript."

11 "Transcript of Tribune Interview," *Chicago Tribune*, March 16, 2008, at http://www.chicagotribune.com/news/opinion/chi-obamafullwebmar16,0,2950570.story.

12 Ibid.

13 Ray Gibson and David Jackson, "Rezko owns vacant lot next to Obama's home," *Chicago Tribune*, November 1,

2006, at http://www.chicagotribune.com/news/politics/chi-0611010273nov01,1,2716725.story.

14 Gretchen Reynolds, "Vote of Confidence," *Chicago Magazine*, January 1993, at http://www.chicagomag.com/Chicago-Magazine/January-1993/Vote-of-Confidence/.

15 Mary Wisniewski, "Rezko accuses ex-partner," *Chicago Sun-Times*, February 24, 2008, at http://www.suntimes.com/news/metro/rezko/810572,CST-NWS-rezko24.stng.

16 Tim Novak, "Broken promises, broken homes," *Chicago Sun-Times*, April 24, 2007, at http://www.suntimes.com/news/metro/355099,cst-nws-rez24a.article.

17 Ibid.

18 Ibid.

19 Ibid.

20 Tim Novak, "Rezmar deals involving Davis Miner law firm," *Chicago Sun-Times*, April 23, 2007, at http://www.suntimes.com/news/metro/353777,CST-NWS-rezside23.article.

21 Tim Novak, "Obama's letters for Rezko," *Chicago Sun-Times*, June 13, 2007, at http://www.suntimes.com/newspolitics/425305,CST-NWS-obama13.article.

22 Ibid.

23 Ibid.

24 Ibid.

25 Ibid.

26 Ibid.

27 *Sun-Times* Staff, "Complete transcript."

28 Ibid.

29 Ibid.

30 Edward McClelland, "How close were Barack Obama and Tony Rezko?" Salon.com, February 1, 2008, at http://www.salon.com/news/feature/2008/02/01/rezko/index1.html.

31 Gibson and Jackson, "Rezko owns vacant lot next to Obama's home."

32 McClelland described the homes in the Kenwood neighborhood as "balconied piles popular with the University of Chicago econ professors looking to blow their Nobel Prize loot."

33 Binyamin Appelbaum, "Obama haunted by friend's help securing dream house," *Boston Globe*, March 16, 2008, at http://www.boston.com/news/nation/articles/2008/03/16/obama_haunted_by_friends_help_securing_dream_house/.

34 Lynn Sweet, "Barack and Michelle Obama earned $991,296 in 2006," *Chicago Sun-Times*, April 16, 2007, at http://blogs.suntimes.com/sweet/2007/04/sweet_blog_extra_barack_and_mi.html.

35 John Fund, "Obama and Chicago Mores."

36 Appelbaum, "Obama haunted by friend's help securing dream house."

37 Ibid.

38 Pringle, "Barack Obama—The Wizard of Oz."

39 Appelbaum, "Obama haunted by friend's help securing dream house."

40 Ibid.

41 David Jackson and Ray Gibson, "Rezko sells lot next to Obama," *Chicago Tribune*, February 24, 2007, at http://www.chicagotribune.com/news/local/chi-0702240237feb24,0,4469899.story.

42 Ibid.

43 Ibid.

44 "Obama's 'Rezko' lot: Obama is one lucky fellow," Rezko Watch, March 23, 2008, at http://www.zimbio.com/pilot?ZURL=%2FObamamania%2Farticles%2F398%2FFolow%2BMoney%2Bbought%2BRezko%Blot&URL=http%3A%2F%2Frezkowatch.blogspotcom%2F2008%2F03%2Fobamas-rezko-lot-obama-is-one-lucky.html.

45 Kenneth P. Vogel, "Obama releases names of Rezko-linked donors," Politico.com, March 15, 2008, at http://dyn.politico.com/members/forums/thread.cfm?catid=1&subcatid=2&threadid=497387.

46 "Obama's 'Rezko' lot."

47 "Top recipients of campaign cash," *Chicago Sun-Times*, April 23, 2007, at http://www.suntimes.com/news/metro/353782,CST-NWS-rezpols23.article.

48 *Sun-Times* Staff, "Complete transcript."

49 "Transcript of Tribune Interview."

50 David Jackson, "Obama: I trusted Rezko," *Chicago Tribune*, March 15, 2008, at http://www.chicagotribune.com/news/politics/chi-obama-rezko-mar15,0,2968927.story.

51 *Sun-Times* Staff, "Complete transcript of the *Sun-Times* interview with Barack Obama." On Obama claiming Rezko raised $50,000 to $60,000 in campaign contributions, see Dave McKinney and Chris Fusco, "Obama on Rezko deal: It was a mistake," November 5, 2006, at http://www.suntimes.com/news/politics/124171,CST-NWS-obama05.article.

52 Chris Fusco and Tim Novak, "Obama cuts Rezko Ties," *Chicago Sun-Times*, January 30, 2008, at http://www.suntimes.com/news/politics/obama/766605,CST-NWS-obama30.article.

53 Jackson, "Obama: I trusted Rezko."

54 "Follow the Money: The Rezko lot (2 updates/questions added)," Rezko Watch, February 10, 2008, at http://rezkowatch.blogspot.com/2008/02/follow-money-rezko-lot.html.

55 David Kidwell, "Governor's wife's deals questioned," *Chicago Tribune*, October 27, 2006, at http://www.chicagotribune.com/news/politics/chi-govwifedeals061027,1,5312198,full.story.

56 Christopher Wills, Associated Press, "After Senate donor's indictment, Obama gives money to charity," December 15, 2007, at http://www.nctimes.com/articles/2007/12/15/news/politics/15_17_5012_14_07.txt.

57 "Follow the Money: Obama contributions donated to charity (Updated)," Rezko Watch, January 31, 2008, at http://rezkowatch.blogspot.com/2008/01/obamas.html.

58 John Batchelor, "Rezko Connections: More Questions for Obama," *Human Events*, March 3, 2008, at http://www.humanevents.com/article.php?id=25282.

59 Chris Fusco, "Obama to donate funds received from Rezko friend," *Chicago Sun-Times*, April 29, 2008, at http://www.suntimes.com/news/politics/obama/920701,CST-NWS-obama29WEB.article.

60 Brian Ross, Rhonda Schwartz, and Avni Patel, "Reformer: Trial Will Reveal 'Cesspool' of Obama's Allies," February 29, 2008, at http://abcnews.go.com/Blotter/story?id=4365942.

Chapter 7. MEET REVEREND WRIGHT

1 "Confusing God and Government," sermon by Reverend Jeremiah Wright, transcript of sermon, Trinity United Church of Christ, Chicago, April 13, 2003, ABC News, at http://abcnews.go.com/Blotter/Story?id=4719157&page=2.

2 James H. Cone, *For My People: Black Theology and the Black Church* (Maryknoll, N.Y.: Orbis, 1984), p. 66.

3 "Obama's Pastor: Rev. Jeremiah Wright," transcript from *Hannity & Colmes,* Fox News, March 2, 2007, at http://www.foxnews.com/story/0,2933,256078,00.html.

4 James H. Cone, *Black Theology & Black Power* (New York: Harper & Row, 1969).

5 Stokely Carmichael and Charles V. Hamilton, *Black Power: The Politics of Liberation in America* (New York: Random House, 1967).

6 Cone, *Black Theology & Black Power,* p. 6.

7 Ibid., p. 31.

8 Ibid., p. 32.

9 Ibid., p. 35.

10 Cone, *For My People,* p. 66.

11 Ibid., p. 67.

12 Ibid., pp. 72–73.

13 Frantz Fanon, *The Wretched of the Earth* (New York: Grove, 1966), p. 67.

14 James H. Cone, *Martin & Malcolm & America* (Maryknoll, N.Y.: Orbis, 1991), p. 225.

15 Cone, *Black Theology & Black Power,* p. 56.

16 "The Day of Jerusalem's Fall," sermon by Reverend Jeremiah Wright, transcript of speech, Trinity United Church of Christ, Chicago, September 16, 2001, ABC News, at http://abcnews.go.com/Blotter/story?id=4719157&page=1.

17 Quoted in Cone, *Martin & Malcolm & America,* p. 1.

18   Ibid., p. 187.

19   Malcolm X, with the assistance of Alex Haley, *The Autobiography of Malcolm X* (New York: Grove, 1965), p. 249.

20   C. Eric Lincoln, *The Black Muslims in America* (Boston: Beacon, 1961), p. 75.

21   Quoted in Cone, *Martin & Malcolm & America*, p. 151.

22   "Transcript: Rev. Wright at the National Press Club," Fox News, April 28, 2008, at http://elections.foxnews.com/2008/04/28/transcript-rev-wright-at-the-national-press-club/.

23   Wright, "Confusing God and Government."

24   Jeff Goldblatt, "Obama's Former Pastor Getting $1.6M Home in Retirement," Fox News, March 27, 2008, at http://elections.foxnews.com/2008/03/27/obamas-former-pastor-builds-a-multimillion-dollar-retirement-home/.

25   Donald C. Reitzes and Dietrich C. Reitzes, "Alinsky in the 1980s: Two Contemporary Chicago Community Organizations," *Sociological Quarterly* 28, no. 2 (June 1987), pp. 265–83, at p. 271. Archived at http://www.blackwell-synergy.com/doi/abs/10.1111/j.1533-8525.1987.tb00294.x?journalCode=tsq.

26   Ibid., p. 268.

27   Interview with Saul Alinsky, "Organizing the Back of the Yards," *Playboy*, March 1972, pp. 59–178. Archived at http://www.progress.org/2003/alinsky8.htm.

28   Obama, *Audacity of Hope*, p. 202.

29   Ibid., p. 203.

30   Ibid., p. 204.

31   Ibid., p. 206.

32   Obama, *Dreams,* p. 141.

33   Ibid.

34   Ibid.

35   Obama, "Why Organize?"

36   Obama, *Dreams,* p. 280.

37   Ibid., p. 274.

38   Noam Scheiber, "Why'd Obama Join Trinity in the First Place?" *New Republic*, April 29, 2008, at http://blogs.tnr.com/tnr/blogs/the_stump/archive/2008/04/29/why-d-obama-join-trinity-in-the-first-place.aspx?CommentPosted=true.

39 David Mendell, *Obama: From Promise to Power* (New York: Amistad, 2007), p. 64.

40 Obama, *Dreams*, p. 282.

41 Jeremiah A. Wright, Jr., *What Makes You So Strong? Sermons of Joy and Strength* (Valley Forge, Pa.: Judson, 1993), p. 107.

42 Obama, *Audacity of Hope*, p. 207.

43 Ibid., p. 208.

44 Niccolò Machiavelli, *The Discourses*, book 1, chapter 25.

45 Rodric J. Bradford, "Hiring Barack Obama," BustedHalo .com, at http://www.bustedhalo.com/features/BarackObama andJerryKellman.htm.

46 Hank De Zutter, "What Makes Obama Run?"

47 Mattias Gardell, *In the Name of Elijah Muhammad: Louis Farrakhan and the Nation of Islam* (Durham, N.C.: Duke University Press, 1996), pp. 240–41.

48 Ibid., p. 241.

49 Ibid., p. 286.

50 Ibid., p. 287.

51 Ibid., p. 282.

52 Charles Bierbauer, "Million Man March: Its goal more widely accepted than its leader," CNN, October 17, 1995, at http://www-cgi.cnn.com/US/9510/mega march/10-17/ notebook/index.html.

53 Ibid.

54 "Minister Farrakhan challenges black men," transcript from Minister Louis Farrakhan's remarks at the Million Man March, CNN, October 17, 1995, at http://www-cgi.cnn .com/US/9510/megamarch/10-16/transcript/index.html.

55 See, for instance: "Despite Obama's Criticism of Million Man March, Race-Obsessed Hannity Tries to Paint Him as Bigoted Soulmate," posted on News Hounds, April 20, 2008, at http://www.newshounds.us/2008/04/20/despite_ obamas_criticisms_of_million_man_march_race_obsessed_ hannity_tries_to_paint_him_as_bigoted_soulmate_of_farra khan.php.

56 De Zutter, "What Makes Obama Run?"

57 "Wright & Obama helped Organize March with Louis Farrakhan," Gateway Pundits, April 2, 2008, at http://

gatewaypundit.blogspot.com/2008/04/wright-obama-helped-organize-march-with.html.

58   Louis Farrakhan Biography, Biography.com, at http://www
.biography.com/search/article.do?id=9291850.

59   Frank Madison Reid, III, Jeremiah A. Wright, Jr., and Col-
leen Birchett, *When Black Men Stand Up for God: Reflections
on the Million Man March* (Chicago: African American
Images, 1976), p. 10.

60   Ibid., p. 13.

61   Gardell, *In the Name of Elijah Muhammad*, pp. 205–6.

62   Ibid., p. 206.

63   Edward McClelland, "How close were Barack Obama and
Tony Rezko?"

64   Dennis Walker, *Islam and the Search for African-American
Nationhood: Elijah Muhammad, Louis Farrakhan and the
Nation of Islam* (Atlanta: Clarity, 2005).

65   Gardell, *In the Name of Elijah Muhammad*, pp. 206–7.

66   Ibid., p. 207.

67   Quoted in Ronald Kessler, "Obama Attended Hate America Sermon," NewsMax, March 16, 2008, at http://www
.newsmax.com/kessler/Obama_hate_America_sermon/2008
/03/16/80870.html.

68   Richard Cohen, "Obama's Farrakhan Test," *Washington
Post*, January 15, 2008, at http://www.washingtonpost
.com/wp-dyn/content/article/2008/01/14/AR20080114020
83.html.

69   Jake Tapper, "Who's Scrubbing the Trinity United Church of
Christ Website?" ABC News, March 31, 2008, at http://blogs
.abcnews.com/politicalpunch/2008/03/whos-scrubbing.html.

70   Transcript, *Bill Moyers Journal*, PBS, April 25, 2008, at http://
www.pbs.org/moyers/journal/04252008/transcript1.html.

71   "Transcript: Rev. Wright at the National Press Club," Fox
News, April 28, 2008, at http://elections.foxnews.com
/2008/04/28/transcript-rev-wright-at-the-national-press-club/.

72   Dana Milbank, "Could Rev. Spell Doom for Obama?"
Washington Post, April 28, 2008, at http://blog.washington
post.com/roughsketch/2008/04/obamas_pastor_reignites_
race_c.html.

73 Barack Obama, "On My Faith and My Church," Huffington Post, March 14, 2008, at http://www.huffingtonpost.com/barack-obama/on-my-faith-and-my-church_b_91623.html.

74 Kessler, "Obama Attended Hate America Sermon."

75 "Fact: Obama Did Not Attend Services on July 22," Obama presidential campaign website, posted March 16, 2008, at http://factcheck.barackobama.com/factcheck/2008/03/16/fact_obama_did_not_attend_serv.php.

76 Remarks of Senator Barack Obama, "A More Perfect Union," Philadelphia, posted on Obama's presidential campaign website March 19, 2008, at http://my.barackobama.com/page/content/hisownwords.

77 "Transcript: Obama Press Conference on Jeremiah Wright," Fox News, April 29, 2008, at http://elections.foxnews.com/2008/04/29/transcript-obama-press-conference-on-jeremiah-wright/.

78 "Transcript: Barack Obama on 'Fox News Sunday,'" Fox News, April 28, 2008, at http://www.foxnews.com/story/0,2933,352785,00.html.

79 Aaron Klein, "Obama's New pastor quotes 'F— AmeriKKKa' rap song," World Net Daily, May 4, 2008, at http://www.worldnetdaily.com/index.php?fa=PAGE.view&pageId=63377.

80 Father Michael Pfleger, Senior Pastor, St. Sabina Church, Chicago, listed on the "People of Faith" testimonial page of Obama's 2008 presidential campaign website, at http://faith.barackobama.com/page/content/faithtestimonials.

81 Ray Long, Ray Gibson, and David Jackson, "State pork to Obama's district included allies, donors," Chicago Tribune, May 3, 2007, at http://www.chicagotribune.com/entertainment/chi-0705030035may03,0,7803217.story.

82 "Barack Obama: Putting Faith Out Front," Christian Science Monitor, July 16, 2007, at http://www.csmonitor.com/2007/0716/p01s01-uspo.html?page=2.

83 Jay Levine, "Minister Louis Farrakhan Speaks at St. Sabina's," CBS 2 Chicago, May 25, 2007, at http://cbs2chicago.com/local/louis.farrakhan.nation.2.337213.html.

84 "Priest threatens to 'snuff out' legislators," Capitol Fax

Blog, May 30, 2007, at http://thecapitolfaxblog.com/2007/05/30/priest-threatens-to-snuff-out-legislators/.

85   Susan Hogan, "Cardinal Rebukes Pfleger for 'Threat,'" *Chicago Sun-Times*, June 8, 2007. The article appears not to be archived on the *Chicago Sun-Times* website, but is documented and discussed at FreeRepublic.com at http://www.freerepublic.com/focus/f-news/1846964/posts.

86   "Father Michael Pfleger at Jackson Square, Aug. 29, 2007," posted on YouTube.com, September 2, 2007, at http://www.youtube.com/watch?v=tt-Y2qFtkU0.

87   "Local Priest Worried That Public May Not Be Ready for Obama," WBBM News Radio 780, Chicago, January 16, 2007, at http://www.wbbm780.com/pages/185206.php?contentType=4&contentId=290430.

88   Leonard G. Horowitz, *Emerging Viruses: AIDS & Ebola—Nature, Accident or Intentional?* (Standpoint, Idaho: Tetrahedron, 1996).

89   Harriet A. Washington, *Medical Apartheid: The Dark History of Medical Experimentation on Black Americans from Colonial Times to the Present* (New York: Doubleday, 2006).

90   Cliff Kincaid, "Obama Pastor's AIDS Charge Mimics Soviet KGB Disinformation Campaign," report published by America's Survival, Inc., at http://www.usasurvival.org/docs/ASI_Report_on_Wright.pdf.

91   Associated Press, "Soviet Disavows Charges that U.S. Created AIDS," *New York Times*, November 5, 1987, at http://query.nytimes.com/gst/fullpage.html?res=9B0DE0DE1730F936A35752C1A961948260.

92   "'White people want to wipe us out'—Researcher, author insists AIDS a weapon of genocide," *Final Call*, July 30, 2002, at http://www.finalcall.com/perspectives/interviews/dr_felder07-30-2002.htm.

93   Margaret Ramirez, "Louis Farrakhan backs Obama for president at Nation of Islam convention in Chicago," *Chicago Tribune*, February 25, 2008, at http://www.chicagotribune.com/news/chi-farrakhan25feb25,0,6391391.story.

94   Aaron Klein, "Hillary believed she'd win 'cause she's white," World Net Daily, May 29, 2008, at http://www.wnd.com/index.php?fa=PAGE.view&pageId=65625.

95 Lynn Sweet, "Obama 'deeply disappointed' in Father Michael Pfleger," *Chicago Sun-Times*, May 29, 2008, at http://blogs.suntimes.com/sweet/2008/05/obama_deeply_disappointed_in_f_1.html.

96 "Clinton team demands Obama act on pastor attack," AFP, May 29, 2008, at http://afp.google.com/article/ALeqM5izZw_Pt7BvA5fS0GjNV4m7AcoW0g.

97 Lynn Sweet, "Obama on quitting Trinity United Church of Christ," with press conference transcript, *Chicago Sun-Times*, May 31, 2008, at http://blogs.suntimes.com/sweet/2008/05/obama_on_quitting_trinity_unit.html. All quotations from Obama's press conference of May 31, 2008, come from this source.

PART THREE: THE CANDIDATE IS THE MESSAGE

1 The Chris Matthews sequence televised on MSNBC's *Decision '08* on February 19, 2008, with Texas state senator Kirk Watson can be viewed on YouTube.com at http://www.youtube.com/watch?v=jj4VK9wVAi0.

2 Eric Zorn, "He's billed as a kingpin, yet can't bowl," *Chicago Tribune*, April 3, 2008, at http://www.chicagotribune.com/news/local/chicago/chi-zornapr03,0,7128655.column.

3 Ibid.

4 Marshall McLuhan, *Understanding Media: The Extensions of Man* (New York: McGraw-Hill, 1964), p. 309.

Chapter 8. THE CULT OF PERSONALITY

1 Abraham Katsman, "Obama is no moderate: His radical position on 'abortion' after birth," *Jerusalem Post*, April 3, 2008, at http://www.jpost.com/servlet/Satellite?cid=1207159750412&pagename=JPost%2FJPArticle%2FShowFull.

2 Paul Bedard, "More an Architect than a Bridge Builder," *U.S. News & World Report*, May 1, 2007, at http://www.usnews.com/blogs/washington-whispers/2007/5/1/more-an-architect-than-a-bridge-builder.html.

3   Arnold Beichman, "Ralph McAllister Ingersoll, RIP—Obituary," *National Review*, April 5, 1985, at http://findarticles.com/p/articles/mi_m1282/is_v37/ai_3719782.

4   Tim Graham, "Radical Writer I. F. Stone Wasn't a Paid Soviet Agent: He'd Perform Tasks for Free," News Busters, September 30, 2006, at http://newsbusters.org/node/8003.

5   The issue of I. F. Stone's relation with Soviet spies is discussed in Paul Berman, "The Watchdog," *New York Times*, October 1, 2006.

6   Frank Marshall Davis, *Livin' the Blues: Memoirs of a Black Journalist and Poet,* p. 289.

7   "Backin' Black," *On the Media*, NPR, and interview of Christopher Hayes conducted by Brooke Gladstone, February 23, 2007, at http://www.onthemedia.org/transcripts/2007/02/23/06.

8   Howard Wolinsky, "The Secret Side of David Axelrod," *BusinessWeek*, March 14, 2008, at http://www.businessweek.com/bwdaily/dnflash/content/mar2008/db20080314_121054.htm?campaign_id=rss_daily.

9   Ibid.

10   Patrick T. Reardon, "The Agony and the Agony," *Chicago Tribune*, June 24, 2007, at http://www.chicagotribune.com/features/magazine/chi-070620axelrod-htmlstory,0,3477242.htmlstory.

11   Ben Wallace-Wells, "Obama's Narrator," *New York Times*, April 1, 2007, at http://www.nytimes.com/2007/04/01/magazine/01axelrod.t.html.

12   Ibid.

13   Christopher Hayes, "Obama's Media Maven," *Nation*, February 6, 2007, at http://www.thenation.com/doc/20070219/hayes.

14   Wallace-Wells, "Obama's Narrator."

15   Obama Messiah Blogspot, Internet homepage at http://obamamessiah.blogspot.com/. This section first appeared as Jerome R. Corsi, "Is Obama the Messiah?" World Net Daily, February 23, 2008, at http://www.wnd.com/index.php?fa=PAGE.view&pageId=57090.

16   First reported at Jerome R. Corsi, "'Obama messiah' creator:

How far will 'cult' go?" World Net Daily, March 27, 2008, at http://www.wnd.com/index.php?pageId=60093.

17 Deepak Chopra, "Obama and the Call: 'I Am America,'" Huffington Post, http://www.huffingtonpost.com/deepak-chopra/obama-and-the-call-i-am_b_80016.html.

18 Brad Wilmouth, "Matthews: Obama Speech Caused Thrill Going Up My Leg," February 13, 2008, at http://newsbusters .org/blogs/brad-wilmouth/2008/02/13/matthews-obama-speech-caused-thrill-going-my-leg?q=blogs/brad-wilmouth/2008/02/13/matthews-obama-speech-caused-thrill-going-my-leg.

19 Dan Gearino, "Oprah says Obama's tongue 'dipped in the unvarnished truth,'" Quad-City Times, December 8, 2007, at http://www.qctimes.com/articles/2007/12/08/news/local/doc475b3520cfbbf148217551.txt.

20 J. R. Dunn, "Obama as Liberal Messiah," American Thinker, January 14, 2008, at http://www.americanthinker.com/2008/01/obama_as_liberal_messiah.html.

21 J. R. Dunn, "Hollywood's Red Decade," American Thinker, November 16, 2007, at http://www.americanthinker.com/2007/11/hollywoods_red_decade.html.

22 Jon Swift, "Barack Obama's Achilles Heel," JonSwift.Blog spot.com, February 13, 2008, at http://jonswift.blogspot .com/2008/02/barack-obamas-achilles-heel.html.

23 Matthew Mosk and Jose Antonio Vargas, "Clinton Camp Charges Obama 'Plagiarism,'" Washington Post, February 18, 2008, at http://blog.washingtonpost.com/the-trail/2008/02/18/clinton_camp_charges_obama_wit_1.html.

24 "Just Words. Just not Obama's," YouTube.com, posted February 17, 2008, at http://www.youtube.com/watch?v=8M6x1H08aFc&eurl=http://blog.washingtonpost.com/channel-08/2008/02/post_2.html.

25 Lisa Ferri and Olivia Sterns, "Patrick: Plagiarism Accusation Against Obama 'Extravagant,'" ABC News, February 19, 2008, at http://abcnews.go.com/GMA/Vote2008/story?id=4310143.

26 Ibid.

27 "Obama plagiarizing again?" YouTube.com, posted February 19,

2008, at http://www.youtube.com/watch?v=NVtg2T4XR7w& feature=related.

28   Nedra Pickler, Associated Press, "Obama Says Borrowed Lines Not a Big Deal," ABC News, February 19, 2008, at http://abcnews.go.com/Politics/wireStory?id=4306620.

29   Larry J. Sabato, "Joseph Biden's Plagiarism; Michael Dukakis's 'Attack Video'—1988," *Washington Post*, Copyright 1998, at http://www.washingtonpost.com/wp-srv/politics/special/clinton/frenzy/biden.htm.

30   Seymour Glass, "Bamboozled: How Obama has been Plagiarizing Spike Lee/Malcolm X," Direct Democracy, February 21, 2008, at http://www.mydd.com/story/2008/2/21/143317/391.

31   See *Malcolm X*, director Spike Lee, at http://www.imdb.com/title/tt0104797/.

32   "Barack Obama: There Will Be Bamboozling," YouTube.com, posted February 20, 2008, at http://www.youtube.com/watch?v=YuB_W8o_UsU&eurl=http://www.mydd.com/story/2008/2/21/143317/391.

33   Jan Freeman, "Hoodwinked," *Boston Globe*, February 10, 2008, at http://www.boston.com/bostonglobe/ideas/articles/2008/02/10/hornswoggled/?page=2.

34   See Visionaries, "We Are the Ones," at http://www.amazon.com/Are-Ones-Weve-Been-Waiting/dp/B000HEYZFU/ref=sr_1_2?ie=UTF8&s=music&qid=1206470405&sr=1-2.

35   Alice Walker, *We Are the Ones We Have Been Waiting For* (New York: New Press, 2006).

36   See page for *The Matrix*, directors Andy Wachowski and Larry Wachowski, 1999, at http://www.imdb.com/title/tt0133093/.

37   " 'Yes We Can' Song," by DipDive, at http://www.dipdive.com/.

38   "Yes We Can—Barack Obama Music Video," YouTube.com, posted February 2, 2008, at http://youtube.com/watch?v=jjXyqcx-mYY.

39   "Michelle Obama Takes Heat for Saying She's 'Proud of My Country' for the First Time," Fox News, February 19, 2008, at http://elections.foxnews.com/2008/02/19/michelle-obama-

takes-heat-for-saying-shes-proud-of-my-country-for-the-first-time/.

40 "Michelle Obama: 'For the First Time in My Adult Lifetime, I am Really Proud of My Country,'" Breitbart.tv, February 18, 2008, at http://www.breitbart.tv/html/49244.html.

41 "Michelle Obama: First Time proud of USA," YouTube .com, posted February 18, 2008, at http://www.youtube .com/watch?v=LYY73RO_egw.

42 Jim Hoft, "Oops! She Did It Again! . . . Michelle Obama's 'Proud of My Country' Twofer (Video)," Gateway Pundit, February 20, 2008, at http://gateway pundit.blogspot .com/2008/02/oops-she-did-it-again-michelle-obamas.html.

43 "Michelle Obama Takes Heat for Saying She's 'Proud of My Country' for the First Time," Fox News.

44 Ibid.

45 Quoted by Michelle Malkin, "Michelle Obama's America— and mine," MichelleMalkin.com, February 20, 2008, at http:// michellemalkin.com/2008/02/20/michelle-obamas-america-and-mine/.

46 Michelle LaVaughn Robinson, "Princeton-Educated Blacks and the Black Community," a thesis presented to Princeton University in partial fulfillment of the requirements for bachelor of arts in Department of Sociology, 1985. Initially, Princeton University said the thesis would be withheld from the public until after the 2008 presidential campaign. A copy, however, has appeared on the Internet and is available for download at http://www.scribd.com/ doc/2305083/PrincetonEdcated-Blacks-and-the-Black-Com munity.

47 Christopher Hitchens, "Are We Getting Two for One?" Salon.com, May 5, 2008, at http://www.slate.com/id/2190589/.

48 Lauren Collins, "'I want to rip Bill Clinton's eyes out. Kidding! See, that's what gets me into trouble,'" *Guardian*, May 4, 2008, at http://www.guardian.co.uk/politics/2008/ may/04/barackobama.

49 David Mendell, *Obama: From Promise to Power* (New York: Amistad, 2007), p. 258.

50 Ibid.

Chapter 9. A FAR-LEFT DOMESTIC POLICY

1   Brian Friel, Richard E. Cohen, and Kirk Victor, "Obama: Most Liberal Senator in 2007," *National Journal*, January 31, 2008, at http://nj.nationaljournal.com/voteratings/.

2   David Wright and Sunlen Miller, "Obama Dropped Flag Pin in War Statement," ABC News, October 4, 2007, at http://abcnews.go.com/Politics/Story?id=3690000.

3   Jill Stanek, "Top 10 Reasons Obama Voted Against Illinois Born Alive Infant Protection Act," *Illinois Review*, January 10, 2008, at http://illinoisreview.typepad.com/illinois review/2008/01/top-10-reasons.html.

4   Abraham Katsman, "Obama is no moderate: His radical position on 'abortion' after birth," *Jerusalem Post*, April 3, 2008, at http://www.jpost.com/servlet/Satellite?cid=120715 9750412&pagename=JPost%2FJPArticle%2FShowFull.

5   State of Illinois, 92nd General Assembly, Regular Session, Senate Transcript, 20th Legislative Day, March 30, 2001, at http://www.ilga.gov/senate/transcripts/strans92/ST033001.pdf, pp. 86–87.

6   Senator Obama, Voting Record Score, NARAL Pro-Choice America, at http://www.prochoiceamerica.org/elections/state ments/obama.html.

7   Barack Obama before Planned Parenthood Action Fund, July 17, 2007, transcribed by Laura Echevarria at http://lauraetch.googlepages.com/barackobamabeforeplannedparent hoodaction. A video of Obama's speech has been archived on "One Million for Planned Parenthood" at http://www.imoneinamillion.com/.

8   Ibid.

9   Transcript, "More Campaign Happenings," March 29, 2008, at http://transcripts.cnn.com/TRANSCRIPTS/0803/29/bb.01.html.

10 Statistics cited in Marie Jon', "Barack Hussein Obama refused: 'I do not want to concede,'" RenewAmerica.com, March 9, 2008, at http://www.renewamerica.us/columns/jon/080309.

11 "Abortion and the Black Community," posted on Black Genocide.org, http://www.blackgenocide.org/black.html.

12 Blackwell and Corsi, *Rebuilding America,* p. 98.

13 John McCain, Voting Record Score, NARAL Pro-Choice America, at http://www.prochoiceamerica.org/elections/state ments/mccain.html.

14 Frank Main, "Man who shot intruder arrested," *Chicago Sun-Times,* January 9, 2004.

15 Ana Mendieta, "Wilmette police chief gets an earful on handgun ban," *Chicago Sun-Times,* January 14, 2004.

16 Quoted by Wayne LaPierre, Executive Vice President, National Rifle Association, "Barack Obama's Slippery Oratory," NRA Official Journal, 2008, at http://www.nra publications.org/SG/index.asp.

17 Dave Workman, "Lethal blow for gun control," *Chicago Sun-Times,* November 28, 2004.

18 LaPierre, "Barack Obama's Slippery Oratory."

19 Quoted on Slate.com by a reader, "Sgt. Rock," who posted a comment, "Obama and the 2nd Amendment," on April 20, 2008, at http://fray.slate.com/discuss/forums/thread/1149796 .aspx.

20 Kenneth P. Vogel, "Obama linked to gun control efforts," Politico.com, April 19, 2008, at http://www.politico.com/ news/stories/0408/9722.html.

21 "Every Handgun Is Aimed at You," book notice posted at BanHandGunsNow.com, at http://www.banhandgunsnow .org/everyhandgun/index.html.

22 Josh Sugarman, Introduction to *Every Handgun Is Aimed at You: The Case for Banning Handguns* (New York: New Press, 2002), at: http://www.banhandgunsnow.org/everyhandgun/ intro.html.

23 Associated Press, "Obama Supports Individual Gun Rights," February 15, 2008, at http://www.breitbart.com/article.php? id=D8UQTAS80&show_article=1.

24 Abdon M. Pallasch, "Laws alone can't stop violence: Obama," *Chicago Sun-Times,* April 25, 2008, at http://www.suntimes .com/news/politics/obama/914970,CST-NWS-obama25.article.

25 Erich Pratt, "Obama to Get the Dems 'Barack' into the

Business of Gun Control," GunOwners.org, at http://www
.gunowners.org/press08/obama.htm.

26 Barack Obama, "Remarks of Senator Barack Obama: Tax
Fairness for the Middle Class," September 18, 2007, at http://
www.barackobama.com/2007/09/18/remarks_of_senator_
barack_obam_25.php.

27 James Pethokoukis, "Obama Pushes for Higher Investment
Taxes," writing in "Capital Commerce" in *U.S. News &
World Report*, September 19, 2007, at http://www.usnews
.com/blogs/capital-commerce/2007/9/19/obama-pushes-for-
higher-investment-taxes.html.

28 Ed Morrissey, "Video: Obama's redistributionism on capital
gains taxes," HotAir.com, April 17, 2008, at http://hotair.com/
archives/2008/04/17/video-obamas-redistributionism-on-
capital-gains-taxes/.

29 Transcript, Democratic Debate in Philadelphia, *New York
Times*, April 16, 2008, at http://www.nytimes.com/2008/
04/16/us/politics/16text-debate.html?_r=3&adxnnl=1&oref=s
login&pagewanted=all&adxnnlx=1208437269-fKtTgU17/
E3aJWBZu-oKGw&oref=slogin.

30 "Hillary Clinton on Health Care," OnTheIssues.com, at
http://www.ontheissues.org/2008/hillary_clinton_health_care
.htm#1990s_Hillarycare.

31 Transcript, Democratic Candidates' Debate, South Carolina,
April 26, 2007, MSNBC, at http://www.msnbc.msn.com/
id/18351716/.

32 Ibid.

33 Barack Obama, "The Time Has Come for Universal Health
Care," speech delivered to the Families USA Conference,
Washington, D.C., January 25, 2007. Posted on the Inter-
net by Deborah White, "U.S. Liberal Politics," About.com,
at   http://usliberals.about.com/od/extraordinaryspeeches/a/
ObamaHealthIns.htm.

34 Transcript, The Democratic Debate in Cleveland, *New
York Times*, February 26, 2008, at http://www.nytimes
.com/2008/02/26/us/politics/26text-debate.html.

35 Paul Krugman, "Clinton, Obama, Insurance," *New York Times*, February 4, 2008, at http://www.nytimes.com/2008/02/04/opinion/04krugman.html.

36 Barack Obama, press release, "Obama, Hegel, Cantwell, Smith Hail Committee Passage of the Global Poverty Act," February 13, 2008, at http://obama.senate.gov/press/080213-obama_hagel_can_1/.

37 Cliff Kincaid, "Obama's Global Tax Proposal Up for Senate Vote," Accuracy in Media, February 12, 2008, at http://www.aim.org/aim-column/obamas-global-tax-proposal-up-for-senate-vote/.

38 United Nations Millennium Declaration, resolution adopted by the General Assembly, Fifty-fifth Session, at http://www.un.org/millennium/declaration/ares552e.pdf.

39 Phyllis Schlafly, "Obama's sovereignty giveaway plan," World Net Daily, February 22, 2008, at http://www.worldnetdaily.com/index.php?fa=PAGE.view&pageId=56959.

40 Investing in Development: A Practical Plan to Achieve the Millennium Development, United Nations, Millennium Project, 2005, at http://www.unmillenniumproject.org/reports/index.htm.

41 Jeffrey D. Sachs, *The End of Poverty: Economic Possibilities for Our Time* (New York: Penguin, 2006).

42 William Easterly, "A Modest Proposal," review of *The End of Poverty* by Jeffrey D. Sachs, *Washington Post*, March 13, 2005, at http://www.washingtonpost.com/wp-dyn/articles/A25562-2005Mar10.html.

43 Lee Cary, "Obama's Global Tax," *American Thinker*, February 19, 2008, at http://www.americanthinker.com/2008/02/the_global_candidate_proposes.html.

44 Barack Obama, 2008 Presidential Campaign, Top Contributors, OpenSecrets.org, at http://www.opensecrets.org/pres08/contrib.php?cycle=2008&cid=N00009638.

45 David Edwards and Jason Rhyne, "No hand over heart from Obama during national anthem," RawStory.com, October 22, 2007, at http://rawstory.com/news/2007/Obama_doesnt_put_hand_over_heart_1022.html.

46 Mark Finkelstein, "Obama: No Hand on Heart for National Anthem," NewsBusters.org, October 20, 2007, at http://newsbusters.org/blogs/mark-finkelstein/2007/10/20/obama-no-hand-heart-pledge-either-will-msm-notice.

47 E-mail from Senator Barack Obama quoted in Christopher Hayes, "Smearing Obama by E-Mail," *Nation*, Campaign '08 Blog, November 8, 2007, at http://www.thenation.com/blogs/campaignmatters?bid=45&pid=249994.

48 John Kerry and Vietnam Veterans Against the War, *The New Soldier*, ed. by David Thorne and George Butler (New York: Macmillan, 1971).

Chapter 10. OBAMA'S ANTIWAR, ANTI-ISRAEL FOREIGN POLICY

1 Bill Glauber, "Remembering Obama's Speech," National Public Radio, March 25, 2008, and the accompanying article, Don Gonyea, "Obama Still Stumps on 2002," National Public Radio, March 25, 2008, both at http://www.npr.org/templates/story/story.php?storyId=88988093. For a text of the speech, see "Barack Obama's Iraq Speech," Wikisource.org, at http://en.wikisource.org/wiki/Barack_Obama's_Iraq_Speech.

2 President George W. Bush, Remarks by the President to Members of the Knesset, Office of the Press Secretary (Jerusalem), White House, May 15, 2008, at http://i.usatoday.net/news/mmemmottpdf/bush-knesset-may-15-2008.pdf.

3 "Bill Clinton Challenges Obama's Stance on the Iraq War," video clip of President Bill Clinton's comments captured by MSNBC and posted for viewing at http://www.redlasso.com/ClipPlayer.aspx?id=980890fe-9b73-4b99-b391-d2accda7b689.

4 Gonyea, "Obama Still Stumps on 2002."

5 Ibid.

6 Ibid.

7 Ibid.

8 Lynn Sweet, "Obama said 'no' to Iraq money in theory, 'yes' in reality," *Chicago Sun-Times*, January 14, 2008, at

http://www.suntimes.com/news/sweet/739563,CST-NWS-sweet14.article.

9 Ibid.

10 James W. Pindell and Rick Klein, "Obama defends votes in favor of Iraq funding," *Boston Globe*, March 22, 2007, at http://www.boston.com/news/nation/articles/2007/03/22/obama_defends_votes_in_favor_of_iraq_funding/.

11 Transcript, "The Democratic Debate in Las Vegas," *New York Times*, January 15, 2008, at http://www.nytimes.com/2008/01/15/us/politics/15demdebate-transcript.html?pagewanted=print.

12 Ibid.

13 Remarks of Barack Obama: "A New Beginning," Chicago, October 2, 2007, at http://www.barackobama.com/2007/10/02/remarks_of_senator_barack_obam_27.php.

14 Lou Cannon, "Reagan-Gorbachev Summit Talks Collapse as Deadlock on SDI Wipes Out Other Gains," *Washington Post*, October 13, 1986, at http://www.washingtonpost.com/wp-srv/inatl/longterm/summit/archive/oct86.htm.

15 Joseph Cirincione, "The Greatest Threat to Us All," *New York Review of Books*, March 6, 2008, at http://www.nybooks.com/articles/21054.

16 Ibid.

17 National Intelligence Council, "Iran: Nuclear Intentions and Capabilities," November 2007, at http://www.dni.gov/press_releases/20071203_release.pdf.

18 See, for instance, James Phillips, "The Iran National Intelligence Estimate: A Comprehensive Guide to What Is Wrong with the NIE," Heritage Foundation, January 11, 2008, at http://www.heritage.org/research/MiddleEast/bg2098.cfm#_ftn1.

19 Report by the Director General, "Implementation of the NPT Safeguards Agreement and relevant provisions of Security Council resolutions 1737 (2006) and 1747 (2007) in the Islamic Republic of Iran," International Atomic Energy Agency, February 22, 2008, at http://www.iaea.org/Publications/Documents/Board/2008/gov2008-4.pdf.

20 "North Korea-Syria nuclear ties: déjà vu all over again,"

Foreign Policy, September 14, 2007, at http://blog.foreign policy.com/node/6251.

21 National Public Radio, "Mystery Surrounds Israeli Strike in Syria," *All Things Considered*, September 19, 2007, at http://www.npr.org/templates/transcript/transcript.php?storyId=145 37546.

22 David E. Sanger, "Bush Administration Releases Images to Bolster its Claims About Syrian Reactor," *New York Times*, April 25, 2008, at http://www.nytimes.com/2008/04/25/world/middleeast/25korea.html?hp=&pagewanted=all.

23 Cirincione quoted in Ewen MacAskill, "US claims North Korea helped build Syria reactor plant," *Guardian*, April 25, 2008, at http://www.guardian.co.uk/world/2008/apr/25/usa.nuclear.

24 Aaron Klein, "Obama advisor: Israel must give up its nukes," World Net Daily, May 1, 2008, at http://www.worldnetdaily.com/index.php?fa=PAGE.view&pageId=63031.

25 Quoted by Haider Rizvi, "Israeli Arsenal Vexes Nuclear Negotiators," AntiWar.com, May 21, 2005, at http://www.antiwar.com/ips/rizvi.php?articleid=6033.

26 Ed Lasky, "Obama Keeps Hiring Anti-Israeli Advisors," *American Thinker*, May 16, 2008, at http://www.americanthinker.com/blog/2008/04/obama_keeps_hiring_antiisraeli.html.

27 Robert M. Goldberg, "McPeak on Display," *American Spectator*, March 24, 2008, at http://www.spectator.org/dsp_rticle.asp?art_id=12937.

28 Colonel Merrill A. McPeak, "Israel: Borders and Security," *Foreign Affairs*, April 1976, at http://www.foreignaffairs.org/19760401faessay10180/colonel-merrill-a-mcpeak/israel-borders-and-security.html.

29 Text of interview with Gen. Merrill A. "Tony" McPeak, *Oregonian*, March 27, 2003, at http://www.oregonlive.com/special/iraq/index.ssf?/special/iraq/0327mcpeak.html.

30 Aaron Klein, "Hamas terrorists make 2008 presidential pick," World Net Daily, April 14, 2008, at http://worldnet daily.com/index.php?fa=PAGE.view&pageId=61631.

31 Aaron Klein, "Hamas terrorists join Jimmy Carter fan club,"

World Net Daily, April 13, 2008, at http://www.wnd.com/index.php?pageId=61496.

32 "McCain Takes Shot at Obama for Hamas Support," Fox News, April 25, 2008, at http://elections.foxnews.com/2008/04/25/mccain-takes-shot-at-obama-for-hamas-support/. A video of Senator McCain's remarks to Fox News about the Hamas endorsement of Obama can be seen on YouTube: "Hamas Endorses Obama, McCain Responds," posted on YouTube.com, April 26, 2008, at http://www.youtube.com/watch?v=43zgOHLHep4.

33 Philip Klein, "Stop Believing Obama," *American Spectator*, May 12, 2008, at http://www.spectator.org/dsp_article.asp?art_id=13194.

34 "Obama: Anniversary of Israeli Independence," Speech at the 60th Anniversary of Israeli Independence at Washington, D.C., posted on YouTube.com, May 8, 2008, at http://www.youtube.com/watch?v=jATQU2qh1m4.

35 "Obama: World wants to see U.S. lead," CNN Election Center 2008, May 8, 2008, at http://www.cnn.com/2008/POLITICS/05/08/obama/index.html.

36 "Memo from McCain Adviser Salter," *Time*, May 8, 2008, at http://thepage.time.com/memo-from-mccain-adviser-salter/.

37 Tom Baldwin, "Barack Obama sacks adviser over talks with Hamas," *Times* (London), May 10, 2008, at http://www.timesonline.co.uk/tol/news/world/us_and_americas/us_elections/article3897414.ece.

38 Ibid.

39 Aaron Klein, "Obama aide wants: Foreign adviser's 'anti-Israel policies,'" World Net Daily, January 29, 2008, at http://www.worldnetdaily.com/news/article.asp?ARTICLE_ID=59930.

40 Jeffrey Goldberg, "Obama on Zionism and Hamas," Atlantic.com, May 12, 2008, at http://jeffreygoldberg.theatlantic.com/archives/2008/05/obama_on_zionism_and_hamas.php.

41 Aaron Klein, "Hamas worried its praise harming Obama," World Net Daily, May 14, 2008, at http://www.worldnetdaily.com/index.php?fa=PAGE.view&pageId=64247.

42 CNN/YouTube Democratic Presidential Debate Transcript,

CNN, posted July 24, 2007, at http://www.cnn.com/2007/POLITICS/07/23/debate.transcript/index.html.

43 Corsi, *Atomic Iran,* pp. 68–69.

44 Ibid., pp. 15–16.

45 Marc Ambinder, "The White House Changes Targets," TheAtlantic.com, May 16, 2008, at http://marcambinder.theatlantic.com/archives/2008/05/the_white_house_changes_target.php.

46 Ed Henry, "Dems fire back at Bush on 'appeasement' statement," CNN, Election Center 2008, May 16, 2008, at http://www.cnn.com/2008/POLITICS/05/15/bush.dems/index.html.

47 Mike Glover, Associated Press, "Obama criticizes McCain, Bush on appeasement talk," May 16, 2008, at http://www.breitbart.com/article.php?id=D90MSV5G0&show_article=1.

48 Senator Barack Obama, transcript from *Meet the Press,* MSNBC, May 4, 2008, at http://www.msnbc.msn.com/id/24445166/.

49 JPost.com Staff, "Ahmadinejad: Israel a 'stinking corpse,'" *Jerusalem Post,* May 8, 2008, at http://www.jpost.com/servlet/Satellite?cid=1209627040670&pagename=JPost%2FJPArticle%2FShowFull.

50 Scott Johnson, "Obama's Unrealistic Realism," Power Line, May 16, 2008, at http://www.powerlineblog.com/.

CONCLUSION

1 Michael S. Dukakis, "A New Era of Greatness for America," speech accepting the nomination for the presidency of the United States, Democratic Party Nominating Convention, Atlanta, Georgia, July 21, 1988, at http://www.4president.org/speeches/mikedukakis1988acceptance.htm.

2 Transcript from CNN's Election Center, *Time* in partnership with CNN, May 6, 2008, at http://thepage.time.com/transcript-from-cnns-election-center/.

3 Joe McGinniss, *The Selling of the President 1968* (New York: Trident, 1968), p. 26.

4   Ibid., McGinniss quoting national Republican chairman Leonard Hall, p. 27.

5   Edward L. Bernays, *Propaganda: The Public Mind in the Making* (New York: Liveright, 1928), pp. 101–2.

6   Transcript from CNN's Election Center.

7   Dick Morris and Eileen McGann, "Hillary Has No Shot at the Nomination," published at NewsMax.com on May 7, 2008, at http://www.newsmax.com/morris/Obama_hillary_clinton/2008/05/07/94165.html.

8   "Transcript: Obama Delivers Victory Speech in North Carolina," *Washington Post*, May 6, 2008, at http://www.washingtonpost.com/wp-dyn/content/article/2008/05/06/AR2008050603099.html.

9   Mike Soraghan, Manu Raju, and Jared Allen, "Obama takes campaign to House floor," *The Hill*, May 8, 2008, at http://thehill.com/leading-the-news/obama-talks-to-superdelegates-on-house-floor-2008-05-08.html.

10 Jon Cohen and Dan Balz, "U.S. Outlook Is Worst Since '92, Poll Finds," *Washington Post*, May 13, 2008, at http://www.washingtonpost.com/wp-dyn/content/article/2008/05/12/AR2008051201073.html?hpid=topnews.

11 Douglas Brinkley, *Tour of Duty: John Kerry and the Vietnam War* (New York: William Morrow, 2004).

— INDEX —